Dear Liberty

DEAR LIBERTY

Connecticut's Mobilization for the Revolutionary War

RICHARD BUEL, JR.

Wesleyan University Press   Middletown, Connecticut

COPYRIGHT © 1980 BY RICHARD BUEL, JR.

MAPS: MILT JOHNSON

THE PUBLISHER GRATEFULLY ACKNOWLEDGES THE
SUPPORT OF THE NATIONAL ENDOWMENT
FOR THE HUMANITIES TOWARD THE
PUBLICATION OF THIS BOOK.

Library of Congress Cataloging in Publication Data

Buel, Richard, 1933–
Dear liberty.

Includes bibliographical references and index.
1. Connecticut—History—Revolution, 1775–1783.
2. Connecticut—Militia—Mobilization. I. Title.
E263.C5B83   973.3'09746   80-14511
ISBN 0-8195-5047-7

DISTRIBUTED BY COLUMBIA UNIVERSITY PRESS
136 SOUTH BROADWAY, IRVINGTON, NY 10533
MANUFACTURED IN THE UNITED STATES OF AMERICA
FIRST EDITION

For Joy

Contents

Tables

Maps

Preface

THIS BOOK grew out of a problem I encountered while writing *Securing the Revolution*. The prospect of renewed warfare between Great Britain and the United States during the 1790s produced more anxiety in some national leaders than in others, and though this was not in itself surprising, the pattern of these variant responses differed widely from what one would expect. The South, with its large slave population, and with the memory still painfully sharp of British forays into its interior, might in theory have suffered greater apprehension than the North, which had no potential enemy within its gates and which had succeeded in forcing the surrender of one sizable army when it ventured beyond the reach of British naval support. In fact, with the notable exception of South Carolina, the opposite occurred. Somehow, the war of the Revolution had hit the North harder than the South.

The literature shed no light on why this had happened. Economic factors had certainly helped to determine the responses of the regions, and of the statesmen who represented them, both during and after the war. Beyond this, I could find no answer to my question. I decided, therefore, to make my own investigation.

At first, I hoped to address the subject in terms of the continent as a whole. But in the course of writing a paper on state mobilizations (presented to a conference at the National

Archives) I realized that the matter was too complex for treatment on a grand scale. In the absence of a national market, there is no way to explore a national political economy. One must work at the state and local levels. Luck had placed me within reach of an unusually full revolutionary state archive, and of the Jeremiah Wadsworth papers. The first of these reconciled me to a state-focused study; the second convinced me that Connecticut's wartime experience was unique at the same time as it was intertwined with the political, economic, and military fortunes of the whole northern region.

In the hope of finding a southern counterpart, I spent a year investigating revolutionary records in Virginia. My plan was to present a comparative study. But I found little symmetry in the kinds of documentation that survive for the two states. Since the Connecticut material proved infinitely richer, and since few of the issues it raised have received attention, I decided to let it stand alone.

To traditional military historians, a full-length study of the Revolutionary War as it affected only one state, and at that a state which suffered a mere 151 battlefield fatalities on her own territory (according to the most recent tally),[1] may seem too narrow to be generally useful. I would reply that previous studies have concentrated so closely on formal politics or military operations as virtually to ignore other aspects of the wartime experience, aspects that affected more people more continuously than did the ins and outs of politics or those brief, violent episodes, the famous battles. I do not discount the importance of military operations: indeed, they form a substantial part of my account. But I am interested in them primarily for their effect upon recruitment, procurement, and popular morale. Connecticut, though she saw little fighting on her own ground, provides a particularly clear illustration of that other side of life in wartime. And for this reason, I believe that the following study illuminates far more than the one corner of revolutionary America it focuses upon.

The faults in this work are mine; the credit for its virtues I share with the numerous institutions and individuals that helped me with its production. Grants from the National Endowment for the Humanities, from the American Council of Learned Societies, and from the Colonel Return Jonathan Meigs First (1740–1823) Fund—which was created by Dorothy Mix Meigs and Fielding Pope Meigs, Jr., in memory of that soldier of the Revolution whose home was in Middletown, Connecticut, from 1740 to 1787—supported my research and writing. The Dietrich Foundation's gift to Wesleyan University of early American imprints on microprint put many important resources within immediate reach. I received invaluable help and hospitality from the staffs of numerous libraries, including those of the Archives Division of the Connecticut State Library, the Connecticut Historical Society, the Beinecke Library and the Sterling Memorial Library at Yale, the New York Historical Society, the American Antiquarian Society, the Alderman Library at the University of Virginia, the Russell Library of Middletown, and especially the Olin Library at Wesleyan University. I am particularly obliged to Robert Schnare, Christopher Bickford, Ruth Blair, and Joan Jurale. Jane Tosto, Edna Haran, Bryna Goodman, June Urquart, Monica Murray, and Jane Muskatallo typed various parts of the manuscript. John Barber, Julie Liss, and Monica Murray helped with the collection of the statistical data that appear in tabular form. Four former students—Barry Craig, Harold Selesky, Michael Zuckerman, and Philip Zea—taught me much about the subject of this book when I was first exploring it. I am grateful to Merrill Peterson, Joseph Kett, William Abbott, and particularly Robert D. Cross for the productive year I spent in Charlottesville, Virginia. Bernard Bailyn, Michael Kammen, and Jack Greene have supported the project since its inception. I have benefited greatly from the critical reading given parts or all of the manuscript by John Shy, Don Higginbotham, George Billias, Stanley Lebergott, Willard Wallace, Harold Selesky, and my father, as well as from their encouragement. I owe a debt of gratitude to them all. But my greatest debt, as always, is to my wife, Joy Day Buel, whose hand has helped shape every page.

Haddam, Connecticut

Dear Liberty

PART ONE

Introduction

CHAPTER ONE

Revolutionary Potential

IN 1763, Britain's North American colonies emerged from the Seven Years' War with new confidence. At first Americans had doubted their ability to withstand the enemy, and during the early years of the war they had met some crushing defeats at French hands. Now, only a few years later, the colonists reveled in the knowledge that Britain could not have expelled the Catholic powers without their help. With that knowledge came a sense of security such as they had never known. The clergy, giving thanks for the Peace of Paris, expatiated upon the glorious prospect thus opened for the extension of British liberty and Protestant Christianity throughout the continent. They saw the hand of God in a victory won despite bitter adversity, from which they inferred God's further intention "to maintain and diffuse among Mankind the blessings of humanity, freedom and religion."[1] Some orators did sound an occasional warning. One Anglican clergyman feared that Americans would celebrate their new immunity from foreign attack by indulging in domestic contention and disorder; others, that sudden prosperity might tempt them to extravagance. But the dourest Jeremiah preferred the perils of peace to the hazards of war. James Lockwood, minister of the First Church of Wethersfield, saw America's deliverance from the menace of Catholicism as God's renewal of covenant with his chosen people and, if Americans maintained the moral heights they had reached during the war, as a prelude to Christ's thousand-year reign on earth.[2] And though such grand millennial hopes were confined to evangelicals, everyone felt the spirit of optimism they expressed.[3]

Connecticut and the Peace of 1763

Connecticut had particular reason to rejoice, for she occupied a uniquely privileged place in the Empire. For one hundred years, she had governed herself as an independent republic. Under the charter issued by Charles II in 1662, she had developed the most popular form of government on the continent. Twice a year the freemen elected two deputies to represent their towns in the General Assembly. Each September they nominated a slate of twenty men from whom they would select their governor, deputy governor, and twelve assistants in the following April. The governor exercised few powers in his own right, but the part he played in the Council, or upper house of the legislature, gave him a voice in framing the colony's laws. As a member of the Council, he also shared in the Assembly's power of appointing judicial and military officers.[4] In most colonies, an authority resident in Britain, usually the Crown, named the governor, who could veto legislation and appoint judicial and military officers with the concurrence of the Council. Quite often, the Crown appointed the Council members too. Except for Rhode Island, no other colony enjoyed so much freedom from British supervision as Connecticut. And though less than half of her adult males qualified as freemen,[5] in no other colony did they go so frequently to the polls to elect, hence possibly to change, their lower house. The men in the militia (in theory, everyone between the ages of sixteen and fifty, though many were exempt from actual service) also nominated their company officers by popular vote.[6] Of all the mainland colonies, Connecticut possessed the most republican institutions.

At the time, of course, not everyone admired republicanism. The dominant ideology of eighteenth-century Britain deplored the excesses of the Commonwealth period, and the pace of Connecticut's development had raised the specter of similar disorders there. Though the original settlements along the Connecticut River and Long Island Sound had grown slowly, the elimination of hostile Indians during King Philip's War had opened eastern Connecticut to settlers, while the pressure of the French to the north made it attractive as a place where they felt comparatively safe from attack. During the late seventeenth and early eighteenth centuries the population expanded at an unprecedented rate, mostly because of migration from Massachusetts. There followed a series of challenges to the authority of the older towns, which some blamed on the republicanism of the government. They would have preferred a closer tie to the English church and state and regretted that the colony seemed to have neither a traditional elite nor the institutions through which it could have exercised power.[7] But only a few people held this view, and certain factors persuaded them to go along with the majority who approved the status quo.

The tighter hold that Britain took on her colonies after 1748 had dramatized the advantages of Connecticut's autonomy;[8] and, more important still, throughout a period of rapid, sweeping change, the colony's leaders had won the people's confidence in their ability to keep society stable. They did so, furthermore, despite the absence of either a staple or a central distribution point for imports from Europe, the bases for the development of elites in the other colonies.[9] The power of Connecticut's leadership depended almost entirely on its control of the Council.[10] Because the nominating procedures favored candidates from the more populous areas, the older towns, particularly those in the Connecticut River Valley, were overrepresented. The electoral procedures furthermore virtually guaranteed reelection of incumbents. The requirement that freemen vote for nominees according to their seniority on the Council, rather than according to the number of nominating votes they received, favored the continuance of those already in office, and the continuity of its composition gave the Council a disproportionate influence over the rest of the political system. The Council could always postpone an action initiated by the

lower house, and a long enough postponement, given the
frequent change of personnel in the popular branch, often
meant tomorrow's loss of enthusiasm for today's proposals. A
prolonged opposition to the popular will would, even then,
have precipitated a change in the Council,[11] but the fast pace of
development in Connecticut helped keep such confrontations to
a minimum.

Because electoral procedure thus favored seniority, the
Council took on the appearance of a meritocracy. The people
saw it as a body in which deserving men worked their way up
the nomination list until, should they live long enough, they
succeeded to the posts of governor and deputy governor. The
popular view in turn encouraged the Assembly to bestow other
offices besides elected ones upon the councillors. Most councillors held judgeships in the superior and county courts; councillors also came to occupy Connecticut's highest military posts;
and the practice extended even to the granting of lesser judicial
and military commissions to prominent deputies.[12] Few objected; on the contrary, many thought that plural officeholding
for long, contiguous periods by a predictable few might give
their otherwise decentralized system a firmer foundation.

Connecticut's economy was less enviable than her political
structure, mostly because she had no staple product suitable for
direct trade with Europe. Nonetheless, by the middle of the
eighteenth century she had carved her own niche in the economy of the western Atlantic. She produced livestock, "provisions" (mostly salt meat), and lumber, the greater part of which
she exchanged in the West Indies for sugar products and bills of
exchange on Europe. She sent flour, lumber, New England
rum, and "Stores for Muling" to Gibraltar and the North African coast (Barbary), flaxseed to Ireland, and lumber and potash
to England. But the bulk of the European manufactures that
Connecticut consumed she purchased in the larger neighboring
ports of New York, Newport, and Boston and paid for with
sugar products or bills of exchange.[13] Her surplus, though
small, combined with the surplus of the other northern colonies
to become more than the British Islands could use, even before
the mid–eighteenth century. The foreign islands, particularly

the French and Dutch, took up the slack, however, while recurrent colonial wars created a periodic demand closer to home, since Connecticut's salted meat (considered the best on the continent) made ideal army provisions.[14]

Despite her political superiority and economic competence, one chronic problem plagued Connecticut. By the mid–eighteenth century, her population had taken possession of almost all her land. In 1750 an acute need for more space prompted the reassertion of a long-dormant claim to territory west of New York. The charter of 1662 extended Connecticut's western boundaries to the South Seas, but Charles II had soon qualified this lavish phrasing. He conveyed to his brother, the duke of York, title to all lands between the Connecticut River and the Delaware. Connecticut and New York had no difficulty in agreeing on the border between them, which they drew along lines that remain little altered today. That done, nothing was heard of Connecticut's western claim for eighty years. Even in 1681, when Charles II granted William Penn a vast domain that overlapped some of Connecticut's original grant, the colony made no protest. Her existing boundaries seemed ample to fill all needs for many years to come. No one foresaw the rapid growth that would begin at the end of the seventeenth century, fill up eastern Connecticut by 1730, and lead to settlement of the western wilderness by 1750.[15]

As long as Connecticut retained unallocated land, she had a source of capital on which one generation could draw to provide for the next. The exhaustion of this source in the 1740s, distressing enough in itself, coincided with a costly war that saddled the colony with a debt she could not pay.[16] Her one hope for solvency rested in a prompt payment from Parliament for expenses incurred during 1745 in the reduction of the French fortress at Louisbourg, but mercantile interests in both Britain and America delayed action on that score by demanding a guarantee that the money would be used to reform the much-depreciated old tenor currency. As a result, Connecticut received reimbursement too late to save her currency from chaos;[17] Parliament responded to the disaster (which overtook not Connecticut alone but also Rhode Island) with the Currency Act of 1751, restricting the power of the New England colonies to issue paper money;[18] and Connecticut found herself suddenly bereft of both means that she had hitherto used to form indigenous capital.

It was at this point that the claim to lands west of New York emerged as an issue. The first petition for a grant was presented to the General Assembly in 1750. A torrent of similar petitions, with hundreds of signers, followed.[19] Besides land hunger and penury, the people had the prospect of war with France to spur them on. The mainland colonies wanted to establish as many settlements as possible in the interior before open conflict broke out. France was already putting pressure on the upper Ohio, and Pennsylvania's Quaker leadership made that government a possibly weak link in the chain of defense. Those who craved land saw Pennsylvania's weakness as Connecticut's opportunity. Surely the imperial government would prefer settlement by families whose men had proved their military worth at Louisbourg.[20] Connecticut's government took no official stance on the matter, but individual legislators advised the petitioners to establish land companies, to sell stock, and, with the proceeds, to buy up Indian titles. The Delaware and Susquehannah companies formed and acquired titles to lands between the rivers denoted by their names, as well as to lands further west.[21] In 1755, they asked the legislature to endorse a petition to the Crown for incorporation as a separate colony, and the General Assembly at once complied.[22]

The primary purpose of organizing companies and issuing stock was to aid emigration. By selling shares, companies could raise the capital to finance parties of emigrants. The growing number of potentially landless people would readily take the necessary risks in exchange for free land. The stockholders would reap their long-term reward either from a rise in the price of still-unoccupied territory that they hoped would follow the first wave of successful settlement or from the use of their stockholders' rights to settle their children in the west.[23]

Though the companies did not have time to establish settlements before the war began, they resumed their efforts the moment peace returned. Settlement, indeed, preceded petitioning the Crown. By the mid-1750s, both companies had gone so far in the acquisition of Indian titles and the assertion of their claims as to goad Pennsylvania's proprietor into an appeal for imperial authorities to defend his title.[24] But the companies did not fear Penn, though they lacked his influence with Whitehall. They knew that he had also to combat an attack on his charter by an antiproprietary party in Pennsylvania which blamed him for the Seven Years' War.[25] The Connecticut land companies saw their first priority as the settlement of the western lands before Penn could put his people there, a perception based on the assumption that possession would force the Crown's consent to their claim. Secure in this belief, between 1760 and 1762 they actively promoted settlement.[26]

They were aided in their ambitions by the prosperity that resulted from the Seven Years' War. Because Parliament had for once paid Britain's debt to the colonies promptly, Connecticut could give her bills of credit a remarkably stable value. Parliament began making payments in 1757. After 1758, Connecticut was in a position to deposit her share in a London bank and to sell bills of exchange on her sterling account for bills of credit.[27] The currency that the bills of credit acquired through their use in settling sterling debts created a broader demand for them than before. Though British contractors do not appear to have dealt as much as they might in American supplies, the generous bounty offered to the colonies for each man recruited enabled Connecticut to make ample provision for her troops in the field. And, thanks to the soundness of the currency, the benefits from government contracts extended throughout the colony.[28]

Unfortunately the activity of the companies offended the powerful Six Nations at a time when imperial officialdom wanted good relations with the Indians. Sir Jeffery Amherst, British commander in North America, and Sir William Johnson, superintendent for Indian affairs, pressed Connecticut's Governor Thomas Fitch to stop further encroachment.[29] Fitch, who came from the western coastal town of Norwalk and identified with conservative merchants who had no interest whatever in territorial expansion, promptly issued a proclamation that settlers would incur the king's displeasure if they persisted. The companies took no notice until Secretary of State Egremont intervened, when they did agree to desist. Some settlers, however, defied both the governor and the companies and continued to occupy the western lands until an Indian raid in October 1763, part of Pontiac's Rebellion, wiped out most of them.[30] A special order-in-council required Fitch to remove the remainder,[31] and the tragedy effectively discouraged further attempts. On October 7 a royal proclamation closed the area to European settlers indefinitely.[32]

The companies had to abandon their plans for the time being, but those under pressure to emigrate could still find opportunities elsewhere. Cheap land beckoned them in New York, New Hampshire, Nova Scotia, and present-day Maine. Still better bargains awaited the buyer in the lands under dispute between New York and New Hampshire (present-day Vermont), provided he did not mind the uncertainty of his title.[33] This war, unlike the last, had generated the capital to finance emigration. The expansion of the money supply, and the still-increasing pressure of population on space, inflated land values. Whole families could sell to buyers eager to capitalize on local improvements and could use the proceeds to resettle where land was more plentiful. Excessive emigration from any one area might lower land prices again, but in that case a decline in the pressures for emigration would balance the decline in value.[34] Even those who owned no land could earn the money to buy some in a new settlement. They had only to take advantage of the large bounties offered for military service.[35] Circumstances had changed, and emigrants no longer had much need for the backing of the Susquehannah and Delaware companies.

Though people had been moving away from Connecticut since the seventeenth century, most scholars agree that mass emigration began about 1760.[36] At that time, it did not threaten the stability of Connecticut's institutions. Indeed, some people thought that the end of internal expansion would mean the end of the disorders that had accompanied it. Other colonies may have enjoyed greater prosperity and faced fewer adjustments in the immediate postwar period, but Connecticut's charter privileges and republican social order seemed to most of her residents ample compensation for their economic disadvantages. Connecticut, they felt, did not need to struggle for liberty. She had long possessed it.[37]

The Dawn of Revolutionary Consciousness

In 1763 the most foresighted would never have dreamed that one decade could transform Connecticut into a revolutionary society. But in 1775 Connecticut entered the fray with an enthusiasm unsurpassed by any other colony. The years between had wrought a great change in her. The other colonies also changed, of course, the mainspring of all their transformations being Britain's policy toward them. Some of them, particularly New York, Rhode Island, and Massachusetts, had found themselves singled out for especially harsh treatment, while Connecticut came under no regulation that was not common to all.[38] Nevertheless, the measures by which the British government sought to tighten up its colonial administration had a profound effect there.

Connecticut received an early intimation of the trouble ahead. On July 9, 1783, Secretary of State Egremont informed Governor Fitch that the navy had instructions to enforce the navigation acts. In 1764 the Sugar Act revived the policy of placing a prohibitive tax on foreign sugar imports to the mainland colonies, imposed a tangle of new regulations on colonial trade, and established an admiralty court in Nova Scotia before which officials could libel seizures uninhibited by local disapproval. Those who continued to smuggle now ran a much higher risk, but those who complied with the law soon protested the low price their produce fetched in the overstocked markets of the British islands.[39] Because it forced them to trade in the Caribbean on highly disadvantageous terms, the Sugar Act left the colonies whose economies depended on West Indian trade with diminished means to pay the large debts their wartime prosperity had led them to contract in Britain. In Connecticut, the scarcity of remittances then raised the price of bills of exchange in relation to the bills of credit. This accelerated the retirement of the public debt but threatened the liquidity of the economy since the Currency Act forbade Connecticut to reissue her wartime bills of credit. And the pressure of private debts, together with the retirement of the bills of credit, caused a sharp decline in the value of real estate.[40]

The colonists in general, and Connecticut in particular, could have weathered the blows inflicted by the Sugar Act but for its sequel. The Stamp Act, which proposed to raise a large revenue in specie by a direct tax, would clearly deliver the coup de grace to the economy. It set the colonies to some hard thinking about their constitutional relation to the imperial government, including the political implications of a system whereby the British Parliament could lay taxes on men not represented there. In contemporary terms, it raised their political consciousness. British subsidies during the Seven Years' War had allowed them to think of Parliament as sharing their broader interests, and for eighteenth-century Americans, shared interest constituted the essence of the representative relationship. They were accustomed to think of it as ensuring that the governors could not injure the governed without injuring themselves.[41] The Stamp Act shocked them into the recognition that, in the matter of taxation, the members of the British House of Commons possessed an interest diametrically opposed to their own. Every penny of tax laid on Americans would be a penny less laid on themselves and their constituents. The colonists did not deny their obligation to contribute to the Empire. But they had thought the profits of the American trade, largely engrossed by Great Britain, contribution enough. Now Britain demanded more, and since Americans knew how staggering a public debt she had to pay they might well ask where that demand would end. If they conceded Parliament's right to lay a stamp tax, they would have conceded its right to lay others. And they saw that the weight of taxes imposed upon them could increase indefinitely without causing any immediate discomfort to the government and people of the mother country.[42]

Connecticut played no major role in the development of

the new political consciousness. Though her newspapers carried essays on the Stamp Act and on the question of Parliament's right to tax the colonists, she made only one contribution to the wider imperial debate. This was a pamphlet entitled *Reasons why the British Colonies in America, should not be charged with internal taxes*. Governor Fitch, together with a committee drawn from both houses of the legislature, had drafted it in the summer of 1764 when the colonies first learned that the ministry contemplated a stamp tax. Thanks largely to Fitch, *Reasons why* sidestepped the question of whether or not Parliament had constitutional power to tax Americans and concentrated on the argument that parliamentary taxation would take away their traditional privileges.[43] The pamphlet also gave currency to the distinction between internal and external taxes, an idea that Charles Townshend would use against the colonists in the Townshend Duties. In its October session, the Assembly endorsed the pamphlet and ordered its transmission to Parliament.[44]

The moderation of *Reasons why* betrayed the government's conviction that the status quo endowed Connecticut with certain benefits and that it behoved her to preserve them by avoiding fundamental questions about the sovereignty of Parliament. The people, on the other hand, were less interested in the preservation of charter privileges than in how to cope with the problems that the new imperial policies raised. When they learned that the Stamp Act had passed into law, they gave open expression to their fury. At first, they focused it upon Jared Ingersoll, who returned from England in 1765 to be the colony's official distributor of stamps. His arrival touched off a series of demonstrations, mostly hangings in effigy.[45] It soon appeared, however, that some people meant to force his resignation. In recognition that the colony had reached a crisis, and in response to pressure from the more radical Council members that the colony be represented in the Stamp Act Congress, Governor Fitch called an emergency session of the legislature in mid-September.[46] As Ingersoll rode toward Hartford to attend it, a party of five hundred mounted men carrying barrel staves intercepted him at Wethersfield. They were part of a three-

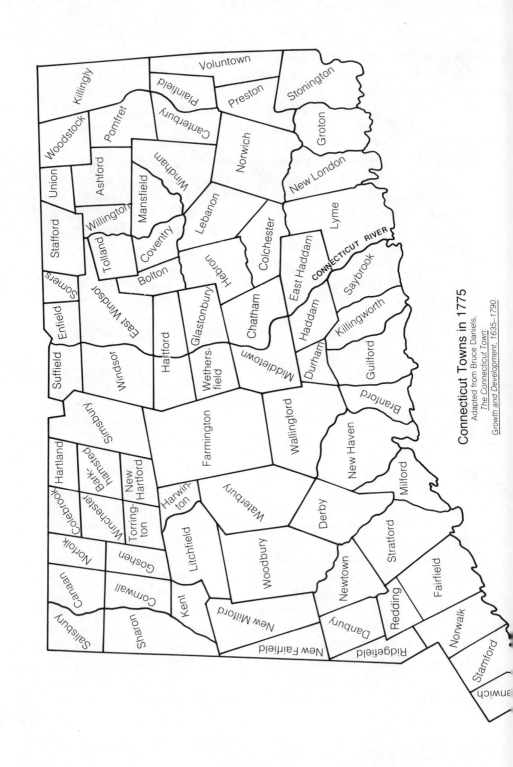

Connecticut Towns in 1775
Adapted from Bruce Daniels,
*The Connecticut Town:
Growth and Development, 1635–1790.*

pronged force moving in from the eastern towns of Windham, Norwich, and New London to demand that he resign. Somewhat to their relief, he did.[47] But the General Assembly, meeting shortly thereafter, roundly condemned them as rioters.[48] Nor did the next Assembly wholly abandon the restraint its predecessor had shown in responding to the Stamp Act. Though the members framed a series of resolves condemning it as unconstitutional, many favored compliance, at least to the extent of abstention from all business that would require stamps.[49] Fitch even took the oath that the Stamp Act required of all colonial governors, an oath to enforce the law in his jurisdiction, though he had received no official order to do so.[50]

Fitch knew that his action would stir controversy. His Council divided over the issue, and the eastern assistants refused to attend the ceremony.[51] In a pamphlet entitled *Some reasons that influenced the governor to take, and the Council to administer the oath, required by the Act of Parliament* (Hartford, 1766) Fitch said he had done it in order to safeguard the colony's charter privilege of electing magistrates. As the division within the Council showed, his reasoning appealed most strongly to western Connecticut. If Great Britain should ever void Connecticut's charter, New York could lay claim to all the land west of the Connecticut River. And there were reasons to think that the British government would support such a claim.

The Crown had recently upheld New York over New Hampshire in a dispute concerning lands west of the Connecticut River.[52] Would it not support her again if Connecticut lost her charter through opposition to the Stamp Act? At one blow, Whitehall could defang a nest of dissenters and strengthen a royal colony ruled by one of the most strictly centralized governments in America.[53] Fitch had taken a calculated risk: he knew his oath would divide the colony but hoped it would bring the stronger section to his side. Western Connecticut contained more towns and more property than the eastern part, and he expected it would respond *en bloc* to this issue.

Throughout the eighteenth century, the western towns had seen their eastern counterparts as breeding grounds of trouble. In the 1730s eastern entrepreneurs had formed the

New London Society for Trade and Commerce which had issued its own banknotes until the legislature, fearing for the charter, had dissolved it.[54] The New Light disturbances of the 1740s had also originated in the east, and though they later spread to the western churches, division there had led not always to the formation of New Light groups but sometimes to the establishment of Anglican churches.[55] In recent years, the principal support for the Susquehannah and Delaware companies had come from eastern Connecticut,[56] which had long since reached the point of overpopulation. Western Connecticut's river and coastal towns, by contrast, had integrated with a wider market economy that permitted intensive as well as extensive growth. And the west's new inland towns had still not reached the stage where emigration offered the only alternative to a lower standard of living. The people there had little interest in the Susquehannah Company, and less in whether or not the new imperial policies inhibited the formation of capital for emigration.[57] All in all, Fitch had reason to hope that western Connecticut would support his decision to take the oath.

The April election of 1766 proved him mistaken. He and the four councillors who had administered the oath found themselves ousted from office. An organization named the Sons of Liberty had engineered their removal, no mean achievement in view of Connecticut's election procedures. Since Fitch and his adherents had already gained their places on the nomination list, their reelection seemed inevitable. Any person who voted for a nonincumbent had to wait for the end of the meeting and to accept what consequences arose from having everyone witness his dissent.[58] Moreover, he knew he would act in vain if he acted alone. On this occasion, the Sons of Liberty had coordinated the opposition. At a colonywide meeting in Hartford on March 25, 1766, the majority voted to remove Fitch and the four councillors and to replace them simply by moving the other nominees up the list. Thus William Pitkin of Hartford, the deputy governor, became governor, while Jonathan Trumbull, from the eastern town of Lebanon, second in seniority among the remaining assistants, took Pitkin's place.[59]

The Sons of Liberty had brought off this difficult maneuver because the Stamp Act had aroused such rage, but Fitch's party refused to see it as anything more than a slick bit of electioneering. In 1767 they made strenuous efforts to promote the reelection of the five men. They tried to incense the western towns with the observation that the east now dominated the Council. Various writers in newspapers combined paeans on the superior wealth and population of western Connecticut with predictions that easterners would "ravage the Government, by pretended principles of Liberty," until all the assistants came from their own ranks. They advised westerners to confer the status of freeman liberally on men who would vote solidly for Fitch and his friends.[60] Even this naked appeal to sectional jealousy failed. The Sons of Liberty had judiciously maintained parity between the sections on the Council and had even won over the Anglican minority in the west by elevating William S. Johnson to the upper house.[61] Though the west had lost its majority, and the fifty-six-year-old Trumbull from the east seemed likely soon to succeed the aging Pitkin as governor, many westerners feared possible domination by eastern Connecticut less than they feared that the British ministry would construe the return of Fitch as a sign of submission to parliamentary taxation.[62]

The Stamp Act had moved the people of Connecticut to their depths, but moved them as yet only to defend the original imperial relationship. Some day, they knew, the American colonies would assume independence from Britain, but there was no hurry. They clung to the hope that Parliament had offended inadvertently. Though the Declaratory Act that accompanied the repeal of the Stamp Act shook their faith a little, they tried to see it as a face-saving device. The use of British soldiers to repress Prendergast's tenant rebellion in eastern New York caused some discomfort, too, though it affected Massachusetts more than Connecticut.[63] The reduction of the duties on foreign sugar troubled Connecticut more, but still not enough to elicit a protest. Like the Sugar Act of 1764, the new act stated Parliament's intent to raise a revenue from America.[64] Since, however, reduced duties permitted resumption of lawful commerce with the foreign islands, the act also offered a way to resolve the liquidity crisis that British policy had thrust upon the colonial economy. And though Britain derived considerable revenue from the reduction,[65] in principle Parliament had only regulated trade. The colonists had always conceded its right to do that.

Between the repeal of the Stamp Act and the summer of 1767, Britain continued to veil her acts in ambiguity: they made Americans uneasy, nothing more. With the creation of an American Board of Customs Commissioners and the imposition of duties on certain articles of British manufacture, known subsequently as the Townshend Duties, Britain dropped the veil. Americans now saw all too clearly that, no matter how they felt about it, Parliament meant to raise an increasing revenue from them.[66] John Dickinson's famous "Farmer's Letters" pointed out the crucial difference between the sugar duties, which Americans had accepted, and the Townshend Duties, which they opposed: one was a regulation of trade, the other a tax. Submission to a tax in the form of the Townshend Duties would open the door to an infinity of others. When Dickinson urged the colonists to form nonimportation associations,[67] he thought thereby to preserve the old empire, not to destroy it. But the experience of forming and maintaining the associations of 1768 to 1770, in the teeth of Britain's displeasure and all the repercussions that implied, accustomed Americans to exertion and endurance in the cause of liberty. It forced more and more of them to admit that they would have to seek liberty beyond the old order. Out of that travail was born a leadership ripe for revolution.

Again Connecticut began by playing a passive role in the drama. Various bodies passed resolutions thanking Dickinson for his useful distinction between a tax and a trade regulation; several towns endorsed the principle of a nonimportation agreement; and in June 1768 the General Assembly petitioned the Crown against the new duties;[68] but no one showed much disposition to act. Though a nonimportation agreement would have helped, among other things, to liquidate private indebtedness, more than a year passed before the merchants concluded one. Perhaps they reflected that few people in Connecticut were in a position to consume any English goods, dutied or otherwise. Connecticut imported so little that at first her merchants felt they could leave the construction of associations and the framing of agreements to the larger ports.[69] Only in June 1770 did they take action to censure Newport's abandonment of the agreement.[70] Shortly afterward they opposed New York's attempt to pull its teeth, and, when their remonstrance had no effect, resolved to boycott the renegades.[71] This was action, but not effective action. Connecticut had too small a share of the market to give her much influence even if she had been able to enforce her resolutions, and in fact she was not able. Peddlers could easily infiltrate her territory for the New York merchants; English goods began to seep through, and Connecticut merchants backed down.[72]

Inglorious a fate as the association suffered in Connecticut, the patriots could tell themselves that it had collapsed not of its own weight but under attack by the British government. The attack had begun with an announcement that the ministry intended to repeal all duties except the one on tea.[73] Simultaneously, the customs commissioners in Boston circulated manifests to the principal ports which alleged that Boston merchants had violated their agreement. These documents deliberately slanted facts and figures. They played on discrepancies between the Boston agreement, which permitted the importation of certain goods, and the agreements of other major ports, which barred them.[74] Boston did have its violators. The imperial officials and British troops there provided incentives that some could not resist and a promise of protection from reprisal. Indeed, it was tension between colonists and soldiers over the subversion of nonimportation that led to the Boston Massacre.[75] Nevertheless, the Boston manifests gave the merchants in other ports an excuse to defect, an excuse they had ever more reason to seize as the retirement of private debts allowed the resumption of importation. New York appears to have found the temptation irresistible when Parliament waived the Currency Act of 1764 and allowed her to issue £120,000 in legal tender.[76] And Britain used the stick as well as the carrot. Parliament discussed reviving a sixteenth-century statute on treason committed outside the realm as a weapon to fight nonimportation, while the ministry considered asking Parliament to outlaw nonimportation associations.[77]

The defeat of nonimportation taught the majority what a few had already guessed: that Britain meant to tax the colonists and that the partial repeal of the Townshend Duties represented a tactical retreat rather than a major concession.[78] They construed the mother country's actions as evidence of jealousy, jealousy of the glorious destiny that victory in the Seven Years' War had opened to her colonies.[79] They still preferred to avoid a confrontation; they were ill prepared, and it seemed unnecessary since they had achieved some immediate objectives. They had persuaded Parliament to repeal all the Townshend Duties except the one on tea, which would not raise much revenue. The merchants continued to boycott the dutied tea, and the public supported them because they had access to smuggled Dutch tea.[80] Meanwhile, the heroic efforts of Britain to subvert the associations had ironically reassured the colonists that she was not invulnerable to them. They emerged from the contest with a dangerous complex of convictions. They felt that Britain's intentions left no room for American liberty; that a basis existed for united action by the mainland colonies in response to a common threat; and that such action could have an effect.

Connecticut's Deepening Radicalism

In Rhode Island and Massachusetts, the new consciousness expressed itself in dramatic acts of defiance. In Connecticut it took the more subtle form of a gradual change in attitude toward the Susquehannah Company. Before 1768, most people assumed that if the Susquehannah Company succeeded it would establish a separate colony in the west.[81] But after 1768 people began to view the company as an instrument Connecticut might use in asserting her own claim to western lands. The change reflected a new inclination for aggressive expansion, born of the recognition that the future held extraordinary challenges that would call for extraordinary resource. Those who controlled the company came round to this view in the wake of the furor over the Townshend Duties and Britain's hard-line response to it.[82] Aided and abetted by the usually conservative Council, the company's directors led Connecticut on an untried path fraught with possibilities and perils.

In 1768 the large Indian cessions negotiated by Sir William Johnson at the Treaty of Fort Stanwix presented a puzzling choice to the Susquehannah Company. The Penn family began at once to sell off land with an eye to preempting the company's claim.[83] The special order-in-council of June 15, 1763, would seem to have barred the company from following suit. But in December 1768 the company decided to construe the Treaty of Fort Stanwix as a repeal of the order-in-council and to establish settlers on company lands before spring. The company offered extensive rights to the first 240 people to go. In addition to free acreage, provisions, and tools, the first 40 settlers could have their pick of the land plus a bounty of five pounds if they took possession by February 1, 1769. At the same time, the company petitioned the General Assembly for a grant of title,[84] apparently on the advice of the colony's highest officers. The Council endorsed the petition at once, but a majority of the House, hesitant to run headlong into a course that could embroil the colony in controversy with the Penns, postponed action until May.[85]

In the interim it became clear that the Penns meant to resist the company's intrusion, by force if necessary. John Penn, the proprietor's nephew and governor of the province, ordered the authorities in Northampton County to arrest the company's advance settlers. Thirty-one of them were seized and bound over to trial in the Pennsylvania courts.[86] This made the company's petition more urgent. Though the directors sent forward a second wave of two hundred settlers and offered rights to an additional three hundred,[87] they feared that they could not maintain this flow of immigrants unless the colony backed them. Meanwhile, the dangers of following where the company and Council would lead had become clearer. The military occupation of Boston signaled the intention of the imperial authorities to bear down hard on any colonial troublemakers. In May, therefore, the new legislature defeated the company's petition by a small margin in the lower house. Even so, it accomplished that defeat only by disqualifying all members of the House who were also members of the company.[88]

The decision satisfied neither the company nor its opponents. The company's adherents objected because it put them at a disadvantage in the contest for the Susquehannah lands. The company's opponents, on the other hand, felt that the narrowness of the margin left them open to the risk that a small increase in their adversaries' influence might even now tilt the balance in the company's favor. They were particularly disturbed by the consequences that would flow from a grant to the company and by the Council's unanimous support of it.

Company spokesmen claimed that they wanted nothing more than a transfer of right from the colony to the company. They even offered to post bond on the pledge that the colony would "not be put to any expense to support the claim." But their opponents knew that if the colony made the grant she would of course become a party to any subsequent dispute.[89] They knew, too, that a grant would stimulate settlement; that settlement would increase the number of friends and relatives of settlers at home in Connecticut; and that those friends and relatives would increase the pressure for Connecticut to assert her jurisdiction. In August 1769 the 191 settlers on company land petitioned the Assembly for recognition as a separate county. Anticipating a need to defend their claim by force, they sought to have the violence they would then commit legalized in advance.[90] The company could make the proposition of extended jurisdiction attractive with the argument that the lands to the west of theirs would also become vendible and that the sale of them would bring money into Connecticut's treasury.[91] Then, once the company controlled the legislature, it could renege on any bond it had posted promising not to involve the colony.[92]

Opponents of the company saw the tendency of events and tried to make the public see it too. In a pamphlet entitled *Doct. Gale's Letter to J. W. Esquire*, Benjamin Gale deplored the amount of influence that the company had already acquired in the legislature. Several other pamphleteers and newspaper writers echoed him, stressing the expense to the colony should the company become involved in controversy over the grant.[93] But they brought their biggest guns to bear on the question of the company's title, which they saw as the chink in its armor.[94] The very request for a grant confessed the illegitimacy of the claim. If the colony held title to those lands, by what right could the legislature bestow them on one exclusive group?[95] The company's request implied a quid pro quo: give us the Susquehannah lands, and we will help to establish Connecticut's claim to yet more western territory. The company's opponents, however, hoped to curb the ambitions of both company and colony by questioning whether Connecticut had land to give in the first place. They pressed the point successfully enough to cause the General Assembly to appoint a committee for the purpose of gathering evidence on the question.[96]

Events in the settlement helped them at first. In September 1769 fighting broke out between the Pennsylvania authorities and the Connecticut settlers, and in November the Pennsylvanians took John Durkee, the leader of the settlement, prisoner. Shortly after, the leaderless remnant surrendered to a large posse and signed an agreement to vacate the land within three days.[97] During the winter of 1770, the only settlers the company could entice were a bunch of frontier rowdies, a remnant of the Paxton Boys who, in the wake of Pontiac's Rebellion, acquired notoriety by murdering friendly Indians. At odds with the proprietor, they were happy to accept grants to the rich Susquehannah lands on the liberal terms of the company. But their presence made for trouble, and they had several bloody clashes with the Pennsylvania authorities in 1770.[98] Such episodes made it hard for the company to attract settlers, free land notwithstanding, and by the beginning of 1771 the future looked so bleak that the company voted to sound out the proprietor about resolving the controversy at law.[99]

That spring, however, the company's prospects improved. More than four thousand freemen, none of them, allegedly, with a direct interest in the Susquehannah Purchase, signed a petition urging the Assembly to press the colony's claim.[100] The petition marked the failure of all attempts to deny that a claim existed and set in motion an irreversible sequence of events. Opponents in the legislature delayed action by demanding that the evidence gathered by the committee of 1769 be sent to Britain for legal opinions on the colony's right, but the General Assembly openly asserted its belief that company lands did fall within the charter boundaries.[101] The petition and the resolve encouraged a second influx of migrants that brought the Connecticut settlers to a strength sufficient to overcome the fort held by the proprietary interest. Since the proprietor could not immediately challenge the company's settlement of the land because the Pennsylvanians had momentarily lost interest in defending his claim, settlement passed easily into permanent occupation.[102]

The petition of 1771 has not survived. Except for oblique contemporary references, our knowledge of it derives from a newspaper article written three years later by Roger Sherman.[103] It is not hard to guess why no one preserved the petition. In it, an effective majority of Connecticut freemen asked their government to embark on a course that risked offending the imperial authorities. Both the men and their government would want to disassociate themselves from it if British officialdom should react harshly. The question remains of why the company should have succeeded in breaking a two-year political deadlock at this particular time. The evidence is inconclusive, but it is certain that the collapse of nonimportation had forced a growing number of people to accept the view held by leaders in the company and the Council that Connecticut could achieve true liberty only through that independence from Britain which would make the charter meaningless.

The company had gained a decisive advantage in 1771, yet Connecticut still approached the extension of jurisdiction cautiously. The legislature continued to postpone action on the petition,[104] reluctant to draw the ministry's fire unnecessarily and hesitant to divide the colony on the eve of a possible crisis. The company had established possession and could wait to extend jurisdiction until more people consented to the wisdom of the move. Their number would undoubtedly increase as the Susquehannah settlements grew and as relations with the mother country worsened. Even the violence that had followed New York's attempt to assert jurisdiction in Vermont might enhance interest in the company's enterprise by discouraging migration to the north.[105] In 1773, when the legal opinions that the colony had sought (and paid for, handsomely) proved favorable, the legislature resolved to use them in persuading the proprietor to yield. In January 1774 the Assembly at last extended jurisdiction, but only because Penn had finally recruited supporters to defend his claim.[106] Pennsylvanians had also realized that, should the Empire dissolve, possession would be more than nine points of the law.

The political storm raised by the extension of jurisdiction confirmed the wisdom of the legislature's former caution. Twenty-three towns sent delegates to a convention at Middletown in 1774 with instructions to reverse the decision, and they framed resolutions demurring at the expense and risk involved in pressing the claim to the western lands before the privy council had handed down an opinion.[107] The remonstrance eventually drafted by the Middletown Convention made it clear that the risk they envisioned was loss of the charter.[108] Like its predecessor of 1766, the convention attempted to change the composition of the Council to one less biased toward the company. The conventioneers wanted the removal of Governor Trumbull, who had succeeded Pitkin in 1769, and the reappointment of Fitch with his supporter Ebenezer Silliman.[109] In these aims they failed, for none of the existing councillors lost his place.

Nevertheless, the convention had one result. In an effort to placate those who still wanted Great Britain to decide the land controversy, the General Assembly resolved in May to petition the Crown for the appointment of commissioners who would settle the boundary between Connecticut and Pennsylvania west of the Delaware. They asked that both parties retain the right of appeal and that the decision of the commissioners "be prosecuted to a final issue . . . as soon as conveniently *may be.*"[110] This was a gesture only. Connecticut had had enough experience with appeals to the privy council to know that no final decision would be made for at least ten years. Besides, early in May the news had arrived of the Boston Port Act, and the Assembly must have realized that the final crisis was at hand.

If the Port Act had been an isolated response to an isolated incident, Connecticut might have continued to think in terms of preserving the imperial connection. But the people found it too much of a piece with other recent changes in policy. There was the announcement in 1772 that the members of the Massachusetts Superior Court would receive their salaries from the Crown rather than the province, a move that would make the American judicial system an instrument of imperial control. There was the appointment of a royal commission empowered to investigate the *Gaspee* incident and to remove suspects to England for trial. These two acts had helped to promote the intercolonial network of committees of correspondence which Connecticut had joined during 1773.[111] Then came the Tea Act, easier to deal with in some respects. Though it had tempted people to consume duties tea rather than Dutch tea, and so to acknowledge Britain's right to raise an American revenue, the common threat it presented had called forth a common response. And when Britain singled out Boston, whose governor had made it impossible for her to resist peaceably, for harsh and particular punishment, most people in Connecticut understood that their rights hung in the balance too.[112] If any remained whose misty-eyed backward view of the Empire's golden days kept them from seeing that its end approached, the Administration of Justice Act and the Massachusetts Government Act, both of which threatened all the chartered colonies, gave them no further excuse for their blindness.[113]

Preparations

The Coercive Acts helped to unite Connecticut in opposition. The General Assembly at once denounced the Port Act and asserted the right of colonies "to be governed by their General

Assembly in the article of taxing and internal police." Though
they prudently decided not to enter the resolves in the legislature's journals until they were sure that the other colonies had
responded likewise, the resolves did appear in the newspapers.[114] Many of the towns echoed them at meetings where
they condemned Parliament, pledged to support Boston with
supplies, and sometimes established their own committees of
correspondence.[115] Farmington went a step further and burned
the Boston Port Act before a liberty pole "forty-five feet
high."[116]

Other signs of incipient revolt appeared. In early July,
Francis Greene, who had signed a laudatory address to Governor Hutchinson of Massachusetts just before Hutchinson's departure for England, encountered hostile mobs at Windham
and Norwich. At Norwich he appealed to a magistrate, none
other than Samuel Huntington, the future president of Congress, who refused to help; at Windham, the people justified
themselves as righteously provoked since Hutchinson had been
a "principal agent" in procuring the recent acts of Parliament.[117] In early August, three hundred persons from Litchfield County joined a mob at Great Barrington, Massachusetts,
which obstructed court sessions and perpetrated the kidnapping
of Jared Ingersoll's cousin.[118] And though the colony's authorities did threaten to prosecute the ringleaders of this riot, they
condoned other acts and threats of violence toward suspected
Tories. A mob descended on Samuel Peters, the Anglican
clergyman at Hebron, interrogated him, and searched his
papers for copies of letters he might have written "unfriendly to
the rights and privileges of this Colony." Peters had indeed
written unfriendly letters, but they found no copies of them.
They did, however, find a series of resolves he had framed
which endorsed the Tea Act and condemned the towns of
Windham and Farmington for rioting. These they published,
together with a promise, which they forced from him and
which he subsequently broke, to intervene no further.[119]

Peters received gentle treatment compared to some. Abijah
Willard, one of General Gage's councillors, arrived at Union,
Connecticut, to collect some debts. Two Windham attorneys

openly refused to help him. A mob then seized him, imprisoned him for the night, and the next day carried him forcibly to Brimfield, Massachusetts, where a meeting of four hundred people threatened to throw him in Newgate Prison (formerly the Simsbury copper mine). They were taking him back to Connecticut to carry out the threat when he resigned his office.[120] In early September, Doctor Beebe of East Haddam suffered a tarring and feathering for refusing to swear to a mob that his "principles and practice" suited theirs. When he demanded prosecution of the offenders, Joseph Spencer replied that he saw no point in issuing a writ he could never execute without calling in outside force.[121]

Violence and abuse made the biggest splash, of course, but a more important development that summer was the quiet gathering of grass-roots support for an effective nonimportation movement. Connecticut had learned from the disintegration of the first. In early June, its Committee of Correspondence asserted that a general congress should take precedence over "every other measure":

> The resolves of merchants or any individual town or Province, however generously designed, must be partial . . . on the other hand, every measure recommended, every resolve come into by the whole united Colonies, must carry weight and influence with it on the mind of the people, and tend effectually to silence those base insinuations which our enemies are ever ready to throw out, of interested motives, sinister views, unfair practices, and the like, for the vile purposes of sowing the seeds of jealousy between the Colonies.[122]

The other colonies concurred, and a continental congress met in Philadelphia that September. The Hartford Committee of Correspondence also called for delegates from all Connecticut's towns to meet at Hartford on September 15. Towns from every county but Fairfield sent representatives. They voted to supplement any nonimportation agreement proposed by the Continental Congress with a pledge not to purchase or consume proscribed commodities and promised that any merchant who tried to anticipate nonimportation by ordering large quantities of English and West Indian goods in advance would fail in his attempt.[123]

Many of the clergy proved as active in resistance as their secular brethren. Several of them used the colony's fast day, August 31, to launch polemics against the Coercive Acts in which they identified civil liberty and religious liberty as one cause.[124] The established clergy had stronger incentives to support the patriots than ministers of other denominations. If Parliament assumed the right to regulate the colonies more closely, it might extend that right to include establishment of the Church of England in place of the Congregational church. The dissenters had less to lose. Indeed, the existing laws penalized some of them so heavily as to make Israel Holly speculate that America's problems were sent to punish that sin. Levi Hart of Farmington also thought sin was the cause, the sin of enslaving the African.[125] Yet, while the members of the clergy differed in identifying the root of the trouble, most of them agreed on the need for resistance. Benjamin Trumbull of North Haven even acquired a certain notoriety for his interest in military matters.[126] Only the Anglicans were silent and by their silence increased the suspicion that at heart they did not believe in the concept of American rights. The one clergyman who openly deplored the general unrest attracted censure.[127]

In late 1774, an incident in Massachusetts gave Connecticut a chance to show that she could and would take stronger measures than a boycott. On September 3 a report reached Connecticut that the troops sent to enforce the Port Act had clashed with the Massachusetts militia. Connecticut mobilized spontaneously, and some men set out for Boston. They turned back when they learned that, though Gage and his men had seized the Medford powder magazine, they had shed no blood.[128] Nevertheless, the incident impelled Gage to fortify Boston Neck. The ranks of New England's militia included the majority of its adult males, and no one knew better than he that their service in the Seven Years' War had schooled a whole generation of them in the techniques of North American warfare.[129] He had reason to fear that their political feeling, especially if it had reached the point where they would gather and march from distant places in response to provocation, would translate into military action with ease. The colonists, however, interpreted his action as one more sign of Britain's intent to use force.

Preparations to meet that force with force were already well underway. Four months before Gage showed his hand, the General Assembly had commissioned two independent military companies, organized two new militia regiments, and ordered an inventory of the colony's artillery.[130] Now someone suggested that the colonies "raise an *Army of Observation*" for deployment around Boston.[131] This was further than the Continental Congress would go until it received a response to its addresses, to its petition to the king, and to its newly formed Continental Association. But the General Assembly of Connecticut, less willing to wait, went ahead and authorized a program of military preparedness on an unprecedented level. The legislators ordered the militia to train for twelve half days before May 1, 1775, each noncommissioned officer and private to be paid six shillings for his time. They organized four more militia regiments, provided for a general inventory and repair of weapons, ordered the mounting of cannon at New London, and required the colony's entire armed force to muster at the end of November. These preparations would cost money. In addition to the customary tax of a penny on the pound, the government emitted £15,000 in bills of credit.[132]

No amount of money, though, could make up for the lack of good powder. Without powder, the colonists would remain at the mercy of the British. That is why the seizure of the Medford magazine moved New England so profoundly. During the autumn, the patriots of Massachusetts had worked at the wholesale secretion of military stores in and around Boston. In December, the patriots of New Hampshire and Rhode Island had seized the large stocks of powder and artillery at Fort William and Mary in Portsmouth and at Fort Wolcott in Newport.[133] Connecticut had no large military installation to plunder. And though every colony had begun to encourage the domestic production of powder, no reliable source had emerged so far. It soon became clear that the towns could not comply with the General Assembly's order to double their powder and shot without recourse to outside supplies.[134] In early 1775 the Council decided to lay the foundation for such recourse. To call an emergency session of the legislature would draw unwanted publicity. To wait for the next regular session, on the other hand, might give the British naval commander time to deploy vessels in every harbor on the coast, as some said he had orders to do. Therefore, the Council acting alone commissioned Nathaniel Shaw of New London to send fast sailing ships to the West Indies for powder and shot.[135]

Throughout the autumn and winter, Connecticut readied for war. At the same time, almost all the towns formally adopted the nonimportation agreement framed by Congress and elected committees of inspection to enforce the Association.[136] A few inland towns, which had little contact with the outside world, took no action. Two of the towns along the western border, Ridgefield and Newtown, publicly rejected the Association. The Tories of Danbury succeeded in briefly reversing an earlier vote by the town to adopt it, and some of the freeholders in Redding and New Milford openly dissented from the adoption voted by their towns.[137] Minority protests could be left to the communities in which they occurred, but majority rejection called for a weightier response. On February 14, 1775, a convention of Fairfield towns met to censure Ridgefield and Newtown and to recommend that patriots "withdraw and withhold all commerce, dealings, and connection from all the inhabitants of these two Towns" save those who had supported the Association.[138] When two persons from Ridgefield, who arrived in Wethersfield that same night, broadcast a boisterous justification of their town, some prominent citizens joined in drumming them out of town under the escort usually provided for "strolling ideots, lunaticks, &c."[139] Even in western Connecticut, loyalists did not exist in sufficient numbers to pose a real threat to the Association or to any other patriot enterprise.

By the beginning of March, when Trumbull called the legislature back into session, little remained to do. The legislators met for only eight days. They investigated charges against a few militia officers accused of disloyalty to the cause,

commissioned officers for the new regiments, and filled an un-
usual number of vacancies for field officers created by resignations on the eve of hostilities.[140] During peacetime, when the
militia had more an administrative than a military function,
field officers rarely resigned. But between May and October of
1774 four of them did, and eight more followed suit soon after.
Age or infirmity accounted for some of the resignations. But a
few, including those of William Samuel Johnson, Aaron Eliot,
and Thomas Fitch, had definite political overtones. No harm
came of them. On the contrary, the withdrawal of men unable
or unwilling to serve only strengthened the militia. In just one
year, Connecticut had moved from a divisiveness that bordered
on violence to an appearance of unanimity. As a result, her
leaders faced the future with more confidence than perhaps
they should have felt.

PART TWO

War

AMERICANS WAITED through the winter of 1775 to learn how Britain had responded to the Continental Association and to the petition from Congress. Many still believed that she would repudiate the ministry sooner than drive the colonies to fight.[1] But the end of January brought news that shattered their hopes. The king in his speech to Parliament of November 30 had complained of a "daring spirit of resistance and disobedience to the law" prevailing in Massachusetts Bay and had declared his own "steadfast resolution to withstand every attempt to weaken or impair the supreme authority of this Legislature over all the Dominions of my crown." The House of Lords and the House of Commons had both acclaimed this policy in their replies.[2] The colonists now knew that the ministry would enjoy the freedom to pursue coercive measures. The exact nature of those measures remained in doubt until the beginning of April, when they learned that the ministry intended to reinforce Gage in Boston, to restrict New England's commerce, and to outlaw the fisheries. Though Parliament did not act on the commercial proposals at once, Americans felt sure that they would pass. A joint address from both houses in early February had described Massachusetts as a colony in rebellion and had reaffirmed their determination to enforce Parliament's authority.[3]

Long before the beginning of April, the Provincial Congress of Massachusetts had commenced preparations for war. The arrival of several large men-of-war at Boston in mid-December had indicated how the king meant to maintain the authority of his Parliament,[4] and as early as February the Massachusetts Congress began to raise an army, to procure supplies, and to acquaint the other colonies with her circumstances.[5] Though both sides had incentives to strike before the other could gather its strength, both had even more incentive to make the other fire first. Massachusetts knew that she could not count on the support of other colonies unless she took a purely defensive stance.[6] And Gage still felt uncertain that the policy of force commanded the necessary political support in Britain. When the men-of-war arrived, he did march some detachments into the countryside to familiarize his troops with the terrain. In late February he even tried to seize some military supplies in Salem. But he had obviously told his men not to start a fight, for they allowed a mere show of strength to drive them back.[7] Gage made his attempt to seize the Concord magazine only after he received explicit orders from England.[8] Fortunately for the colonists, those orders did not arrive before news of the ministry's policy and Parliament's support for it had told them as plainly as possible that they could no longer avoid war.

CHAPTER TWO

Commitment

THE NEWS that British troops had shed blood at Lexington raced across southern New England. Joseph Palmer of the Massachusetts Committee of Safety dispatched a report from Watertown at 10:00 A.M., April 19. Twelve hours later, it reached Providence, Rhode Island. By eight the following morning, it had arrived in Newport.[1] In eastern Connecticut, it reached Brooklyn by 11:00 A.M., Norwich by 4:00 P.M., and New London by 7:00 P.M. Traveling westward along the coast during the night, the report came to Lyme's committee at 1:00 A.M. on the twenty-first, Saybrook's at 4:00, Killingworth's at 7:00, and Branford's at noon. New Haven heard the news later that afternoon and sent it forward to Fairfield. Fairfield received it at 8:00 A.M. on the twenty-second and sent it forward to New York.[2] Hard on its heels came word of the battle at Concord and the British retreat to Boston under the galling fire of the Massachusetts militia. False report kept pace with true, creating confusion everywhere about what really had happened.[3] But by Sunday, April 23, when Palmer's message reached New York, all but most remote northwestern communities knew that the long-smoldering dissension between royal and provincial forces had flamed into open conflict at last.

Enthusiasm

Tradition holds that Israel Putnam heard the news while tend-ing his fields on the morning of April 20. Without returning to the house, he sprang on a horse and rode hard to Cambridge, arriving on the twenty-first to find an army already assembling before Boston and in time to attend a council of war.[4] Others showed the same eagerness. Connecticut's Committee of Corre-spondence, writing on the twenty-first to the Massachusetts Provincial Congress, declared: "The ardour of our people is such, that they can't be kept back."[5] Still, it was just as well that not everyone acted so impulsively. Gage had chosen to strike during the spring, when supplies were low everywhere. If the 3,716 Connecticut men who marched within the week had gone on horseback,[6] they would have found little forage for their mounts either along the way or at Boston, where the spring grasses would not appear until late May. The men alone could scarcely be provisioned. Their march from Connecticut to eastern Massachusetts would take about a week. Each town sending a contingent had to find not only supplies but also the horses and wagons to carry them, no easy matter. Though a few towns had their men on the way by that turbulent Sab-bath, most contingents did not start before the last week in April.[7]

Forty-six of the colony's seventy-two towns sent troops toward Boston, and three towns in southwestern Connecticut sent 139 men to New York on hearing that the British meant to reinforce the small garrison there.[8] The town of Fairfield sent men to both places. Twenty-seven towns did nothing at all, not necessarily because of disaffection. Loyalist sentiment does partly explain why only three out of ten towns in Fairfield County answered the summons and why Waterbury sent no men,[9] but geography dictated the pattern of response as often as politics. East of the Connecticut River, all but two towns, Groton and Somers, sent detachments. By contrast, in the most remote county of Litchfield only little Norfolk responded. Many northwestern towns undoubtedly heard that the General

Assembly had called an emergency session for the twenty-sixth almost as soon as they heard about the fighting and guessed that it would end in a commitment to a sustained effort. These towns might well have decided to complete their spring chores while they could, rather than to sacrifice the crops in the cause of temporary relief for Boston. Many of the newer, poorer towns in the northwest could ill spare enough to feed the men until they reached Cambridge, let alone to keep them supplied in the field. But in the absence as yet of any commissary system, the towns would have to maintain the flow of supplies as long as their men were in arms. These considerations prompted Colonel Isaac Lee's decision to hold the men of older, more prosperous Farmington back from a pointless trek to Boston.[10] His judgment was vindicated when two-thirds of Connecticut's marchers returned in ten days, driven back before they reached their objective by reports of scant provisions at Boston.

Those who had wisely waited for government direction did not wait long. Within a week the legislature resolved upon a seven-month army of 6,000, almost one-quarter of the 26,260 militiamen reported by the colony in 1774.[11] This substantial force was to be raised on the ambitious scale of 100 men to a company. Though the militia had developed into a rudimentary selective service system during the late colonial wars, Connecticut still relied on the personal influence of the officers, backed by public opinion, for the voluntary recruitment of men to serve beyond her borders. Wherever the authorities expected to find recruits hard to come by, they multiplied officers. Before Lexington and Concord swept away most people's lingering hope that war was avoidable, the Massachusetts Provincial Congress could recruit in companies of no more than fifty men.[12] To stipulate one hundred men to a company revealed a confidence that the spirited response to this crisis would maintain the same pitch when the call came to sign on for seven months. Though the little evidence we have shows that even a brief exposure to army life left many men reluctant to reenlist,[13] that confidence proved justified. Lieutenant Colonel Roger Enos recruited 101 men in three days.[14] By the end of

May, six regiments of a thousand men each had formed. Never again in the course of the Revolution would troops enlist so readily for so long.

The mobilization of 1775 owed its success to more than the ignorant enthusiasm of untried men. The colonists really believed that they had the military and political advantage of their opponents. Past experience had shown that European armies labored under extraordinary difficulties on American soil. "Americanus" in the *Connecticut Gazette* of December 1774 had canvassed them in detail:

> there is not a power in Europe, formidable and numerous as their armies are in that country [*sic*], able to send and support an army of thirty thousand men in America . . . for various reasons, obvious at first view—the length of the voyage, sure to render the great part of troops embarked, unfit for service, on their arrival—the immense charge of transporting provision and of every kind of warlike stores, such a distance—and the great number of recruits, constantly wanted, to supply the losses, by sickness, death, or desertion, and which are not to be procured, nearer than from that distance.[15]

On only one occasion had any European force above ten thousand men ever conducted operations in the interior of North America, and then not without strong support from the colonists. The vast distances to traverse, and the difficulty of procuring provisions and transport where few had settled, made the obstacles almost insuperable. Hence the bravado of a "gentleman in Connecticut" who claimed in a letter of May 2, 1775, to feel "no apprehensions from General *Gage's* ever being able to penetrate into the country thus far, if he was even reinforced with fifty thousand men."[16] Few colonists then expected to face even as many as twenty thousand. The ministry had deliberately refrained from asking for much increase in the armed forces. And Americans thought that any attempt to mount a massive attack on them would undermine the political supports of the British government. Lastly, the morale of the British troops stationed in North America since 1763 had sunk so low as to inspire neither awe nor even the conviction that they wanted to fight.[17] On the whole, the colonists felt confident that, despite their inexperience, they could overcome a professional European army through superior numbers and irregular tactics.[18]

Even so, that belief gained more currency in Connecticut than in Massachusetts, Rhode Island, and New York. Those colonies knew from the start that the war would be fought on their ground. Connecticut thought so, too, which helped the work of recruiters there. Connecticut recruiters could also exploit economic factors. The colony's economy, in crisis for the past ten years, had come nearly to a standstill between the congressional nonimport, nonexport, nonconsumption Association and Lord North's policy of restraining New England commerce.[19] Just as the few remaining options seemed about to disappear, along came the prospect of jobs in the army. We have only a partial knowledge of wages paid during the early 1770s, but what evidence there is suggests that the package offered a fully equipped recruit in the seven-month army compared very well with the three shillings a day he could earn as an unskilled laborer at the peak of the farming season.[20] Though privates were paid only forty shillings a month, they also received fifty-two shillings for a blanket, knapsack, and clothing; ten shillings for a musket, bayonet, and cartouche box; and food worth at least fifteen shillings a month. Given the month's advance pay he pocketed upon enlistment, the man who could equip himeslf (and no others were accepted) would start out with slightly more than five pounds in cash. It would take him six to eight weeks to earn such a sum at farm labor, even during the peak season, and he would still have his food and clothing to buy.[21] Yet another advantage, not just to the recruit, was the legislature's promise to pay in a £50,000 emission of bills of credit. Money had begun to flow freely again.[22]

That Connecticut heard few voices raised against her military policies, and could silence those few with ease, also helped recruitment. Alone among the colonies, Connecticut moved from peace to war without having to reconstruct her political institutions. Because her committee system did not have to bypass stubborn loyalist officials, her government could concentrate on organizing the people for the coming struggle. In

Rhode Island, the governor and several councillors had resisted the Assembly's call to arms.[23] In Connecticut, however, circumstances gave those few high-ranking officials who would have done the same no chance to speak. When the Assembly met on April 26, the members received reports from David Trumbull, the governor's son and special emissary to Massachusetts; from a member of the Massachusetts Provincial Congress, and from sundry travelers heading west. All agreed that the British had fired first and that all colonies must support Massachusetts.[24] It now remained only to dispose of the possibility that Gage would repudiate the acts of his subordinates. At the legislature's request, Governor Trumbull wrote to Gage inviting him to give his account of events and to suspend hostilities. The two most influential advocates of moderation in the legislature, Erastus Wolcott and William Samuel Johnson, were deputed to carry the letter, and for a moment Massachusetts feared that Connecticut meant to abandon her. But Gage's reply removed that doubt,[25] and Connecticut had taken advantage of Wolcott's and Johnson's absence to develop her mobilization plans unhindered. Even in the western part of the state, where strong loyalist opposition persisted, it had little effect on recruitment.

The seizure of Ticonderoga and Crown Point also helped to silence the moderates. During the Seven Years' War, these posts had been bitterly contested because of their strategic importance to control of the waterways between New York and Canada. When the war ended, Britain had left a large store of artillery and ammunition there under a token guard. In 1775 artillery and ammunition were what the colonists needed most, especially if they were to drive Gage out of Boston. Besides, the possession of these posts would secure the northern frontier against the enemy. Tradition credits Benedict Arnold and Samuel Holden Parsons with conceiving the attack at a chance meeting near Hartford on April 27. Arnold was on his way to Boston with a volunteer company, and Parsons was returning with a report on the situation there for the emergency session of the legislature.[26] The advantage of capturing the posts before they could be reinforced was obvious. As soon as Arnold propounded the idea to the Massachusetts Committee of Safety, they made him a colonel and authorized him to raise a regiment in the western part of the state.[27] With equal ease, Parsons persuaded some influential Connecticut legislators to join him in borrowing £300 from the state treasury on their personal security, for use in raising men in western Massachusetts and the New Hampshire Grants.[28] On the morning of May 10, Ethan Allen, whom the Connecticut Committee of War had appointed to command the expedition, together with Benedict Arnold led eighty-one men in a surprise attack on Ticonderoga. The garrison of forty-eight troops surrendered without serious casualty on either side.[29] On the eleventh, Crown Point fell unresisting into the hands of a smaller party under Seth Warner.[30]

Success raised new problems. To ensure surprise, neither the Continental Congress nor New York, within whose jurisdiction both posts lay, had been consulted in advance. As a safeguard against subsequent repudiation by Congress, Connecticut had kept the expedition "unofficial." The revolutionary government of Massachusetts, already totally committed to the war, had shown less caution. Arnold's commission gave him a claim to legal authority that neither Ethan Allen nor the Committee of War could match, which produced a dispute over command almost ruinous to the enterprise.[31] The New York government presented another hazard. New York was the weakest political link in the chain of colonies from New Hampshire to South Carolina. The small size of her lower house made it susceptible to executive influence. As a result, the Assembly failed to provide a focus for popular resistance, and the burden of mobilizing the people fell on extralegal committees which had to struggle against loyalist opposition at every turn. The loyalists questioned the authority of New York City's committee to obey the First Continental Congress and call for the election of delegates to the Second. They also questioned its right to summon a Provincial Convention that would supplant New York's regular government.[32] Only in May had the news of Lexington and Concord swung the pendulum of local opinion far enough in the committee's favor to permit the calling of a revolutionary congress, and New England's decision to take

Crown Point and Ticonderoga without consulting New York might swing it back again.[33]

On May 23 Connecticut received a resolution passed by the Continental Congress approving the captures.[34] Unfortunately Congress also ordered that the posts be abandoned as too hard to hold, a decision which Connecticut's leadership immediately protested. While Trumbull wrote urging Congress to reconsider, a delegation from the General Assembly composed of Nathaniel Wales, Jr., Thaddeus Burr, and Pierpont Edwards tried to persuade the New York Congress to undertake responsibility for the defense of the northern frontier.[35] But a report from Arnold dated May 23, warning that the British, with their Indian allies, were advancing south along the lakes, aborted this attempt to involve New York. Connecticut's immediate response was to dispatch 400 men and 500 pounds of powder to Ticonderoga.[36] Soon afterward, having received an invitation from New York to occupy the forts, she sent forward Colonel Benjamin Hinman with an additional 600 men. Pleased as Connecticut was to learn that Congress approved these actions, the fact remained that she had obtained no help from her neighbor other than a pledge of provisions.[37]

New York's inability to man her own posts in this crisis raised the suspicion that she pursued a policy not of involvement but of neutrality, a suspicion fed by subsequent events. When the sixty-four-gun British ship *Asia* arrived in New York on May 27, the New York Congress sanctioned her provisioning by a naval contractor; later, it permitted the small British garrison in the city to embark for Boston, and ordered the return of all arms, accoutrements, and military stores either pilfered or sequestered from the magazine at Turtle Bay.[38] Connecticut's leaders must have itched to take a hand in New York's government, using the two regiments then gathering at Greenwich under David Wooster, but dared not risk it on their own, particularly as Hinman's regiment on the lakes would have to depend on New York for provisions. They had to wait and fret while New York fiddled. In mid-June, when the news came that four of the regiments sent from Europe to reinforce Gage were headed for New York, the Continental Congress urged that Conneticut troops occupy the city. Soon afterward, amended reports gave the British destination as Boston, not New York, whereupon the New York Congress politely suggested that Wooster march his troops eastward instead. Wooster, however, ignored their recommendation, occupied the town, and seized the stores at Turtle Bay.[39] Reluctant as they were to become a certain battleground in the coming conflict, New Yorkers had either to acquiesce or to risk antagonizing the entire continent.

Conneticut's enthusiasm for the cause seemed to lend itself less readily to the reinforcement of Massachusetts than to the occupation of New York. Though on May 4 the Massachusetts Provincial Congress called on Connecticut for three to four thousand men to help drive Gage out of Boston, only two regiments under Joseph Spencer and Israel Putnam received orders to march. A little later, in response to reports that Gage would soon receive reinforcements, the newly formed Council of Safety, which would exercise executive power throughout the war, ordered out two more companies of Parson's Sixth Regiment at New London together with two and a half tons of powder, which was even scarcer than men.[40] But until she knew for certain that the reinforcements were bound for Boston, Connecticut had several reasons to keep some troops back. Since the New York Congress had made no effort to mobilize, Connecticut would have to take sole responsibility for the defense of her western flank should the British commence operations in that vicinity. For this reason she was reluctant to commit the bulk of her forces to Boston until she was certain the British were concentrating there.

Connecticut also wished to guard New London against possible naval bombardment. On the eve of Lexington, Vice Admiral Samuel Graves had only twenty-four ships. But two of them, stationed at Newport under Captain James Wallace, had threatened to level the town if Rhode Island sent Boston any of the troops voted by its legislature.[41] This threat aroused apprehension in other coastal communities too, which may explain why the two Connecticut towns nearest to Newport—

Stonington and Groton—sent almost no men in response to the
Lexington alarm.[42] And the fear of attack increased with time.
In May, Wallace used his large complement of sailors to man
tenders that could pursue colonial ships into the shallow waters
of New England's coast. Soon they began seizing provision vessels too.[43] No wonder Connecticut reserved some of Parsons's
men at New London in order to cover the arrival, expected at
any moment, of powder shipments from the West Indies.[44] If
Wallace found out that this vital commodity had reached an
unguarded port, what was to stop him from destroying it?

Only on June 17, the very day of the Battle of Bunker
Hill, when the Council of Safety learned that the British reinforcements had indeed landed in Boston, did they send forward
Parsons's remaining 600 men. Two companies from Wooster's
regiment were summoned east to take their place.[45] But Massachusetts almost immediately signaled a need for yet more
men. On June 25 her Provincial Congress, convinced that the
ministry had singled her out for vengeance, appealed to the
neighboring colonies for help. The appeal avoided setting
quotas and left each colony to decide what she could do. It did,
however, note the military opinion that 30,000 men would be
needed to contain an enemy force of 10,000. Massachusetts felt
she could supply only 13,600 and pleaded with Connecticut to
help supply the remainder.[46] Trumbull summoned the legislature to consider the matter, but this time with less striking results. The General Assembly authorized only two additional
regiments of 700 men to serve for five months, a restraint engendered more by the fear that Congress would not accept the
cost as a Continental expense than by the exhaustion of
Connecticut's resource. Still, if the second largest colony in New
England could spare less than 5,000 men to the siege of Boston,
an army of 30,000 was clearly beyond reach.[47]

Preemptive Warfare

No matter how many troops had gone to Boston, two constraints would have prevented the use of them to expel the Brit-

ish throughout 1775. A chronic shortage of artillery and especially of powder made offensive warfare a luxury that the
revolutionaries could not afford.[48] And the carnage that the en-
trenched American troops had inflicted on their exposed enemy
at Breed's Hill encouraged no one to court a reversal of the
roles played on that day.[49] Bunker Hill had taught Americans
that their best strategy was to occupy strong points, then wait
for the British to attack. The army besieging Boston had been
deployed with this in mind, though circumstances did not in
fact favor the patriots as highly as before. The enemy had the
advantage of concentration, while Washington had to spread his
troops over a broad front.[50] As it turned out, he need not have
worried about his extended lines. Bunker Hill had its effect
upon the British too, and they refused to attack on disadvantageous terms. The stalemate that ensued gave the revolutionaries a welcome breathing space in which to mold an army
from a mass of raw recruits. If it continued, however, it could
inflict irreparable damage on the cause.

The belief that victory would come quickly and cheaply
had inflamed the initial enthusiasm for the Revolution; the loss
of that belief might so disenchant the people as to put out the
fire forever. Washington felt especially concerned lest the cost
of maintaining his men through the autumn should hinder the
raising of a new army when the old one's time had expired. He
toyed in the late summer with the notion of an attempt to take
Boston by storm,[51] but a Council of General Officers put a
quick end to this dream. The ruinous consequences that would
follow if they should fail, and their hope that the reverses already suffered by the British at Boston would cause a change of
ministries, made them unwilling to risk all on one throw of the
dice.[52] At the same time, something had to be done to reconcile
the people to the cost of a new army. Fortunately, the patriots
had already begun exploring the possibility of seizing other
"Bunker Hills" of indisputable strategic value. The targets that
appeared most eligible for the purpose were New York and
Quebec.

New York gave access to the Connecticut and New Jersey
coasts and to the river that linked New England with the rest of

the continent. New York contained three sizable islands and good sources for provisions. New York also had a large population, much of which continued to show little enthusiasm for the Revolution. Given the difficulties Howe had encountered at Boston, he might decide to move there. Not only were provisions hard to come by in Boston and the quarters worse than cramped, but the town lay open to a number of surrounding high points like Breed's Hill and the Dorchester Heights. In August, the possibility that Howe would leave Boston for New York led Washington to acquiesce in Governor Trumbull's decision to keep Charles Webb's five-month regiment along the coast.[53] Trumbull wanted protection against Wallace's men-of-war, which had actually landed a small contingent at New London on July 26. He had also to contend with some dozen ships that were removing stock from neighboring islands.[54] When the ships first left Boston, Washington had feared that they might represent the beginning of a British attempt to occupy New York. And though it soon appeared otherwise, the possibility of such a move remained a worry, particularly as, at the request of Congress, Wooster had just sent northward David Waterbury's regiment, which represented more than half of Wooster's men.[55]

The ability of neighboring revolutionaries to occupy New York before the British could arrive led the patriot leadership to concentrate instead on Quebec, where they could entertain no such hope. Other considerations recommended the northern outpost as well. The weather would keep it safe for half the year, and for the other half the town's fortifications would give its defenders the power to withstand superior numbers. During the Seven Years' War the French had held Quebec until 1759 and lost it then only because the British colonists had overwhelmingly supported the attackers. Possession of Quebec would guarantee the northern flank of the colonies against either a British invasion or a British-incited Indian attack. On June 27, therefore, Congress authorized Philip Schuyler, commander in the north, to enter Canada in force if he thought the move practicable and not "disagreeable to the Canadians."[56] So bold an action did not appeal to Schuyler's temperament, but

reports of the British garrison's weakness, and of many Canadians who would defect, converted him to the scheme.[57] By
early August, every day lessened the likelihood that Governor
Carleton would receive reinforcements from Europe. Meanwhile the return of the foraging fleets to Boston, the building of
barracks, the forays after fuel, and various reports from deserters or spies combined to make Washington sure that the
British meant to winter there. He decided to aid Schuyler's Canadian venture and ordered that 1,200 men detached from his
army at Boston be marched to Quebec through central
Maine.[58]

Considering that three of the five senior officers on this expedition, namely, Benedict Arnold, Roger Enos, and Return
Jonathan Meigs, hailed from Connecticut, her contribution of
100 men seems meager. In fact she played a larger role than ap-
pearances suggest, since Washington had decided to replace
some of the men sent from Boston to Canada with the five-
month regiment retained by Connecticut.[59] His call for these
men unfortunately coincided with the appearance of a second
foraging fleet. The first had confined itself to spiking a few cannon at New London, plundering several undefended islands,
and seizing a bit of shipping; the second bombarded Stonington
on August 29.[60] This attack should actually have reduced the
fear of Wallace, for it was singularly ineffectual. As a local
clergyman wrote to his daughter, "(wonderfull, even to as-
tonishment) not one human Person [was] killd, only one
wounded, now almost well—not one house or building brot
down, nor greatly damaged . . . nor any dumb creature killd
or hurt, save one Cat, I am told."[61] But the coastal towns took
alarm and clamored for protection. On September 4 the Council of Safety ordered Webb's five-month regiment, including
the three companies held in reserve for New York, to deploy
along the coastline.[62] On that same evening, Trumbull received
Washington's directive commanding that these men march to
Cambridge.

Understandably, Trumbull demurred. In a letter written
on September 5 he pointed out how grave a threat the foraging
fleet posed. But Washington was adamant. He invoked a con-

gressional understanding that the militia, not the Continental troops, should defend the coast and insisted that the men come at once. Connecticut had to obey, lest "advantage . . . be taken against the Colony should we refuse to send them."[63] But she resented the demand that local needs give place to continental needs, the more so because two problems had arisen in the defense of her coastline. One concerned the obstacles she had encountered in the attempt to develop a seagoing force powerful enough to challenge Britain's. The other was financial.

In contrast to the speed with which she raised an army, Connecticut procrastinated in fitting out a fleet. Not until July did the legislature order even two armed vessels to guard the coast, and then only after Wooster complained that his operations in New York had suffered from the lack of them.[64] A committee appointed by the Council of Safety to examine ways and means of fitting out the vessels indicated reasons for the delay. On August 2 it reported that "the people are differently minded about the measure, many thinking that as it is impossible for us to compare by sea with the British ships, &c., it will but provoke insult and expose our sea coasts and vessels inward bound to greater danger."[65] The committee in fact exaggerated the British navy's capability. Shallow waters prevented it from deploying heavy armaments along large parts of the east coast. That is why Wallace's largest vessel was a twenty-gun sixth-rater and why he deployed so much of his manpower in shallow-draft tenders.[66] This factor, together with their own superior knowledge of the rugged, largely unmarked tidal waters, should have allowed the colonists to challenge Britain's naval superiority along the shore. But the committee assessed public opinion rightly. To fit out the *Spy*, a fast-sailing reconnaissance ship, proved easy, as she need not expect to do battle with a man-of-war.[67] Numerous delays, however, and a mutiny inspired by doubts that the vessel was seaworthy, obstructed Connecticut's efforts to equip the sixteen-gun *Minerva*.[68] After months of work to get her ready, the brig made one brief cruise on the Sound in December before she was decommissioned.[69]

The need for economy further hampered the defense of the

coast that autumn. The eight regiments Connecticut had already supplied represented an advance of £150,000 to the cause.[70] To meet the expense, the legislature had issued half as many bills of credit in the first few months of hostilities with Britain as it had in the entire course of the Seven Years' War.[71] Though Congress had voted a partial reimbursement, the money had not yet arrived. Connecticut's leadership feared that if the colony continued to contract debts faster than Congress repaid her, the people would grow disillusioned. And the warnings of their delegates to Congress against unauthorized advances to the common cause made them also fear that, should the war end with a majority of the colonies in debt to Connecticut, those who had advanced the least might ignore their obligations to those who advanced the most.[72]

Political and economic prudence both dictated that Connecticut scale down her military efforts, yet a refusal to protect the coast would damage the movement as seriously as continued overspending. The shelling of Bristol, Rhode Island, on October 7 and the destruction of Falmouth (now Portland, Maine) on October 18, the first execution of Graves's savage orders to devastate the coast, had certainly verified the need for coastal defense.[73] Fortunately, a favorable conjunction of circumstances during the autumn of 1775 enabled Connecticut's government to deal with the dilemma by resorting to means that gave more reassurance than protection but cost correspondingly less.

The British had too few ships for winter maneuvers, hazardous at any time, to appeal to them now. Besides, as Connecticut perceived, Rhode Island was busy hobbling Wallace's force at Newport. Though not privy to Graves's orders that attacks on Connecticut yield to the objective of a foothold at Newport,[74] the leadership knew that Wallace had threatened to destroy Newport if the colony did not withdraw its troops from Aquidneck Island. He hoped this would force Newport to support the British in their attempt to gain control of all the island with its quantities of livestock.[75] But apart from the fact that Newport had lost considerable influence by her eagerness to provision Wallace, the revolutionary government guessed that he was bluffing. After all, to carry out his threat would injure those friendly to the British without hurting their enemies much. Accordingly, the Rhode Islanders would agree to no more than the removal of troops from the town itself. This meant that the British obtained only enough provisions to maintain the force immediately under Wallace's command, for which slight gain they became virtual prisoners in Narragansett Bay.[76] Forays elsewhere could be punished by severance of supplies. Because Connecticut might reasonably hope to be left alone until spring, she could afford for the moment to treat the matter of coastal defense as a political rather than a military problem. The government therefore confined its efforts to the borrowing of cannon for the ports and to the ritual of cruising the *Minerva*.[77]

Connecticut had less success in adjusting to the strains imposed by the Canadian expedition. During the summer and autumn of 1775, as Schuyler gathered the necessary force for an invasion of Canada, he had leaned heavily upon Connecticut. New York had been slow to raise her battalions, Massachusetts was still concentrating on Boston, and factional rivalry paralyzed the New Hampshire Grants.[78] When Schuyler made his weakness known, Connecticut sent him £15,000, a large supply of powder, and over the course of several months, almost two thousand additional men.[79] Despite this dependence on her, Schuyler quarreled with Connecticut's officers and offended her men as Washington never had.

It is fair to say that the New Yorker faced greater difficulties than the Virginian. The task of moving a large force up the lakes to Canada posed problems more tangled than any that arose in the course of maintaining an army at Boston. Washington's attempts to weld an amorphous mass into an army had actually received some help from the surroundings. He could assume the support of a society willing to reinforce military authority whenever necessary, and the enemy's nearness provided the men with a powerful incentive to accept discipline.[80] Moreover, no one had ever disputed his role as commander-in-chief. Schuyler lacked these advantages. The enemy was too far off and too weak to attack. His unruly army had assembled at a wilderness post far from the constraints of civilization. As a New Yorker, he found the distrust that Connecticut felt for his province transferred to his person. And he had also to contend with Wooster, twenty years Schuyler's senior and a major-general in the Connecticut militia, who resented his relegation to the inferior rank of brigadier in the Continental army.[81]

It is also true, though, that Schuyler went out of his way to ruffle people's feelings. Connecticut would be his sole support until mid-August, since Congress had neglected even to vote funds before the beginning of the month.[82] Yet Schuyler objected to the liberal daily rations granted Connecticut's troops by the General Assembly and accused their provisioning agent of waste and embezzlement.[83] In early August he appointed Walter Livingston, a fellow New Yorker and kinsman, to supervise and restrict the issue of stores.[84] He made his greatest mistake, however, when he quarreled with the colony's high-ranking officers, who alone commanded the goodwill of their men.

It is instructive to contrast Schuyler's handling of the militia's reluctance to muster under the Continental articles of war with Washington's response to the same problem. Observing that it would be "vain to attempt to reason away the Prejudices of the whole Army," Washington forbore to press the issue any further than Connecticut's officers would willingly go.[85] As a consequence, he kept their loyalty. Schuyler's approach brought less happy results. The Connecticut regiments remained distinct not only in form but in fact. This appeared when Wooster called a court-martial on his own authority and undertook to discharge men from the Connecticut regiments as if he possessed an independent command. But Schuyler made a bad business worse when he took issue with Wooster's action before Congress,[86] ensuring that his complaints would filter back to the Connecticut troops. And he openly baited Wooster, whose cooperation he needed to persuade the men to march north, with this petty note:

Being well informed that you have declared, on your way to this place, that if you were at *St. John's,* you would march into the

Fort, at the head of your regiment, as it is just that you should have an opportunity of showing your prowess and that of your regiment, I have desired General *Montgomery* to give you leave to make the attempt, if you choose. I do not wish, however, that you should be too lavish with your men's lives, unless you have a prospect of gaining the Fortress.[87]

While it is true that Wooster left much to be desired as an officer, Schuyler showed poor judgment in pursuing the quarrel with him.[88]

In the end, partly through Schuyler's blunders, the army that advanced on Canada in the autumn of 1775 resembled an armed rabble more than a cohesive force. Only the New Yorkers and Canadians acknowledged his authority at all, and then perfunctorily.[89] By the time he reached Montreal, the greater part of the Connecticut seven-month regiments had melted away, the men pleading sickness. Sickness there was, fostered by crowded, unsanitary barracks, lack of tents for shelter, and a poor diet for which the Connecticut soldiers blamed the cut in their rations ordered by Schuyler. But the rate of sickness was so much higher among the Connecticut men than among the New Yorkers as to suggest a form of desertion.[90] Schuyler certainly thought so and as usual said so, too. On November 20 he wrote to Congress reporting on 200 Connecticut troops recently discharged as invalids, "not one willing to re-engage for the winter service" or to do any work within their present term:

> Of all the specificks ever invented for any, there is none so efficacious as a discharge for the prevailing disorder. No sooner was it administered, but it perfected the cure of nine out of ten, who, refusing to wait for boats to go by way of Fort *George*, slung their heavy packs, crossed the lake at this place, and undertook a march of two hundred miles with the greatest goodwill and alacrity.[91]

Vindictive to the end, he refused to give food for the journey to any of those returning home.[92] That two-thirds of the Connecticut troops left the service in this manner does them no credit; but Schuyler, who had himself pleaded sickness as a reason to stay in the rear throughout the campaign, was ill placed to censure them.

The New Army

The Americans lost more than half their men in the unsuccessful bid for Quebec on December 31, yet the city remained an inviting objective to them. Carleton had gathered together the scattered units that remained under his command in Quebec before the Americans arrived, but his force had grown no stronger. If Arnold and Wooster could receive fresh troops in time, they might still capture the undermanned garrison before spring broke the ice and British reinforcements arrived.[93] Even before Congress learned of the defeat, it had voted to send nine more battalions to Canada, and two battalions from the middle colonies had already started for Albany. On January 17, when the news arrived, Congress decided to offer an extraordinary bounty of six and two-thirds dollars, together with a month's advance pay, to every soldier who enlisted in the northern army. The next day, it advanced $12,500 to each colony then raising a battalion for Canada.[94] One of these was Connecticut.

Connecticut had received the news from Canada on January 16. On the eighteenth, Governor Trumbull called for volunteers and within a week had raised the bounty and terms of service to meet the specifications of Congress.[95] Charles Burrall was appointed colonel of the prospective regiment. On February 1 the Council of Safety agreed to advance the bounty to recruits, ordering John Lawrence, the colony's treasurer, to station himself in northwestern Connecticut and prepare for the inundation of volunteers that the Council expected.[96] It did not come. By the end of March, only one of Burrall's companies had passed Albany on its way to Canada. Schuyler warned that thinning ice might prevent others from following, and indeed Burrall's regiment does not appear in the returns of the northern army until the middle of May, after Quebec had been relieved and the siege abandoned.[97]

Connecticut fell short of her obligations for many reasons.

A dispute among field officers held up recruitment from the start. Major Nathaniel Buell refused to serve under Lieutenant Colonel Edward Mott. Though Mott had rendered distinguished service in the previous northern campaign, to those from northwestern Connecticut he was an eastern outsider. As soon as he saw that the very people from whom the regiment should come would never accept him, Mott magnanimously resigned, but precious time had been lost.[98] Then again, a winter march to Quebec entailed severe hardships. It would take time for a man to equip himself to withstand them,[99] and why should he when a more attractive alternative existed? Connecticut was under requisition to supply four two-month militia regiments for service around Boston in addition to her Continental quota.[100] Militia service, both briefer and, in this case, closer to home, competed with long-term enlistments for Canada. And the cost of both at once rendered impossible a hopeful suggestion from Washington that the colony boost the number of those who volunteered for Canadian service by doubling the one month's advance pay already offered.[101] But perhaps the most serious obstacle to recruitment was that Burrall sought his men in the area which Hinman and David Waterbury had tapped for the preceding campaign, and the likeliest prospects had heard too many veteran's stories of Schuyler's harsh treatment. Burrall's regiment might never have formed at all but for assurances from the officers that, once in Canada, the men would be out of Schuyler's jurisdiction and would most likely be commanded by the popular Charles Lee.[102]

The difficulties met by those who sought the reenlistment of Continental troops at Boston had other causes too. In the autumn of 1775, when Connecticut embarked on the attempt to recruit the new army from the ranks of the old, no one expected trouble. Thanks to the new Continental establishment, Connecticut owed some eight hundred less men than she had supplied in the spring.[103] She should have had no added costs to bear, since pay and provisions were supposed to come from the Continental treasury. Furthermore, Congress had authorized Washington to designate all officers in the new army, so that he could use the knowledge gained during the last campaign to rusticate the less effective ones and to place those who had proven themselves where they could best use their influence with the men. The only apparent impediment to recruitment was the requirement of service for twelve months rather than seven, and even that might prove an attraction to some. Where but in the army could a casual laborer receive a guarantee of twelve months' wages at comparable rates? If any further temptation were needed, however, the promise of cheap uniforms and a furlough for all soldiers who signed on again would surely supply it.[104]

Alas, these apparent assets turned out to be liabilities. Though the colony owed fewer men to the Continental army, the departure for Quebec of two popular officers, Benedict Arnold and Return Jonathan Meigs, and the disgrace of a third, Roger Enos, hurt the recruitment drive.[105] Nor did the decision of Congress to assume all costs of the new army suit the Connecticut rank and file. Still as parochial as when they refused to muster under the Continental articles of war, they objected to Continental pay as Continental control. The colony's government sought to appease them by dispatching most of its reimbursement money to the camp at Boston,[106] but on December 1, when their term of service expired, the troops began to abandon the lines. They took their arms and ammunition with them, even more vital at the time than their persons.[107] The officers used "threats [and] persuasion" to prevent the wholesale defection of men, and the army did recover some of the pilfered equipment through "the Activity of the People of the Country who sent back many of them that had set out." Nevertheless, more than eighty got away, and on December 12 the Connecticut troops departed *en masse*, though their officers had assured Washington that they would stay until relieved by the Massachusetts and New Hampshire militias.[108]

Washington was furious. In private, he spoke of the "dirty, mercenary spirit" of the Connecticut troops.[109] In public, he exercised restraint, but he let Governor Trumbull know that he felt betrayed. Congress agreed. Eliphalet Dyer reported from Philadelphia that the "poor Connecticut troops have lost (here) all their fame and all their glory. you will scarce hear anything but execrations against them."[110] Not that the gap left by their flight created more than a momentary danger. Though the American lines, already outnumbered, would have faced hopeless odds if Howe had received reinforcements before he did, the neighboring militia came into camp so promptly that by the end of December the army had recovered its strength.[111] Washington knew, too, that the Connecticut troops had not permanently deserted the cause. But he felt sure that they had tried to force their government to raise the terms that Congress had offered new recruits and that all New Englanders who hung back from reenlistment acted on the same ignoble principle.

Congress had not changed the wage scales adopted by New England's governments in 1775 except to raise the pay for captains and subalterns. It had, however, tried to cut the costs of maintaining the army by abandoning the practice of offering bounties. In 1775 a fully equipped Connecticut recruit had received £3.2s. In 1776, unless he were marching to Canada, he would receive only twelve shillings for a blanket, and about one-fifth of his monthly wages would be withheld to pay for his clothing. All those who condemned the Connecticut troops for their behavior perfectly understood that they were dealing with a strike for better pay. But they thought it inadmissible, for two reasons.[112]

First, a military showdown had become inescapable. The colonists had long cherished the hope that when England heard what had happened in Massachusetts her people would petition Parliament and the throne with even more determination than in the 1760s, during the movement for parliamentary reform, and force a change of ministry.[113] A nearly unanimous voice of popular disapprobation might shake the North ministry's hold on Parliament. Nothing less would do it. And by the autumn of 1775 informed colonial leaders knew that the response had fallen short of the volume needed to bring down North.[114] His ministry would increase its use of force, and the colonists must prepare to fight a major war on terms of Britain's choosing. The times called for Roman virtue rather than fair-weather patriotism, and Connecticut's desertion had raised a doubt that

Americans possessed virtue. Tory advocates of submission played on that doubt for all it was worth.[115]

The second reason for the abuse directed at Connecticut was that she appeared to other colonies, particularly her nearest neighbors, to have profited by the outbreak of war. The raising of a large army for Massachusetts and northern New York had reversed some long-standing economic relationships. Formerly a mere satellite to the centers of international commerce, Connecticut became the supplier on whom all others depended. The change had both economic and political causes. Eastern Massachusetts had lost agricultural self-sufficiency some time before and no longer had a surplus with which to support a large army.[116] The attempt to starve the British out of Boston, especially given the presence of the Royal Navy, made it hard to continue importing food from the middle and southern colonies. New York preferred to send her agricultural surplus to the West Indies since the Continental commissaries could pay only in bills of credit that would be worthless if the British won. Not until Graves ordered that all colonial provision vessels be seized and sent to Boston did southern New York decide to abandon these shipments and supply the continent instead.[117] Even then, Connecticut had the advantage of closer proximity.

As early as May 1775 the Provincial Congress of Massachusetts realized that the neighboring colonies would become economically indispensable. Hitherto doubtful of their paper money, Massachusetts now accepted it as legal tender.[118] Possession of these bills, particularly Connecticut's, would give Massachusetts a claim on the surplus food of other areas, a surplus that might become her only resource. The speculation proved sound. Joseph Trumbull, Governor Trumbull's oldest son, having provisioned Connecticut troops at Boston on a scale no other New England commissary could match, went on to fill the needs of the Massachusetts commissary. The success of Connecticut's commissary so impressed Washington that he recommended the appointment of Trumbull as commissary general of the army, to which Congress agreed without hesitation.[119] Since Congress planned to finance the war with Continental bills of credit, of which each colony would pay a proportional share,[120] Connecticut could now hope to be transformed from chronic debtor to general creditor. "Cato," writing in the *Connecticut Gazette,* pointed to the advantages the colony enjoyed:

> The greater part of the money that is issued to defray the enormous expenses of the war, is expended among us—We have a market for the productions of our farms, and good pay in hand, which is not the case with any of the southern provinces. What vend, for instance, has Virginia for her Tobacco, the great source of her wealth? or indeed any of the adjacent provinces, for the productions of their land? and yet they have their equal part of the charge to defray.[121]

The other colonies thought so, too, and thought that when men stood to gain so much from the cause it ill became them to desert the lines out of greed.

On the home front, the benefits conferred by traffic with the army had their effect. Governor Trumbull told Washington that the "late extraordinary and reprehensible conduct of some of the troops of this Colony, impresseth me, and the minds of many of our people, with grief, surprise, and indignation." He went on to say "that the people of the towns where most of the men belong, were so greatly affected with their unreasonable conduct, that they would readily march to supply their places."[122] An emergency session of the legislature tried to make other amends. It passed an act subjecting deserters to fines and imprisonment and provided that exemption from the poll tax would henceforth be granted only to those who had served out their terms. The legislature also established a reserve force of minutemen, consisting of one-quarter of the militia together with "as many other able bodied effective men not included in any militia roll." Each man had to equip himself with arms, ammunition, and knapsack, for which purpose he would receive eight shillings. He must attend training for one half day a fortnight at one shilling a drill. Severe penalties were imposed on "inimicals," defined as those who gave the enemy provisions or information, or enlisted in the British army, or encouraged others to enlist. By the same law, any person who, "by writing or speaking, or by any overt act," libeled or defamed Congress or the General Assembly could be disarmed, disenfranchised, fined, and imprisoned. The legislature commissioned two armed sloops and four row galleys and retained the *Spy* for public service. Finally, it provided that all those who reenlisted for 1776 would enjoy immunity from imprisonment for debt.[123]

This was amends indeed. Washington, deeply impressed, hailed the proceedings of Connecticut as a model for other New England colonies.[124] Meanwhile, the frosty reception accorded in most communities to those who had disgraced the colony by deserting, added to the discovery that they would not receive prompt payment for service in 1775 unless they reenlisted for 1776, sent many of them scurrying back. The returns may exaggerate the process: on December 30 the five Connecticut regiments are shown at one-third strength, and little more than a week later, at 90 percent strength. The arrival of the short-term militia undoubtedly accounts for part of these figures. Nevertheless, by the end of February the Connecticut regiments stood at three-quarters of their own complement.[125]

The reconstitution of Connecticut's forces did not solve all Washington's manpower problems, for reenlistment went slowly elsewhere, too. But since the Ticonderoga ordnance was on its way to Boston by sleigh and sufficient powder had now arrived from abroad, an attack on the city had at last become possible. There were strong incentives to launch one before Howe could receive reinforcements. In mid-January Washington called on all the New England governments (except Rhode Island) to supplement their Continental regiments with thirteen more, pledged to serve until April 1.[126] Connecticut attempted to raise her quota of four without offering more than a token bounty of four shillings and sixpence to each man who provided his own gun and blanket.[127] The government's insistence that recruits receive a three-dollar advance on their wages to buy themselves "necessary clothing &c" caused some delay. The treasury was bare, Washington could not help with a loan, and the money had therefore to come from the $12,500 reimbursement to Connecticut for the advance she had made to Burrall's regiment.[128] Still, by the beginning of March, when Washington was ready to pressure the British by occupying Dorchester Heights, Connecticut had sent him three more regiments, almost complete.[129]

The fourth militia regiment that Washington had called for went to New York, apparently with his tacit consent. By the end of 1775, New York politics had taken an alarming turn. The revolutionary Provincial Congress had lost all control over the southern parts of the colony most prone to British sympathies. When the Westchester County committee reported that a gang of Tories had threatened to kidnap the county's foremost patriots, the Provincial Congress ignored them. In desperation, the committee appealed to Connecticut for help,[130] which Connecticut gave in a form that raised more problems than it solved. Using the appeal as his excuse, Isaac Sears led a hundred men into New York City on November 22. They destroyed the press and types of the Tory printer James Rivington and carried off the mayor, a justice of the peace, and the Tory pamphleteer Samuel Seabury.[131] In many minds their violent intrusion confirmed the charges of Seabury and other Tories that the extremism of New England's republicans endangered New York more than the designs of the British.[132]

It is hard to tell for sure how much Sears's expedition influenced the course of events, but when the new Provincial Congress assembled in December neither Richmond (Staten Island) nor Queens (on Long Island) had sent representatives. Reports said that the *Asia* had armed the Tories in both places and encouraged them to oppose "in military manner . . . the measures taken by the *United Colonies.*"[133] Any other provincial congress would have taken strong action, but that of New York buckled when the *Asia* and two newly arrived cohorts trained their guns on the city. On December 21 its members told the Continental Congress that they feared to act.[134] They toyed briefly with a scheme for reconciliation propounded by Governor Tryon, then adjourned. When Washington heard shortly afterward that the British in Boston were fitting out ships to venture south,[135] he naturally thought Howe meant to join with New York's armed loyalists. If he secured a foothold there, it would be hard to dislodge him.

Washington immediately ordered Lee to raise volunteers in Connecticut for an expedition to secure Richmond and Queens.[136] In the meantime, Congress had responded to the communication of December 21 by ordering that five to six hundred men from Connecticut and New Jersey enter New York to disarm the Tories in the two offending counties. Then, thinking better of it, Congress revoked the order and decided instead to use the continentals under Lord Stirling's command in New Jersey.[137] Experience suggested that they would more likely disarm the Tories peacefully, and indeed they had done so by the third week in January.[138] Unhappily for New York, this did not end the risk of intervention by Connecticut. Acting on Lee's request, on January 12 the Council of Safety called for two regiments to form under Colonels Waterbury and Andrew Ward. Congress ordered them disbanded, but Trumbull ignored the order.[139] On the twenty-first, the New York Committee of Safety sent a message begging Lee not to march any large body of Connecticut troops into New York lest the intrusion provoke local residents to violence.[140] Lee had no ears for their appeal. Reports had reached him that a detachment under Sir Henry Clinton had sailed from Boston for New York on the twentieth.[141] At this point the Continental Congress, guessing that the situation had become too explosive to stand Lee's rough handling, rushed a committee to New York which obtained her consent, albeit a reluctant one, to the introduction of Connecticut and New Jersey troops and to the fortification of lower Manhattan and western Long Island.[142]

The Spoils of Victory

Having raised six Continental regiments and five militia regiments within two months, Connecticut could honestly claim to have helped drive Howe from Boston. When he evacuated the city on March 17, patriot spirits rose everywhere. The belief

that American soldiers could stand up to the British army had
been justified. Those in Britain who called for peace with the
colonies, whether out of sympathy for them or unwillingness to
pay the cost of war, would now plead a stronger case. And the
French would receive encouragement to continue their covert
shipments of arms and powder in defiance of all that their old
enemy might say or do.

Yet the withdrawal was not all gain. It meant that the
enemy could regroup and seize the initiative at some other strategic point along the coast. Clinton's venture southward to try
the mettle of the Carolinas furnished an example of the options
that the British retreat had opened to Howe. He had also
regained the power of surprise and Americans could no longer
be sure where he would strike. For a time, Washington thought
Howe's abandonment of Boston might be a ruse to draw off
American forces just before he launched an all-out attack on
Massachusetts Bay. On the other hand, New York seemed
more likely to be Howe's ultimate destination. Obliged to cover
both possibilities, Washington had to leave the bulk of his army
at Boston, at least until the army transports and men-of-war
laid up in Nantasket Road had made their departure. But he
also ordered six regiments to New York. It being mud time,
they took ten days to reach Norwich in Connecticut and almost
three more to complete the journey.[143] Had British warships
patrolled the Sound, they would have taken longer. If Howe
had chosen to sail his troops to New York, he could have
reached it well ahead of Washington's men. The patriots were
finding that they paid for their recapture of Boston in uncertainty and uncomfortable vulnerability to chance.

Washington saw the inherent peril of the new circumstances. As soon as the British evacuation seemed imminent, he
wrote asking Trumbull "immediately to throw two thousand
men into that city [New York] . . . to maintain the place until
I can arrive there with the army under my command." He also
asked New Jersey for another thousand men.[144] On March 14
Connecticut's Council of Safety advised Trumbull to order the
commanders of seven militia regiments to call for volunteers for
New York, as was customary when raising expeditionary forces

to serve outside the colony. If none came forward, they were to detach the necessary men immediately. As its authority for this unprecedented assertion of power, the Council invoked a colony law authorizing the governor to detach men from the militia "for the relief . . . of any . . . places attacked." It appointed Colonels Gold Selleck Silliman and Matthew Talcott as field officers but left the matter of company officers to them. Fifteen hundred men who had followed Lee to New York in January, and who were then preparing to return home, received orders to stay where they were until discharged by Congress.[145]

They had not long to wait. Silliman's battalion reached the city on March 29. Talcott had further to come and had difficulty in procuring guns and money, but his men were not far behind and arrived on April 1. Silliman had made a point of detaching some of his men, perhaps to test the loyalty of certain western regiments; perhaps to demonstrate the power of the government in the wake of Washington's victory at Boston; perhaps both.[146] It is clear that he could have attracted sufficient volunteers had he cared to try. The militia recognized the necessity. A British contingent in New York would threaten the southwestern part of Connecticut far more than the occupation of Boston had done. And the men knew that, unless the British appeared at New York immediately, they could return home as soon as the Continental troops arrived. The first units appeared on March 30. The main body of troops, though they did not leave until the twenty-seventh and were delayed along the way by a false alarm that Howe had gone to Newport, came in by the middle of April.[147] Only five regiments remained at Boston to guard against the possibility of a British return.

Whether or not the British gained a foothold in New York, the shift in the focus of the war would exacerbate Connecticut's troubles. Until now, the desire to economize had led the government to provide for coastal defense more ritualistically than realistically. But the collapse of Rhode Island's truce with Wallace in January—marked by the raids on Prudence Island and Point Judith and the burning of Norfolk, Virginia—had revived a fear that the Royal Navy would carry out its threat to devastate the coast.[148] Pressure mounted for the government to send the larger towns all the men and ordinance necessary to hold men-of-war too far off for them to give a landing party covering fire. In January and February the legislators made what they hoped were gestures in the right direction. They commandeered the Salisbury ironworks, which belonged to a reputed loyalist, Richard Smith, to cast cannon for the towns.[149] They increased the guards allocated to New London to some three hundred. They speeded up construction of the four new galleys they had authorized and of the fortifications at Groton and New London.[150] But the people wanted more than gestures. On February 14 Samuel Mott reported to the Council of Safety "the universal opinion and expectation of the people, that at least one regiment of men be raised to guard the coast" between Stonington and the Connecticut River. "Less than that number will, by all that I can learn, not give content," he wrote. "Judges of our Court" had told him that if the enemy should gain "any considerable advantage of us, by reason of our neglect . . . we should have reason to blame ourselves for it."[151]

The British withdrawal from Boston did, of course, diminish the danger momentarily. Throughout the war, major troop movements by sea put a strain on the Royal Navy's resources that lessened its power to prowl the coast.[152] But as New York became an objective, Connecticut could expect an increase of enemy activity in the Sound that would offset temporary gains. That is why Ezek Hopkins's Continental fleet received a glad welcome at New London on April 8 even though he had let H.M.S. *Glasgow*, outgunned by more than a hundred cannon, escape him in the early morning hours.[153]

The encounter prompted Hopkins to offer Connecticut the thirty-six cannon he had captured in the Bahamas in exchange for the use of the colony's two ships. Washington, who had wanted thirty pieces for New York, was told that he could have what was left when Connecticut had supplied her need.[154] Meanwhile, Rhode Island and Pennsylvania had also entered claims for the cannon. An unseemly tussle ensued, in the course of which Congress ordered Connecticut to send fourteen of them to Pennsylvania.[155] Trumbull told Congress of Connecticut's "uneasiness, disappointment, and surprise at this."

> [W]e had [he wrote]—relying upon the faith of [Congress] . . .
> proceeded to lay out a large and expensive plan of fortifications,
> got the works in considerable forwardness, provided carriages,
> mounted cannon, and all going on with the utmost dispatch, for
> the purpose of making an effectual defence; now to be thus at
> once so suddenly, unexpectedly, and without a hearing, stripped
> naked and left defenceless, without a possibility of present relief,
> as must inevitably be the case if that number of cannon be taken
> from us, we think extremely hard and unaccountable, and flatter
> ourselves that, upon a reconsideration of the matter, the . . .
> resolve will be altered . . . especially when we consider no Col-
> ony has exerted itself more in the common cause, and none re-
> ceived less assistance from the Continent.[156]

In other words, the government had better leave the people some means of defense if it wanted them to go on supporting the cause. On June 24 Congress responded with a resolution that New London receive twenty-two cannon and 300 guards at Continental expense. No further action followed this munificent gesture, though Congress did suspend the demand that fourteen cannon go to Philadelphia. Most of the disputed ordnance presumably stayed in Connecticut;[157] certainly Washington never saw any of it. Nor did he embroil himself further in controversy: he, at least, understood the occasional wisdom of putting political expedience before military needs.

The Council of Safety tried to cut corners in guarding the coast by ordering that a reserve force from the eastern and central regiments stand "in readiness to march on the shortest notice for defence in any invaded place or places in this or the neighbouring Colonies." Only two companies were ordered to immediate active service.[158] Yet this became the occasion for the first complaints about the institution of a draft. Why, when Silliman's detachment had submitted without demur? Perhaps because these men were being summoned to the unglamorous task of fortifying New London, and the time they would serve had not been specified. Nevertheless, the necessity of a draft, no matter what "uneasiness among the people" it occasioned,[159] and for more reasons than the defense of the coast, began to make itself understood.

Howe had proceeded to Halifax and now stood poised, either to relieve Quebec or to attack New York or both. If Washington reinforced the northern army, known to be in serious trouble, he would weaken New York's defenses. He based his eventual decision to take that risk on the assumption that "our affairs in Canada can derive no support but what is sent to them . . . [while] the Militia may be called in here."[160] Thus, in April, when he sent a substantial part of his troops north, he instructed Trumbull to organize Connecticut's militia so that "Assistance may be had on the earliest Notice of an approach by the Enemy."[161] The legislature promptly formed the troops of light horse attached to the militia into five cavalry regiments and ordered that one-quarter of the inland regiments and one-third of the coastal regiments embody as minute companies. Unless enough volunteers came forward, the recruiting officers would draft men. But no one need serve against his will, except in dire emergency. The draft meant only that if a man declined to march when ordered he incurred a ten-pound fine. The legislature also guaranteed that no drafted man would serve more than three months, having apparently learned from experience that vagueness on this point encouraged refusal.[162]

If Connecticut hoped that she had now done all that could be asked of her, she was disappointed. Just as Congress had conceded the leaving of the cannon at New London in order to assuage Connecticut's apprehensions, so now it saw fit to reassure Massachusetts and Rhode Island that the departure of the army had not left them defenseless. In late April, acting on a report that sixty ships commanded by Howe and carrying 12,000 Hessians had sailed for Boston, Congress recommended that Rhode Island's state regiments receive Continental pay and that three new regiments from Massachusetts, New Hampshire, and Connecticut reinforce the five remaining in Boston.[163] The report itself, relayed to Congress by Thomas Cushing, seemed sufficiently implausible to be discounted. It would take more than sixty transports to carry 12,000 men, and Howe would have more sense than to send troops just off the boat from Europe straight on to Boston. At that season of the year, he would most likely give them time to rest from the journey at Halifax. The truth, however, mattered less than the belief of the Massachusetts leadership that Britain meant to wreak revenge upon the colony.[164] That Congress perceived both aspects of the situation appeared in its response. Congress revealed its doubt that any real danger existed by using the scare as an opportunity to find out if troops would enlist for more than a year at a time. New Hampshire, as a less-developed frontier colony with little surplus manpower, was exempt from the experiment. But Massachusetts and Connecticut were told to ask their men for a two-year commitment.[165]

By the time Connecticut received this latest congressional requisition (which she immediately passed into law),[166] Americans had at last learned the magnitude of the force that the British ministry would send against them. They had known since January that Britain might employ foreign troops.[167] but not until dispatches arrived from Arthur Lee in May did they know exactly what to expect. Lee's letters contained the texts of treaties in which certain German states agreed to provide Britain with mercenary soldiers. The ministry planned to send 26,000 more troops by the beginning of the next campaign. Along with the 8,000 already in Canada and Nova Scotia, these men would be deployed in three divisions: one in Canada, a second in New York, and the third in the South.[168] Though Lee's letter itself was withheld from print in order to maintain his usefulness as a spy, other reports in plenty informed the colonists that Britain planned to hurl up to 50,000 troops at them.[169] No European power had ever sent so numerous a force across the Atlantic. The news must have made many hearts skip a beat and many minds entertain the passing thought that they would never have taken up arms if they had known that the war would reach these dimensions. For the leadership, however, there was no going back. Britain considered them traitors, and they must either fight, or die on the gallows.[170] The scale of the offensive even encouraged them in one respect. Britain could not support so great a burden for more than a year without hurting. If they could only keep her from winning a decisive victory for that period of time, her people at home might grow disgusted with the costs to them and force a change of ministries.[171]

The Connecticut legislature certainly did not falter in response to the news. After providing for recruitment of the two-year regiment and embodiment of nearly a quarter of the militia, it passed a series of acts that pointed toward independence. The acts deleted all mention of the Crown in oaths, writs, commissions, and processes. The General Assembly assumed a former Crown prerogative and invested the county courts with admiralty jurisdiction. It also decided to outdo the recommendations of Congress and Washington by raising two state regiments, both to be at Washington's command if the governor agreed.[172]

Determining what bounties to offer presented a problem. Having heard from the delegation to Congress that the continent probably would not repay Connecticut for the unauthorized bounties she had given in 1775,[173] the legislature did not mean to go further into debt. Besides, to offer more to volunteers for the state regiments than to recruits for the continental army would make it hard to fill up the two-year regiment for Boston. So the legislature offered a £3.2s. advance, only £1.2s. of which would count as a bounty. Even so, the legislature had to finance these measures, as well as the bounties offered producers of powder and salt, by emitting £60,000 in bills of credit redeemable in 1781.[174]

At the end of the session, the legislature directed that an address "be printed and dispersed and . . . read and published in all the religious societies in this Colony," exhorting the people to arm and prepare. "All able-bodied men who are not of the standing militia, and such as have been dismissed from common military exercise" were ordered to "form themselves into companies," to choose officers, to equip themselves, and to stand ready. In support of the call to arms, the address also presented a moral appeal couched in the familiar rhetoric of Protestant Christianity, which had far greater power to inspire both leaders and people than opposition ideology. Reminding the people "that all human care, efforts and exertions are but fruitless attempts for our security and defence, and will prove vain

and abortive unless attended with the blessing of Heaven," the
address went on:

> Wherefore, in this day of darkness and threatening calamity, it is
> most earnestly recommended to and pressed upon all persons of
> every rank and denomination in this Colony, to promote and cul-
> tivate charity and benevolence one towards another, to abstain
> from every species of extortion and oppression, sincerely to re-
> pent and break off from every sin, folly and vice, to live together
> in peace, love and harmony among themselves, to look up with
> earnest importunity to Heaven for help, success, salvation and
> deliverance, and with careful attention to the use of means hope
> and trust in the Lord of Hosts, who presides over universal na-
> ture, guides and governs all, and we [need] not fear or be dis-
> mayed at all the attempts or numerous hosts with which we are
> threatened.[175]

Moral force, in other words, would count as much as military
skill in the war against the mother country.[176]

Meanwhile, Congress, in consultation with Washington,
had worked out a plan to double the Continental army by adding twenty thousand six-month men, or "new levies." Six thousand would go to the northern army, ten thousand to New Jersey, and the remainder to Washington in New York. Seven
thousand of these men were to come from Connecticut.[177]
Congress had wholly exempted Rhode Island and had asked
populous Massachusetts, in deference to its fears of reprisal, for
only five thousand. Congressional delegate Oliver Wolcott objected to the requisition as unrealistically large and Governor Trumbull protested that a Connecticut stripped of men
might lose the ability to produce enough food for the army.
Nevertheless, in response to the prodding of Congress he dutifully called the legislature back into session, and the legislature dutifully provided for nine new battalions, projected
slightly above the usual strength to ensure a full complement
eventually.[178] The legislature did not hesitate in this extremity
to offer higher bounties than Congress had suggested (£6 to
recruits for Canada, £3 to recruits for New York, plus the usual
£1.2s. for blanket, knapsack, and arms), and Trumbull defended them as essential to success. For one thing, "the pres-

sure of country business was such as . . . was not to be left
without great difficulty"; for another, the premium offered recruits for Canada had to be doubled because the men knew that
the army there had smallpox; and so it went, one increase leading to another.[179] To finance all this, the legislature authorized
yet another emission of bills of credit up to £50,000, redeemable in 1782. At the same time, it instructed its delegation to
Congress to press for a declaration of independence and a formal plan of union.[180]

Showdown

Without a doubt, the Connecticut leadership had risen to the
occasion. But would the people follow them this time? There
were disturbing signs that they might not. British recruiters
busy in western Connecticut met with no small success. On
May 12 Captain Seth Harding of the *Defence* intercepted a sloop
carrying eight men to Long Island to join one Peter Fairchild,
who had fled his home in Redding after an incident in which he
obstructed a local militia response to Silliman's call.[181] Several
of the captured eight confessed that they belonged to a British
recruiting network based on Long Island. They said that a British officer in disguise had circulated rumors of a large force
about to attack the coast, so that timid folk would be tempted
to get on "the right and safe side of the controversy" by joining
the enemy.[182] This information dismayed the leadership all the
more because it coincided with the discovery of just how strong
a campaign the British would mount.[183] The Fairfield County
patriots should have had no difficulty in dealing with the conspirators: their activities had been outlawed since December,
and local authorities had the power to enforce the law. Yet the
problem persisted into the summer of 1776, when the Council
of Safety became so alarmed as to prohibit traveling without a
pass and to make civil officers—grand jurors, tithingmen,
sheriffs, and constables—share with the military the responsibility for checking the identity of strangers. The larger towns

were also ordered to post night watches as a guard against clan-
destine movement after dark.[184]

One incentive for such restrictions was the Council of
Safety's desire to conceal how slowly the new levies formed.
The returns of Washington's army tell the story. The new
levies were first mentioned on July 13. Of the fifty-six companies authorized, only thirty-four were listed, numbered at
1,796. A week later, they numbered 2,178, and by July 27 they
stood at 2,494. But the rate of new arrivals barely kept pace
with the rate of sickness. Returns for August 3, the last complete ones before the Battle of Long Island, show 554 sick and
only 2,307 men fit for duty.[185] After more than a month of effort, the new levies for New York stood at no more than half
strength. The two six-month regiments sent north under Brigadier David Waterbury had the same history of inadequate recruitment and poor performance. They straggled into the lake
region in the middle of August, far too late to prevent the retreat from Canada or the evacuation of Crown Point, and still
far from complete.[186] Andrew Ward, the commanding officer
of the two-year regiment, which had been recruiting for almost
a month longer than the others, had early on reached the conclusion that the army should accept volunteers for three or four
months instead of demanding two years. Without some concession, he despaired of filling the ranks.[187]

As usual, many factors contributed to the poor showing.
Smallpox was one of them. Reports of an epidemic raging
through the northern army frightened away recruits to Waterbury's regiments. Governor Trumbull told Congress that not
"one in twenty" of the Connecticut troops had immunity and
that in their eyes the smallpox towered as "a more terrible
enemy than the British troops."[188] Seeing no hope of sending
an effective force north without first reassuring the men, Trumbull dispatched John Ely, a doctor widely known and trusted
for the success of his inoculating hospital on Duck Island, to
report on the state of the army.[189] Ely's account did correct the
exaggerations of rumor, but so late that troops did not begin to
head north until the beginning of August.[190] Similar rumors of

smallpox at Boston may have discouraged enlistment into Ward's regiment, assigned to that town.[191]

On June 28 the arrival of Howe's First Division at New York panicked Washington into a frantic plea for new levies.[192] The unforeseen result was again to obstruct recruitment. Since the regiments had only begun to raise men a week before, few were ready to go. The Council of Safety therefore dispatched three regiments of light horse. But six hundred horses put an impossible burden on Washington's limited forage, and since most of the men were unwilling to serve as foot soldiers he had to dismiss them.[193] Meanwhile, the diversion of so many men and horses from haying meant that those who stayed behind found their services in such demand as to discourage enlistment. Connecticut spokesmen in general agreed that the competition for harvest laborers hurt recruitment for the six-month regiments.[194] Nor did it help that on July 12 three British men-of-war had run past the fortifications on Manhattan Island and gained control of the Hudson River. That incident impelled Connecticut to send men to help put down an insurrection of Tories in Dutchess County and Washington to request that the state's three new galleys be dispatched to the Hudson.[195] Yet these were only incidental problems.

The grand obstacle to recruitment was the awesome scale of British operations in New York. When the detachment sent south for an attempt on Charleston returned, and when the Hessian reinforcements from Europe arrived, Howe would have over twenty thousand men to deploy around New York. Burgoyne also had a large force moving south along Lake Champlain in an attempt to make juncture with Howe. When Ward's regiment heard of the order reassigning it to service in New York, Ward told Trumbull that the officers feared it would prove "very disagreeable to their soldiers to march anywhere but to Boston," an admission with honesty alone to recommend it.[196] Men like Thomas Seymour began to ask if the colony should abandon voluntary enlistment and resort wholly to preemptory detachment.[197] The Council of Safety, not yet ready to agree, temporized by giving the governor authority to circularize the selectmen, civil officers, and committeemen in every town, urging them to promote enlistment with the utmost vigor.[198] They felt that detachment would sacrifice quality to quantity; they believed that a republican army of willing citizens must always be better than a reluctant, foot-dragging horde; and, from the little evidence we have, it seems that local leaderships agreed. For example, Thomas Mumford reported from Groton that "a number of us advanced to the amount of fifteen dollars to each volunteer that would immediately inlist, besides which, I engaged myself to supply the families of any such needy volunteers with provisions during their absence; and if, when they returned, they were unable to pay, I would freely give what I had so advanced."[199]

We shall never know if their faith in the continued feasibility of a volunteer army would have been justified. On August 7 Washington learned that the Hessians had begun to arrive in New York along with Clinton's and Cornwallis's troops from the south. Washington thought that the enemy, supported by a powerful fleet, would soon stand at thirty thousand, while he had little more than thirteen thousand men deployed from Amboy to Long Island, many of whom were sick. In his extremity, he sent out a call for immediate support from neighboring militia. Even so, he asked for only five regiments from Connecticut, mindful in the midst of crisis that his last summons had damaged recruitment for the new levies and anxious to avoid repetition.[200] But when the Council of Safety heard of his desperation, it suspended the effort to fill the six-month regiments and extended the levy to nine additional regiments, including the Nineteenth and Twenty-second east of the Connecticut River.[201]

This did not mean that the members of the Council had given up on the new levies. They probably thought that some of the militiamen who marched to New York would now volunteer. The harvest was almost done, and a man who enlisted could claim a bounty that he would not otherwise receive. They also continued to encourage volunteers. At Norwich, an independent company of veteran guards received orders to head for New York with "as many more as will inlist to the number of ninety-three including officers."[202] And on August 12

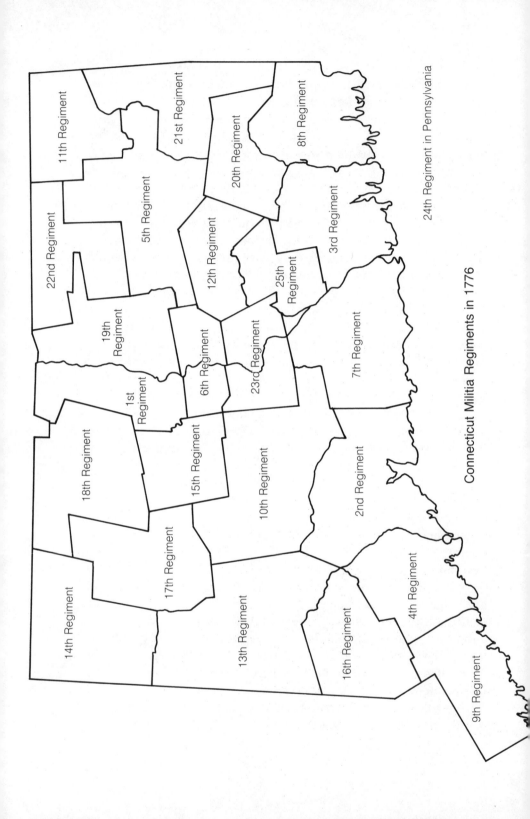

Connecticut Militia Regiments in 1776

Trumbull sent another circular to the towns near New York, urging the authorities "to imbody all the householders not obliged to do duty in any training band, in order to march forthwith to *New York.*"[203] But now that Washington stood in such need, the Council was at last willing, if all else failed, to use compulsory detachment.

Only fragmentary evidence of the mobilization survives, but it suggests that in some towns the response was tremendous. On August 19 Thomas Seymour reported from Hartford that the "general . . . method adopted by the Militia here, that none would go, unless all went, to *New York,* has stripped us so much of men and arms, that the inhabitants feel themselves under some apprehensions, considering the number of prisoners here and the guard we are obliged to keep every night."[204] Other towns proceeded with more restraint, yet wherever the militia hung back the volunteers came forward.[205] In the course of a journey Jeremiah Wadsworth made from New York to New Haven at the beginning of September, he remarked on how "amazingly stripped of Inhabitants" the coast appeared.[206] Surviving payrolls indicate that the regiments showed commendable speed as well. Most of the first four requisitioned on the seventh arrived before the eighteenth. Units from those ordered out by the Council of Safety streamed in from the middle to the end of the month. Washington took heart. At last his own strength increased faster than that of his enemy.[207]

Other states besides Connecticut had sent troops, of course, but Connecticut sent one-sixth of the reinforcements Washington received. And thanks to the initiative of her government, the flow seemed likely to continue. On the eve of the Battle of Long Island, Washington said he had received nine of the fourteen Connecticut militia regiments ordered forward, "averaging about 350 men" (or 85 percent complete, according to the Council's calculations).[208] There is evidence that the other five regiments came in at roughly the same strength during the battle.[209] These raw militiamen played no direct part in the drama on Long Island. But by manning the works in New York, they freed the Continental regiments and the partially trained new levies for the fighting.[210]

Connecticut's contribution did not end there. After the British landed a substantial force at Long Island on August 22, Washington wrote to Trumbull suggesting that "your Government . . . throw a Body of about one thousand or more Men across the Sound, to harass the Enemy in their rear or upon their Flanks." He hoped that they might also keep the livestock, a hundred thousand head of cattle and somewhat more sheep, from falling into enemy hands.[211] Washington's message did not reach Lebanon until the twenty-seventh, and the Council of Safety took the precaution of sending Benjamin Huntington and John Ely across first to see what reception the island's inhabitants would give such a force.[212] On that same day, Washington's army suffered defeat and the New York Convention sent Connecticut an urgent request for "assistance in removing the inhabitants and stock from *Long-Island*."[213] Though it could not have reached the Council later than August 31, the members did not act until the following day, when Huntington returned. Then they made up for lost time, calling out eight more militia regiments—a force almost three times the number suggested—and ordering the guards stationed at New London under Colonel Erastus Wolcott to embark for Long Island. Evidently the Council meant to create a major diversion. The news of Washington's retreat to Manhattan changed the picture, however, and the Council halted embarkation.[214] When it appeared that, despite their cries for help, Long Islanders did not really want to fight,[215] Connecticut abandoned the expedition, though she did authorize Wolcott to use men to guard the transports from New London and Groton that were carrying refugees and stock from the island.[216]

The eight regiments called on September 1 were not sent home. The Council of Safety decided on its own initiative to march them to New York, together with two regiments of horse that had not served in July and with the Seventh Regiment from the hitherto exempt coastal communities between New Haven and Saybrook.[217] This action may have followed rumors that the Connecticut militia had begun to desert from New York. More likely it signified a recognition that British control of Long Island gave Howe the power to launch an attack across the Bronx or Westchester that could isolate the army from the rest of the continent. The militia stationed at New York must have seen the danger, which, far more than lack of equipment or need to plant the winter wheat, may account for the dwindling of manpower that Washington so bitterly lamented.[218] Members of the Council of Safety undoubtedly saw it, too. The New York Convention had pointed out the possibility some weeks before and had proposed that Connecticut send a force of 6,000 to wait in Westchester County and attack from the rear if the enemy tried any such maneuver.[219] Washington had sent the proposal to Trumbull, with a note saying that it "might be productive of the most salutary consequences" but that it should not supersede the obligation to supply 5,500 new levies.[220] He might have spared those cautionary words. At that moment, Connecticut could not possibly have sent men to Westchester. Recruitment for the six-month regiments was proving difficult enough. Only in September, when the need for such a force had grown desperate, did the colony act. Then it acted decisively, to the point of stripping Wolcott's regiment of two companies, on the understanding that those of the Groton and New London militia regiments who could not march to New York at once would take their places.[221]

In the second week of September, Connecticut's mobilization reached its peak. The only militia regiments not under marching orders were the Fourteenth in the northwestern region, held in reserve to defend the Salisbury foundry against possible Tory uprisings, and the Twenty-fourth in distant Westmoreland County, the Susquehannah Company's lands. Though we lack precise figures, we can estimate the manpower harnessed as in Table 1. The grand total of 18,915 may contain redundancies because of the use of returns over a six-month period. On the other hand, the numbers recorded do not take full account of those who supported the army as carters, drovers, draymen, and quartermasters or of those who helped to rescue people and stock from Long Island. Assuming the figure of 18,915 to be reasonably accurate, it still represents only 72 percent of the total militia reported by the colony in 1774 or,

Table One
Connecticut Mobilization, May–November 1776

Continental Army [b]

Unit	Commander	Men
	State	
10th Cont.	Parsons	672
17th Cont.	Huntington	615
19th Cont.	C. Webb	600
20th Cont.	Durkee	615
22nd Cont.	Wyllys	615
	Burrall	653
	Elmore	443 [a]
	Ward	498
	Bigelow's artillery	25
	New Levies	
1st. Conn.	Silliman	485
2nd. Conn.	Gay	511
3rd. Conn.	Sage	570
4th Conn.	Selden	575
5th Conn.	Douglas	666
6th Conn.	Chester	624
	Bradley	661
(N.L.)	Swift	556
(N.L.)	Mott	592

Militia [b]

Unit	Commander	Men
	First Wave (Aug.)	
1st. Reg.	Newbury	511
2nd Reg.	Thompson	527
4th Reg.	Lewis	343
6th Reg.	E. Talcott	398
9th Reg.	Mead	312
10th Reg.	Baldwin	566
13th Reg.	Hinman	313
15th Reg.	Strong	483
16th Reg.	Cook	181
17th Reg.	Sheldon	304
18th Reg.	Pettibone	306
19th Reg.	Pitkin	391
22nd Reg.	Chapman	383
23rd Reg.	M. Talcott	288
Volunteer Companies		199
		5,620
	Second Wave (Sept.)	
3rd Reg.	Ely	335
5th Reg.	Storrs	261
7th Reg.	Graves	266

Naval Forces

Type	Vessel	Men
	Public Vessels [b]	
Galley	Shark	55
	Whiting	55 (est.)
	Crane	55 (est.)
	Trumbull	68
Brig	Defence	150 (est.)
Sloop	Spy	45
		428
	Privateers [c]	
American Revenue		25
Broom		70
Gamecock		50
Two Brothers		60
		205

20th Reg.	Rogers	256
21st Reg.	Douglass	259
25th Reg.	Throop	231
Horse	Backus	141
Horse	Sheldon	199
		2,686

Grand total   18,915

[a] Connecticut's component estimated.
[b] Calculated from the highest figure reported between May and November 1776 on returns or muster rolls.
[c] Only vessels commissioned during the spring and summer listed.

SOURCES: *SOI*, pp. 22–41
AA, 1:763–64, 2:327–30, 479, 907–10, 1132, 3:425
RCM, passim
Louis F. Middlebrook, *Maritime Connecticut during the American Revolution* (Salem, Mass., 1925), 2:passim

assuming a 5 percent increase in the militia roles between 1774 and 1776, only 69 percent of the militia in 1776.[222] Nonetheless, Connecticut had given her all to the cause. From what can be learned from fragmentary militia returns throughout the war, roughly 25 percent of the adult males under fifty were unfit for military duty at any given moment.[223] If we make this assumption about the Connecticut militia in the summer of 1776, then the state had 91 percent of its able-bodied militia under arms. Though 18,915 men comprised only 45 percent of Connecticut's estimated male population between the ages of sixteen and fifty, they probably approached the limit of those the state could equip for the field.[224]

It might be argued that the state should receive no credit for the militia who abandoned the lines at New York, whom Washington himself described as better gone. But the bulk of these regiments remained at their posts until the third week of September, when they were discharged. We must remember, too, that many of those who left earlier were genuinely sick. Some never reached home. Contemporary reports say that worried relatives coming to care for their sons and brothers jammed the roads to New York and so obstructed military movement that the Council of Safety could no longer close its eyes to the need for proper military hospitals.[225] The performance of the men who mustered can sometimes be questioned, perhaps, but not the commitment of their government. By September 1776, Connecticut had put forth to the limit of her ability.

CHAPTER THREE

Exertion

SEPTEMBER 1776 marked both the peak of Connecticut's mobilization and the moment when the foundations of popular enthusiasm began to crumble. Americans had thought they would win the war in a matter of months. Instead, though Howe had still achieved no final victory, he had twice subjected the revolutionary army to a humiliating defeat (first at the Battle of Long Island, and again at New York) while receiving less damage himself than a mere provincial militia had inflicted on British troops the year before. Unless he made some gross error that would allow Washington to strike a swift, conclusive blow, Howe would certainly stay to mount another campaign in the spring. Those who had believed that Britain could not sustain her vast army beyond a year had miscalculated. On September 16 the members of Congress tacitly admitted their mistake when they put aside their ideological reservations and yielded to Washington's demand for a standing army. They had come to agree that, short of the vastly superior numbers which experience had taught them not to expect, only a well-trained, permanent force could hope to defeat Howe, and they authorized the establishment, for the duration, of eighty-eight 728-man regiments, eight of them to come from Connecticut.[1]

If any congressman cherished a secret doubt or hope that he and his fellows had responded not to facts but to fear, he lost it before the year ended. Except in the engagements at Harlem

Heights and White Plains, Howe continued to hurt the continentals far more than they hurt him. When he advanced through New Jersey to the Delaware, the people's ready submission to royal authority indicated that his army could easily control enough territory to support itself. And Washington's victories at Trenton and Princeton, though they led to the recovery of most of the ground lost, would not deter the British from undertaking another campaign. They had too nearly grasped success to give up now, especially when it looked so doubtful that the revolutionaries could recruit another army. Unless Americans could show at least the capability to raise a permanent force, they could hardly expect the British to pack up and go home.

Cause for Despondency

That autumn, Connecticut had to digest more than one unpleasant fact. At the same time as people began to realize that the war would last longer than expected, they also became aware that Connecticut was about to lose advantages she had enjoyed since April 1775. The new prosperity went first. Throughout the summer of 1776, letters between Joseph Trumbull and Jeremiah Wadsworth show that their main problem at that time was how to absorb a surplus efficiently and cheaply. Hence, Wadsworth's complaint that "Our farmers still clamour about the flower [sic]—and are determined to . . . make me their Pack-Horse."[2] In early September, he spoke for the first time of finding it hard to buy grain for the army. This had less to do with the damage bad weather had done to the harvest than with a shortage of hands to sack the old grain and thresh the new.[3] As a rule, a farmer who fell behind through illness would have received help from neighbors better situated. But this year the constant movement of men from the farm to the army, from the army to the farm, had put everyone behind. Everyone needed help that no one could spare. The immediate task before most farmers should have been to plant winter wheat, but they had neither the time nor the labor to set about it. In a letter to Joseph Trumbull, Wadsworth warned that worse than misfortune to the army would follow. The "sufferings of the Husband-men will be incredible unless speedily relieved," he wrote.[4]

To compound the problem of declining supply, the stock evacuated from Long Island made extraordinary demands on forage.[5] The constant motion of the army, because it increased the number of draft horses and oxen required for transportation, also increased the amount of forage consumed. Then, in this year of all years, the slaughter of pigs that usually took place in November and December, in order to save on expensive winter feed, was delayed for want of certain essential commodities. Before refrigeration, people valued salt meat as healthier, safer food in hot weather than fresh meat. The war increased its value still more, since an army could not long function without it in any circumstances, and especially under siege. Yet now, when the fodder to be saved and the profits to be gained seemed more desirable than ever, the state lacked enough salt and barrels to do the job.

The shortage of barrels arose because most of the coopers had marched with the militia;[6] the shortage of salt, because Americans were cut off from the source of supply. In 1775, the northern colonies had not yet felt the pinch. When the British closed the fisheries, the salt laid up for their use during 1774 had been diverted to meat packing.[7] In addition, some importation from the West Indies remained possible despite the Royal Navy's blockade of the American cost.[8] But by the autumn of 1776, the little salt obtained in this way no longer met the requirements of both army and household. Every household also needed salt to preserve food for its own support. As the competition between public and private needs grew fiercer, the Council of Safety declared the shortage a threat to "the publick peace and safety of the State." In early October, it ordered that five hundred tons of shipping be impressed to procure salt under armed convoy.[9] Shortly afterward, the British seized a large cache of salt at New Rochelle,[10] and existing supplies fell lower still.

In September the commissary agents began to complain of

rising prices. Sometimes the temporary shortage of a commodity caused the rise, but more often the shortage of labor and the concomitant demand for higher wages had pushed prices up.[11] In 1775 the challenge had been to regulate the flow of produce. Trumbull had fought to control popular access to the market and to defend his monopoly of purchasing from attack in the legislature. He saw a danger that competition among commissary agents would inflate prices and precipitate an alternation of gluts and shortages.[12] By the autumn of 1776, however, the challenge was to find any produce at all. Connecticut suddenly lacked all the commodities most needed by the army. Trumbull's agents could not draw on the nearest places, because all New England and New York labored under the same difficulties. And in October the movement of British men-of-war up the Hudson, together with the capture of two Connecticut galleys stationed there to defend communications, had cut off New Jersey and Pennsylvania as sources of supply.[13] The strain on Connecticut's economy did ease up in the following month when New Jersey became the center of British operations, but the commissary gained nothing by this. As soon as producers realized that the commissary needed them more than they needed the commissary, they did not hestitate to break contracts and to demand higher prices, which Trumbull had to let his agents pay.[14]

Meanwhile, the Continental and state bills of credit began to depreciate. In the first months of the war, both had been welcome to an economy hitherto short of currency, and in Connecticut the bills had circulated at par. Recently, however, the signs of depreciation had become unmistakable. Those offering paper money found themselves asked to pay higher prices than those offering specie, even for plentiful commodities such as fresh pork and corn.[15] Aware that the bills of credit were no more than promises to pay *if* the Revolution succeeded, and less confident of success since the defeats of Long Island and New York, sellers guarded themselves from the danger that the bills would become worthless. The decline in the value of money led enterprising people to engross goods needed by the army in order to protect their assets, which in turn forced the revolutionaries either to pay more for the continent's resources or to do without. During 1776, as emissions of currency increased to meet increasing costs, the money supply expanded to a degree that, together with the cessation of European imports, diminished the demand for it and decreased its value further.[16]

Devaluation occurred by common consent in the marketplace, and only those who held on to the bills as a fixed asset sustained any disproportionate loss. Nevertheless, the leadership deplored the phenomenon. It reflected an unfavorable judgment on the Revolution and advertised the increasing difficulty of persuading the people to support it voluntarily. Though procurement continued, the government had to mortgage more and more of its future resource in order to retain the cooperation of producers and soldiers. And should the debt grow so large as to seem unpayable, the people might turn irrevocably against the cause.

Faced with so unhealthy a prospect, the legislature tried a quick cure. In the October session it declared that Continental and state bills must be accepted as legal tender. Anyone accounting them at a lower value than specie would forfeit his due in a transaction. This measure attacked a symptom but not the ill itself. Next, in an attempt to meet the graver threat that all procurement would cease, the legislature authorized the governor and Council of Safety to impress necessities for the army from those who had engrossed them. The authorities could force sale at a price to be determined "by two indifferent judicious men under oath appointed for that purpose."[17] In the November session, the legislature gave these powers of impressment, at first confined to the governor and Council, into many more hands. Clothing, butter, and cheese could be commandeered by an assistant or two justices of the peace; salt, by the civil officers and selectmen of any town; wheat and flour, by Deputy Commissary Wadsworth. The passage of a comprehensive measure to regulate prices did away with the earlier need to appoint appraisers, and vigorous embargoes against unauthorized exportation where intended to ensure that adequate supplies remained within the state.[18]

These measures were no sooner passed than found wanting. The influx of Continental and state currencies had created a regional market that no one state government could control. In November 1776 Massachusetts called for a convention of the New England states at Providence, in the hope that together they could find a remedy for their individual powerlessness. At first, Connecticut hung back. In mid-December, however, the state suddenly acquired other than economic incentives to attend (as we shall see), and the delegates from Connecticut made a significant contribution. They helped to formulate the economic policies that the convention eventually presented to its constitutents. These included the recommendation that the states finance their war efforts through loans rather than further currency emissions "unless . . . there be an absolute necessity of an immediate supply, and the money cannot be procured upon loan." The convention also urged the states to "levy such taxes upon the inhabitants as their abilities will bear" and to call in their bills of credit on time. It established a comprehensive price schedule for New England and recommended that each state enforce by law the suggested controls upon engrossers and the general public.[19]

Connecticut promptly adopted the convention's price regulations, which closely followed those outlined in November and provided for both a state loan office and a modest tax. But Connecticut also emitted more currency, a sure sign that she found it ever harder to meet the demands of the war. In accordance with the recommendations of the convention, the new currency now bore interest.[20] Congress had specifically condemned the emission of state bills of credit at interest because the practice might further depreciate the Continental currency.[21] In Connecticut, the event bore out the fear. By the following May, the General Assembly raised the prices of most necessities.[22] The chronic economic problems accompanying the war had yet to find a solution.

Not only had prosperity suddenly slipped through Connecticut's fingers, but by October 1776 the enemy had come uncomfortably close to home. As long as Washington held New York against Howe, the British could not move from the western end of Long Island. Their preoccupation with the revolutionary army allowed a Continental regiment, aided by a few Connecticut troops, to remove refugees and stock from the island more or less with impunity,[23] but that was the sole advantage the patriots gained from the situation. All the schemes advanced for keeping control of eastern Long Island proved impracticable. A force large enough to hold its own against Howe, even if Connecticut had one to send, could not subsist on the island without supplies from the mainland.[24] In other words, it would find itself at the mercy of the British navy. Evacuation seemed the only practical course, even though it would give the British victory by default. At first, it looked as though they had little to gain from such a victory: the resources of the island alone would solve only a fraction of their supply problems and at a cost of so angering local residents as to ensure their loyalty to the patriot side.[25] No one foresaw the aftermath of the battles of Long Island and New York, when Long Island became the center of a British recruiting network that spread across New York and western Connecticut and promised to make easy for the British what the patriots had thought they would find hard, the replacement of losses from their ranks.

As soon as he knew of it, Washington authorized an expedition "to check and suppress, if possible, a practice so injurious and detrimental to our cause." He ordered that a brigade of Massachusetts militia, then on its way to reinforce him at New York, turn aside at Fairfield for the purpose.[26] The raid never took place, partly because Governor Trumbull intervened. Trumbull had heard that the notorious Major Rogers was gathering troops at Huntington (near Lloyd's Neck) for an attack on a Continental depot at Norwalk. He decided that before the expeditionary force set out it should increase from twelve hundred to two thousand men and disperse these marauders as well. Though he kept the Massachusetts militia waiting about for reinforcements until it was too late for the raid as originally planned, he never obtained the extra men.[27] No one but Washington had eight hundred fully equipped soldiers to send, and he could not spare any part of his army. After the retreat from New York City in September, his strong position on Harlem

Heights protected him from frontal assault; yet he still had to guard the rear. To cover himself at Westchester without weakening his defense at Harlem Heights, Washington concentrated his main force at Kingsbridge where it could quickly reinforce either place should the British attack. All troops not deployed at these two points, such as the second wave of Connecticut militia commanded by Gurdon Saltonstall, were spread out along the sixteen miles of Westchester's coastline up to Connecticut.[28]

What happened next made the people of Connecticut feel more vulnerable than ever. On October 12 the British landed a force at Throg's Neck. Though they had picked a good spot for the troops to disembark, the surrounding marshes blocked the way to the mainland. A few days later, they transferred the men to Pell's Point. Before Washington could be sure that this landing was anything more than a feint, he decided to shift the greater part of the army from Kingsbridge to White Plains.[29] Howe's recruiters in Westchester, already a thorn in the patriot side, became still more dangerous when three British men-of-war passed up the Hudson on October 9 on their way to the Highlands.[30] If those ships made juncture with a sufficient number of Tories along the river to Albany, Washington might find an insurrection threatening his rear. At White Plains, the army would stand the best chance of keeping Howe from joining with the Tories and of halting British recruitment on the mainland.[31] At the same time, it could maintain the lines of supply to New England and to the northern army above Albany. The move would leave Fort Washington exposed to the enemy, but in the circumstances that seemed the lesser of two evils. If the British could be induced to attack, it might even lead to another Bunker Hill.

As an extra safeguard against insurrection, Washington ordered some of the Massachusetts militia to Tarrytown. He then appealed to Trumbull for Connecticut militia to join them, and once again Connecticut responded. The legislature sent two companies of Hartford militia, and a troop of horse under Elisha Sheldon, toward Fishkill,[32] none of which ever reached their destination. When Washington saw that Howe meant to attack him at White Plains, he diverted them to the main army there.[33] In so doing, he rendered the western frontier of Connecticut defenseless. The only forces left to oppose Howe if he decided to advance along the coast of Connecticut were two militia battalions at the Saw Pitts (modern Port Chester), both below full strength, and the two Massachusetts militia battalions, previously detained at Fairfield, which were now marching to join the main army.[34]

After an inconclusive engagement at White Plains, Howe decided that he could not force Washington to fight a general action in Westchester's hilly interior and that he should lay siege to Fort Washington instead. But an invasion of Connecticut might well have occurred to him as an eligible option; it certainly occurred to the state legislature, then in session at New Haven. A frantic General Assembly tried to form a new corps of men on the southwestern frontier. The order went out that "as many of the militia as are fit for service and of other householders, etc., able-bodied . . . men," in four adjoining militia districts should immediately convene under David Wooster to join the militia from Durham and Wallingford. Trumbull received authority to pardon all those who had dodged service in August if they would now swell Wooster's ranks,[35] and on October 31 he told Washington that Wooster would probably command four hundred infantry with one hundred fifty horse and the local militia.[36] From all accounts, though, this force was not ready to meet the enemy until mid-November.[37] Had Howe bypassed Washington at White Plains and advanced along the coast, or had he chosen to exploit Washington's withdrawal to North Castle by invading Connecticut, Wooster could have done almost nothing to stop him.

From the standpoint of Connecticut, it looked almost as if Washington were inviting Howe to occupy the state. His deployment at the beginning of November of Parsons's brigade along Kingstreet, a road in Rye running parallel to Connecticut's border, made some amends,[38] but even then his intention seemed less to protect the frontier than to cover the commissary agents while they moved their supply lines inland and to guard the few soldiers at the Saw Pitts from marauders. Although

Washington probably recognized and regretted the political consequences of appearing to abandon Connecticut, he had little option until Howe withdrew. Before all else he had to keep his army together. During the march from Kingsbridge to White Plains, desertion reached epidemic proportions. If Washington spread his men thin in an attempt to guard both Westchester and Connecticut against incursion by Howe, many who did not succumb to the enemy would probably succumb to temptation and follow the other deserters. He had to choose, and he chose to concentrate and to guard Westchester.

The Tories at Westchester would have infinitely more attraction for Howe than the Tories in Connecticut. They could receive strong British support from the river with virtually no hindrance from New York's feeble government. In Connecticut, by contrast, most of the Tories lived inland, at places such as Ridgefield, Redding, and Newtown, out of the reach of the British navy. Furthermore, Connecticut had already shown a willingness to deal with her Tories and displayed no sign of flagging. The October session of the legislature, in response to a petition from New Haven, empowered "the civil authority, selectmen and committees of inspection" to remove any suspected defector at their own cost. In any town where the civil authority itself came under suspicion, a special committee supported by the militia would do the job.[39] If Howe abandoned New York and invaded Connecticut, he would exchange friendly territory, with solid strategic advantages, for very uncertain ground. Washington felt sure that Howe knew it and that Connecticut might safely trust to the protection afforded by her lack of attraction for the enemy.

Though Howe's withdrawal to Kingsbridge relieved Connecticut's anxiety at the time, in the long run it compounded the state's military problems by stripping her of all defense. Washington rightly guessed that Howe would angle for political credit at home by attacking the revolutionary Congress at Philadelphia. On November 6 Washington's Council of War decided to divide the army and send the greater part at once to New Jersey.[40] The troops who crossed the river between November 9 and 10 came primarily from the middle and southern states, but the force that they joined in New Jersey included a Continental regiment, a regiment of new levies, and a militia regiment from Connecticut.[41] Meanwhile, most of the Connecticut regiments remained on the east side of the river with the rest of the army, again divided in two parts. One division marched under William Heath's command to Peekskill to hold the Highlands against attack. Parsons's brigade, containing four Connecticut Continental regiments, went with this group.[42] The remainder of the army, including James Wadsworth's brigade (six regiments of new levies), stayed in Westchester under Charles Lee. Attached to it were Wooster's new force and the remnants of Saltonstall's eastern militia, now no bigger than a sizable company.[43] Lee's troops constituted the sole remaining hope for Connecticut if the enemy should look her way, and they too would soon march elsewhere.

Washington had already told Lee that, if the British committed their troops to New Jersey in force, he should cross with his men to the west bank of the river, "leaving the Militia and Invalids to cover the Frontiers of Connecticut &c. in case of need."[44] On November 15 Fort Washington surrendered to Howe. The loss to the Americans included more than one-half of Philip Bradley's Connecticut regiment of new levies, sent from New Jersey at the last moment as reinforcements.[45] Howe sought to capitalize on his victory by throwing the greater part of his men into an immediate attack on New Jersey. On December 1 Lee followed him with most of the Connecticut troops under his command. On December 9 the part of Parsons's brigade stationed on the east bank of the river at the Highlands was ordered to New Jersey with Heath.[46] This left only Fellows's brigade, together with Wadsworth's new levies, never strong and weakened still more by the removal of one regiment, to guard Westchester and help Wooster's militia in case of a British attack.[47]

This new deployment of troops gave Connecticut the more concern because of two other developments. First, as Howe withdrew, the enemy had stepped up its activities along the coast. Until November, Connecticut had held the initiative in that area. The continuous passage of refugees to the mainland kept intermittent military operations going and kept the Americans supplied with useful intelligence of enemy plans and movements.[48] When the British on Long Island threatened to disrupt the movement of supplies to the army at New York, Connecticut threatened counterraids. She even planned a naval force with which to challenge British supremacy at sea.[49] But Howe's landing at Throg's Neck forced her to think of better ways to defend her coastline. The General Assembly asked Congress to deploy "two battalions, at the expence of the several United States . . . along the sea coast of this State," ordered all stores moved inland, and put all coastal regiments on alert, plus the Wallingford, Durham, and Norwich regiments near New Haven and New London.[50] These precautions seemed adequate for the moment, especially since Howe's demand for contributions to the Westchester enterprise had weakened the Long Island loyalists.

In early November, quantities of stock, and particularly horses, began to disappear from the coastal towns during the night.[51] The government did no more at first than recommend that sentries stand guard and raise the alarm if marauders appeared.[52] Reports that the British were preparing for an expedition aimed at Rhode Island caused more concern, but Washington discounted them, convinced that the enemy would not willfully seek the hardships of a winter campaign in New England.[53] As November passed with no sign of a fleet, the general anxiety diminished. On December 1, however, ten big men-of-war appeared off Montauk Point. Governor Trumbull learned of their presence at the same time as he heard that a large fleet of transport ships had passed Hell Gate heading down the Sound.[54] Howe had sent Clinton and six thousand men to seize Newport, a good place from which to launch an invasion of Massachusetts when the next campaign began.[55] Clinton may or may not have intended to make a feint at Connecticut along the way; in any case, on December 5 bad weather drove both fleets into Niantic Bay, just west of New London. There they lay until the seventh, and the Council of Safety ordered several regiments into New London to guard Continental and state stores. Then the weather improved, the enemy bore eastward, and the Council canceled the order. On the ninth, when news arrived of the British landing on Aquidneck Island, the regiments were sent instead to Rhode Island.[56]

New Londoners undoubtedly heaved sighs of relief when the British moved off, but in fact the occupation of Aquidneck Island left the state open to attack on three sides. The enemy held posts from Newport to Westchester and had the naval power to strike anywhere along the Connecticut coastline from the sea or along the western frontier from the Hudson. Even the northern frontier was not immune. Arnold's defense of Lake Champlain had ended in defeat at Valcour Island, and though he had delayed the enemy long enough to ensure that the northern states need fear no invasion from that quarter during the remainder of 1776, the British had won control of Lake Champlain. They would certainly use their advantage in the next campaign, and in the meantime they might launch an expedition south from Canada along the Connecticut River. This plan, suggested as a possibility by the Tory Creon Bush, had appeared in all the Connecticut newspapers during May.[57] If it were carried out, where could the state turn for help? The Continental army had gone to New Jersey, apart from which its time of service would expire on December 31. And the small force of new levies that comprised her principal defense would disband on December 25.

Connecticut had embarked on the war with confidence. In 1776, through heroic effort, she had mustered almost all her able-bodied men. Now, at the beginning of 1777, Connecticut found herself exhausted, discouraged, and in greater danger than ever.

The Leadership Falters

For the first time since Connecticut entered the war her government lapsed into indecision and confusion. No one could agree on solutions to any of the urgent problems confronting them. For example, what should be done about the many political prisoners held there since 1775? Some were hostages, taken by order of the Continental Congress as pawns to bargain with if the British should ever capture some prominent patriot; most were New York Tories, removed to Connecticut during the summer of 1776 to prevent their collaboration with the enemy. With every report of British gains, both groups became more openly unruly, and their rowdiness encouraged the emulation of Connecticut Tories who might otherwise have kept still.[58] The disturbances they provoked, such as the noisy brawl set on by Governor William Franklin at Middletown, caused more nuisance than danger.[59] But that winter Connecticut acquired additional reasons to seek the return of as many as possible. Widespread shortages had begun to make providing for them difficult.[60] And those prisoners who were men of means, with families left behind in British-controlled territory, often slipped strategic information to the enemy through servants delivering necessaries from home. The discovery that David Matthews, the Tory mayor of Albany imprisoned at Litchfield, had written to advise a British invasion of Connecticut, heightened everyone's anxiety; and there were ominous indications that his act revealed but the tip of an iceberg.[61]

The leadership also had reason to fear that the Tories might acquire undue influence as people grew disenchanted with the war. Articles in the public prints complaining of high prices and extortion, letters charging that mobilization of the militia in August and September had penalized the poor and left the rich alone, and beleaguered patriot defenses of Washington's decision to avoid a general action at White Plains, all betrayed the people's loss of heart.[62] The note of discouragement sounded still louder in private correspondence. David Trumbull, not much heartened by Howe's withdrawal from White Plains and Carleton's abandonment of the northern campaign for the winter, wrote to his brothers, "What have the Enemy attempted this season that they have not executed?"[63] When the governor's own family found pessimists within its gates, morale had sunk low indeed.

At the end of 1776, unnerved by the general listlessness, the patriot leadership took alarm at the Howe brothers' offer of

an unconditional pardon for all who swore "peaceable obe-
dience to his Majesty." Together with Carleton's ostentatious
display of leniency when he paroled prisoners taken in Canada,
the offer conjured up an image of a loving, forgiving mother
country which the disheartened might find all too appealing. In
December, Governor Trumbull toyed with the idea of calling
for town meetings "to inspirit the people, know their sentiments in the present days," and ask them would they "yield
up their lives and properties and sacred liberties to the imperi-
ous demands of *Britons,* and submit to that base, ignominious
yoke of slavery . . . or will they . . . stand forth in the cause
of their country, and engage in the glorious struggle?"[64] But
nothing came of it.

The legislators, however, did attempt to remove some of
the causes for dissatisfaction and complaint. Recognizing the
injustice of a militia system that allowed so many exemptions,[65]
recognizing also the need to change what had been an administrative institution into one that could take the field, they undertook a thorough reorganization of the military. They set out to
see that the state could if necessary deploy all her resources in
her defense. In December they passed a law forming "all male
persons" from sixteen to sixty "not included in that part of the
militia called the train-band" into alarm companies. These
companies could choose their own officers and had the same
military obligations as the regular militia. They had to attend
training as prescribed by law and to answer when their officers
called. Virtually every able-bodied man in Connecticut could
now be summoned to take up arms at any moment. To avoid
wholesale economic disruption in the event of an alarm, the
legislature directed the officers to section each company in four
equal parts, "taking care that persons of the same office, family,
business, trade or occupation, be divided as much as may be
and placed in different divisions." Each division should decide
by lot the order in which they would take turns of duty; then
the individuals within a division should repeat the process.
Lastly, to ensure that the men took the field quickly in an
emergency, the state's twenty-five militia regiments were
formed into six brigades commanded by brigadiers and two di-

visions commanded by major generals. David Wooster and Jabez Huntington were named as major generals, while Erastus Wolcott, Oliver Wolcott, James Wadsworth, Gurdon Saltonstall, Gold Selleck Silliman, and Eliphalet Dyer received appointments as brigadiers. The colonels of the regiments could appoint adjutants for administrative duty so as to free field officers for active command.[66]

Unfortunately, the legislature undercut its own reforms, first by lowering the fine for refusal to march from ten pounds to five pounds, then by rescinding the requirement that all officers and freemen abjure the Crown and swear allegiance to the state government before January 1.[67] The excuse that dissenters had raised scruples of conscience begged the question. The law could have been amended to satisfy the small group concerned, rather than repealed. In any case, in a national emergency the safety of the majority should have come before the qualms of the few. Critics of the action later said that it showed a pusillanimous reluctance to burn bridges for a cause that had come to seem precarious, but they did not speak out until just before the next election.[68] So public a display of faintheartedness by the very men they looked up to as leaders must have put the finishing touch to the people's loss of faith during that discontented winter.

Worse than faintheartedness drove the government to bungle the other emergency that arose in December, when they found the state tugged in two different directions. Clinton's force on Rhode Island threatened the whole of southern New England, which sparked many proposals for a large army to strike and destroy it before it could strike them. Meanwhile, to the westward, with Washington in full flight across New Jersey and Howe advancing upon him, an unexpected opportunity arose to attack the enemy's overextended supply lines. Charles Lee wasted precious time on an attempt to make Heath surrender some of his men for the purpose, instead of going straight to Washington's aid as ordered.[69] When Heath refused, Lee approached the New York Convention. New York claimed to have no spare manpower but agreed to approach Connecticut, the next nearest source, for men to carry out Lee's plan.[70]

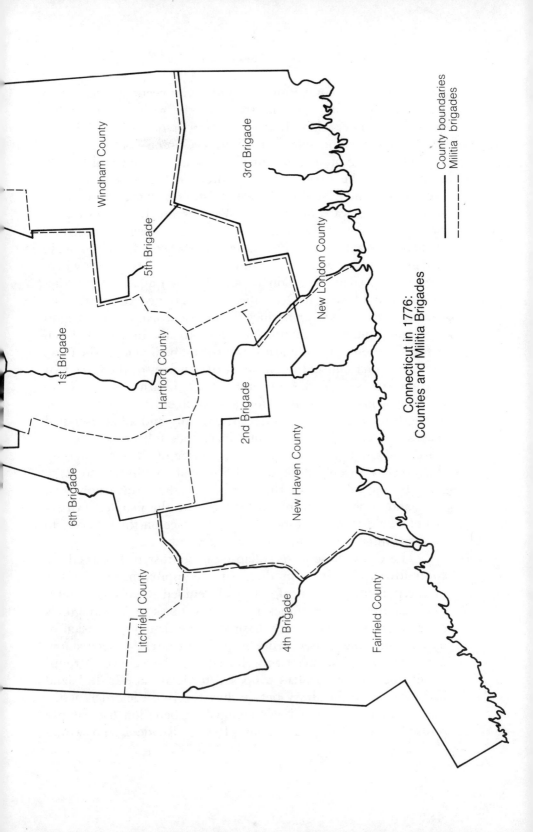

Connecticut in 1776:
Counties and Militia Brigades

—— County boundaries
----- Militia brigades

Windham County

3rd Brigade

5th Brigade

New London County

1st Brigade

Hartford County

2nd Brigade

6th Brigade

New Haven County

Litchfield County

4th Brigade

Fairfield County

Faced with competing demands, Connecticut decided to skimp on attacking Clinton and give the greater part of her resources to Lee, whose bravado the leadership admired. Howe seemed more vulnerable than Clinton. Clinton held the advantage of position on a large, fortified island; Howe could be surrounded in the open field. A force of six thousand Massachusetts and New Hampshire militia were even then marching westward to reinforce Washington. It seemed logical to divert them to Providence, while western Connecticut rushed men across the river as fast as she could. In this way, troops would arrive with maximum speed at both places where they were needed. The Convention of New England States that met in Providence on December 25 sanctioned the plan. The convention reasoned that, since Connecticut had already begun to recruit four three-month battalions to fill the gap between the dissolution of the old army and the embodiment of the new, the men so far enlisted might form the nucleus of the force that Lee and the New York Convention wanted.[71] Instead, the Connecticut legislature called for a volunteer force of brigade strength to serve two months. Urging "any and all able-bodied men . . . west of Connecticut River, cheerfully to spring forward and offer themselves for the service of their country on this great occasion," it appointed a special committee "to carry into the several parts of this State . . . the resolve now past . . . and endeavour to rouse and animate the people." All recruits would receive a forty-shilling advance on their wages, to be distributed by the members of the committee.[72]

These grandiose plans collapsed in confusion. It was all the committee could do to produce a force approximately the size of a regiment; the goal of a brigade eluded them completely. Lee's capture on December 13 and the news of Washington's retreat across the Delaware dissipated the first bright vision of opportunity and undoubtedly helped to cause the poor showing.[73] Perhaps it was just as well that the Massachusetts troops which the convention had proposed to detain at Rhode Island had marched to Danbury before they received the order, while the commander of the New Hampshire battalion had simply refused to obey it.[74] But their place at Rhode Island would have to be supplied by men from Connecticut, particularly since Washington, misinterpreting Trumbull's plea for some experienced general to take charge there as a request for the appointment of Connecticut officers, had sent forward Benedict Arnold and Joseph Spencer.[75]

Connecticut could not now deploy the mere token force of men, men who would serve the briefest possible term, that the Providence convention had envisioned. Later sessions of the convention increased Connecticut's quota to 1,092 men, more than she could readily produce.[76] The state was in sad disarray. The appeal for volunteers competed disastrously with recruitment for the three-month regiments. Furthermore, the distracted legislature had waited too long to ask that the new levies at Westchester stay until their replacements came. By the time a committee arrived to make the request, Wadsworth's brigade had dissolved.[77] Meanwhile, the task of finding replacements for Erastus Wolcott's battalion of coast guards, whose time would be up at the end of the year, had become urgent.

In this emergency, the one complete three-month regiment, providentially raised in the New London area and commanded by John Ely, received orders to replace Wolcott's men until a relief guard could be drafted from the five neighboring militia regiments. As soon as relief arrived, Ely's regiment could march to Rhode Island to join the three large companies raised for service there.[78] It went a long way toward filling the requisition, on paper at least, though it did assume that operations in Rhode Island would have concluded by the end of March.

The plight of the western frontier proved harder to relieve. When Wooster's militia and the new levies retired at the end of the year, almost nothing stood between Connecticut and the British at New York. Wooster had ordered ten companies of the Ninth Regiment to replace the men who had left, and these, together with such members of the two-month volunteers and the remaining three-month regiments as could join him at once, represented the sole defense of the state.[79] Fortunately, Washington's victories at Trenton and Princeton gave the British other things to think about for a while, besides which a new and unexpected source of help had appeared. Acting on Washington's orders that he station his men where they could press on the British at New York, Heath had recrossed the Hudson on December 23 to take up a position in Westchester.[80] This tided Connecticut over the dangerous period from December 25, when the terms of almost all her forces in the field ran out, until mid-January when the three-month regiments were ready to replace them. Still, everyone was uncomfortably aware that luck had done more than good judgment to bring her through.

Furthermore, Connecticut had failed to find recruits for the new army that Congress had resolved to raise. Economic considerations had done much to persuade Congress that the advantages of a standing army outweighed the dangers. In every troop shuffle a large quantity of arms, ammunition, camping equipment, and clothing disappeared with those who went home, and it was not easy to replace them for the new arrivals. America had nowhere near the capacity of European economies to produce these articles quickly and cheaply. The adoption of a permanent force would plug this drain on vital resources and would also save the continent a great deal of the marching money paid out every few months under the present system.[81] More important still, it would diminish the disruption of agriculture that occurred every time men marched between farm and camp. In the previous summer and autumn, Connecticut had suffered so grievously in this respect that Governor Trumbull warned the people they had only two choices: a standing army, or the "certain prospect of being devoured by FAMINE."[82] Despite the obvious advantage, not to say the necessity, of such a force, Connecticut's government could not persuade men to volunteer for it.

Political mismanagement had helped to cause their reluctance. Congress wanted to ensure that a new army would stand ready to replace the old one at the end of 1776. Knowing that the men's dislike for the officers put over them had obstructed recruitment late in 1775, Congress changed the procedure that made the appointment of officers its own prerogative. Under the new system, each state government would appoint all officers of the line below the rank of general officer.[83] Now, however, the state governments began to show a maddening inability to make the necessary decisions. Some, and Connecticut among them, did not want to act without recommendations from Washington and his generals. Recommendations were therefore made. In Connecticut, they immediately became controversial because several areas were not represented in them, and the legislature argued for weeks before deciding that all parts of the state would not send recruits unless all parts of the state had a proportional share of officers.[84] At the beginning of November, Washington had received not one commission from any state for officers, and the work of recruitment could not begin without them. Recruiting orders were at last issued on November 19, when commissioners from Connecticut arrived in camp to name the state's officers.[85] By then, Howe's vigorous campaign in New Jersey had divided the army and scattered the men across the countryside. How could the new army now come from the ranks of the old, as Congress had hoped?

Even if the commissioners had found the army accessible, they might not have found the men willing to reenlist. Though spirits had improved among the officers since the retreat from New York, the men's morale declined as the winter approached.[86] Baggage and camp equipment had been lost in that retreat and in the subsequent confused, hasty movement of the army. The men would have to suffer through the bitter weather without tents for shelter, without even proper clothing. Summer uniforms had worn out, and few winter replacements existed.[87] Congress tried to turn this to advantage by promising all men who reenlisted in the permanent army a new suit of clothes annually, an offer that helped wherever the power to keep the promise existed.[88] In many places it did not. Clothing remained scarce well into 1777, despite the capture of prizes carrying supplies of it.[89] In any case, the army's rapid movement would have made distribution difficult. The perpetual motion of the American soldier's life made trouble for him at every turn. It denied him regular pay or food and in the absence of an effective hospital system, left him destitute if he became sick.[90] Altogether, the closing weeks of 1776 would have been an inauspicious moment to recruit for any length of time, let alone an unspecified period.

When Congress conceived the new army, recognizing that the uncertain length of service would hinder recruitment, it promised no less than a twenty-dollar bounty and one hundred acres of land to every man who enlisted for the duration.[91] The New Englanders were not impressed. In 1776 the new levies had received such large bounties from their several states that prospective recruits found the proposition no inducement. Massachusetts and Connecticut rejected the bounty outright as inadequate and on their own initiative increased the men's wages from two to three pounds a month. Connecticut added the further offer of a blanket for each man.[92] Both states rescinded these offers, however, when Washington complained that differential pay would create hopeless jealousy between state lines.[93] Meanwhile, Congress decided to allow the choice of three years as an option to service for the duration. Connecticut's legislature tried to insist that those who chose limited service receive only the twenty dollars, but in 1777 Congress made them eligible for the land bounty, too.[94] Subsequently, when the New England states met at Providence in late December 1776, they decided that they could not raise their quotas without raising the bounties they offered. They promised each recruit thirty-three dollars in addition to the twenty from Congress, along with a blanket and with refreshments to be supplied at prime cost.[95] Governor Trumbull tried to justify this by claiming that the massive mobilization of 1776 had driven prices higher in New England than elsewhere. Whether this was true or not (and Washington doubted it), inflation together with the depreciation of Continental and state currencies had certainly eroded much of whatever financial incentive for enlistment had once existed. And potential recruits had grown wary of taking themselves out of the labor market for an indefinite period of time at fixed wages.[96]

Connecticut's legislature tackled the problem by adopting some of the measures to support the credit of the currency recommended by the Providence convention. But the legislature hesitated to tax the people, though a surplus of money clearly existed. With eightpence already due between December 1776 and May 1777, to ask for over fourpence more would have raised the level of taxation above one shilling in the pound. Only twice had taxes gone higher, and that was during 1758 and 1759, in the first flush of a wartime prosperity guaranteed by parliamentary reimbursement. Twenty years later, the people's state of mind made their compliance doubtful, and the legislators instructed constables "not to enforce the collection immediately on such as are not now of sufficient ability to discharge the same."[97]

Connecticut's government preferred borrowing to taxation. In October 1776, Congress had in fact suggested borrowing as a way to finance the war without printing more money. The continent would agree to borrow $5 million of the money already in circulation at 4 percent and in quantities of no less than $300.[98] The General Assembly in Connecticut immediately named its treasurer, John Lawrence, as Continental loan officer, too. When the necessary forms had not arrived from Philadelphia by the end of the year, the Assembly authorized Lawrence to give receipts guaranteed by the state for any money subscribed. In case the $300 minimum should discourage investors, it also provided that, if the federal loan should fail, he might borrow £80,000 against the state's credit at 4 percent and in denominations as low as £10.[99] Unfortunately, the depreciation made people unwilling to lend at such low rates of interest.

Reluctance to tax and inability to borrow made it nearly impossible for Connecticut's treasury to pay the nominal value of the bounties promised. The state had been drained of funds by the expense of two previous campaigns and by the recent advance of £10,000 to equip a battalion of light horse commanded by Elisha Sheldon.[100] A congressional grant of $133,000 toward recruitment brought some hope of relief, but the money came in late and was less than promised. The Continental loan office, which should have supplied $33,000, had succeeded in attracting very little money. In order to pay the bounties, the legislature authorized Lawrence to execute £60,000 of "notes or bills under his own hand and office" at 4 percent, redeemable in three years.[101]

No sooner had the state tackled the lack of bounty money and clothing (with only minimal success, at that) than a fresh obstacle sprang up. Smallpox broke out in the army at New Jersey. Washington well knew how this would hurt enlistment and knew that the only help for it was to inoculate the whole army, but he shrank from a step that could put his men out of action for up to four weeks, take away his option of an attack on New Jersey and Long Island, and give the British an opportunity they might use to deadly advantage.[102] Nevertheless, by the beginning of February he saw that he must take the chance. The pox was raging through his men. Where was the point of struggling to raise a permanent army if disease should decimate its ranks before it even took the field?[103]

It is hard to determine how Washington's orders affected enlistment in Connecticut. They were kept as secret as possible, but word must have leaked out that enlistment meant inoculation. Certainly everyone knew that the army in New Jersey had smallpox, for Trumbull had to promise a detachment of militia ordered to Peekskill that they would not be sent across the river.[104] Had there been a smallpox epidemic within the state, of course, inoculation might have appeared an incentive. What evidence there is, however, suggests that, though the return of infected captives from New York had spread the disease, Connecticut's government preferred to isolate cases as they arose rather than to risk further spread by inoculation. Statutes against the practice were strictly enforced as late as May.[105] Even those who believed in and wanted it would probably not have chosen to have the army hospital department, currently in bad odor, perform the procedure.

Apart from these disadvantages, the militia and volunteer corps inevitably appeared more attractive than the Continental army. The state needed defenders, and local service required enlistment for only specified, short terms. In January 1777, Connecticut had four three-month battalions and a regiment of two-month volunteers stationed in New York and Rhode Island. British control of the Sound, the constant movement of enemy ships along the Connecticut coast, and sporadic raids for livestock had also forced the General Assembly to authorize two more regiments. The first, for coastal defense, would serve one year; the other, for general defense, would serve as long as the war should last.[106] The Council of Safety sought to avoid a conflict with recruitment for the permanent army by replacing the two-month militia at New London with men who had already enlisted in the line, but the order for inoculation of all Continental troops made this impossible to carry through. Though four companies of Ely's three-month battalion at Rhode Island came back to fill the breach,[107] their protection would last only until their discharge on March 15. The Council of Safety therefore had also to order a one-month draft on part of the Third and Eighth regiments, supplemented by a voluntary company drawn from the Twentieth. Then, when Major-General Spencer, commanding the army in Rhode Island, called for reinforcements to attack British positions, the Council felt that it must at least replace Ely's men. It ordered a six-week draft of five companies from the four eastern regiments which had seen the least action so far. Finally, on March 15, the three-month troops stationed along the New York coast and at Peekskill went home, and the gap they left had to be filled by another draft of two thousand men from the western regiments for six weeks.[108]

Forming a Permanent Army

Do what she would, Connecticut could not gather the army that all friends to the cause believed essential. In early March, Samuel Holden Parsons admitted to Washington that only 1,380 men had enlisted in the nine Continental regiments assigned to the state.[109] Washington, appalled, learned that three of the Connecticut regiments, those of John Chandler, Heman Swift, and Charles Webb, had only 80 men each; that a fourth, John Durkee's, had only 140 men; and that the other four were less than half full.[110] That the additional regiment assigned the state by Congress, under Samuel B. Webb's command, also fell

short came as less of a shock. When Washington had refused to
let him compete with the Connecticut line by raising the Continental bounty from twenty to fifty-three dollars, he had expected Webb's regiment to fill up last. He had spoken so
eloquently on the evils of New England's decision to give ten
pounds more than Congress in bounty money that the Assembly at last agreed to extend the same offer to Webb's recruits.[111] Coming as it did at the end of February, this concession unfortunately added to the burdens of the state treasury
and ate into the funds just received from the continent as an aid
to recruitment. Nor did it seem likely to increase the influx of
men, considering the lack of enthusiasm so far. After three
months of effort, Connecticut had reached only 20 percent of
her quota. Many of the recruits had yet to be inoculated, and
most of them were still dispersed throughout the state.

The spectacle of their impotence to recruit for the army
provoked the first sustained criticisms of the state's civil leaders.
Carping about the military leadership was as old as the war.
Complaints about their officers from men unused to army life
had first gained popular credit in the autumn of 1775, when the
army at Boston did not immediately defeat the British,[112] and
the succeeding campaign had improved no one's prestige. Of all
Connecticut's high-ranking officers only Wooster remained
popular, largely, it seems, by dubious means that made poor
soldiers of his men.[113] General Silliman, whose reputation
plummeted because of backbiting as malicious as it was un-
deserved, illustrates the more common experience.[114] Now the
legislature's turn had come. In the middle of March, when everyone could see that the state was not meeting her Continental
quota, the *Connecticut Journal* burst into controversy over where
to lay the blame. In March, it ran three articles blaming the
current legislature, which had spent four weeks and over a
thousand pounds in appointing officers of Continental regiments along geographic lines, contrary to the recommendations
of Washington's general staff. "A Freeman" called this "a chief
cause, our part of the Continental army is not yet filled up" and
bitterly contrasted it to the performance of the legislature in
April 1775, which had raised six thousand men in three weeks.

What could people do about it? Prune the legislature of reluctant patriots in the forthcoming election, he said. "Plain Dealer" agreed and urged that the people put men "determined to contend while life lasts, and extricate their country from slavery, or perish in its ruin, at the helm of our affairs."[115]

The Council of Safety did not need the prodding of the *Journal*. One day before the first of these articles appeared, the Council framed an address to the towns on "the slow progress made in filling up the continental battalions" in which it proposed to assign each of them a troop quota. The Council meant to awaken a sense of local responsibility and to involve town authorities, their prestige as yet little jolted by the bumpy course of the war, in recruitment for the continent. To this end, "the civil authority, selectmen and military officers, and all friends to the liberties of mankind" were "requested and exhorted to exert themselves to the utmost, and that immediately, as they regard the welfare and salvation of their country, in incouraging and procuring the quotas of their respective towns to engage in said service." The towns were asked also to help their recruits cope with depreciation by appointing committees to "make proper provision for their families . . . at the prices stated by law."[116] It took several days to make copies of the address and to fix the respective quotas. Just before the towns received them, they heard of the British raid on Peekskill. On March 22, the same day the Council had drafted two thousand men to replace the three-month men who had gone home, the British attacked with 550 men and destroyed all the Continental stores accumulated there.[117] Nothing could have underscored the Council's appeal more heavily. And nothing could better have shown the limitations of the volunteer system. Though many towns immediately expressed their willingness to offer handsome bounties to recruits,[118] the rate of enlistment for the Connecticut line during the first two weeks of April remained roughly the same as in the preceding months. (See Table 2.)

Washington had already asserted the need for a compulsory draft.[119] But the right of government to detach men at all, even for short periods, had been called in question over an in-

Table Two
Recruitment of the Connecticut Line, November 1776–December 1777

	Huntington 1st Reg.		C. Webb 2nd Reg.		Wyllys 3rd Reg.		Durkee 4th Reg.		Bradley 5th Reg.		Douglas Meigs 6th Reg.		Swift 7th Reg.		Chandler 8th Reg.		S. Webb Add'l. Reg.		Monthly Total		
	War	3 yrs.	War	3 yrs.	War	3 yrs.	War	3 yrs.	War	3 yrs.	War	3 yrs.	War	3 yrs.	War	3 yrs.	War	3 yrs.	War	3 yrs.	Total
Nov. '76	1		1		10	7	6	1	9	2	17	2							44	12	56
Dec. '76	14	2	2	3	18	2	18	7	12	13	23	4							87	31	118
Jan. '77	31	31	28	42	34	14	27	8	45	25	37	12	12	40	2	3	2		218	175	393
Feb. '77	28	48	21	9	47	25	24	15	76	51	30	26	26	43	14	1	24	16	290	234	527
(8 mos.)						2		1													3
Mar. '77	16	34	14	27	17	16	16	12	28	17	29	14	37	60	36	11	23	38	216	229	448
(8 mos.)								3													3
Apr. '77 (1st half)	9	14	3	16	9	23	20	10	27	6	23	22	13	31	29	17	15	21	148	160	319
(8 mos.)						2		4		1		1		1							9
(1 yr.)		2																			2
Apr. '77 (2nd half)	22	48	8	12	29	32	17	34	9	16	34	9	15	23	34	42	19	20	187	236	611
(8 mos.)	6			32		24		29		5		17		28		40		2		183	
(1 yr.)		5																		5	

																				13	
(1 yr.)																				13	
Jun. '77	5	7	6	7	16	9	9	9	15	7	9	6	14	11	13	4	13	14	101	73	234
(8 mos.)	4	3		3	2	7	7		3		7		6		14		3		49		
(1 yr.)	11																			11	
Jul. '77	1	3	1	3	1	3	1	1	4	1	1	1	3	4	3		3	4	21	15	39
(8 mos.)									1				1		1		1		3		
Aug. '77	2	8	2	3	3	3	1	1	3	1	1	6	6	8	5	7	5	4	31	28	67
(8 mos.)	2						3		5		3						8		8		
Sept. '77	1	8	1	4	2	9	1	1	9	1	1	5	5	8	8	3	39	1	39	17	61
(8 mos.)	1			3	1	1	1		1		1						5		5		
Oct. '77	1		1	6	1		1		1	1	1	1	1	1		1	12		12	4	16
Nov. '77		1			1		2	2	2	6							9	2	9	6	15
Dec. '77	1	1	1	3	2	2	2	2	1	12	2				4	2	26		26	6	32
Grand Total	462	331	517	382	487	523	545	491	281												4,019

NOTE: Commissioned and noncommissioned officers excluded.

SOURCE: *RCM*, 148–252. Compiled by John Barber and Monica Murray.

cident that had taken place in January. At the time, the legislature had ordered a two-month draft of men to guard the New London area. Colonel Dyer Throop, the officer concerned, had sent a file of men to carry off sundry persons named in his order, whether they would or no, apparently in defiance of the law which allowed them to pay a fine in lieu of service. Some of them subsequently appealed to the Council of Safety, which sought to temporize. It upheld Throop in that his course had conformed to "a special act and order of the General Assembly necessary for the immediate safety and defense of the forts and garrison at New London" and therefore did not "come under the former or late acts of Assembly respecting fines and penaltys upon refusal in case of detachment." On the other hand, the Council ordered that anyone so detached who was not "of the militia" and who was over forty-five be discharged on the grounds that the new militia law had not taken effect when the legislature ordered the detachment.[120] This diplomatic solution, while it quieted controversy, did not help to increase the yields from subsequent detachments. Two-thirds of the two thousand men ordered to Peekskill for six weeks apparently chose to pay a fine rather than march.[121] When drafts for six weeks and two months met such resistance, legislators were understandably loath to draft men for three years or the duration.

The campaign was about to begin; something had to be done, and quickly. On April 12 the Council of Safety hit on the device known as classing. The board ordered that "the commission officers of every company in each town, and field officers residing therein . . . divide and class all the men of each company, within the same, into as many equal numbers of classes" as there were deficiencies in the town's quota. The classes should "include all persons formed, or to be formed by law, into Alarm companies." Each class should then be convened by its officers and "earnestly invited, freely to inlist . . . one able man into some company of our eight battalions." Failing this, within three days the officers must "without further order . . . draft . . . one suitable and able man from each of said divisions, who shall be joined to the nearest and most convenient company in any of said eight battalions where he may be needed . . . to be held therein until the first day of *January* next, unless sooner discharged." [122] The provision for discharge reflected an undimmed hope that voluntary enlistment would come with time. And the classing system still stopped short of ironclad coercion. Each man drafted would receive a three-pound bounty in addition to Continental wages for eight months' service, "provided he shall voluntarily engage in said service (before marching)." Draftees could also buy an exemption for five pounds, "such penalty [to] be applied to procure a fit person to inlist into the Continental army, or to take the place of such person so declining and incurring said penalty according to the provision of said law." [123] Nevertheless, the Council had moved closer to compulsory recruitment.

The Council was eager to take this step without waiting for the new legislature to assemble. It had received reports that the enemy might raid the Continental magazines at Danbury, which since the last campaign had become an important depot for provisions, camp equipment, and hospital stores. [124] Danbury had been chosen because it was near all positions the Continental army was likely to take up between the Highlands and Horseneck (modern Greenwich), yet comparatively safe from enemy attack. [125] Any raiding party bent on Danbury, no matter which way it came, would have to traverse some twenty-five miles of rough terrain. That would mean at least two days of marching, plenty of time for the men already under arms to concentrate and for the civilian population to turn out in Danbury's defense. It would also help the defenders that the raiders had to leave the shelter of British naval support. In normal circumstances, a raid on Danbury should have provided the perfect opportunity for Americans to revenge themselves for Peekskill.

Circumstances were not normal. While we know that the militia draft of two thousand men from Danbury and its environs had drawn a disappointing response, enough men were gone away to weaken the area's defenses. The loss could have been partly set off by sending Continental recruits to Danbury for inoculation, as Washington suggested, which would have made the town a rendezvous for all coming from the east. But

most of the Connecticut recruits had completed their inocula-
tions, and such as were in the vicinity had neither arms nor ammunition.[126] At the same time, despite strong repressive measures, pockets of disaffection in western Connecticut continued
to trouble the patriots. Most of the suspicious persons sent east
early in 1776 had returned on parole for the lean winter months
and soon set to work again. The authorities meted out harsh
punishment to British recruiters when they could catch them.
Moses Dunbar, for example, convicted of treason by the Superior Court, was hanged at Hartford on March 19 in an effort to
discourage his fellow subversives.[127] Yet Washington's intelligence agents in New York continuted to report "large and
weekly supplies of fresh provisions" coming to the British from
western Connecticut, not to mention large numbers of people
there accepting Howe's offer of protection.[128] Along the coast,
attempts to prosecute local Tories in the county courts brought
open threats of reprisal raids that would be launched from Long
Island.[129] In late April, the interior of western Connecticut invited attack.

Two thousand men landed at Compo (now Westport) on
the afternoon of April 25. Except for a brief skirmish as they
moved inland, they marched across country to Danbury without opposition, arriving at 4:00 P.M. the next day.[130] Only fifty
continentals and about a hundred militia waited there, and they
judged it wiser to join the populace in sequestering supplies
than to offer an opposition clearly hopeless. Peekskill could
send no immediate help: the British had sailed eighteen vessels
up the river toward the Highlands to prevent reinforcement
from that quarter.[131] Connecticut's new militia law of December 1776 was about to meet the first test of its adequacy.

Major General Wooster, receiving word of the attack at
New Haven early on the twenty-sixth, headed west at once.
He left his junior officers with orders to send their men forward
as fast as possible. Silliman had summoned his brigade the
previous evening. Though they were unable to assemble until
early the following morning, Silliman then marched them at
once toward Redding, where Wooster and Arnold caught up
with him. Their combined forces numbered six hundred. The

general officers agreed to split up: about four hundred men
under Arnold and Silliman would block the retreat at Ridgefield, while Wooster led the remainder in an attack on the rear
to draw off enemy fire. Alas, Wooster attacked before the men
in front had fully engaged the enemy, received a mortal wound,
and left his forces in hopeless confusion. Arnold nevertheless
threw up hasty barricades at a strong point in the road through
Ridgefield, inflicted heavy casualties on the British, and impeded their retreat. That night, the British had to bivouac a
mile from Ridgefield.[132] They had an uneasy wait. For all they
knew, the militia was gathering strength with every hour that
passed. They may also have heard that Alexander McDougall,
in command of a considerable force at Peekskill and aware that
so large a raiding party at Danbury precluded any danger to his
garrison, was marching twelve hundred men toward Bedford to
cut off that line of retreat.[133]

The next day, when the British tried to make for the fleet
at Norwalk, they encountered another obstruction. Silliman
and Arnold, reinforced by a company of Continental artillery,
had taken up a strong position at a bridge over the Saugatuck
River in Wilton. Anxious not to repeat their bitter experience at
Ridgefield, the British column forded the river above the bridge
and marched off, double-quick, past the Continental and Connecticut troops waiting on the right bank. By prompt action,
and by using their position on the bridge to full advantage, the
Connecticut troops might still have cut off their retreat, but it
was beyond the powers of either Arnold or Silliman to make
them face British regulars without protection from fortifications
and support from artillery. They settled for harassment in the
rear, right up to the moment when the soldiers regained their
ships.[134] This strategy avoided heavy American losses while
giving the impression, not wholly false, that the British had
fled in terror. British casualties amounted to roughly 5 percent
of their men: twenty-four killed, twenty-eight missing, and
ninety-two wounded—not too much to pay, perhaps, for a raid
that destroyed five thousand barrels of provisions, together
with most of the revolutionary army's tents, and put the Americans to the expense of moving all magazines further inland.[135]

But the British officers felt that they had barely escaped and would not lightly hazard any more such ventures.

Neither did the Americans celebrate any triumph. That the enemy could stay four days inside Connecticut without meeting total destruction lowered the state's estimation of her military power and heightened the people's feeling of vulnerability. Surely there had been enough time for the militia of four western regiments, the Fourth, Ninth, Thirteenth, and Sixteenth, to have turned out and met the enemy, particularly after McDougall sealed off their escape to the Hudson. Since the preceding December's reorganization, these four regiments alone had a potential of four thousand troops.[136] Yet it looked as if no more than eight hundred men had mustered from Connecticut. Enlistment in the Continental army, notoriously in arrears, could not be pleaded in extenuation, and the March 20 draft of two thousand men to reinforce Peekskill had affected only half of the regiments that should have succored Danbury.

The most ingenious excuse offered for the militia's laggard response came from an anonymous writer in the *Connecticut Courant*, who attributed it to the absence of most of the state's officers in the Continental army.[137] It seems more likely that the reluctance of some to abandon the spring planting, especially those whose service the previous autumn had kept them from sowing winter grains, had combined with the disaffection of others to cause the poor turnout. We must not forget that disaffection held back more than the few who felt it. To people who could not know where the British would strike but knew too well that disloyal neighbors would point out their property for reprisal if opportunity arose, staying at home might seem the only safe course.[138] It is also true that Silliman's orders requiring his brigade to rendezvous at Fairfield in effect obstructed the immediate deployment of those men who did respond to the call. If the British had been obliged to fight their way into Danbury, as well as out of it, they might not have been able to extricate themselves in time.[139] McDougall's brigade would have caught up with them, and more of the militia from politically sound parts of the state would have reached the scene of action.

In the event, whatever their dissatisfactions, the British had succeeded in Danbury at least to the extent of increasing the difficulties encountered by recruiters for the continent. People had thought their state not important enough to attract a major attack; now they knew better. When Governor Trumbull wrote to Washington on May 4, his words reflected the change in public thinking. He complained that "This State is . . . more in consideration of the enemy, as it is the great source, among the New England states, of provisions both for the army and the country; and by their frequent attacks on the different parts, they know they keep us in alarm, and so much divert us from our husbandry as will soon reduce us to that want which both the army and country must sensibly feel."[140] The same changed view echoed in the requests for special reinforcements that poured in from towns all over the state, both coastal and inland, each one sure it would be next. Even Salisbury in the remote northwest trembled for itself. The iron foundry, with its proximity to the Hudson River and to a clutch of active Tories in the Rhinebeck region, made the town an irresistible target, or so its nervous residents thought.[141] Governor Trumbull himself panicked to the extent of believing rumors that the British would execute the plan of Creon Bush, which was to march through the country and rendezvous with Carleton on the Connecticut River.[142]

With every corner of Connecticut appealing for protection, the government decided that the shoreline had first call. On the twenty-ninth, the Council of Safety alerted the four regiments nearest New London and Groton. On May 4 orders went out to draft one-quarter of the Second and Fourth brigades for service along the coast west of New Haven and one-quarter of six northeastern regiments, together with Stonington's regiment, to defend the eastern coast.[143] Still insecure, Trumbull then sent Washington an additional request for two Continental regiments to cover the shore. Pending a reply, he ordered Parsons to use his continentals for that purpose.[144]

Washington could not accede, given his chronic shortage of men. On May 11 he replied that though "the Enemy will harass our Coasts and injure the maritime Towns, with their shipping and by sudden debarkations of small parties of Men . . . whilst they have the entire command of the Water," a rendezvous on the Sound between the British and Carleton was unlikely. He pointed out that he could not station guards everywhere the enemy might land without hopelessly dividing the revolutionary army and losing the war.

> The Enemy have certainly some Capital Object in view [he wrote], either Philadelphia or Hudson's River. Till their designs are unfolded, all the Troops from this and the more Southern States must Assemble in this Quarter, to prevent their possessing the Former. Those raised in the Eastern States, except such as were ordered immediately to Ticonderoga, must march to Peekskill, to prevent them possessing the latter and the important passes thro' the Highlands. Should they be able to carry those and the Fortifications for the defence of the River, we all know the important and fatal consequences that would follow.

Washington concluded that, given the weakness of the army as it stood in May, "I cannot comply with your request for two regiments to remain in the State at this time."[145] He could promise only that, when all the eastern states had delivered their quotas to Peekskill, he would "post a respectable number about the white Plains, to act as an Army or detachment of Observation &c . . . from which your state, as far as I am able to judge, will be more likely to be protected, against any Capital attempts of the Enemy than any other."[146] As if this vague offer were not sufficiently disappointing, Washington had also to refuse Connecticut's request for some of the newly imported cannon, far superior to those cast at Salisbury.[147]

Neither Trumbull nor the General Assembly denied the logic of Washington's reasoning. But his answer did not make recruitment for the Continental army any easier, particularly as the British hovered about the coast throughout May.[148] Still, they had to try. The alternative was an indefinite continuance of the present discomforts and difficulties. A strong body of men around Peekskill would certainly help, and a concentration of Continental troops to the north of New York could put enough pressure on the garrison around Manhattan to discourage harassment of the coast. The new legislature that met in early May appeared eager to make a better showing than its predecessor. First, it passed a number of measures to provide incentives for influential men to help with recruitment. One of them stated that "any two men . . . who shall procure an able-bodied soldier or recruit to inlist into either of the continental battalions . . . shall be exempted from actual service and from all drafts during the term for which they shall so procure each soldier or recruit to enlist."[149] The effectiveness of this, of course, would depend upon convincing people that exemptions were worth the effort to gain them. Therefore, the legislature went on to modify the Council's plan for classing. If the Continental battalions were not complete by May 26, the commanding officers in every class that failed to produce a recruit would draft each member of that class in succession, to serve eight months, until someone enlisted. If and when someone did, he would receive the three-pound bounty along with Continental and state premiums of clothing, wages and allowances, and up to twenty pounds of the money paid in fines by draftees who declined to serve.[150]

The proclamations of the governor and Council of Safety in March and April, together with the act of the Assembly in May, do appear to have spurred recruitment forward. Of the men who joined the new Army in 1777, 48 percent did so between April 15 and June 30 (see Table 2). Yet the provisions for compulsion seem to have been used sparingly and reluctantly. The number of short-term recruits never rose above thirty percent, and what little evidence we have of classing in practice suggests that it aroused great indignation, particularly since the officers empowered to class the population usually exempted themselves.[151] Most local officials preferred to increase the incentives to enlist, even for short-term service, by raising the bounty to a point where someone must find the advantages greater than the disadvantages. The informal collection of bounty money from local residents, particularly the wealthier ones, occasionally practiced in 1776, received a new impetus in 1777 from the legislature's grant of exemption to those who hired replacements. The classes seem to have adopted the principle within themselves, as did whole towns.[152] As a result, though most men who joined up in 1777 enlisted under the threat of the draft and under considerable pressure from their community, they usually accepted the bounty and so qualified as volunteers.

Still it was not enough, and still the Continental ranks were undermanned. Washington, who had expected the Connecticut regiments to reach at least 85 percent strength, found that by mid-July all but one remained below 70 percent and recruitment had ground to a halt (see Table 2).[153] The civil and military authorities kept on prodding the towns, but few of them did their full share.

Competing Demands

Though the Danbury raid had thrown all Connecticut into panic, the government continued to honor Washington's demand that the Continental army come first.[154] The decision to detach militia for the defense of the coast, rather than to enlist for the two state regiments authorized the preceding December, did not compete with the main objective but complemented it. Most men accepting short-term service in the militia would in no circumstances have considered a longer period. Recruitment for state regiments that asked men to commit themselves for a year or the duration would have offered more serious competition. If a man could choose, he would almost certainly prefer a state regiment to the Continental army. A soldier in a state regiment had more hope of remaining within reach of help from friends or relatives should need arise, and a shorter term of service gave him better protection from galloping depreciation.

In May, however, the legislature abandoned restraint and ordered that recruitment begin for two regiments, commanded by Roger Enos and John Ely, their terms to run until January 1778. It also ordered a company of rangers to protect the southwestern frontier, where loyalist raiders made frequent inroads on livestock.[155] None of the men who enlisted in these units would act under pressure of classing or threat of a draft, nor would they receive the generous bounty offered to Continental recruits. Yet no one doubted that the ranks would fill.[156] Several factors had impelled the decision. Once the legislators had realized that Connecticut would get little protection from the Continental army during the coming campaign, they decided that they must find some means of defense less ruinous than the constant shuffling of men between farm and camp. Meanwhile, the success of a recent raid from Connecticut on the British magazines at Sag Harbor had increased their need for protection from reprisal.

Parsons had first conceived this raid as a way of both taking revenge for Danbury and boosting public morale. On May 21 Lieutenant Colonel Return Jonathan Meigs embarked at Guilford with 220 men in thirteen whaleboats, escorted by two armed sloops. An unarmed sloop followed to bring off prisoners. Meigs reached the northern peninsula that same evening. Dragging eleven boats across the narrow neck of land, he took 130 men and struck out in the dark for Sag Harbor on the southern peninsula. He reached it at midnight. At 2:00 A.M., he attacked the 60-man garrison. Without a single casualty, the expedition destroyed "Twelve brigs and sloops, one an armed vessel with twelve guns, about one hundred and twenty tons of pressed hay, oats, corn and other forage, ten hogsheads of rum and a large quantity of other merchandise." Meigs returned to Guilford on the following afternoon with all his men safe and "with ninety prisoners, having in twenty-five hours, by land and water, transported his men full ninety miles."[157]

Congress, elated by an exploit that made partial amends for the humiliations at Peekskill and Danbury, singled Meigs out for special commendation and "an elegant sword."[158] Connecticut responded ambivalently. Revenge was sweet, but what if the British revenged themselves in turn by a surprise attack on New Haven or New London? When recruitment for the state regiments began in June, therefore, the community pressure that had done much to enlist men for the Continental army would now, and particularly in the coastal towns, exert itself to fill the ranks of local defenders. This diversion of energy had perhaps no immediate effect on the Continental army. The communities concerned had enough manpower to satisfy both local and Continental demands, because the disruption of commerce and fishing had left so many men out of work. But the government had planted the seed of a tendency to put local needs before Continental needs.

That tendency appeared again during the summer of 1777. Nothing had prepared Americans for the threat that then materialized to the north. Convinced that Philadelphia remained the primary objective of the British, Washington had assumed that, unless Howe received reinforcements from Europe, he would have to fetch the Canadian army down by sea to make up his losses in the preceding campaign.[159] In late May, when intelligence suggested that a major offensive was building up around Lake Champlain, Washington interpreted the activity reported as a feint to distract his attention. If Burgoyne intended to come down the lakes toward Albany, surely Howe would meet him with an expedition up the North River. Instead, Howe seemed to be preparing to strike across New Jersey toward Philadelphia. Certain that Howe's objective had not changed, Washington continued to build up his army around Morristown with men detached from Putnam's command in the Highlands.[160]

Israel Putnam took the news from Canada more seriously. A major offensive in the north would mean that the British objective was no longer to take Philadelphia but to cut off New England from her southern allies. If so, the key to their success lay in the Highlands. In mid-June, Putnam appealed to Connecticut for militia to replace the men withdrawn by Washington.[161] Because a contingent of Connecticut's Continental recruits was even then on its way to Peekskill, and because enemy activity in the Sound was consuming everyone's attention,[162] Connecticut took no immediate steps. Reports that British troops were gathering about the lakes produced somewhat more response. The colonel of the Fourteenth Militia Regiment in northwest Connecticut received orders to draft half his men for the reinforcement of Ticonderoga, but learned that the post had been abandoned before they could march. When the news came that Howe's forces had suddenly withdrawn from New Jersey, the Council of Safety told the militia to stand by, the brigadiers to start making up cartridges, and four of the six brigades to draft a quarter of their men, "to be properly . . . equipped, with suitable officers thereto appointed, and to hold themselves in readiness to march on the shortest notice." In response to another request for reinforcements from Schuyler, one-half of Oliver Wolcott's Sixth Brigade received standby orders. All the regiments in Silliman's Fourth Brigade, the one closest to the Highlands, also stood ready to march. Lastly, Enos's and Ely's newly formed state regiments received orders to relieve the local militia then guarding the coast.[163]

Within a week of the alert, Wolcott heard that Ticonderoga had been abandoned and that half of two regiments in his brigade, Burrall's and Jonathan Humphrey's, should head north at once. On July 14 he replied that his requisition on Humphrey's regiment had produced no more than a company and that Burrall's was "considerably deficient." "The men attempt to justify themselves on acco. of the season's being busy," he wrote, "and say they will fight the enemy nearer home."[164] Some had already served six weeks at Peekskill during the planting season; others had had their farming interrupted by the Danbury alarm. And Governor Trumbull told Washington that "the distrust of being commanded by officers whose conduct in evacuating the posts at Ticonderoga was so much censured, inclined the men to incur the fine in the case, rather than turn out with the freedom and spirit they would otherwise have done." Certainly the militia officers in the Sixth Brigade, to judge from the complaints against them, inspired no confidence in the men. Trumbull felt sure, however, that "our militia . . . will turn out with much better spirit to defend the pass of the enemy through the Highlands, than to go northward in their present situation."[165]

This optimistic statement would meet no test for some weeks. Washington had decided that Howe meant to abandon Philadelphia for an attempt to seize control of the Hudson River. He reinforced Peekskill and positioned his army so that he could come to Putnam's aid. In early July, he advised Putnam to call for militia. Silliman may even have sent a small detachment,[166] though reinforcements from New Jersey, as well as the new Continental recruits, arrived in time to spare most of them for the moment. If the Highlands were attacked, they would have to go. But this time, instead of having the militia engage the enemy while the Continental army came up, the army would hold the line while the militia deployed. The plan was the more desirable as haying and harvest were about to begin, and the farmers wanted to make up for the previous year's neglect.

On July 24 Howe's fleet sailed, not up the Hudson but out to sea, destination unknown. The move did not take Washington wholly by surprise. Deserter reports had prepared the way enough to keep him from a total commitment to Peekskill. Still, by mid-July he had positioned most of the army within reach of that point, and now it seemed that Philadelphia was Howe's objective after all. Washington began to call the troops back. Only two thousand continentals remained with Putnam when Washington sent him the alarming intelligence that Howe's fleet, sighted off the Delaware on July 30, had stood eastward out to sea on the thirty-first.[167] This raised the question that its sailing in the first place had been an elaborate ruse to draw off the army before Howe's entire force descended on the Highlands. Washington advised Putnam to call for militia from Connecticut and New York at once.[168]

As it happened, Putnam had already issued a call for a modest reinforcement of five hundred Connecticut militia. He had seen an intercepted letter which suggested that Howe no longer had designs on Philadelphia.[169] Trumbull received the request at almost the same moment Schuyler called on him for a thousand men. He passed Schuyler's request to Washington, suggesting that he reinforce Schuyler from Peekskill while the Connecticut militia joined Putnam.[170] Another report, following hard on the heels of the first, asked for two thousand reinforcements to halt Burgoyne's advance.[171] The Council of Safety decided to consult the Convention of New England States, then meeting at Springfield, Massachusetts, which advised that Connecticut should reinforce only Peekskill. The

Council still felt uncomfortable about refusing, and discussions of the northern campaign formed the sole topic at its meetings of August 4 and 5. Yet the only result was a call for an emergency session of the legislature.[172]

The news that Howe's fleet had sailed eastward focused attention on the threat to the Highlands from the south. Putnam responded on August 3 with a frantic call for three thousand Connecticut militia.[173] The western brigadiers answered before the Council of Safety had time to act. Silliman ordered his two northern regiments to Peekskill, with a detachment from Enos's regiment and some light horse, and Oliver Wolcott ordered all those from the Fifteenth, Seventeenth, and Eighteenth regiments who had not served before to join them. The Council of Safety endorsed their actions and ordered four hundred men from Erastus Wolcott's First Brigade, with three hundred men from Andrew Ward's Second Brigade, to make for Peekskill on horseback.[174]

Trumbull now believed, and reported to Washington and Schuyler, that Connecticut had sent three thousand men to Peekskill.[175] Considerably fewer in fact appeared there. We know that only four hundred men from the three regiments of the Sixth Brigade answered the call and that at first Enos's battalion would not go beyond Bedford in New York because they refused to leave the southwestern frontier defenseless.[176] We know, too, that even those who reported to Putnam did not stay long. Worried about their crops, and seeing no fleet at that moment, they wanted to go home. Putnam told Washington that he could "as well reason with a strong Northwester as with these [men]."[177]

Washington's reply excoriated "the conduct of the Militia of Connecticut, who because they find no enemy at their doors, refuse to assist their Neighbors." Though he had no immediate fear for the Highlands once the British fleet had failed to appear at the Hook by August 7, he still thought that Howe would land somewhere in New England to coordinate operations with Burgoyne. To go further south than the Delaware in the full heat of the summer would risk his men's health. Washington considered the Highlands vital to preventing a juncture between Burgoyne and Howe, and he hesitated to reinforce the northern army unless he could count on the Connecticut militia to assist Putnam. He instructed Putnam to "inform Governor Trumbull of these circumstances, and to call upon him for a certain number of Militia to continue in the Service for Three months at least, that we may know what we have to depend upon."[178]

Several factors led Putnam to temporize in executing the order. Shortly after he received it, he learned that Howe had landed in the Chesapeake. He also knew that the Connecticut militia had honest cause for complaint. For two years in a row they had been under continuous requisition, and many had much to do on their farms if they were to recoup last year's losses. One could not expect them to relish hanging about at Peekskill on the off chance that Howe would return or that Clinton, with his token force of four thousand in New York, would launch an attack. If necessary, his two thousand continentals could have held out against Clinton until Connecticut reinforced them. Besides, more than any other state militia, Connecticut's western regiments were forever answering calls to serve outside their own state. The last time they had reinforced Peekskill, their reward had been the Danbury raid. Seeing their low spirits and afraid that they would demoralize his continentals, already fainthearted to judge from his general orders, he dismissed most of them within a week.[179] As a play for their future goodwill, he ordered Parsons to lead some four hundred men in an attack on the Tories on Long Island, the bane of the Connecticut coast. But the raid did not take place until late August and then failed.[180] Putnam also deployed some of the Connecticut troops along the southwestern frontier,[181] and in this he did confer a real benefit.

Even so, when he next needed reinforcements Putnam found that his gestures had counted for little. On September 8 Congress ordered him to detach fifteen hundred men to help Washington at Philadelphia. McDougall's brigade marched on the sixteenth,[182] leaving Putnam with only six to seven hundred men. He then learned that Howe had defeated Washington at Brandywine, while reinforcements from Europe, ru-

mored to number ten thousand men, had begun to arrive at
New York. The two developments together made it likely that
Clinton would act independently to support Burgoyne. Indeed,
Clinton seized the initiative before most of the reinforcements
had disembarked. On September 12 a large body of British and
Hessian troops invaded Bergen County, New Jersey, which
diverted McDougall's brigade from its march to join the main
army. Putnam at once called on Connecticut for three thousand
troops to serve until January 1, 1778. Two days later, he sent a
second call.[183] By September 25, Clinton's reinforcements had
all arrived, and though they numbered closer to two thousand
than the ten thousand feared, the chance that Clinton would attack the Highlands seemed more certain all the time.[184]

Connecticut did not answer Putnam until September 30.
Perhaps the continued presence of Parsons's brigade at White
Plains lulled her into a false sense of security. On September
27, however, Putnam told Trumbull that the detachments he
had sent Washington had left a gap that forced him to recall
Parsons to Peekskill.[185] The southwestern frontier and Westchester County now lay open to attack. On the same day, Parsons wrote to tell Silliman of his withdrawal and warned him
that Clinton planned a foraging excursion throughout the defenseless area.[186] On the thirtieth, the Council of Safety be-
latedly ordered Silliman to move one-quarter of the Fourth and
Ninth regiments to Horseneck to protect the southwestern
frontier. The Council also ordered that the First and Second
brigades draft three hundred men each for two month's service
at Peekskill, and Trumbull ordered Enos's battalion to join
them.[187] Not until two weeks after Putnam's first appeal had
the government bestirred itself to call for half the men he
requested, and at that with orders to serve only until the end of
November rather than the end of January.

The unfortunate impression of crying wolf that Putnam
had given in August may have contributed to the government's
lethargy in answering his call, but a plan for a glorious expedition against the British garrison at Newport had more to do
with it. Governor Trumbull apparently thought it up.[188] He
saw that the dispersal of the enemy's force presented an unpar-

alleled opportunity to pick off part of it by a "secret" attack. Howe and Burgoyne were occupied elsewhere, and a rising demand for British manpower southward might draw even more men away. Furthermore, after nine months of garrison duty, relieved by one foray on the mainland,[189] the troops that remained would not be in crack form. The raiders might confidently expect to face dispirited men out of training, and few of these at that. Massachusetts and Connecticut easily secured the consent of Rhode Island. Twice that summer, once before Howe's departure from New York and again in the three weeks between the sighting of him off the Delaware capes and his arrival in the Chesapeake, it had looked as if he might make Rhode Island the springboard for a grand attack on the New England states. But the success of Trumbull's plan would depend on how much Massachusetts ventured, and she took until late September to make her arrangements.

Meanwhile, Connecticut's Council of Safety used the power given it by the General Assembly to raise a battalion of 810 men under Samuel McClellan for thirty-one days of service in Rhode Island. To encourage enlistment, the Council appealed for volunteers and appointed John Douglas, brigadier of the Fifth Brigade, as its commander.[190] This left Connecticut still seven hundred men short of the number promised the enterprise, and the Council decided to meet the demand by reshuffling men deployed along the coastline. The Council relieved Ely from duty there, added a company of watermen and another of matrosses to his regiment, and ordered them to join the Rhode Island expedition. Next, the state would have to find provisions and baggage transportation.[191] No wonder that the governor and Council of Safety, engrossed with the exciting prospect before them, had little time for an appeal from a general who had shown himself prone to panic.[192]

Defeat out of Victory

Despite her distraction, Connecticut did play a part in the defeat of Burgoyne at Saratoga. In August, Congress had removed Schuyler from the northern command and replaced him

with Gates. The Connecticut leadership immediately responded by sending Gates more help than he requested.[193]
Gates's greater popularity partly accounted for the about-face,
but it had also become clear that the strained extension of
Burgoyne's supply lines left him open to attack as never before.[194] An emergency session of the legislature ordered two
battalions of 728 men each, for two months' service, together
with "one half of the troops of light horse within this State, not
now in actual service," to join the northern army at once. To
ensure that this force would form quickly, the Assembly
fixed the precise numbers of officers and men to come from
each of the six militia brigades. The western brigades, responsible for guarding the southwestern frontier against raids from
Long Island or Westchester and for reinforcing Peekskill, had a
token quota to meet. Quotas for other brigades ranged from 240
(the Second) to 331 (the Third and Fifth).[195] To show it meant
business, the legislature offered volunteers a ten-pound bounty
but also issued a blunt directive that the ranks be filled if necessary "by an indiscriminate peremptory draught from the able-
bodied effective men" and that if any drafted person "shall neglect to march . . . and shall not procure some able-bodied
man in his room within twenty-four hours . . . not making
reasonable excuse to the satisfaction of the officer who drafted
him, [he] shall be considered as a soldier in the army for the
time aforesaid and treated as such."[196] In this, the legislature
came the closest yet to outright compulsion.

Colonels Jonathan Latimer of New London and Thaddeus
Cook of Wallingford commanded the two regiments. A general
abstract of only one survives in its entirety. Though some of
the company rolls may not reflect casualties, the information
they do give suggests that many companies marched at close to
full strength and that the regiments formed within the last week
of August, apparently by drafting. In one week Latimer's regiment had achieved 80 percent of the strength established for
Continental regiments.[197] Both regiments won honor in the
field. Under the command of Benedict Arnold, they were heavily engaged in the crucial actions near Stillwater on September
19 and October 7.[198]

As the summer ended, more Connecticut militia joined the march north. Along with about one hundred and fifty others, between three and four hundred members of Burrall's Fourteenth Militia Regiment set out for Bennington in August, though they had gone no farther than Massachusetts when they learned that the New Hampshire militia under General Stark had defeated the British detachment there.[199] Again, in late September, an appeal for men to help cut off Burgoyne's retreat reached Oliver Wolcott as he was presiding over the Litchfield County Court. When he called for volunteers from his brigade, members of the court not only echoed him but, together with some gentlemen of the bar, declared that they would go themselves.[200] Such a display of personal commitment by civil authorities encouraged about three hundred men to volunteer and to serve at least long enough to swell the growing numbers of troops that convinced Burgoyne to surrender.[201] Though they had not earned the laurels that crowned the battalions of Latimer and Cook, these men too had done their bit.

If the achievement of Burgoyne's surrender had depended on keeping Clinton back below the Highlands, Connecticut would have emerged from the action covered with blame rather than trailing some of the glory. Up to October 3, when Clinton had begun moving up the river in order to relieve Burgoyne, Putnam had received no Connecticut militia. The Council of Safety then tried to make up for lost time by ordering that the four western brigades send detachments to Peekskill "with all possible dispatch without regard to fines."[202] The wording suggests that the Council left the respective commanders to decide how many men should go. In his order to Silliman, Trumbull spoke of "all Able Bodied Effective Men" and enclosed blank commissions for the organization of volunteer companies. Major General James Wadsworth, Wooster's successor, called for one-half of two regiments in the Second Brigade and a general turnout of the First Brigade. Putnam, bypassing the established chain of command, appealed directly to the colonels of regiments along the western boundary for as many men as they could muster.[203]

The cry for help was heard at last, but too late to save the forts on the west bank. The first division of Connecticut militia did not arrive at Peekskill until October 9, by which time the British had taken Forts Montgomery and Clinton, while Putnam's men had retreated to Fishkill.[204] The delay occurred largely because Silliman, crediting a rumor that three thousand enemy soldiers were advancing on the western frontier, had sent regiments to Ridgefield first instead of straight to Peekskill.[205] If the British had planted this rumor, it served them well. For a moment before the sidetracked regiments reached Putnam, no army stood between Clinton and a passage upriver to Albany, and the Americans faced the unpleasant prospect of racing him there on land in an effort to prevent his union with Burgoyne.[206] Fortunately, it took the British several days to maneuver their transports through the chevaux-de-frise obstructing the way, and Burgoyne surrendered before they could reach him.[207] By the time the two thousand or more additional militia had arrived, the British fleet had ranged along the river burning the stores at Poughkeepsie, Livingston Manor, Kingston (the seat of the new state government), and the Continental Village at Peekskill.[208]

As commanding officer at the Highlands, Putnam must have felt himself dishonored. Though a military court of inquiry subsequently blamed the loss of the forts on "the want of an adequate force" rather than on any negligence or misconduct by the commanding officers,[209] Putnam knew it would reflect on him. The moment he learned that Burgoyne was about to surrender, he halted the march north and began to consider a move downstream toward New York City in the hope of obliging Clinton to forfeit either his position in the Highlands or his base in Manhattan.[210] The plan received a tentative endorsement from Washington. Shortly afterward, when Howe ordered Clinton to evacuate the Highlands in order to reinforce the army near Philadelphia, Washington withdrew his approval of Putnam's plan and called instead for reinforcements to counterbalance those Clinton would send Howe.[211] Most of these men should have come from Gates. To make sure that they set out with all possible speed, Washington sent Alexander Hamilton, his trusted aide-de-camp, posthaste to New York. Gates put up the predictable resistance: Burgoyne's surrender had turned him into something of a prima donna, and he hated to see his command whittled down. Recognizing that Gates had acquired a degree of political influence he could not safely ignore, Hamilton avoided a direct confrontation by ordering Putnam to send most of his continentals to Washington.[212] But Putnam, desperate to redeem his reputation, had worked out a plan to attack New York City which depended on his keeping all his troops. It called for splitting the eight thousand men under Gates and Putnam into two divisions, one of which would move down the west bank of the river and stand ready to help Washington if necessary, while the other would advance on New York from the east. A remaining thousand men would stay at the Highlands.[213] The scheme struck Hamilton as quixotic and Washington as tangential to the necessity of stopping Howe before he controlled the Delaware.[214] Putnam, however, could not bring himself to give it up.

At the beginning of November, though Hamilton had made it clear that Washington would never agree to the proposed attack, Putnam sent his aide-de-camp Jesse Root into Connecticut to appeal for volunteers. He hoped at least to retrieve some of the militia he had hastily discharged in late October.[215] When Hamilton presented his demand, Putnam's bubble burst. Protesting that he would have only three hundred men left to him, he balked. The knowledge that compliance would make him look small in Connecticut when he failed to deliver on Root's extravagant promises of victory undoubtedly fed his intransigence. And a mutiny of one brigade that refused to cross the river until the soldiers received their back pay gave him an excuse for delay.[216] Not until it became unmistakable that Hamilton had Washington's authority did Putnam take any notice whatsoever, and at that he sent only a thousand men. He also retained the Connecticut continentals and sent Washington the New York units, in direct controversion of Washington's orders.[217] Then he wrote to tell Governor Trumbull that because his force had shrunk to two thousand, he needed a substantial reinforcement to secure the southwestern frontier and harass the enemy.[218] And for its own reasons, not unlike his, Connecticut's government agreed.

Connecticut's Council of Safety had lost considerable prestige when the secret expedition to Rhode Island ended in fiasco. The enterprise had rested on a block of misconceptions. The enemy stood two thousand men stronger than anyone had supposed.[219] As for the element of surprise expected to derive from close secrecy, that hope soon vanished. After the recall of Ely's battalion and Trumbull's appeal for volunteers, the most unobservant person would have seen something afoot.[220] Perhaps it was just as well that in the end the attack never took place, but the bad coordination that had combined with bad luck to cause its collapse brought contempt on those who had planned it.

Though the rendezvous had been set for the second week in October, Connecticut's full force was not ready in time.[221] On the sixteenth, when the men assembled at last, a shortage of boats became evident. A day's delay to adjust this oversight stretched into three because of bad weather. By the nineteenth, all was ready. Then, as a detachment of Massachusetts troops commanded by General Palmer and Colonel Lovell rowed to their rendezvous, the enemy saw them and fired. This brought final ruin on the hope of surprise, and the Americans abandoned their attempt for the night because of a southerly wind that would have put their boats at the mercy of the men-of-war anchored two or three miles to windward. Bad weather forced the postponement of another strike planned for a different point of the island on the twenty-third. Many of the Massachusetts and Rhode Island militia began to leave, "as twas said, thro fear they should be detained on the Island beyond their limited time." Yet another assault was planned for the twenty-sixth. By then, however, sickness and desertion had reduced the attack force below the numbers of the defenders. A council of officers met and concluded that disaffection of the troops compounded by unfavorable weather made it impossible to continue the enterprise.[222]

At the moment when Putnam's proposal arrived, the Council was ready to clutch at any straw to retrieve its prestige and gain something in exchange for the state's huge exertions, something closer to home than Saratoga. On November 18 it ordered 600 militia to join Putnam together with Ely's state regiment, which had just returned from the Rhode Island fiasco. Enos's regiment was already under Putnam's command.[223] But many of the men did not share the Council's feelings. The western militia, receiving its sixth (for some, seventh) call to arms within a year, dragged its feet.[224] Ely's battalion would barely reach Putnam before the terms of half his force had expired.[225] On November 27, with only 247 Connecticut militia to help, Putnam tried to lure the British garrison at Fort Independence into an ambush. Meigs's regiment paraded before the fort as a decoy. The British sallied forth but unfortunately not in such a way as to enter the trap that Putnam had set up. Eventually he had to withdraw his force from the environs of Kingsbridge without encountering the enemy. He had nothing to show for his efforts but Colonel James Delancey, commander of a loyalist corps, seized at the town of West Chester by a scouting party.[226]

On December 4, when Ely's regiment finally arrived, Putnam's strength had so dissipated that he had to settle for a minor attempt on Long Island. There, at least, the chances still looked good for a raid as effective as the one that Meigs had led in May. Report said that the island's regular troops had gone to New York, leaving only untried loyalist militia behind. The enemy had stockpiled wood at the eastern end of the island, some for building barracks in New York City, the remainder for winter fuel for the Newport garrison. Laborers were even now loading it on transports. A complicated plan evolved. Meigs would lead a detachment against the loyalist regiment at Jamaica; Parsons would make for the eastern end of the island to destroy the transports and wood stores, and Webb would land slightly to the east of Meigs, to support either him or Parsons as necessary.[227]

The plan failed. Bad weather kept Meigs on the mainland, and by the time Parsons arrived at the wood depot most of the ships had sailed. He took only one vessel carrying timber; the rest sought the protection of two armed sloops nearby. Worse still, the *Schuyler*, with Colonels Samuel B. Webb, John Ely, and sixty-three others on board, fell into the clutches of an enemy sloop, the *Falcon*, on her way from New York to Newport. As Webb told the story to General Heath:

> at the dawn of the day . . . we were off Satalkut [*sic*]—when we discovered a Ship crowding all Sail for us, being to Leeward we had only one chance to escape, which was by running the Vessel ashore, no time was lost, the Vessel grounded on a Beach about 200 Yards from shore, the boat was hove out, before we could get her from the Vessel the Surf ran so amazingly high that she fill'd and Sunk,—with much difficulty we regained the Vessel—by this time the Ship had come to within half a Mile of us and was pouring in her Broadside—in this cruel Situation we were obliged to Strike.

Though the rest of Webb's and Parsons's divisions returned safely to the mainland with twenty prisoners, having killed eight and wounded ten, the Americans had come off worst in the exchange.[228] After all the time and energy spent on marching Ely's men from the east to the west of Connecticut, not to mention the expense of calling out an extra battalion of militia, Putnam had succeeded only in destroying one timber vessel and taking a handful of prisoners, hardly compensation for the loss of sixty-five Americans, including two important colonels.

If anything could make the matter worse, it was that Putnam had neglected more important duties for these adventures. On December 2 Washington had written to him emphasizing the importance of the Highlands. "These facts are familiar to all, they are familiar to you," he wrote, ordering Putnam to "employ your whole force and all the means in your power for erecting and completing . . . such works and obstructions as may be necessary to defend and secure the River against any future attempts of the Enemy." The letter concluded with a specific injunction against the sort of action attempted on December 9. "The troops must not be kept out on command, and acting in detachment to cover the country below," he wrote, "which is a consideration infinitely less important and interesting."[229] Putnam must have received this letter before he launched the Long Island expedition, which made it all the more inexcusable. He did not reply to Washington until December 16. Even then, he would only promise that "The troops of this place shall be Removed to Fish Kill Agreeable to your Orders as Speedily as possible." Though he said that "Nothing in My power shall be wanting to secure the River against Any further attempts of the Enemy," he did not wish to strip Connecticut's western frontier of all covering forces, particularly as the terms of Ely's and Enos's battalions were almost up. Thus he authorized Samuel Parsons to retain 150 continentals in the area.[230]

As it turned out, Washington did not mind leaving a small covering force in Westchester provided the reconstruction of fortifications in the Highlands went forward.[231] But the charges of New York and New Jersey officials that Putnam had mismanaged his troops in the Highlands, coupled with his own apparent willingness to sacrifice the strategic interests of the continent for the peripheral interests of Connecticut, shook Washington's faith in him. Despite his exoneration by a court of inquiry, Washington removed him from command there on March 16, 1778.[232] Spencer too resigned his commission, though a special board appointed by Connecticut, Massachusetts, and Rhode Island had cleared him of responsibility for the Rhode Island fiasco.[233] The campaign of 1777 had ruined the careers of two of Connecticut's three major generals in the Continental army.

PART THREE

Attrition

SARATOGA MARKED a turning point. The battle set in motion a series of events that drew all three of the major European powers into the conflict. Great Britain had hitherto concentrated all her might upon America itself, but the entry of France and later of Spain forced her to spread her resources thinner.

Even before the Franco-American treaties became general knowledge in America, Connecticut newspapers predicted that the victory at Saratoga would encourage France and Spain to lend help more directly than before.[1] And as soon as Congress ratified the alliance, it broadcast its own belief that French recognition of American independence virtually guaranteed success for the Revolution: "At length that God of battles, in whom was our trust, hath conducted us through the paths of danger and distress to the threshold of security. It hath now become morally certain, that, if we have the courage to persevere, we shall establish our liberties and independence."[2] At the same time, Congress did not want people to rely on France for their victory. That might result in their winning freedom from one power only to fall captive to another. The address therefore exhorted Americans to renew their exertions: "Your foreign alliances, though they secure your independence, cannot secure your country from desolation, your habitations from plunder, your wives from insult or violation, nor your children from butchery. . . . Arise then! to your tents! and gird you for battle!"[3] Nevertheless, in the eyes of Congress the alliance had brought the end of the war into view. After "one severe conflict" which they expected to end in the expulsion of all British troops, America would pursue her splendid destiny in peace and freedom.[4]

Though Americans were right to think that the support of France would cause profound changes in the nature of the war, they were disappointed in the hope of a sudden conclusion. Once the British recovered from the initial shock, far from finding the Franco-American Alliance a deterrent, they found that it made their persistence in waging war against the colonies easier to justify. The ministry could argue that Britain must either withstand her old enemy's bid for influence in North America or forfeit her status as a great power. Everyone could see, furthermore, that the war might at last begin to pay. The inroads that the cost of it made on Britain's productive system had for a time raised doubts that she could continue the fight much longer.[5] There seemed little hope of return from the huge outlays she had made, beyond the seizure of a few colonial ships. There were no places in the North worth pillaging, and, if there had been, the desire to win back American hearts would have inhibited the act.[6] But French involvement, and Spanish if that should occur, opened the prospect of many rich prizes to be taken, both from the ships that carried their commerce and from their thriving, far-flung empires.[7] Not for another four years, when the British at Yorktown met another defeat as crushing as Saratoga, would they give up the war at last.

In the meantime, they changed their strategy completely. They abandoned the attempt to control any territory in the North except for the islands scattered between New York and Rhode Island and an outpost in northern Maine. The military potential of the region was such that any conquest would cost more than it would repay. With the exception of New Hampshire and Maine, the northern colonies would yield the conqueror little that differed from her own native produce. On the other hand, Britain still coveted the West Indies and the southern states for the staples grown there that would not grow at home. The wider diffusion of the population in the South, the presence of slaves there who might turn on their masters if Britain gave them the chance, and its proximity to the Caribbean also made that area appear worth conquering. With these considerations in mind, the British shifted the focus of their operations from the northern to the southern theater.[8] Though Clinton continued to dream of recapturing the Highlands and of forcing Washington to fight on terrain unfavorable to his forces, he lacked the means to do it.[9] Washington took no chances, and the ministry, preoccupied with the defense of islands already under Britain's control as well as with the acquisition of others, kept ordering detachments for campaigns in the West Indies and the South. In the North, Clinton could embark on nothing more ambitious than an attempt to divide Washington's force at the Highlands by harassing Connecticut and New Jersey.[10] In these peripheral areas, the war settled into a war of attrition that proved particularly wearying to the people of Connecticut.

CHAPTER FOUR

Signs of Strain

ON APRIL 17, 1778, Governor William Tryon of New York sent Governor Trumbull a draft of several bills before Parliament in which Britain resigned the power to tax the colonies and created a commission, subsequently led by the earl of Carlisle, to restore the ties between herself and America.[1] For Connecticut, this was the first sure sign that the nature of the struggle would change.[2] On April 23 Trumbull sent a blistering rejection. Noting that "a vague, half blank, and very indefinite draft of a bill *once . . .* read before *one* of *three bodies* of the legislature" hardly constituted grounds to infer any serious intention to conciliate, he went on:

> There was a day when even this step from our acknowledged parent state might have been accepted with joy and gratitude. But that day, Sir, is passed irrevocably. The repeated insolent rejection of our sincere and sufficiently humble petitions, the unprovoked commencement of hostilities, the barbarous inhumanity which has marked the prosecution of the war on your part in its several stages, the insolence which displays itself on every petty advantage, the cruelty which has been exhausted on those unhappy men whom the fortune of war has thrown into your hands,—all these are insuperable and eternal bars to the very idea of concluding a peace with Great Britain on any other conditions than the most absolute and perfect independency.[3]

On the surface, the vigor of this statement suggests that, since the victory of Saratoga, Americans interpreted all pacific gestures from Britain as confessions of a weakness which allowed them to take a hard line. But Trumbull's bravado had another dimension. He went on to charge that Parliament's real object in debating these bills was "to disunite the people, and lull us into a state of quietude and negligence of the necessary preparation for the approaching campaign."[4] Fear had nourished the suspicion. In common with most of the American leadership, Trumbull feared that if Great Britain did reestablish political ties with America the foremost patriots would swing for it. And he feared that any offer of reconciliation, even one that required some yielding of points in dispute, would prove irresistible to a people that had borne the burden of war for three full years. They might refuse the lure at first, but if the enemy could drag out the war for long enough they would take it in the end. In spite of Saratoga and the prospect of a Franco-American alliance, it seemed to Trumbull that the British had time on their side.

Economic Difficulties

Early in 1778 an economic crisis erupted that endangered the whole patriot enterprise. The first warning signs had appeared months before, in the form of increasing complaints about the shortages of money and provisions. At the time, however, it seemed possible to trace both problems to political rather than economic roots.

In the spring of 1777, Congress had yielded to the general complaint about Joseph Trumbull's administration of the commissariat and had promised to reorganize it. Within his home state, Trumbull could control the political antagonism he had aroused in holding down prices and keeping supplies moving. Elsewhere, the special advantage conferred on Connecticut as principal supplier to the army had stirred a jealousy he found harder to combat.[5] By 1777, those who wanted to exclude both Trumbull and Connecticut from the commissariat could cite the sharp rise in the costs of procurement as proof of his inefficiency. The real cause, of course, was the depreciation. Continental money had dropped to half its original value during the first few months of the year, which doubled the price of all goods and services.[6] Yet a congressional committee reporting in April 1777 tried to blame this on Trumbull's agents, whom they charged with "a want of ability or integrity" in "raising the prices of the articles they purchase by bidding upon each other, under the idea of receiving commissions or compensation proportioned to the sums they expend."[7] The report did not specify Trumbull as the target of its criticism but implied so strong a disapproval of his administration as to leave no doubt that the committee thought him culpable.

There were grounds for some of the charges. One of Trumbull's New Jersey agents, Carpenter Wharton, unquestionably mismanaged public supplies and paid exorbitant prices.[8] Congress had asked Trumbull in January to investigate Wharton, but Trumbull, pressed with business, did not suspend him until May, and it was June before Congress at last removed him from office.[9] This affair led the Committee on the Conduct of the Commissaries to recommend the department's reorganization into districts governed by new regulations and directly responsible to Congress.[10] The "new arrangement," submitted to Congress in June, separated the work of purchase and issue so that those charged with purchasing could give all their attention to that task. Thus the commissary general of purchasers would sink to the level of an administrative bureaucrat. Though he would continue to supervise the system, he could no longer appoint his deputies, save temporarily should he remove one for misconduct.[11] Congress also imposed many new restrictions on the purchasing agents, restrictions designed to enforce a rigorous accountancy, and answered Trumbull's request that his entire department receive liberal commissions with an order that put it on salary instead. With depreciation rampant, and his agents already threatening to resign on the grounds of poor pay, Trumbull felt as if Congress had slapped his face. After several vain attempts to negotiate modifications, he resigned in anger from his post as commissary general of purchases.[12]

William Buchanan of Baltimore replaced him. Buchanan

had attracted the attention of Congress with a proposal to supply the army "by Contract at a certain price per ration." His further proposal for district control over purchasing had inspired the new appointment of three distinct deputy commissaries for the northern, middle, and southern districts.[13] During the critical campaign of 1777, it seemed that no one could fill Trumbull's shoes better than Buchanan, particularly as the scene of action moved south toward his home ground. But it soon emerged that he depended largely upon New England for such vital supplies as salt and meat; and for flour, the staple commodity of Pennsylvania and Maryland, he turned as much to New York, Virginia, and Connecticut as to the territory where he wielded most influence.[14] Meanwhile, Congress found that Trumbull's agents would not adapt to the new dispensation. Jeremiah Wadsworth refused to assume the position of deputy commissary general, and Peter Colt would agree to act only if Congress modified some of its regulations.[15]

Colt's demand reached Congress in the middle of the rush to evacuate Philadelphia. Not until October 4 did the delegates find time to consider it. When at last it dawned on Congress that, among other things, Colt was telling them either to do as he asked or find themselves without meat for the army that winter, a panic set in. Congress gave way to almost all Colt's requests at the same time as it empowered Putnam to appoint a replacement should he refuse to serve.[16] Putnam apparently construed this as an authorization to approach Wadsworth again.[17] Wadsworth, however, was not tempted, not even by the modified regulations. He had already decided that the task of laying in supplies for the coming campaign would far exceed the ability of the newly arranged commissariat, and he left Colt to carry on as best he could.[18]

A further complication arose when Connecticut's governor and Council of Safety appointed, first, Joseph Trumbull, then, when he refused, Henry Champion, as state commissary general "to purchase beef and pork."[19] By putting former commissaries in the position of competing with Colt for limited supplies, Connecticut had impeded procurement for the continent.[20] The action reflected the deep offense taken by the inner circle of the state's leadership at the maneuvers of a congressional clique apparently bent on clipping the wings of the Trumbull family. Previously responsible for denying John Trumbull a proper date on his commission as deputy adjutant to Gates, this coterie had shaken up the commissary system with little aim save the displacement of Joseph from office. At least, to judge from the speed and ease with which Congress subsequently abandoned the new arrangement, it served no other vital purpose.[21]

Such factional jealousy and connivance might easily have ruined the patriot cause. All that saved the day was a belated recognition by Congress that the continent needed Connecticut's help. Under Buchanan's administration, Washington's army never held more than two days' worth of food at a time, which severely restricted his options in dealing with Howe that autumn and brought his men to the verge of starvation at Valley Forge.[22] Even before the winter began, Congress knew it must placate the Trumbulls. On November 4, apparently unaware that Colt was acting as deputy commissary for the eastern department, Congress granted Connecticut's governor and Council of Safety not only the right to appoint a deputy commissary but also the right to "direct" him. The word "direct" implied a discretionary power to modify the new arrangement.[23] In January the governor and Council used this generous concession to effect a unilateral modification. They claimed a strict necessity in the matter which implied that Congress had made complete hash of the commissary,[24] but Congress dared not show pique. While some members worked privately to pacify the governor and his son,[25] President Laurens tendered Governor Trumbull a formal apology for a congressional circular that had failed to observe protocol in addressing him.[26] And at the end of January, Congress resolved to approve "the conduct of the governor and council of safety of Connecticut, in the appointment of Mr. Champion, and their other measures for providing public stores and provisions."[27] By the middle of February, when Congress asked Jeremiah Wadsworth to replace Buchanan, that chastened body virtually allowed him to dictate his terms.[28]

Wadsworth's appointment as commissary general smoothed over the factional squabbling that had aggravated the problems of procurement. Still more important, it helped to resolve a profound disagreement that had appeared within the ranks of the revolutionary leadership over the question of how to arrest the depreciation.

In spite of all attempts to control depreciation, by July 1777 the Continental dollar had lost two-thirds of its nominal value as a result of the declining demand for it.[29] Purely economic factors now began to play a larger part in depreciation than the fear that the Revolution would fail, which is why the victory at Saratoga would not help as much as some hoped.[30] The disruption of normal patterns of exchange, either through the closing of courts to creditors who sought to collect their debts or through the cessation of most overseas commerce, depreciated currency simply by slowing down economic activity to a point that diminished the need for money.[31] So did the government's efforts to boost the procurement of scarce goods through embargo and impress laws. But all these developments hit with greater force because of the surplus money in circulation.

Surplus money, though only one of several reasons for depreciation, received the most attention from the leadership. They did not want to admit in public that depreciation implied any doubt of the Revolution's ultimate success. The excess paper money offered a less embarrassing explanation. By the end of 1777, the states and Congress together had issued an unprecedented $72 million. The consequent glut of depreciating money stimulated economic activity where it was least wanted, since those who held currency could protect their holdings only by using it to engross the goods most needed by the army. A vicious circle formed: too much paper money caused depreciation, depreciation exacerbated shortages, and shortages compelled still greater emissions of paper money (at least, if the government were to continue procuring with the people's con-

sent). To blame depreciation on surplus money not only accounted for the problem acceptably, it also suggested a remedy.
Americans could not hope for normal commercial relations with
Europe while the British blockaded their coast, but they could
try to reduce the surplus of money.

The undertaking proved more complex than it sounded.
The superabundance of paper had three separate causes. First,
in addition to a congressional emission of $38 million by the
end of 1777, the state governments had emitted approximately
$34 million.[32] Besides this, every colony still circulated money
from the late colonial period. It is true that the quantum of colonial paper shrank rapidly in relation to the newer emissions
and that in Connecticut, by 1778, it made up only 15 percent of
the total.[33] Nevertheless, it often passed at a premium among
the disaffected or the doubtful, who hoped that currency sanctioned by the Crown would not be repudiated if Britain won.[34]
Finally, the surplus currency was not evenly distributed but
concentrated in certain areas. Joseph Trumbull's reliance on his
home state for army provisions during 1775–76 had caused
larger disbursements there than elsewhere. In addition, eastern
New England now had to buy cereals from Connecticut, while
New York looked to her for whatever supplies of salt, clothing,
and West Indian produce continued to trickle in.[35] Money from
these states augmented the stream of currency flowing into
Connecticut for Continental purposes.

Congress tried to develop national policies to increase the
demand for paper. Hitherto reluctant to open the courts to
creditors for fear of alienating debtors, it advised the step in
November 1777.[36] Because the Continental money had already
lost much of its nominal value, debtors were delighted to retire
their obligations with it, but their doing so neither increased
the demand for paper nor placated their creditors. The only
way left to keep supply down and demand up seemed to lie
through taxation and borrowing, which presented other problems. Who would invest at fixed interest when depreciation
would more than likely exceed any earnings accrued? In any
case, it made no sense for one or a few states to retire their
Continental money while the rest sat back and watched. The

sums would be too large and the burdens assumed too uneven. Recalling the state emissions would also make difficulties. State paper usually passed at a higher rate than Continental paper. State issues had both due dates and taxes established to fund them; Continental issues, all except the first few, had neither.[37] And the disparity in value of state and Continental bills tended to increase whenever a state attempted to retire her own emissions by taxation. Raising the demand for one currency depressed the demand for the other and accelerated its depreciation.

Lacking a national government with power to tax, what the country needed was a coordination of policy between the state governments. When the New England states and New York met in convention at Springfield in August 1777, they recommended that all participants agree to retire their own currencies by funding them as loans, while pledging to support the future war effort out of current taxes.[38] But the scheme could not work unless "similar measures . . . be adopted by the other United States."[39] Congress, fully aware of the importance of public credit to the war effort, proceeded to devise a policy which in many ways followed the recommendations of the Springfield convention. Congress urged the states to issue no more paper money, to call in their previous emissions "where there is sufficient quantity of continental bills of credit for the purpose of a circulating medium", and to raise $5 million through taxation in 1778, the burden to be apportioned among them "having regard to their present circumstances and abilities."[40] Evidently Congress had a high opinion of Connecticut's circumstances and abilities, for 12 percent of the total burden fell on that state, more than a fair share in the opinion of her leaders.

Since the projected $5 million still fell short of the expected costs for 1778, Congress proposed two further measures. One provided for confiscation of loyalist estates, which would achieve two desirable ends: the amassment of a considerable resource and an accelerated demand for currency.[41] The other authorised a loan. For several reasons, borrowing became the cornerstone of the financial policy adopted by Congress in the autumn of 1777. Neither taxes nor confiscation could raise the money that Congress needed in time. Loyalist property could not be sold until all creditors had received their due. The legislature dealt with this problem by declaring the owners legally dead and by putting their estates into probate, but probate took time.[42] As for taxes, the Connecticut legislature could not act on the recommendations of Congress until the following February and then would not set the first due date earlier than June 1.[43] Borrowing also seemed a politically shrewder expedient than taxation. In funding their paper money, the states would presumably have to pay interest on the capital sum besides meeting the requisition of Congress. Connecticut's share of $5 million would require an unprecedented tax of two shillings on the pound, while funding her outstanding state currency would require paying interest on approximately $1.4 million.[44]

Given the depreciation, it might seem unrealistic to aim at borrowing $20 million. In February 1777, Congress had raised the interest on continental loans to 6 percent; yet by September no more than $4,011,544 had been subscribed.[45] In the meantime, however, a more promising scheme took shape. When word arrived from Paris that France would renew her 2 million livre subsidy, Congress offered to pay interest on all loan office bills subscribed up to March 1, 1778, in bills of exchange on France at 6 percent of the nominal amount.[46] Taking depreciation into account, this meant a return of up to 30 percent in cash.[47] Congress had reason to expect that investors would inundate the loan offices with money during the time specified and that the amount in circulation would correspondingly shrink. The shrinkage, together with the retirement of state paper, would arrest depreciation and even cause a modest appreciation that might make investment at the loan office attractive without extraordinary incentives.[48]

Once more, circumstances defeated expectation. For one thing, the moneyed interests for whom these policies angled had learned from the depreciation to hold as little cash as possible. Concentrations of capital in the hands of a few great merchants no longer existed, and those who did hold cash were not so ready as they might once have been to buy bills of exchange on France.[49] They had little use for them as long as the British navy obstructed commerce with Europe. Besides, they may have heard that Congress only had sufficient foreign funds to pay interest on approximately $5 million nominal dollars and only gambled on being able to procure further subsidies.[50] Of course, there were those who subscribed with other ends in view than the bills of exchange. Some acted solely out of patriotism. Others banked on the success of the Revolution and the consequent appreciation of paper money. Even so, the loan scheme failed, and its failure sabotaged the rest of Congress's financial policy by forcing a choice between the issuance of yet more currency and the abandonment of the cause.

Equally disastrous, though less far-reaching, was the recommendation of Congress that the states draft regional price regulations on lines laid down by the Providence convention.[51] Though the Springfield convention of 1777 had advised the repeal of laws against monopoly or oppression and laws enforcing price regulation agreed to by the Providence convention, Congress knew that whenever the northern states had complied, prices had risen out of sight.[52] For this to happen again would endanger the financial policy adopted for 1778, a policy based on the assumption that expenses could be held down at least to their 1777 level.[53] Public opinion also appeared to favor price regulation. Assuming that a debt contracted with depreciating currency would be paid at par, it behooved the people to cooperate in holding prices firm. Otherwise the many who had to pay the public debt would have to bear an additional burden for the benefit of a few.[54]

When the representatives of the states from New Hampshire to Pennsylvania met at New Haven in January 1778, they took only a week to agree on a comprehensive scheme of prices. The scheme allowed for intraregional variation and sanctioned a general increase of anywhere from 75 percent to 400 percent on 1775 prices, depending on the article. In an address to the states, the participants explained that they had "endeavoured to avoid too great a revulsion" by "accommodating this regulation as much as may be to the conveniences of immediate practice." They saw the proposal as a holding action based on the expectation that "when the juditious and spirited exertions of the several legislatures shall have reduced the quantity of the circulating medium" through loans, taxation, and the retirement of the state emissions, "the prices will naturally fall from the high rates at which we have stated them, to their original standard."[55]

Connecticut legislators embraced the new recommendations gladly. Since the autumn of 1777, they had wrestled with runaway prices while trying to abide by the rules of the Springfield convention. They had tried to limit demand by requiring licenses for the purchase of any commodities "except in small quantities for [one's] own use and consumption." They had ordered the governor to draft a proclamation against oppression in the marketplace, to be read by all ministers to their congregations.[56] But neither these nor other measures of the kind had the slightest effect. When the legislature met in special session during February, the delegates were ready to change their tack. They adopted the recommendations of the New Haven convention and promised to enforce them, not only by imposing fines or forfeitures but by disqualifying violators from holding office or maintaining suits at law. After March 20, no one could commence or maintain a legal action who did not first swear he had obeyed the Regulation Act. Proven violators who could not pay fines would have to serve in the army or navy.[57]

This was price regulation with a vengeance, and it came at a bad moment. Even if the plan to reduce the amount of currency had succeeded by early 1778, real price rises must have occurred, given certain factors that the New Haven convention seemed not to recognize. For instance, the price of almost all agricultural produce rose every spring as the stores laid in since the preceding harvest were used up. The Connecticut legislature could not have chosen a worse time for a price freeze than March 20. The legislators must have assumed that any seasonal price rise would be more than offset by the declining volume of the currency. But in this they failed to allow for other anomalies of the regional economy. The disruption of the New England commissariat had seriously diminished supplies of salted meat in public magazines, creating an extraordinary demand for alternative stocks of live cattle and feed to fatten them. The military exertions of states like Connecticut and Massachusetts during that year made further inroads on the stores of food.[58] And after November 1777, the presence of Burgoyne's Convention army about Boston compounded the problem. The army itself numbered a mere five thousand, but Massachusetts had to raise fifteen hundred men to guard them, and the two forces together consumed eight thousand rations a day. Added to the other disruptions, this inevitably brought severe shortages and ever-higher prices.[59]

The legislature had also disregarded Governor Trumbull's warning that price regulation would discourage production. His prediction that "the farmer will cease to till the ground for more than is necessary for his own subsistence—and the merchant to risk his fortune on a small and precarious prospect of gain," seemed to come true when the Regulation Act took effect, and the farmers indeed withheld their produce.[60] The legislature, unconvinced, clung doggedly to the measure. The Council would not accept Trumbull's suggestion of an emergency session to repeal it. When the new legislature met in May, it sent representatives to Massachusetts to persuade that large and influential neighbor to adhere to price regulation.[61] The report of a Wadsworth agent that the Massachusetts lower house favored the measure more than the upper house suggests that there too it had popular support.[62] Only a resolve of Congress eventually brought Connecticut to the point of repeal.[63]

Congress too found the action hard. Over several months, Henry Champion had repeatedly asked Congress to advise suspension of price regulation and had warned that it would hamper the purchase of beef for Washington's army. No one listened.[64] Congress clung to the measure as an essential element of the policy it had gambled on. The inability of state loan offices to honor warrants from Congress should have showed that its hopes of borrowing were doomed;[65] yet the members still hunted about for some way to rescue their plan. They saw nowhere else to turn. On April 8, a congressional committee appointed to review the proceedings of the New

Haven convention recommended a forced loan to retire $20 million and an indefinite extension of the deadline for the loan offering interest in bills of exchange.[66] When Congress addressed the people in May, official policy still called for an appreciation of the currency and a reduction of costs through taxation and borrowing.[67] Not until June did Wadsworth's repeated representations of their disastrous results bring a grudging recommendation for the suspension of the Regulation Acts.

Congress might have ignored him even then but for certain other persuasions. When the merchants heard of the Franco-American Alliance they began to accumulate currency in anticipation of renewed transatlantic commerce. This had briefly stabilized prices in the principal ports, which made regulation seem less necessary.[68] And Wadsworth had already told Congress that he could not supply the army during the coming campaign if the law remained in force.[69] Given Burgoyne's surrender, Britain's inability to send enough reinforcements, and the alliance with France, the military picture looked so hopeful that Congress could not resist an attempt to end the war quickly.[70]

Congress never openly repudiated its original plan to save public credit through taxation and borrowing, but practical imperatives obliged more compromises than the suspension of price regulation. Between November 1777 and April 1778, Congress emitted $14 million in notes in order to make ends meet, another blow struck against its own efforts to limit the money supply.[71] Wadsworth hoped to cut costs by paying for contracts upon agreement rather than upon delivery, thus softening the effect of depreciation, and to beat inflation by assembling large stores so that the army's demand for supplies could taper off.[72] His hopes were defeated by the strain that French demands put on American resources, and at the end of the year new emissions totaled $50 million.[73]

Congress knew that it risked its solvency and played into the hands of British propagandists who taunted that "your money is of no value, and your debts so enormous they can never be paid." Congress continued to reply, however, that

America rested on more solid financial foundations than Britain. Besides, given Britain's clear intention to unload her debt on America if she won the war, whatever hardships Americans faced could only grow worse if they turned back.[74]

A Disappointing Alliance

The revolutionary leadership had to make some hard economic choices in the spring of 1778, which left them less optimistic than the people at large. They alone knew how vital it was to continue procuring with the producer's consent, and how likely that a long-drawn-out struggle would end in defeat. For most people, the victory at Saratoga had brought fresh hope. They did not see the more remote possibilities of Congress's economic policies but saw only such events as the appointment of the Carlisle Commission, which they took to mean that the Franco-American Alliance would force the British to relinquish the initiative for the first time since the evacuation of Boston. Though it was not yet clear how that would affect Connecticut, they did expect their fortunes to improve.

As early as April, rumors abounded that the British were contemplating withdrawal.[75] These rumors fed more on speculation than on inside information; nevertheless, the ministry had in fact told Henry Clinton that, after he sent detachments to the West Indies, he should concentrate the remainder of his force in Nova Scotia if he thought their security required it.[76] Though the people did not know the precise nature of these directives, events continued to keep their hopes up. In late May, it became clear that the British would soon evacuate Philadelphia. And though Clinton managed to march his army safely across New Jersey, where he more than held his own at Monmouth Courthouse, a French expeditionary force commanded by Count d'Estaing appeared off Sandy Hook immediately after his arrival in New York. The British had lost their supremacy in American waters and stood to lose their posts in New York and Newport. Clinton had no time now to concentrate his forces in Nova Scotia; he had to settle for reinforcing the Rhode Island garrison while he prepared to defend New York against imminent assault.[77]

As it happened, that assault never took place because of the difficulty of passing the Narrows. Instead, d'Estaing sailed eastward to join the force that John Sullivan was gathering in Narragansett Bay for an attack on Newport. At the time, however, circumstances looked auspicious for Connecticut. The British occupation of Rhode Island had hampered her commerce, Newport being the best vantage point for maintaining surveillance over the Race at the eastern end of Long Island Sound. The coming of the French removed this restriction for the moment and would keep the way permanently open if combined operations against the British force on Aquidneck Island turned out well. Besides, the mere presence of the French fleet off New York had helped relieve a chronic problem over prisoners of war.

Since the winter of 1776–77, reports of the treatment meted out to captive Americans had appalled Connecticut. The horrors described were confirmed by sick and dying prisoners that Howe returned at various times under an agreement which provided for an equal exchange of officers and men by rank. It also allowed each commander to decide which of his captured men should have precedence,[78] but in the winter of 1776–77 circumstances led Howe to take liberties with the established cartel. Knowing that the patriots were trying to raise a three-year army on which the success or failure of his mission might depend, he did not mean to help Washington by returning veterans around whom the new corps would form. Howe began to disregard Washington's stated priorities. He sent back sick men whom Washington could not use, while demanding healthy British prisoners in return.[79] Early in 1777, Washington, unwilling to accept such terms, halted the exchange,[80] while the American prisoners in New York continued to die like flies. A report that the British had offered to sell survivors to the East India Company intensified the anguish of their relatives,[81] who knew that forcible removal to an unhealthy climate would probably finish the deadly job begun by the pestilential conditions in New York.

The people's fury mounted with their grief, especially in Connecticut where proximity ensured continuous reports. In some ways, the government welcomed it. Fury could be used, harnessed to raise morale at a time when defeat and disappointment had brought it low. To this end, the legislature at one point ordered town officials to collect affidavits from returned prisoners describing their maltreatment.[82] They had to take care, though, not to incite more rage than they could handle. For a time, it became nearly impossible to find anyone who would consent to billet British prisoners,[83] and strong political pressure to continue the exchange no matter what the inequalities became a force to reckon with. In January 1777 the Council of Safety endorsed a letter from Governor Trumbull in which he urged Washington to hasten the release of the Connecticut prisoners "before they fall victims to the accursed policy of our inhuman enemies."[84]

When better weather diminished prisoner mortality, and when the suspension of the agreement between Washington and Howe curtailed reports about conditions in the prisons, some of this agitation began to subside. The capitulation at Saratoga, furthermore, meant that, for the first time since the summer of 1776, the balance of prisoners shifted in America's favor.[85] Howe immediately saw that prisoner exchanges might become an important means of replenishing his manpower and in February 1778, when he realized he would receive no reinforcements from Europe, he made overtures for the resumption of the former cartel "without regard to any controverted point."[86] His renewed interest in exchanging prisoners improved their condition. When they became assets to negotiation rather than drains on scarce resources, the British began to show more solicitude for their welfare.[87]

Connecticut welcomed Howe's overtures. As the winter of 1777–78 came on, and with the capture of two highly valued officers, Colonels Samuel B. Webb and John Ely, people renewed their agitation about the prisoners of war. Webb and Ely, in negotiating for their own exchange, provided fresh information about conditions in New York, which drove the Council of Safety to send a representation to Congress urging a general exchange.[88] Trumbull's letter reached Congress just after that body, realizing how much more the British would gain from an exchange than the Americans, had begun to erect obstacles to any resumption of it on the original terms.[89] But Washington wisely intervened. He cautioned Congress to remember that "the prevailing Current of Sentiment demands an Exchange" and that "Were an Opinion once established . . . that we designedly avoided an Exchange, it would be a Cause of Dissatisfaction and Disgust to the Country and to the Army," not to mention a cause "of Resentment and Desparation to our captive Officers and Soldiers." The British could foment this dissatisfaction, he felt, by publishing the correspondence on exchanges, since "in a Business, on the side of which the Passions are so much concerned as in the Present, Men would be readily disposed to believe the worst and cherish the most unfavorable Conclusions."[90]

Though Congress balked at Washington's advice, a substantial exchange did take place in the summer of 1778. Clinton's position in New York, with the French threatening to attack him at any moment and the garrison low on food, made him feel that the last thing he wanted was a sizable body of unexchanged prisoners on his hands. On July 17 all the private soldiers in British prisons, including militia, seamen, and continentals and excluding only those in hospital or "out at work," passed into the hands of the new commissary general of prisoners, John Beatty. They amounted to less than 400 continentals with 687 militia and seamen.[91] Officers were not included in the arrangement. Nevertheless, the principal obstacles to future exchanges seemed to have been overcome, and, thanks to the French, the problem presented by British ill treatment of prisoners appeared on the point of resolution at last.

After July, the yields from the Franco-American Alliance diminished, partly because the failure of combined operations against Rhode Island left the British in control of New York and Newport as winter approached. D'Estaing made the mistake of tarrying off Sandy Hook for eleven days. He would have done better to sail straight to Narragansett Bay where he could have kept Robert Pigot, the commander of the force at Aquidneck Island, from receiving reinforcements.[92] Yet even this error need not have stopped the allies. If they had immediately pressed an attack, they might still have taken the garrison. D'Estaing and Sullivan should have joined up by July 30,[93] but Sullivan kept d'Estaing waiting for a week while he struggled to assemble what he considered the necessary force. Connecticut was partly to blame for the delay. Governor Trumbull, shaken and depressed by the death of his son Joseph on July 23, had not properly responded to Sullivan's appeal for troops until July 28.[94]

When the allies did at last deploy for a landing on August 9, they were interrupted by the appearance off Newport of a British fleet under Lord Howe's command. Again, it is not clear that Howe's arrival need have made this difference. But d'Estaing, convinced that he could only maintain French naval supremacy by engaging Howe before he received reinforcements, decided to offer battle on the tenth. Both fleets maneuvered in the open sea for two days before a violent storm dispersed and damaged them just as they were coming to the point of a general action.[95]

Even so, the allied attack on Newport promised well. Between his arrival at Point Judith and the landing on the ninth, d'Estaing had either destroyed or forced the scuttling of the entire British naval force at Rhode Island, seven men-of-war and a galley.[96] This had allowed Sullivan to press an attack against Pigot. By the time d'Estaing's battered fleet reappeared off Rhode Island on the twentieth, the British forces had withdrawn to Newport and the American siege works were well under way. Just when it seemed that the revolutionaries needed only four thousand French troops and the French fleet to go in and win, d'Estaing would not commit his forces. Anticipating the imminent arrival of Byron's relief squadron from England, he retired to Boston on the twenty-first, thus putting Sullivan's force in jeopardy should Howe reappear with any naval power at all. Sullivan resolved to hold a position on the northern end of Aquidneck Island as long as possible while Lafayette made his way overland to Boston in the hope of persuading d'Estaing

to change his mind.[97] Only when he learned that British reinforcements were moving toward Newport did Sullivan retreat.
Despite a heavy engagement with the enemy on the twenty-
ninth, he removed his army to the mainland on the thirtieth,
reaching it just one day ahead of Clinton's appearance off Newport with a sizable force.[98]

Clinton had achieved superiority in Rhode Island, but he
could not find much to do with it. On September 1 he tried a
strike against New London but abandoned it when contrary
winds prevented him from sailing all his transports into the harbor. He did, however, send out a detachment under Major
General Grey which succeeded in firing New Bedford and
Fairhaven on September 6 and in carrying off stock from
Martha's Vineyard on September 8.[99] Though New London
might congratulate itself on having escaped their fate, Connecticut in general found little consolation in the failure of the
Rhode Island venture. As long as the enemy controlled New
York, Newport, and Long Island, the state faced a danger on
three of her four frontiers. If Newport had been wrested from
the British, Connecticut would have enjoyed at least a respite
from the harsh demands for recruitment and maintenance of a
force to defend the eastern flank. And if, as seemed likely, the
British had then found it harder to keep control of eastern Long
Island, they would have had less time to harass the Connecticut
coast. But the fresh naval reinforcements due to arrive from England at any moment would take away French naval supremacy
in the northwestern Atlantic for the rest of the campaign. With
these advantages, Clinton could maintain his position from
Newport to New York and still send south the large detachments ordered by the ministry.[100] The year 1778 ended with
Connecticut as unsafe as ever.

In one respect, the Franco-American Alliance seemed even
to increase her danger. It gave the British an excuse to embark
on a new strategy aimed at the state's peculiar vulnerability, her
extended coastline. On October 3 a final "Manifesto and Proclamation" of the Carlisle commissioners told the people of Connecticut what to expect in 1779. The manifesto purported to
offer the people themselves the same terms of reconciliation as

Congress had spurned. Much of it, however, consisted of threats. Describing France as "our late mutual and natural enemy," and observing that American Protestantism would find a better friend in Great Britain than in a Catholic power not known for tolerance, the manifesto went on to claim that Britain had fully redressed all legitimate colonial grievances. If the mother country's offer were still rejected, the colonists could expect the worst:

> The policy as well as the benevolence of Great Britain have thus far checked the extremes of war when they tended to distress a people still considered as our fellow-subjects, and to desolate a country shortly to become a source of mutual advantage; but when that country professes the unnatural design not only of estranging herself from us but of mortgaging herself and her resources to our enemies, the whole contest is changed; and the question is, How far Great-Britain may by every means in her power destroy or render useless a connexion contrived for her ruin and for the aggrandizement of France. Under such circumstances the laws of self-preservation must direct the conduct of Great-Britain, and if the British Colonies are to become an accession to France, will direct her to render that accession of as little avail as possible to her enemy.[101]

In case anyone should miss the point of this not cryptic language, a story was planted in the army at New York, a story made for export, that fifteen thousand men would march to reinforce Rhode Island by way of the coast, supported by the British navy and desolating every town they passed through.[102]

Hot on the heels of this rumor came a message from Governor Tryon to Governor Trumbull stating that the British sought to open a barter trade with Connecticut. They offered West Indian produce (rum, sugar, molasses) and tea in exchange for beef. Welcome as the offer might be to those who found their commerce once more impeded by British surveillance, there was no question of acceptance. Not only would the French take offense, but an arrangement whereby the British received necessities in exchange for conveniences (salt and military supplies being exempted from the offer) would have helped to keep the enemy in possession of the very posts that

threatened the state. Though the proposal, like the earlier manifesto, professed the design of reopening "friendly intercourse,"
it was obviously calculated to show up the leadership's vulnerability to economic and military pressure. Hence, it contained a
threat that if the offer were rejected, as Tryon knew it must be,
Connecticut would see her coast so devastated that the people
would fall to their knees and beg for British protection again.[103]
As winter came on, the darkening prospect before the state was
all the harder to bear for its bitter contrast with the high hopes
of the summer gone by.

The Grain Crisis

The French alliance helped to demoralize the people of Connecticut by failing to give them the victory they had thought
within their grasp. And it contributed to a sequence of events
that would create insoluble economic problems, not just for
Connecticut but for the whole nation, problems that would
eventually force the revolutionaries to abandon procurement
only with consent.

Clinton's withdrawal to New York in June 1778 forced the
allies to concentrate in the North in numbers that the region
could not possibly support. That July, Washington assembled
the Continental lines of every state from New Hampshire to
North Carolina about New York. In addition to these,
d'Estaing's expeditionary force consumed ten thousand rations
a day, Sullivan's small army strained the resources of Rhode
Island and its environs, and the Convention army at Boston,
together with its guards, had also to be fed. When the prospect
of combined operations led to a call for additional militia which
took more men away from farm work, the yield from the harvest declined in proportion to the increase in the demand for
it.[104] Nor did the subsequent abandonment of combined operations improve matters much since New England still had to
revictual the French fleet—to provide not only for its daily
needs but also for the time it would spend in the Caribbean.
Besides, the simultaneous presence of the French fleet and the

Convention army at Boston presented the British with so rich a temptation that Washington dared not risk dispersing his army west of the Hudson. On the contrary, as a precautionary measure he began to move some of his brigades east to Hartford.[105]

In the weeks that followed, the movements of the French and British concentrated men in precisely those areas that had the poorest indigenous capacity to supply provisions. With the fisheries disrupted and the normal peacetime patterns of commerce destroyed, the increase in demand caused severe shortages, particularly shortages of grain. Few parts of New England produced much surplus wheat, and the requirements of the horses alone obliged the quartermasters to compete with the commissaries for it.[106] The three brigades at Hartford could not ease the shortage by moving elsewhere: they had nowhere to go that would not be equally straitened. Certainly they could not go to Boston. Massachusetts had so little food to spare that even in September, when it looked as if the British might attack at any moment, the government would not call back the militia for fear of increasing the strain on resource to a breaking point.[107] Had Clinton indeed persuaded the navy to join him in an assault on Boston, it seems possible that the commissary could not have sustained the men through a prolonged defense.[108] The usual problems with carting—its cost, its slowness, its wastefulness—were compounded by the extremes of autumn weather and a shortage of forage.[109] New York, New Jersey, and Pennsylvania, the most feasible alternative sources, had also produced scant crops, partly because of natural causes and partly because of the ravages of war.[110]

One solution remained: an heroic effort to move grain from the South to the North. The disruption of the European tobacco market and the absence of the enemy for a full growing season led to a good 1777 wheat crop in the Chesapeake. The harvest of 1778 also proceeded without interruption. And similar factors produced a surplus of rice in South Carolina. If this flour and rice could be sent north, it would alleviate shortages there.[111] Transportation, however, presented a problem. Southern grain had to be sent by water or not at all. If the enemy should capture the cargo, it would then serve only to help their cause while leaving Americans hungrier than ever. Congress had authorized the movement of provisions once before, in late 1777, when it ordered Virginia to ship flour for the Convention army. But Congress had then acted to some extent out of a hope that the British *would* seize the ships and give the Americans a pretext for breaking the Convention.[112] In any case, on that occasion the supplies were never in fact shipped because of a factional squabble between Patrick Henry and Virginia's deputy commissary for continental purchases.[113]

By the summer of 1778, the complexities of transporting grain by water had increased. The British would certainly exert themselves to seize it; on the other hand, Congress did not want to disappoint an ally who not only subsidized the war effort but also paid for the privilege of fighting in some of the battles. To please France, Congress had to show both the determination to deny Britain any help and the ability to give the French all they needed. What they needed most, of course, was a base in the western Atlantic from which to revictual.[114] Without that assurance, France might lose interest in naval operations. And without naval support the revolutionaries had little hope for ending the war.

The commissariat in Rhode Island had succeeded in meeting the demands of the combined allied forces only by borrowing supplies from Massachusetts and Connecticut, but those states could not continue supplying d'Estaing's great fleet for long without stripping themselves of all resource and all capacity to defend their own coastlines.[115] When d'Estaing withdrew to Boston to revictual it became clear that the region's grain supplies could not keep up with French demand. As soon as Congress knew for sure that the French would tarry in New England and that Wadsworth could not provision both French and American troops without grain from the South, Congress authorized shipment by water.

The decision came at the very moment when France began to lose the naval superiority she had briefly attained. Perhaps it was this that prompted Congress to insist that the shipments travel in convoy,[116] a provision that would inevitably delay the arrival of relief. Vessels loaded and ready to go would have to wait for armed escorts, and a shortage of shipping in the South would make the wait a long one.[117] Meanwhile, the scourge of Hessian fly put the whole effort in question, though eventually the consequences of the pest proved less dire than feared.[118] In the long run, it diminished but did not eradicate the surplus. The inability of Wadsworth's agents to purchase in these states presented an infinitely greater problem. Private buyers set about outbidding Wadsworth's southern agents for every commodity they wanted, and the agents, already short of cash because of the rise in prices, could not fill the army's basic needs.[119] In October Congress went so far as to recommened that the southern states take legal action against the engrossers, but that course could have no immediate effect save as a threat.[120] The grain shipments that did trickle in during the winter came too little and too late to do any real good.[121]

Speculative buying went on in the North too. Even before the French arrived on the scene, the resources that Bostonians had amassed by successful privateering, by importation of West Indian goods, and by Burgoyne's disbursements on behalf of the Convention army encouraged a good deal of private purchasing in provisions as far west as New York.[122] It was hard to control such buying in Connecticut and Massachusetts. The prominent role that Wadsworth and his agents had played in the repeal of the Regulation Act, together with their perennial shortages of cash, had made them so unpopular that producers no longer felt obliged to honor agreements with the commissariat.[123] Wadsworth, who saw the crisis coming, advised a prompt resort to seizure.[124] Colt hesitated to listen. In September, however, desperation drove him to apply for permission to seize in New York, where the threat of a regulation act served to shake loose a few supplies.[125] Another month passed before he summoned the courage to apply to the Connecticut legislature.[126] Then, though the legislature did pass a law permitting seizure upon application to local authorities, the commissary would still have to pay "the market price" upon delivery. Should any argument arise about the price, the commissary would have to submit to an arbitration bound to go against it.[127] Colt had wanted a law enabling seizure at fixed prices, at least until the emergency had passed.[128]

By the autumn of 1778, the failure to draw sufficient relief from the South, coupled with the failure to stop engrossment in the North, had wreaked economic chaos. When interested individuals persuaded d'Estaing that the commissary was not the best agent to revictual his fleet, he commissioned his own agents to buy provisions, particularly flour, with hard cash. They did not scruple to meet the demands of engrossers, who used the money thus obtained to extend their operations into the hinterlands. There they bought up all the remaining supplies, to the total exclusion of the commissary.[129] By October Colt's agents reported that suppliers of flour would accept only specie, and for a while the paper currency stopped circulating altogether. Commissary agents were reduced either to bartering one kind of provision for another or to doing without.[130]

Their inability to provide for the troops provoked disastrous responses from area commanders. For instance, in order to feed Sullivan's force in Rhode Island, the commissary had to cart flour from a depot in western Connecticut which received its supplies from New York, New Jersey, and Pennsylvania. These shipments were being waylaid by the forces under Gates, stationed at Hartford since September.[131] Maddened by the sight of his wretched, starving troops, Sullivan set up his own system of procurement, a move which inevitably increased still more the difficulties faced by Wadsworth's agents.[132] The people had their needs, too, and on November 1 Colt reported that the Connecticut coastline seethed with vessels bartering for supplies to see them through the winter.[133] But relief was in sight. Though French competition had hampered the commissariat, d'Estaing's agents succeeded in supplying his fleet in time for it to sail for the West Indies. If d'Estaing had relied on Wadsworth's agents, he might have had to winter in Boston. That would have made the United States appear a dubious partner in France's pursuit of West Indian ambitions and would have prolonged the strain that French procurement put on American supplies.[134] As it was, the French withdrew, and shortly afterward the Convention army marched south to Virginia. At first, that march caused more trouble than ever since the provisions and wagons diverted by it were badly needed elsewhere.[135] The trouble proved transitory, however, and the benefits promised to be lasting. The prospect improved still more when the three brigades at Hartford received orders to march westward as a precaution against any attempt by Clinton to rescue Burgoyne's men.[136]

Still, in the end these shuffles did not help. Though the departure of the continentals eased the pressure on limited supplies in central Connecticut, their arrival on the Hudson exacerbated shortages there. The mutiny in the Connecticut line that took place shortly afterward had a good deal to do with the scarcity of flour, a scarcity which continued throughout the winter.[137] And when farmers were reduced to using what little grain they still had for human consumption rather than for fattening stock, the grain shortage threatened to lead on to a meat shortage.[138] Between November and January, New England received occasional relief in the shape of a few provision vessels from the Delaware and Chesapeake, but these had slipped through only because the British employed their naval force full-time in the shipping of large detachments from New York to Georgia and the West Indies. Shortly after the New Year, winter weather closed the Delaware and much of the Chesapeake to shipping. The British invasion of Georgia sent what shipping was left in the South scurrying for cover.[139] Fickle weather continued to hinder the overland shipment of the limited surpluses remaining.[140]

Though all New England suffered, the grain shortage hit hardest in the coastal communities of eastern Connecticut, southeastern Massachussets, and Rhode Island. Throughout the winter and spring, the government of Connecticut received an overwhelming number of petitions for grain from the fishing communities of Massachusetts and Rhode Island.[141] In areas like Providence, where troops were heavily concentrated, the soldiers made do with rye and corn. Civilians in urban areas often had to survive on less.[142] But Connecticut was no better off; she could not feed her own garrison in New London or victual the Continental frigate *Confederacy*.[143]

The shortages and disruptions of that winter and spring should have been temporary. Despite the intrinsic limitations of her agriculture, further losses to Hessian fly, and a steady draining off of limited resource to the French fleet,[144] the United States had the potential to supply both her own forces and those of her allies. In a healthy market economy, demand in excess of supply would undoubtedly have produced its own remedy through the incentives for expanded production that rising prices would have generated. When the focus of enemy action shifted to the South, New England and the middle states enjoyed a respite in which they might hope to recover economic equilibrium. What made the shortages of 1778 a lasting problem was the continued depreciation of the currency. Depreciation took away all incentive for producers to increase production until it kept pace with demand.

Insoluble Problems

The French had inadvertently contributed to the financial mess the nation confronted at the beginning of 1779. Though Congress had known for some time that the plan devised in 1777 to halt the depreciation would never succeed,[145] it could not take time to face the fact that its own emissions of currency, conceived as a temporary expedient, threatened to defeat its own purposes. The delegates thought only of the many urgent problems raised by the alliance and the conduct of combined operations,[146] a pardonable distraction since the hope of ending the war seemed real enough. There would be time to sort out the muddle, so they thought, when it was over and independence won. Not until late summer of 1778 did Congress begin to see that French intervention would provide no immediate cure-all,[147] by which time effective action had passed beyond reach.

During 1778, many experienced delegates to Congress had given place to new men unfamiliar with the details of past policies or with the dimensions of the currency problem,[148] which had grown worse than ever. In September 1777, the amount of Continental currency stood at $36 million and the loan office debt at $4 million. By October 1778, both figures had more than doubled.[149] If the state loans to retire state currency were added to the Continental loans, the total would have come to something like $130 million.[150] Now that a general European war loomed, Congress could no longer pin its hopes on a loan from France. Though a new policy was badly needed, the inexperience of the delegates, added to the distractions of the Lee-Deane controversy, kept them from formulating one until the beginning of 1779. Even then, only two features of the plan were new.[151] One was a proposal to withdraw the currency issued between May 20, 1777, and April 11, 1778, from circulation by declaring these notes void unless holders surrendered them to the loan office or exchanged them by a certain date.[152] The other was the establishment of a sinking fund.[153] In addition, Congress asked the states to raise $15 million by taxation. The members hoped that this money, added to the withdrawn issues which would presumably be subscribed to the loan office, would permit them to break the cycle of emission, shortage, and more emission.

In devising strategies to save the currency, Congress had to consider a new side to the problem. In 1777, when the currency had stood at an average value of 3:1, few people had objected to the idea of appreciation to par. Though some were disgruntled about paying at face value a debt for which the public had received considerably less, the feeling provoked nothing worse than demands for price regulation.[154] Expunging the debt did not make sense at the time, particularly since the state would lose much of the value of the extra currency that Trumbull's commissary had brought into Connecticut.[155] By January 1779, however, the picture had changed. The currency now fluctuated between 8:1 and 90:1, depending on where you were and what you wanted to buy.[156] According to a statement by James Watson at Hartford in January;

> the majority of the people of this state wish to see [the money] perish, and I imagine, from the best information I can get, that

throughout the whole New England state[s], there might be found two who would be glad to kill it, to one who would oppose it. What the event will be God knows but the prospect is certainly most gloomy, whether our currency lives, or dies, it has laid a deep foundation for the greatest injustice and consequent distress, & there is too much reason to fear, that it will prove the origin of a *Civil War*. [157]

An extreme view, perhaps, but a radical appreciation of the currency would certainly have alienated many. Though a majority in Congress continued to support appreciation, a growing minority began to speak out against it. They appear to have succeeded in persuading Congress not to aim too high, for its plan missed the mark altogether. [158] Instead of slowing down, the depreciation accelerated. And in February the inevitable happened: Congress issued another $10 million in paper money. [159]

As a consequence, a still graver symptom appeared. The currency ceased to behave as a medium of exchange. For instance, the commissariat found itself less and less able to use money for payment. In March 1779, Wadsworth complained that New England farmers would accept currency for livestock only because they wanted to reduce the consumption of grain by animals, and that commissary agents were frequently obliged to barter for other commodities. [160] Meanwhile, the cities of Boston and Philadelphia acquired a strange ability to pay exorbitant prices for provisions. A barrel of flour costing forty dollars at Sharon in western Connecticut and twenty dollars in more distant areas would cost eighty dollars at Boston. Similar discrepancies appeared in Pennsylvania. They came about because the cities had goods that the countryside wanted. Commissary agents in Connecticut had to pay in a depreciating currency, but agents of the Boston and Philadelphia merchants could offer foreign and West Indian goods that they had acquired through privateering, through what little transatlantic commerce existed, and through their possession of French and British specie. [161] Commodities, not money, became the medium of exchange. The reversion to commodity exchange did not eliminate buying and selling, of course, or the quotation of prices in currency. Money never completely vanished. The limited importation of specie and the retention of some exchange value for paper kept it in circulation. But because paper money never acquired the value conferred by scarcity, it became ever harder to exchange for scarce commodities.

The sickness of the economy in 1779 caused more trouble in Connecticut than perhaps in any other state. Unable to re-open traffic with the outside world as long as the British occupied Newport and unable to buy directly from producers because her officials could not pay in the commodities they wanted, Connecticut found her own salable goods disappearing to Boston. Such a state of affairs aggravated the dislocations and shortages that already existed, and worse: it left Congress powerless to harness what economic activity still existed.[162]

Obviously, there were other ways to procure besides purchase in the marketplace. There was force. Early in 1779, the commissariat in New England did use force to survive the spring shortages and found out that, even as an emergency measure, it had drawbacks. If the official who seized the goods had the local population on his side, the technique could work reasonably well.[163] Because of the activity of Boston purchasers, he rarely did. When the selectmen of Suffield held up the seizure of a small parcel of flour, Wadsworth undertook to settle the business himself. He found that, after submitting to local arbitration and settling all charges, he had paid nearly twice the high prices asked in Boston.[164] Moreover, the power to seize or embargo belonged to so many that the orders of one official were often countermanded by the orders of another.[165] Since these clashes frequently ended in violence, adding to the disorders already plaguing society, local and state officials usually thought it best to accommodate to predominant market forces. That is why New York, which passed remarkably vigorous embargo laws in 1778, yielded a few months later to the demands of Boston buyers for liberal export licences.[166] New York's defection left Wadsworth no alternative but to urge that Connecticut institute some more effective remedy. In April the legislature ordered a town-by-town census of grain with a provision for seizing at fixed prices all supplies not needed for immediate consumption. The measure might even have done something to help had not several engrossers learned of it in advance and promptly exported their surpluses.[167]

The lapse into a barter system had other ill effects. It caused cruel hardship to those of the poor who lived in areas which were not agriculturally self-sufficient. Most people in western Connecticut could partly withstand the pull of the Boston market by keeping some of their wheat for themselves,[168] but their neighbors to the east, who did not grow their own supplies, could not compete for them with city buyers. They weathered the crisis only because the metropolis wanted wheat and flour rather than corn and rye. Though corn and rye were generally considered animal foods, people could live on them if they had nothing else. Some did not have that option. In Boston the flour imported to provision the state's forces arrived in sufficient quantity to prevent widespread distress,[169] In Philadelphia, on the other hand, the poor suffered horribly. Because the surplus purchased by the French had been exported rather than locally consumed, shortages had already caused privation. And when a British raid on the Chesapeake in May threatened to inflict still greater hardship, armed mobs gathered to demand price regulation.[170]

By the spring of 1779, the collapse of the currency had raised the specter of anarchy. As alarmed by this as by its inability to procure sufficient food for the army, Congress tried once more to halt the depreciation. The basic assumption that people would bring in recalled emissions as loans, rather than for exchange, had proven false. Seeing that the currency continued to depreciate, the people had chosen to invest not in loan office certificates but in goods.[171] Meanwhile, a report from the Committee of the Treasury informed Congress that, given the current value of money, the annual expenses of the Quartermaster and Commissary departments had now reached $120 million a year. If depreciation continued to increase at the current rate, the bill might top $200 million by the end of the year.[172]

The agitation in Philadelphia added to a growing body of evidence that some would prefer taxation to loans. On May 21

Congress resolved to requisition the states for an additional $45 million to make a total demand of $60 million. Of this, Connecticut had to raise $6.8 million or 11 percent.[173] Strong as the measure was, it was not enough. By the committee's own estimate, expenses for the remainder of the year would run well in excess of $45 million. Collecting the money would take time, and even if reissued at once it would not meet current demands.[174] Short of borrowing money, Congress had either to emit more currency or to abandon what experience had shown was the only way to finance the war. And beyond a doubt, the continuous emission of more money would destroy the currency.

What Congress urgently needed was an efficacious loan scheme that would bring money into the treasury quickly.[175] A foreign loan would best have served the purpose, but France, the only power with the inclination, lacked the means. A domestic loan appeared equally hard to obtain. What credible incentives could the government hold out, given the continued headlong descent in the value of its money? There was the added difficulty that, if Congress offered tempting terms to lenders in 1779, those terms must be extended backward to include those who had been the nation's creditors since 1776. To do this would vastly increase the cost of borrowing; to do otherwise would be less than just to those who had supported the cause in its infancy.[176] In late June, Congress at last proposed a scheme to set past and future creditors on an equal footing by pegging both interest and principal to the amount of currency in circulation but betrayed its own lack of confidence in the scheme by restricting the loan to $20 million.[177] So low a figure strongly suggested that Congress saw only one certain way to finance the war: more taxation, a course littered with obstacles.

In Connecticut, the prospect of yet higher taxes caused the smoldering dispute over distribution of the burden to flare up fiercely.[178] The exigencies of war engendered the inevitable demand for expansion of the state's tax base, and August 1777 saw the first serious attempt to plug loopholes in the assessment of an individual's liabilities. At the same moment, the imposition of an additional shilling tax brought the total state tax for that year to just under three shillings in the pound.[179] By the autumn of 1778 the people had begun to complain that, though the new method of assessment had increased the tax base, the taxes imposed had increased more. A committee of nine towns in Litchfield County, meeting in early September, asked why unimproved lands and money in hand were exempt from assessment and why assessors made no distinction among the values of dwellings, some worth ten times as much as others?[180] A petition from Norwich raised similar questions and complained bitterly of the weight given to polls.[181] The General Assembly did not act on either memorial in its October session. In a special meeting held the following January, however, it bowed to the Norwich complaint by halving the value that polls between the ages of sixteen and twenty-one would have in the lists, and to the Litchfield complaint by ordering that buildings be listed at 3 percent of value and unimproved lands at 5 percent. Trading inventories, the land of nonresidents, and various luxury items such as coaches, clocks, and plate also became subject to assessment.[182]

The reform came too late. Between January and April 1779 the General Assembly had to raise a tax of ten shillings in the pound on the unreformed lists of 1778. The money was needed to meet the requisition of Congress, the costs of local defense, and the costs of recruiting the state's battalions for the continental line. In February 1779, a two-shilling additional tax, levied the previous November, also fell due.[183] Norwich signaled its discontent with a minor riot in which the rioters broke open the town jail to rescue certain persons arrested for tax delinquency. The incident had no great significance by itself, but a report that local authorities had connived in it gave the government cause for concern because it suggested that the brawl represented more than an outburst of momentary dissatisfaction.[184] Small wonder that when the May General Assembly confronted the requisition from Congress for $6.1 million more, the raising of which would require an additional nineteen shillings in the pound tax, the legislature seethed.[185] The state had been asked to deliver in one year three times as much as the total tax paid during the four preceding years of war or, in other words, to tax at thirty-seven shillings on the assessed pound. The burden that such a requisition would impose on the less affluent could no longer be brushed aside with arguments that money was cheap, that paying taxes would appreciate the value of the remainder, and that in this way the state would accumulate interest-bearing credits against the continent.[186] Though a movement in the lower house for sweeping assessment reform went down to defeat, the popular agitation it expressed boded ill for any attempt to raise Connecticut's share of the Continental requisition.[187]

New Priorities

The magnitude of Connecticut's economic problems sapped her enthusiasm for the cause, as her increasing inclination to put state before continental needs made plain. The tendency had first appeared when the civil leadership had collaborated in Putnam's quixotic operations. It reappeared in a more pernicious form a year later, in the state's response to the matter of completing her quota for the Continental line. The initial fault did not lie with the legislature. When Trumbull presented the members with a requisition from Washington for men to fill out the Connecticut ranks, they responded nobly. Deficiencies in the number of men recruited for 1777, together with the number of returned eight-month men who had to be replaced and the slots made vacant by normal attrition, had left the Connecticut line more than two thousand men below strength.[188] Taking as a starting point the system of town quotas and classing developed in 1777, the legislature provided that any deficiencies remaining after February 20 must be filled in the delinquent towns by preemptory detachment. Preemptory detachment implied the nullification of a clause in the 1777 law which required that, if every man detached chose instead to pay a fine, the detaching officer would have to tap every member of the class before he compelled anyone to march. Besides relieving the officer of a time-consuming obligation, the new law aimed to make the whole process less vulnerable to local pressure. The responsibility for designating men to be detached had passed from elected company officers to field officers named by the legislature. The rights and inclinations of the men were not ignored, however: the law offered a man £5.6s.8d. if he volunteered for ten month's service and permitted anyone "injured by . . . detachment" to appeal to the commanding officer of the regiment.[189]

Good as it looked on paper, the new law gave disappointing results. Though the threat of a draft prompted 484 enlistments in 1778, it produced only 248 detachees as compared with 564 the previous year (see Table 3). Putnam, relieved of command in the Highlands and now charged with the responsibility for filling out Connecticut's Continental regiments, complained to Trumbull that drafts from the brigades of Silliman, Ward, and Oliver Wolcott had produced only 33 men. The two eastern brigades performed as badly, yielding 20 men at the end of April instead of 200. Only Erastus Wolcott's brigade came close to quota.[190]

The trouble was that field officers required to choose detachees often designated those least likely to respond. Charles Burrall explained their dilemma to Trumbull. Every regiment contained ardent supporters of the cause who had already served several times. Every regiment also contained men who had avoided service because of either poverty or disaffection. Fairness to those who had done their part required that commanders now detach those who had not. But these were the men most likely to go over to the enemy or to desert.[191] Burrall's argument, however, ignored the possibility that field officers could have observed priority before equity. Had the Continental army been their first concern, they would not have chosen the least likely candidates for detachment. They deliberately kept their best men for other purposes because their priorities had shifted.

The legislature showed the same bias when it proposed to defend the coast and to meet the temporary requisitions customary since 1776 by calling for a voluntary force of 4,400 one-year men. Volunteers would receive a five-pound bounty if

TABLE THREE
ENLISTMENTS OF PRIVATES IN THE CONNECTICUT LINE, 1777–1780

	1777[a]				1778[a]				1779[b]	1780[a]	
	War	3 yrs.	8 mos.	1 yr.	War	3 yrs.	8 mos.	1 yr.	8 mos.	18 mos. or War	8 mos.
1st Regiment Hungtington	152	256	23	31	6	9	4		22		224
2nd Regiment C. Webb	126	147	58		15	29	15		116		320
3rd Regiment Wyllys	239	201	77		56	42	73	15	39		140
4th Regiment Durkee	182	129	71		24	15	33	1	151		201
5th Regiment Bradley	292	172	59		14	4			70		189
6th Regiment	28o						8o				

8th Regiment Chandler	227	155	109		40	34	26	1	97		192
Additional Regiment S. Webb	122	148	11		20	23			12		147
Total	1,804	1,651	533	31	271	213	176	72	560	134[c]	1,650

Total Enlistments: 7,095

Totals by Year		*War*		
1777	4,019	War	2,209[d]	31.1%
1778	732	3 years	1,864	26.3%
1779	560	8 months	2,919	41.1%
1780	1,784	1 year	103	1.5%

[a] *RCM.*
[b] *SOI*, 100–145, assuming all eight-month men.
[c] Differences between figures in *SOI*, 148–93 and *RCM*, 148–252 passim.
[d] Including all long-term recruits in 1780.

SOURCES: *RCM*, 148–252; *SOI*, 100–93.

they equipped themselves, twenty shillings each calendar month when not on active duty, and an exemption from all state taxes. On active duty they would receive the same pay, rations, and refreshments as continentals, though they were required to serve only three months at a time. When not on active duty, they had to train every fortnight. The legislature then designated six colonels to command the projected regiments, namely, Roger Enos, Thaddeus Cook, Samuel Mott, John Mead, Noadiah Hooker, and Samuel McClellan. They appointed the other field officers but left them to designate the company officers, in the belief that this would assist recruitment.[192] Technically, recruitment for the reserve force should not have competed with recruitment for the Continental line, which ought to have been filled soon after February 20 (the date set for preemptory drafting). The officers felt so reluctant to draft, however, that, during the month when detaching began, a man could still escape the Continental army by volunteering for the less demanding state service at roughly equivalent rates of pay.

Nevertheless, competition does not wholly explain Connecticut's failure to raise more than a third of the men she owed the continent. At the end of March, when the Council of Safety first needed to draw on the reserve force for coastal duty, it had to empower local brigadiers to complete the four companies ordered forward by making temporary drafts on the militia.[193] The same thing happened again in May. Gates sent a requisition for 1,500 men to reinforce the Highlands. The only way that Connecticut could both answer him and provide for her own coastal defense was to detach two battalions of two-month men from the militia. Knowing that an adequate reserve force would have precluded this necessity, the legislature made a last-ditch effort to entice the two-month militia to join by raising the bounty well above that offered the short-term detachee for the continent.[194] This maneuver succeeded no better than others. In June, when the deadline expired, those one-year men who had enlisted were amalgamated into two undermanned battalions and deployed along the coast.[195]

More and more, short-term detachment became the surest

strategy for raising men during 1778. It worked in reinforcing Sullivan at Rhode Island and in helping out the state's coastal defenses during the autumn, a particularly urgent matter after the British threatened to step up their coastal raids. The time of service rather than the size of the bounty had become the men's major consideration. Depreciation lessened the value of money so steadily and so fast that no one who could avoid it would consent to have his wages fixed for any long period of time, regardless of the bounty. Those obliged to bear arms had become more concerned with how to minimize loss than with how to pursue gain. For the same reason, when faced with a choice between state and Continental service, draftees preferred the service closest to home where discipline was less rigorous and friends or family could help to alleviate the hardships of camp life.

The Connecticut government's failure to compensate for the growing unpopularity of the Continental service in 1778 shows how far it had drifted toward a policy of encouraging choices that were bad for the cause. The general assumption that France's entry into the war would lead to Britain's exit, so that Americans need no longer make the same heroic exertions as before, increased the tendency.[196] But long after it had become clear that the British were not giving up, the drift continued to a point where the state government began deliberately to foster a bias against the Continental service.

A complex series of developments had brought things to this pass. Within the inner circles of the leadership, resentment over the way that Congress had treated Joseph Trumbull still rankled, especially after his tragic death in July.[197] At the same time, among those familiar with the complexities of revolutionary finance a suspicion arose that Continental credit would eventually collapse and that Connecticut would suffer disproportionately.[198] Not only had the commissary operation left the state with more than her share of the currency, but the restrictions placed on her commerce after December 1776 reduced her chance of exchanging the depreciating paper for commodities of real value. Even if the British had not cut off Connecticut's waterborne trade, her lack of a major port would have continued her disproportionate accumulation of currency. Traders in the principal ports could more easily exchange currency for commodities of stable or increasing value and could revert to the barter exchange of bulk commodities over short distances, but the countryside needed money. Though the demand for currency declined there too, it remained stronger than in the towns, and currency continued to flow from the commercial centers to the hinterland. Connecticut, still commercially dependent on distant ports like Boston, became the victim of this economic circumstance.[199] And Connecticut's leaders, increasingly concerned about the results to the state if Continental credit should collapse, tried harder than ever to secure repayment of her credits against the continent.[200]

Nevertheless, the leadership alone could not have dimmed the state's ardor for the cause and for Congress had not the people themselves lapsed into despondency. The prestige of Congress declined primarily because of the depreciation of the currency, but the Lee-Deane controversy accelerated the process. At the end of 1777, Congress had recalled Silas Deane from France where he had served since 1776, first as agent for two secret committees of Congress and then as an official representative at court. In December 1778 Deane published a justification of his activities abroad which took the form of a direct attack on the Lee family, two of whom sat in Congress while another two held congressional commissions in Europe. It also constituted an indirect but powerful assault on Congress.[201] His action ignited a blaze of controversy in the public prints that enhanced no one's prestige with its revelation of the bitter divisions that rived the nation's leadership.[202] Though Deane was a Connecticut man by birth and one of the colony's delegates to the First and Second Continental Congresses, members of the state's congressional delegation, including Eliphalet Dyer, William Williams, and Roger Sherman, who had come to distrust his extravagance, joined in promoting his recall.[203] Their hostility expressed itself for the most part in the passive form of a failure to defend him in print.[204] Even so, many of the public who followed the controversy in the newspapers undoubtedly identified with the portrait Deane painted of himself as a victim of congressional mismanagement.

Another sign of popular demoralization was a change of heart toward the army that began partly as a consequence of the success attending recruitment for the long term in 1777. The substitution of a permanent army for a temporary force had put an end to the casual assumption that Connecticut's war effort would always rest in the hands of men who moved easily from civilian to military life. The new strategy caused a division between the military and civilian spheres. The Continental forces ceased to be the extension of the society that armed them and assumed some of the characteristics of a European army. This is not to say that no substantial citizens joined up. The claims filed by the local committees formed to provide for soldiers' families show that many family men did march.[205] The state could offer so few incentives, however, that the army became increasingly a refuge for those from the fringes of society: the young man without much stake in the community, the freed slave, the servant, the adventurer, the social misfit.[206] The officers perceived how unrepresentative the army had grown, and in a memorial presented to the General Assembly during October 1778 expressed their fear that the soldiers would come to be viewed as "a people with separate and clashing interests."[207] But their appeal fell on deaf ears.

Both leadership and people, in fact, had begun to think that the army rendered little if any service to the special interests of Connecticut. The defense of the state's southwestern frontier had suffered in 1777 and again in the spring of 1778, when Washington sent the Connecticut regiments off to the Highlands and Pennsylvania, but at the time there was little protest. Not until the autumn of 1778 did the conflict between the manpower needs of the state and those of the continent burst into open controversy. Governor Trumbull, worried about the threat to the coast, asked Washington to station the Connecticut continentals for the winter "somewhere near the seacoasts, upon the southeastern and western frontiers of this state, where they may . . . serve as a protection thereto."[208]

Parsons, meanwhile, had already advised Washington to quarter two thousand continentals at Danbury, from which base guards might be detached for the coastal towns. Though he admitted that such detachments would wield little military clout, he warned Washington to consider "the great dissatisfaction which will be given the Country if this measure is not pursued."[209] In early November, Washington seemed sympathetic to both requests. But the final arrangements, though they did provide for a large contingent in the Danbury area from which detachments might cover the western coast, did not fulfill any of Trumbull's wishes. Indeed, they left the eastern coast helplessly exposed. On December 12 Trumbull sent a protest to Washington. He urged that permanent rather than movable detachments cover the coast and that the dragoons ordered to Durham be divided between three towns and used for patrols, but in vain. Washington refused to yield on any point.[210]

His refusal coincided with another event unlikely to make the army popular. At the beginning of 1778, Washington had endorsed the idea of compensating the officers for depreciation by promising them half pay for life. Without this, he feared that they would begin to resign in large numbers.[211] In Congress, the proposal met strong opposition from all the New England delegates, and particularly those from Connecticut. When the war began, there had been little difference in New England between the amount of property held by officers and that owned by many of the families whose men served in the ranks. The General Assembly acknowledged this in January 1778 when it ordered the towns, which had taken over the task of protecting soldiers' families from the effects of depreciation, to provide the same guarantee for the families of officers below the rank of brigadier.[212] Why, then, should the officers now receive anything beyond the specie value of the wage set by Congress in 1776, especially since that wage already stood at twice the amount offered in 1775? Why should they be established as a new class of persons privileged to live at the expense of others in a style to which they never were accustomed? The New England delegates presented so united a front

against the idea that Congress had to compromise.[213] According to Connecticut's delegates, that compromise guaranteed
both officers and men a compensation "deemed equal in value
to their wages at the original stipulation." For the officers, this
meant half pay for seven years, while each noncommissioned
officer and enlisted man would receive an additional bounty of
eighty dollars.[214]

The arrangement could not have pleased Connecticut, but
at least it preserved equity. And it gave the Assembly an excuse
to forward to Congress a memorial received in October 1778, in
which the state's officers alleged that the army was in a shamefully bad way.[215] Unfortunately, Governor Trumbull delayed
sending the memorial until the beginning of December,[216] by
which time the situation had grown worse. At the end of December, the governor received a letter from Return Jonathan
Meigs itemizing the many public commitments made to the line
and never met. The men had not received the provisions promised them and had received money in lieu of rations only after
the currency had lost five-sixths of its value. A similar failure to
provide clothing seemed likely to increase the sufferings of the
soldiery in winter. But, Meigs wrote, "the capital grievance is
the trifling value of the wages occasion'd by the depreciation of
our currency." He warned, "If the next Assembly should rise
without positively doing something for them, it is my opinion
that mutiny or desertion will reduce our battalions to nothing
before Spring."[217]

He was right. Four days later, the troops in Jedediah
Huntington's brigade did mutiny. Without orders, they assembled under arms, vowing to march on Hartford and demand redress for their grievances. They did not execute their
design. Putnam bravely confronted the mutineers and convinced them that violence would only jeopardize the measures
for their relief that both Congress and the General Assembly
were then considering. He also warned that the other regiments
might turn out against them. The mutineers decided to disband
and retired to their huts huzzahing for Congress, though not for
the Assembly. When Putnam later arrested the ringleaders,
some of the men concocted a plan to rescue them. A soldier

apprehended while trying to collect volunteers for the attempt was shot dead. With that, the mutiny subsided; the Connecticut line, however, remained restless.[218]

Knowing how the enemy would relish hearing of the mutiny, the authorities tried vainly to suppress the story. It traveled far and wide and undoubtedly helped to increase the popular suspicion of standing armies. Nevertheless, it had one good effect. The General Assembly stopped waiting for Congress to act and initiated its own attempts to appease the men. Putnam sent four of his principal officers, Parsons, Huntington, Bradley, and Meigs, to explain the circumstances of the army to the legislature. They probably did a good deal of apologizing for the mutiny, especially as more money for the army was the last thing people wanted to think about when necessity had just forced the imposition of an unprecedented six shillings in taxes. In the end, the legislators voted the army £105,000 in compensation, £45,000 to be paid on April 1 and the remainder on December 1.[219] The sum did not amount to full compensation; no one could calculate the precise amount due without access to all the Continental accounts. And since depreciation was accelerating, the value of the first payment had dropped 50 percent when it fell due in April. By December, the period set for the second payment, the money had declined to a fourth of its previous value.[220]

The army believed, nonetheless, that it had won a significant victory: after all, it had forced the state to assume a responsibility which she had tried to shuffle off on Congress.[221] The assumption of a responsibility did not, however, guarantee discharge of it. Connecticut found the keeping of her promise a hard task. Though the first payment of £45,000 should have used up only one-sixth of the expected yield from taxes due between February and April 1, the people's preference for paying their taxes in the repudiated currency, which could not be reissued, seriously embarrassed the state treasury. When the government realized what had happened, the legislature decided to ask Congress to exchange £45,000 of the repudiated emissions in its hands.

The application was not sent until April 15, two weeks

after the first payment fell due.[222] In the interval, the Assembly tried to placate the men by guaranteeing that the value of all wages and supplies due under the original agreement would be made good in specie or its equivalent whenever their terms of service expired.[223] But the day had come when the men would be satisfied with nothing but money. On April 10 Parsons wrote to the legislature threatening the mass resignation of officers and disbanding of the Connecticut line if all demands were not soon met. On April 30 he wrote again, blaming the high rate of desertion during the previous winter upon the want of pay.[224] The second letter arrived just as the April session ended, but the new legislature authorized the treasurer to borrow £45,000 at 6 percent repayable in three months. Because the state had to appease the army somehow or abandon all hope of reenlisting the three-year men in 1780, the measure succeeded. In June, when Congress finally offered to lend Connecticut £45,000, she could refuse.[225]

Meanwhile, however, the feeling grew that the army gave Connecticut more problems than protection. Though a detachment of continentals had helped defend Greenwich from attack in February,[226] more often than not when the soldiers were needed they were not there. In late January, reports arrived that the British had begun to concentrate troops on eastern Long Island. The danger they posed impelled Putnam to send 400 continentals to New London.[227] In early March, when the Council of Safety heard that the British strength at Southampton had risen to 2,500 and that carpenters were busy building flatboats for a descent on the mainland, it supplemented Putnam's troops with 640 six-week militia.[228] Putnam in turn ordered another 600 men to the Connecticut coast, though they remained west of New Haven.[229] But soon afterward, with the threat from Long Island still impending, Parsons received orders that the continentals at New London be marched west. Putnam subsequently claimed that Parsons had misunderstood the orders, which applied only to the New Hampshire troops under his command. Misunderstanding or no, on the eve of a major alarm the New London garrison found itself greatly reduced in strength.[230] At the end of the month, various intelligence reports, together with the convergence of two British fleets at Gardiners Island Sound, threw the town and the authorities into a frenzy of fear.[231] They knew they would get little help from the Continental troops.[232]

It soon appeared that the fleets had crossed paths by accident. People also grew easier about the troops on eastern Long Island when it occurred to them that the British could respond to rumor, too, and that they might have wondered if the continentals marched to New London in February were gathering forces for an attack on the island.[233] Nevertheless, recurrent reports of the enemy's hostile intentions and suspicious movements kept the people in suspense throughout April. In their uncertainty, it did not help to know that the continentals would withdraw as the army formed for the opening of the next campaign.[234] Then, toward the end of the month, reports arrived of a major British embarkation.[235] Though it might equally well have been aimed at the Connecticut coast as at the Highlands, Washington did not wait to find out; he simply ordered that all the continentals in Putnam's division march to the Hudson.[236] He also detached some of Gates's two thousand continentals at Providence for service there, and Gates promptly requisitioned Connecticut for 750 militia to replace them.[237]

These facts make it easier to understand why the Connecticut legislature responded coolly to a request that Washington now made. Encouraged by the hope that a French expeditionary force would return to northern waters come summer and that combined operations against the British in New York could succeed, Washington wrote to Connecticut, Massachusetts, and New Hampshire asking "what force of well armed Militia, rank and file, may, in your judgement, be drawn from [your state] by the first of June for three or four Months, if the measure should be found expedient."[238] The warm friendship that Trumbull and Washington had once enjoyed seems from the dwindling of their correspondence to have cooled, perhaps because Trumbull resented the restrictions that Washington had placed on the deployment of continentals. Certainly Trumbull did not exert himself to reply to this latest

request. Instead of taking the lead in the formulation of a spirited response, as he might have done once, he merely submitted
the letter to the legislature. The legislature appointed a committee, and the committee drafted a reply agreeing only to send
one battalion of militia at Continental strength and to complete
the state's quota of Continental recruits. Trumbull signed it on
April 27.[239] He answered Gates's requisition more quickly, and
with an outright refusal. Though Connecticut would support
him in the event of a major British offensive, Trumbull wrote,
the precautionary reinforcements he wanted might better be
drawn from Massachusetts and New Hampshire, states not
constantly subjected to immediate enemy pressure.[240]

The grudging character of this response reoccurred in a
controversy about the state's completion of her Continental
line. The new arrangement of the army, ordered by Congress
at the end of 1778 as an economy measure, had reduced Connecticut's quota by 20 percent.[241] Nevertheless, the Connecticut line remained deficient by eight hundred men, and normal
attrition would increase the number before the campaign was in
full swing. One proposal, apparently drafted by Oliver Wolcott
and supported by a majority of the Council, suggested that the
state try to raise one thousand ten-month men to serve until
March 1780. Wolcott wanted to offer anyone who volunteered
before May 3 a bounty of forty dollars and a guarantee of wages
at specie equivalents to forty shillings a month. Towns which
had not completed their quotas by May 3 would have to draft
as many men as necessary to fill the vacancies.[242] Wolcott and
the Council had obviously concluded that, given the difficulties
they encountered in raising men for the Continental service,
they must aim high if they were to fill the ranks.

A counterproposal by the lower house reveals that the delegates there were willing to give more money for less service.
Their bill would have raised only six hundred men, strictly as
volunteers, and though it offered them a $66.67 bounty it did
not guarantee their wages against depreciation. That the lower
house set so modest a target reflected its determination to receive full credit for the troops Connecticut had supplied to irregular formations in the army. The proposal did not even

prescribe a remedy if the six hundred volunteers were not forthcoming. It merely indicated that something would be done. Yet it was this proposal that became law, and the legislature then went on to cancel out whatever gain Washington might still have derived from it by instructing Trumbull to request the detachment of two Continental regiments for the defense of the coast.[243]

It was just as well for the state's reputation that a minimal response to the appeal for six hundred volunteers obliged the May legislature to reconsider the measure as a whole. The committee formed to draft a new law for completing the Continental battalions pursued its business in a leisurely fashion until late May. At that point McDougall, who feared that the British were about to attack the Highlands, appealed for the Connecticut militia to stand by. Though the legislature ordered one-quarter of its three western brigades to hold themselves in readiness,[244] Clinton seized two strong points below the Highlands before they could be called out. The Continental army, which had covered the southwestern frontier from its Westchester camp during much of 1778, had to retire to the Highlands, leaving the few coast guards in the western coastal towns at the mercy of the enemy. The legislature, mindful of the rumors that the British intended to raid the coast, resolved to meet the emergency by detaching two five-hundred-man regiments and two companies of horses from the interior west of the river. In addition, it hastily adopted the report of its committee on filling the army, which recommended raising the number of volunteers desired from six to eight hundred men and instituting a draft.[245] When Trumbull wrote to Congress at the end of the month, he spoke as if the state had always intended to raise the greater number of men for the army.[246]

The simultaneous attempt to form a large body of state troops did nothing, however, to help raise men for the continent. Though the Assembly ordered that two state battalions of 520 men each be raised to serve until March 1780,[247] the method they chose to attract the men betrayed that they put the home front first. It had become the custom that recruits for both state and Continental service receive large bounties if they volunteered. Six-month recruits for the Continental army would now receive a twenty-pound bounty, while seven-and-a-half-month recruits for the state service who equipped themselves would receive twenty-four pounds. Strictly speaking, the Continental recruits joined on slightly better terms than the state recruits. But in practice the difference in money did not outweigh the advantages of service close to home. More significant still, by ordering that the draft for the Continental battalions begin on July 10 and by omitting all provision that those detached could qualify for bounties by enlisting, the legislature gave even greater incentive for men to enter the state battalions rather than the Continental line. Recruitment for the state battalions would end on July 15. Those in danger of compulsory Continental service with no bounty could still enlist in a state regiment and obtain a bounty.[248]

The legislature had so designed the draft that state ranks would obviously fill before Continental ranks. The legislature, in fact, had come to care less about reinforcing the army than about leaving Continental commanders no excuse to refuse their help if Connecticut were attacked.

CHAPTER FIVE

Exhaustion

THOUGH 1779 opened in the shadow of economic distress, low morale, and the bitter factionalism of the Lee-Deane controversy, the hope of victory revived during the spring. British forces were spread so thin between Rhode Island, New York, and the South as to invite another Saratoga. If the French would divert the necessary naval superiority from the West Indies, it could be done.[1] There was also a hope that Spain would soon either succeed in promoting a peace whereby Britain recognized America's independence or mark the failure of the attempt by entering the war as an ally.[2] Rumors that Spain would soon join the belligerents began to circulate in March, preceding the event itself by a good three months.[3] Besides conferring an overwhelming naval superiority on the allies, such a development would, as Congress pointed out in the address of May 26, give the new nation an opportunity to "form other alliances . . . beneficial to these states."[4]

Then again, bad as the economy looked, there remained a chance that some of the nation's financial problems would come under control. In Philadelphia, for instance, where depreciation had so accelerated that in one three-week period the price of most goods more than doubled, the problem had produced its own solution.[5] A people's committee sprang up to regulate prices, then proceeded not only to halt depreciation but also to cause a slight rise in the value of money, at least within the city.[6] A popular movement in one city would not, of course, effect much improvement in the national economy, but Congress appeared to endorse the idea of more such organizations when it appealed to the people to support measures for appreciating the currency and decreasing the cost of necessities.[7] Should the committee movement fail to catch hold, it still seemed reasonable to expect that compliance with the currency requisition of May 21 would tip the scale. The prospect of a modest appreciation would improve the government's chance of borrowing as it improved the lender's chance of a good return on his money. It even looked as if the commodity shortages which lay at the heart of all the economy's ills might soon be over, thanks to the promise of a bountiful harvest.[8]

Up to this time, the course of events in Connecticut had run parallel to that of the nation. The élan with which she embarked on the war had lost its first freshness, perhaps, but the alienation that would soon creep over the state had little hold as yet. Her new inclination to put local needs before Continental needs appeared only in the priority given to recruitment for the army within her own borders. The legislature unhesitatingly complied with the extraordinary congressional requisitions of May 21 by laying an unprecedented tax of nineteen shillings on the list of 1778. And, because of favorable circumstances, the people acquiesced. First of all, 85 percent of the new tax did not fall due until November and December, by which time farmers would have had ample opportunity to sell their surpluses.[9] Secondly, in May and June when naval supremacy began to slip from Britain in the western Atlantic, Connecticut privateers had enjoyed a rare streak of luck. Their captures allowed them to introduce goods into Connecticut which, together with the prospect of taxes, helped to confirm the demand for money and check the depreciation for the moment.[10] In the early summer, one could still be optimistic. Royal Flint, for example, reported to Wadsworth in July that everyone was working, no one was speculating, city markets were well supplied, and the currency was improving its reputation.[11] There were problems but no cause for despair.

Devastation

It was during July 1779, however, that the problems confronting both state and nation began to get out of hand. In Connecticut, the turning point came with the devastation of the seacoast by an amphibious British force of 2,600 men under Sir George Collier and Governor William Tryon.[12] The first wave hit New Haven on the morning of July 5. Reports of their approach had been received on the previous evening, closely followed by the news that they had anchored off West Haven, but few people suspected their intention. Large fleets heading for Rhode Island had often anchored along the coast on windless nights to wait out unfavorable tides.[13] Not until they saw the boats put off from the ships did New Haveners understand their danger.

The enemy landed in two divisions. The first, consisting of roughly a thousand men under Brigadier General Charles Garth, marched north from Savin Rock. The second division of eight hundred men under Tryon landed on the East Haven side of the harbor. Both met with strong opposition. It took Garth more than eight hours to enter the town. The bridge over the West River was blocked by two field pieces, which forced him to make for the Derby Bridge near West Rock. In the process he found himself hard pressed by the New Haven militia, reinforced by detachments from nearby towns. Tryon's men, who had landed five hours later than Garth's because of a shortage of boats, worked their way up the east side of the harbor during the afternoon with the help of the armed ships, but the militia at Neck Bridge over the Quinnipiac River kept them from joining forces with their fellows.[14]

Once in New Haven, Garth's men made up for lost time. The town was plundered by men from the ships, which came into the harbor on the afternoon tide. And the enemy showed little mercy to the inhabitants, wounding and murdering people, often in their homes, regardless of whether or not they bore arms. So much for the proclamation issued by Collier and Tryon, protesting their forbearance and promising immunity to all who stayed within doors.[15] Still, the spirited resistance put up by the militia may have saved the town from the general conflagration Garth had planned.[16] The raiders burned some stores and vessels at the Long Wharf but left the rest of the town intact. Tradition attributes Garth's failure to execute his design to personal generosity and to the intercession of certain loyalists. The evidence rather suggests he doubted his men's ability to withstand the fury of the militia when they saw New Haven in flames, particularly as the tide and the resistance at Neck Bridge made it hard for Tryon to help him.[17] On the sixth, in fact, Garth evacuated the bulk of his force to East Haven, where Tryon had come under increased pressure from the waves of militia that continued to arrive, some from as far away as Saybrook and Middletown. At East Haven, the scene of a general though inconclusive engagement on the sixth, the raiders burned eight dwellings and three barns, nothing more.[18]

If the British were trying to show off their power to wreak havoc along the coast, they had failed.[19] Their plan had depended on misconceptions. They counted on the ability of the two divisions to help each other, but ten miles of difficult country lay between them. They counted on the navy to support the landing parties, but the ships had to wait on the tide before they could enter the harbor. They counted on the advantages that should have come from an attack launched at two widely separated points simultaneously but found that they had divided their own force more than their enemy's. To cap all, they had chosen one of the most densely populated parts of the coast for their venture, an area far less depleted by wartime migration than coastal communities to the west. The raiders had accomplished some objectives. They had distracted men from the harvest, seized twenty to forty head of cattle from East Haven, and captured or burned most of the shipping in the harbor.[20] This was not much, however, considering the quantity of manpower and shipping deployed.

The British did not make the same mistake twice. On the morning of July 7 they landed two divisions just to the west of Fairfield. This time, they sacrificed numbers to coordination and ease of movement; this time, they enjoyed the advantage of surprise, since from first light to the moment of their landing a fog had shrouded their proceedings;[21] and, as a result, this time they encountered fewer obstacles. The principal fortified point, Black Rock, stood to the east of the town, separated from it by marsh and standing water. They met no such opposition from the Fairfield militia as had blocked them at New Haven. Many of Fairfield's inhabitants had moved inland, troubled by the nearness of the British base at Huntington. The enemy had made frequent forays from this vantage point; two months earlier, a party of marauders had even carried off Brigadier Silliman from his Fairfield home in the middle of the night. Moreover, many of the militia from nearby towns had gone to the aid of New Haven and not yet returned.[22]

Clear as he found his way, Tryon sent a message to the commanding officer in the area, Colonel Samuel Whiting of Stratford, threatening to burn Fairfield if he did not submit at once. Before Whiting received the message, the British began the work of destruction in response to "the fire of the Rebels from their houses." Whiting replied with a splendidly baroque gesture of defiance. "Connecticut having nobly dared to take up arms against the cruel despotism of Britain," he wrote, "and the flames having preceded their answer to your flag, they will persist to oppose to the utmost the power exerted against injured innocence."[23] When the British retired from the town at midday on July 8, they had destroyed 190 structures in Fairfield and the adjacent settlement of Green Farms, including 93 dwellings.[24] They had also proved the seacoast vulnerable. As Whiting put it, "Their invasions & designs are so sudden & unknown that we cannot collect men enough to prevent their Ravaging, plundering, & burning all the Towns upon the Coast."[25]

Washington broadcast a warning that their next objective might be New London.[26] People in both New Haven and Fairfield had reported hearing the raiders talk of it. When three British men-of-war appeared in the harbor, the government hastened to send in reinforcements.[27] Meanwhile, Washington diverted John Glover's Massachusetts brigade, just then approaching New London on their march from Rhode Island to the Highlands, to the defense of the port. This enabled the Council of Safety to spare most of the men from the Third and Fifth brigades from service for the moment, which helped the harvest.[28] But reports that the enemy had 6,000 infantry and 1,000 horse massed along Byrams River on the southwestern frontier moved Major General Wolcott to call up half of the Sixth Brigade on July 9. On the tenth, the Council followed suit, detaching half of the Second Brigade and half of the First Brigade west of the river, together with 300 horse.[29] Washington, who had already sent Parsons to rally the state's militia, ordered Heath's two Connecticut brigades forward from the Highlands to the Bedford-Ridgefield area.[30]

We now know that the British force at Byrams River had no intention of invading Connecticut unless a significant objective appeared. Its real purpose, as Washington suspected, was to draw his army away from the Highlands and keep the interior militia on the defensive at home.[31] Wolcott probably knew of Washington's conjecture and expected that the interior militia would soon be summoned, not to defend the coast but to defend strong points along the Hudson. He knew too that the militia ordered out had already begun to feel restless about the work of harvest left undone at home.[32] When Collier suddenly withdrew, Wolcott felt that to persist in what now appeared an overresponse could do more harm than to skimp on coastal defense, especially at this point in the farmer's year. On July 10 he modified his order of July 9 and asked for one-quarter rather than one-half of the Sixth Brigade. He also advised those detached by the Council of Safety not to march.[33] The Council, though equally aware that it would be unwise to keep the men idling and chafing for nothing, did not feel so sanguine. They may have worried about a rumor that the fleet had reappeared off Branford. Certainly they worried about the effect on morale of constant changes in the men's orders.[34] The Council reduced its detachment of men from the First and Second brigades to one-quarter but went no further to meet Wolcott's advice.

In the event, it proved that Wolcott had leaped to a wrong conclusion. On the evening of the eleventh, Collier's fleet appeared off Norwalk. Just before sunset his men began to land at

Cow's Pasture, a peninsula one and one-half miles to the east of the bridge over the creek that divided the town. Wolcott still had 700 militia there, a good many more than had come to the defense of Fairfield. There was a time that night when the small force that had succeeded in landing before dark might have succumbed to Wolcott's superior numbers had he attacked. He chose instead to wait until he had gathered all his men.[35] This was Wolcott's first independent command in battle, and he probably hesitated to seize the initiative when he had only untrained militia to work with. His decision to wait for Parsons, on his way with a detachment of 150 continentals, proved mistaken. By the time the two joined forces, around six o'clock in the morning, the British had landed a second division to the west and had pushed the militia on both sides to the northern end of the town. Wolcott and Parsons mounted a counterattack which drove them back, but then the ranks of the militia broke. Before Wolcott could regroup, the enemy had burned most of the town and reembarked. Though they had committed none of the atrocities reported at New Haven and Fairfield,[36] they had wreaked ruin on Norwalk. As many as 262 structures were leveled in that raid, 122 of them dwellings.[37]

With this, the attack on the coast ground to a halt. Tryon and Collier had found more fight in these towns than they bargained for, and Clinton thought the losses not worth the gains. If he knew of Heath's movement toward Ridgefield, he may also have seen a chance to strike at the Highlands.[38] But two could play that game, and Washington was already planning to exploit the division of Clinton's forces between the various outposts he had established along the river during June.

In the early morning of July 16, an elite force of light infantry, commanded by Anthony Wayne and including a regiment under Return Jonathan Meigs, stormed the heavily fortified garrison at Stony Point. Stony Point, situated just below West Point, contained only 670 troops, half the number of the attackers. After less than an hour of vicious hand-to-hand fighting, the garrison surrendered. For the first time, American troops had shown that they too could capture a fortified posi-

tion with a bayonet charge. They had also shown that an isolated British detachment could fall to their assault, a point underscored one month later by the capture of the garrison at
Paulus Hook.[39] Both operations gave a great boost to the
morale of the army, whose lack of men and supplies largely
precluded its taking the offensive during the campaign of 1779.

Connecticut, however, felt little the better for these gains.
Clinton had withdrawn his concentration of troops from
Byrams River, true;[40] but since Heath's two Connecticut
brigades had also withdrawn, while Glover's had marched west
to join the main army, the state felt more vulnerable than
ever.[41] There seemed every reason to think the British would
be back. If the recent attacks had indeed represented an attempt
to divert Washington's men from the Highlands, Clinton might
well mount a second, still more devastating attempt with the
same purpose.[42] And if, as many believed, he had the ministry's orders to destroy all the principal towns of Connecticut,
that gave him yet another reason to try again.

The rumor that such orders had been issued made the
rounds in Europe during the spring and filtered through to
America in early July, just before the British raids commenced.
It may account for Hartford's pusillanimous response to the
New Haven alarm. Instead of starting out at once, the Hartford
militia cooled its heels while its leaders ran a panic-stricken
course. They appealed to the Springfield arsenal for cannon,
sent out a special scout to report enemy movements, and in
general behaved as if their town stood in as much danger as
those on the coast. Subsequently, they excused their actions as
a reasonable response to secret information relayed by the
Middletown assistants, Jabez Hamlin and Titus Hosmer, to the
effect that the British ministry had ordered all towns along the
Connecticut River destroyed as well as those along the
Sound.[43] Though they had escaped for the moment, they saw
their town as a possible future target.

These alarms, and the continued presence of British warships at the mouth of the Thames, led the government to send
in a new detachment of militia from the eastern brigades when
Glover's men left New London in July. They avoided calling

on the coastal regiments more than they had to and chose to tap Christopher Leffingwell's volunteer company, men not ordinarily engaged in agriculture, in order to spare the Norwich militia, many of whom farmed for a living.[44] Even so, they had to deflect some precious manpower from the land, a necessary evil that grew worse. Throughout the summer, Governor Trumbull and the members of Congress from time to time received reports of the ministry's designs on Connecticut which, together with continued enemy movements on the Sound and in Westchester, kept the state in constant upheaval.[45]

Washington did not leave Connecticut to face her peril unaided. He halted Glover's detachment in the Ridgefield-Bedford area, and though he refused to post any detachment of the army "within surprising distance of a superior body of the enemy," a force of five hundred continentals remained within a day's march of the southwest frontier for the rest of the year.[46] Massachusetts also helped, sending about a thousand men to serve for one month.[47] Even so, early in August Connecticut resolved to deploy four thousand men in two-month rotations along the coast for the rest of the year. Brigadier Andrew Ward evidently spoke for many when he wrote "that this method is very expensive and Injurious [to agriculture] . . . but not so Injurious as the Destruction of the Seaport Towns."[48]

Concern for the safety of those towns was undoubtedly the main reason for the extravagance of the government's response, though there were other causes too. Events in Stratford during the July raids indicated a weakening of the will to resist. Flanked by New Haven to the east and Fairfield to the west, Stratford had seemed to be in danger from the British fleet on July 9. Some of the frightened townspeople had asked William Samuel Johnson, a personal friend of Tryon and an acquaintance of Sir George Collier, to intercede with the British commanders on behalf of the town. Johnson, who had lived in seclusion since retiring from the Council in 1775, hesitated to act for fear of retaliation when the invaders withdrew. Only the importunities of his neighbors induced him at length to draft a document for their signature in which they promised to protect him from reprisal if he persuaded the British not to harm them.

Before he could go further, the fleet departed. But when

the authorities heard what had happened, they placed the town under martial law, set up a military court of inquiry, and arrested Johnson. Though the court of inquiry recommended clemency for the signers, while Johnson cleared himself of blame and took the oath of allegiance,[49] the incident raised grave enough doubts about the state's political hold on certain coastal communities to make Wolcott risk a large number of his men at an exposed post in Horseneck. In this attempt to maintain political control of the area he went directly against Washington's advice.[50]

Besides obstructing the harvest, the state's decision to keep four thousand men in service indefinitely severely taxed her available manpower. The Council of Safety calculated that, in addition to the matross companies already stationed in the principal towns and the two state regiments for six months authorized in May, more than 2,300 men would be required from the militia on rotation.[51] The government surely had no illusion that such a force could be raised by voluntary enlistment. It must have known that the men who had answered the July alarm did not want to stay in the field a day longer than necessary and that the officers were already embarrassed by the number of desertions.[52] As a further complication, the British raids had upset the schedule for completing the continental quota, which, as we have seen, was in any case designed with an eye to completing the state regiments first. Now all quotas would have to be drafted.

In early August, the officers of the militia brigades found themselves required to detach unprecedented numbers of men for various terms of service. They ran into trouble even in drafting for the two-month service along the coast because those who had gone in mid-July served only one month. Some of the officers would have liked to humor the men by cutting all terms of service down to one month, but that would have struck a further blow at the economy.[53] Though many men detached for the two-month service excused themselves with fines, the brigade commanders knew they could fill their quotas because short-term service precluded service for a longer term.[54]

Recruitment for the state regiments and the Continental

army proved more difficult. By the end of August, Mead's state regiment, assigned to the defense of the southwestern frontier, had reached less than 60 percent of full strength.[55] At that point, another alarm occurred. Toward the end of the month a large reinforcement, said to consist of seven thousand fresh troops, had arrived in New York. Simultaneously, reports came in of shipping and light infantry gathering at Huntington. It looked for a moment as if Clinton were about to embark in earnest on the threatened devastation of the coast. The Council of Safety issued a frantic appeal for Massachusetts militia and ordered that all the brigades form three divisions, the first equal to the last detachment of two-month men and equipped for immediate action along the coast, the other two made up equally of the remainder.[56] Though the panic subsided when it became known that Clinton's reinforcements numbered only about thirty-five hundred and had communicated a fever to the rest of his army, the scare had helped to bring the state regiments to 80 percent of full strength.[57] There, however, they rested.

Drafts for the Continental line did not fare so well. Continental recruiters complained bitterly to Trumbull that the militia officers ordered to detach men were performing that duty in perfunctory fashion, and statistics bear them out. Up through August, only a trickle of recruits found its way to the army. Not until September and October did the ranks receive a sizable addition of 337 men. Though 560 or 70 percent of the quota Connecticut had set herself did eventually join the army (see table 3), 60 percent of them did not arrive until the autumn, after the state had provided for its own defense.[58]

The Currency Collapses

While Connecticut struggled to cope with constant enemy harassment on the home front, she also took part in a national drama, the collapse of the currency. We have seen how continued depreciation during 1779 helped to confirm the imbalance between the demand for grain and the demand for currency that had begun in 1778. Natural disasters and enemy action contributed to the problem, but the root of it lay in a currency which one disgruntled resident of the state described as "no Better than oak leaves & fit for nothing But Bum Fodder."[59] The farmers had no incentive to expand production when payment would take so valueless a form, and coercion just did not work. New York state found that out during the summer of 1779. The harvest there had suffered no real harm, either from nature or from the ravages of war; yet state officials knew that, because the commissary agents had so little to offer in exchange, they might soon be unable to buy grain at all. The legislature therefore passed a law requiring farmers to give up one-eighth of their crop for public purchase. But the assessors appointed to fix individual quotas too often succumbed to local pressure and set ridiculously low ones, while the farmers expressed their resentment by slowing down on threshing. As a result, the measure proved completely ineffectual.[60]

Congress had hoped that taxation would create artificial incentives. Producers would be forced not to hoard but to sell, and it seemed reasonable to hope that they would sell to commissary agents. In September, Henry Champion commented that the heavy taxes due in November and December had certainly made it easier for him to buy cattle with Continental money.[61] And if the demand for money increased enough, its value in relation to goods wanted by commissary agents would stabilize. With the depreciation halted, Continental money would regain its character as a circulating medium and an incentive to producers.[62] News of the $60 million requisition at the end of May did arrest the depreciation in Connecticut briefly. In the long run, however, this demand and its successor, which called for the states to raise $15 million monthly from February to October 1780, helped to make the bills of credit worthless and the marketplace all but useless to the cause.

It was plain from the start that some states either could not or would not pay the requisite taxes. Some could not because they lacked currency. In setting quotas, Congress had tried to allow for the uneven distribution of money, but with less than total success. Henry Laurens, for instance, doubted that there existed within the whole of South Carolina so much currency as the requisition of May 21 asked her to pay.[63] And given her distance from states that did have currency, not to mention the disruption of commerce, she could not earn the money. Virginia did have the money but employed questionable means in the attempt to raise it. Having spent much time and energy during the early years of the war on securing the vast lands in the west to which she laid a disputed claim, Virginia now proposed to meet the requisition of Congress by opening her own land office to sell them off. Her attempt to pay her share of a common debt with what many considered a common asset caused widespread anger and disillusionment.[64]

The northern states, especially the New England states, also had the money to meet the demand, and an incentive too in that, by paying up, they would acquire cheap credits against a final settlement of accounts. Yet they were nearing the limits of their resource, as the example of Connecticut shows. Until June 1779, Connecticut wholeheartedly met each and every congressional requisition. From that time on, the damage done by British raiders and the increasing cost of defending the coast against them cooled her ardor. In October, for the first time, the Assembly complained of the currency quota "as much beyond their due Proportion" and asked that the costs of coastal defense be deducted from it.[65] Congress did not respond until the end of December, when it refused either to change the quota or to "assent to the retaining of any part of the taxes raised for general use." Congress would credit Connecticut's account with the continent for the expense of deploying the militia along the coast for nine months, but this would be computed according to the standard of Continental pay and rations in June 1778 and would not benefit the state until the final settlement. Roger Sherman privately advised Trumbull to reduce the state's quota on his own authority,[66] and Trumbull apparently did instruct the treasurer not to issue warrants for the collection of the tax.

Jeremiah Wadsworth's resignation from the commissariat also had its effect upon the state. He had been threatening to resign for over a year and had continued in the job so long only because Washington and many members of Congress asked him to. His agents could not please everyone, caught as they were between the people's desire to keep down the debt and their equally strong desire to get the highest price for their goods. Since Wadsworth thought it impossible to provide for the army without the seller's consent, his agents usually ended by meeting the seller's demands while the debt rose ever higher. Official criticism of his administration first surfaced in Congress's address of May 26 and again in a resolution of July 9, which authorized the various states to remove persons in the Quartermaster or Commissary departments suspected "of any kind of misbehaviour."[67] Congress realized that to continue supporting procurement with bigger and bigger issues of money would eventually defeat the purpose, and on September 1 it resolved to halt emissions at $200 million.[68] Later that autumn, Congress also resolved to accept Wadsworth's resignation in the belief that, whatever the new system of procurement adopted, some less controversial figure should run it.[69] One result would be that the disbursement of Continental funds no longer favored Connecticut.[70]

Even if all the states had met their requisitions in full, it would not have helped much. Congress never projected enough tax revenue to cover expenses. In making its plans, Congress always assumed that taxation would appreciate the currency, that the difference between receipts and disbursements would be made up by the rise in value of the money, and that people would thus acquire an incentive to invest in the loan office.[71] It refused to recognize that the public opposed appreciation. If the currency had been equitably distributed among them, each man possessing an amount in proportion to his tax liabilities, they might have welcomed a rise in its value. Since it was not, appreciation would leave those who did not have enough to pay their taxes at the mercy of those who had more than enough.

In fact, since Congress continued to spend more than it ever took in, the public need have feared no such event. But that they did fear it appeared in several ways. Wadsworth's agent, Royal Flint, observed in July that "the people grow alarmed about rates, and suppose all the cash they can obtain will be required for public demands." And John Trumbull reported that "many openly declared they would push the tax on the price of their commodities urging that it was unjust to appreciate the money [and] injurious to the poor."[72] The movement for price regulation by popular committee spread beyond the confines of Boston and Philadelphia for the same reason. Begun as an attempt by city folk to gain access to the products of the countryside, in New England it found favor in the country towns as well. In July, a convention at Concord, Massachusetts, resolved first to freeze all prices, then by degrees to reduce them. Later on, New Hampshire and Rhode Island held similar conventions.[73] In Connecticut, the poorer outlying areas took up the movement rather than the central towns: Windham and Fairfield counties, for instance, held conventions endorsing the Philadelphia model because they had the most to fear from an appreciation of debts both public and private,[74] while commercial centers such as Hartford and New Haven resisted the whole idea.[75]

Two circumstances averted a showdown between those who feared a radical appreciation of the currency and those who did not. Congress's declared intention of pursuing a pay-as-you-go policy suggested that its aim was to stabilize the currency rather than appreciate it, and there still seemed to be a chance that the war would end quickly. In the early autumn, rumors spread that d'Estaing was heading north, and Washington tacitly confirmed them when he called on Pennsylvania, New Jersey, New York, Connecticut, and Massachusetts for twelve thousand militia to serve three months.[76] Furthermore, the prospects for combined operations looked particularly good. The enemy was widely dispersed in the northern theater; d'Estaing, by all accounts, was now invincible at sea;[77] and on the domestic front his presence would bring an influx of imported goods and French bills of exchange to increase the incentives of the marketplace.[78]

As had happened so often, both the pay-as-you-go policy and the presence of the French had the opposite effect from that expected. On October 7 Congress asked the states to withdraw the old Continental currency at the rate of $15 million a month between February and October in the coming year.

Connecticut's share of the total requisition would amount to $15 million.[79] When Connecticut heard the news, such a clamor for price regulation arose as the authorities could no longer ignore. The Massachusetts legislature had already suggested that a convention of the New England states and New York meet at Hartford on October 20 to establish uniform prices. Both the time and place had been chosen to coax a reluctant Connecticut into attending, but the congressional requisition did away with most of the reluctance. Connecticut agreed at once with the convention's recommendation that a new meeting take place at Philadelphia the following January, to which delegates would come from states as far south as Virginia, again to fix uniform price regulations.[80] Though Connecticut's government still would not implement the partial rules adopted by the other New England states at the Hartford convention, she promised to observe any price regulation that became general.

None ever did, despite the support of Congress,[81] and just as well. Commissary agents had already felt the pinch of local regulations keenly enough to make them loathe the prospect of a general law. The imminent arrival of the French made matters worse for them. It spurred French purchasing agents to engage in competition with the commissary for scarce provision[82] at the same time as it rendered the commissary, armed with only a depreciating currency, unable to buy wheat at any price. Since the farmers knew that the French would increase the demand for grain and enable them to sell in exchange for imported goods, or for specie and bills of exchange on Europe, they refused to thresh until d'Estaing arrived.[83] Washington's call for militia to support d'Estaing made it clear that extraordinary measures were in order. Connecticut would have four thousand militia to feed, the largest quota of any state. The Assembly promptly apportioned the quantity of grain each town should supply, gave the town authorities a summary power to collect from individuals as they saw fit,[84] and even authorized an advance collection of one-third of the total. Not one bushel of grain was collected. No official dared risk the unpopularity with his fellow townsmen that would have followed an attempt to enforce the law. Twice in November the state ordered men to the coast in response to reports that concentrations of the enemy seemed to threaten an attack;[85] yet still the town authorities procrastinated on the grounds that they need not execute the law until the French arrived.[86]

The lack of grain that autumn exacerbated the rise in demand for cereals that always accompanied the seasonal decline in supplies of grass.[87] Other seasonal factors affected prices too; for example, winter cut the yields from privateering, though there is evidence that, for Connecticut at least, privateering had become less profitable in any and all weathers. The British, set back by d'Estaing's West Indian victories and Spain's entry into the war, grew cautious as Americans grew reckless.[88] But neither high prices nor shortages alone destroyed the currency. D'Estaing's defeat at Savannah and withdrawal to the West Indies dealt the final blow.

The news plunged Americans into despair. When Congress had decided in September to limit further emissions to $200 million, everyone knew that the nation's last hope for solvency lay in a sudden end to the war, or at least a massive reduction in the scale and expense of it. The inability of Congress to supply its purchasing agents with enough money that autumn gave an ominous warning of the rocks and shoals ahead.[89] And when the French failed at Savannah, all prospects of an immediate end to the war disappeared. There remained a chance that eventually the European powers would mediate a peace. Meanwhile, the revolutionaries had somehow to finance yet another campaign.[90]

Though the northern states did not hear of the French retreat until November, Americans had long known that the moment for a joint assault on New York was slipping past. Every day increased the risk that d'Estaing would be frozen in for the winter if he came on, a risk he would never take.[91] Besides this, the British were no longer so invitingly dispersed. The delay had allowed them time to concentrate their forces and fortify New York. In the last week of October, they abandoned their posts on the Hudson River and the position on Aquidneck Island.[92] Ordinarily, Connecticut would have rejoiced, but in the autumn of 1779 these withdrawals appeared to seal the fate of combined operations. By abandoning posts like Newport, the British substantially reinforced New York, bringing their effective troop strength to well over fifteen thousand. Americans knew it would take a force at least twice as large to attack them with any hope of success.[93] With the army already on short rations, how could the northern states maintain any such operation, let alone supply the French? If the government tried to do it by stripping the region of all resource, and if the attack then failed, disaster must follow.[94]

While all these uncertainties were helping to push prices up and up, the first rumors of d'Estaing's defeat sent the value of money hurtling down. On November 18 Colt told Wadsworth that "Merchants & others . . . were determined to exchange their *Square* Dolls for any kind of Produce." Again on November 24 he wrote that "People are running, or rather flying thro the Country, getting rid of their Cash at any rate."[95] With everyone afraid that the currency would collapse before they could convert it to goods, farmers would sell nothing but their perishable stuff and merchants would sell nothing unless "they [were] sure of immediately vesting the Mony in some other Articles of advantage."[96]

Congress had initially responded to the proceedings of the Hartford convention by suggesting that prices be fixed at 20:1 above their level in 1774, but Trumbull now demurred on the grounds that this would "reduce many articles near one half from their present price."[97] One might have expected the rapid drop in the value of money to produce a speculative demand for it. People still had to pay taxes, after all. Though some such activity did take place,[98] most people evidently decided that they stood to lose more by depreciation than by a tax collector's distraint on their goods. At a time when the value of commodities relative to currency had doubled within two months, the wise taxpayer would obviously delay his payments as long as he could.

Given this state of affairs, Congress could hardly expect its requisitions to be met on time even where money was plentiful. The plan to finance the war by orders on state treasuries was finished before it began;[99] not that the money would have made much difference, given the staggering debts accumulated by Continental purchasing agents that autumn which would have to be discharged before producers would sell to them again. Few people would exchange their produce for a promise to pay at some unspecified time in a rapidly depreciating medium—at least, not unless the goods were more perishable than the currency.[100] Some farmers would still sell stock, for instance, because to feed these animals made impossible demands on their supplies of forage. They also thought that the Philadelphia convention might soon agree on a general price limit and that they had better sell while they could still sell high. As Champion reported to Flint in January, "People are determined on no consideration whatsoever to have any fat cattle after the first day of February on hand either to sell at the limited price or to be taken from them for withholding." Champion used the threat of regulation along with the $200,000 that Congress had scraped together to continue through February purchasing cattle for Washington's army, an army reduced to desperation by its lack of supplies in what would prove to be the most savage winter of the war.[101] But this was a temporary expedient at best. A quixotic attempt to raise money by selling sterling bills of exchange on Europe met with almost no takers.[102] Depreciation so far outran all possible yields from requisitions that Congress, with no way to pay its debts, had no way to procure with consent.

Congress now turned to the state governments, not for the cash which they could not supply but for payment in kind. Precedents existed. Quite early in the war, Congress had given the states the responsibility for clothing the men in their lines. And in December of 1779, when the currency would no longer buy flour, Congress had requisitioned some states for wheat.[103] The requisition had marked a shift in the manner of conducting the war. In February 1780, Congress admitted that it had no more resource to fight with. If the struggle were to be sustained, that sustenance would have to come through the direct agency of the states. In a series of resolutions adopted on February 25, Congress laid the states under requisition for most of the supplies the army would need during the coming campaign and for commodities that Continental agents could barter with.

By such means Congress hoped to avail itself of whatever remaining surpluses the continent produced.[104]

Disarray

The bankruptcy of Congress came at a hard time for Connecticut. Her political system had begun to show signs of strain, as for instance in the increased turnover of representatives to the lower house of the legislature. In the four sessions preceding the outbreak of hostilities, 57 to 65 percent of the delegates were repeaters; that is, they had taken part in the preceding Assembly. Another 19 to 28 percent were returnees, or men with some previous experience as legislators. Only 9 to 17 percent were freshmen. In other words, though the people could change the whole composition of the lower house twice a year if they wished, the record shows an impressive continuity in the popular branch. The house elected in April 1775 deviated from this pattern in having a large number of freshmen (22 percent), but the expansion in their ranks occurred at the expense of returnees (17 percent) rather than repeaters (61 percent). From that point on, however, the number of repeaters declined until, by October 1776, they comprised less than half the new House. Nonetheless, they remained the largest component and continued to dominate the Assembly until 1779 (see Table 4).[105]

The declining number of repeaters in the early years of the war probably reflected the preference of the delegates. As the war turned honorific posts into toilsome duties, men willingly stepped down from the legislature when they found their other responsibilities growing heavier. The radical changes in the composition of the Assembly that began to occur in 1779 require further explanation. In April 1779, repeaters formed the smallest component of the newly elected House. At 30 percent, they were outnumbered by both returnees (38 percent) and freshmen (32 percent). So profound a change does suggest grass-roots dissatisfaction. The following autumn saw the pattern reversed again, so that repeaters were once more the largest component in the legislature. The election of April 1779,

TABLE FOUR
PERSISTENCE RATES IN THE CONNECTICUT
LOWER HOUSE, 1773–1784
(Percentage of total delegates by each category)

		Repeaters	*Returnees*	*Freshmen*
May	1773	65	26	9
October	1773	64	19	17
May	1774	58	26	16
October	1774	57	28	15
May	1775	61	17	22
October	1775	52	26	22
May	1776	54	33	13
October	1776	46	32	21
May	1777	43	29	25
October	1777	45	32	24
May	1778	43	35	22
October	1778	54	21	25
May	1779	30	38	32
October	1779	42	39	19
May	1780	36	34	30
October	1780	39	36	26
May	1781	37	38	25
October	1781	52	32	16
May	1782	38	42	20
October	1782	42	31	27
May	1783	48	41	11
October	1783	44	38	18
May	1784	47	44	9
October	1784	57	34	9

SOURCES: *CR*, vols. 14–15; *SR*, vols. 1–5. Compiled by John Barber.

however, marked the beginning of a period extending to May
1782 in which the number of repeaters in any House remained
(with two exceptions) below 40 percent. These figures record
an intense and peculiar pressure building up within Connecticut's political system between the end of 1778 and the spring of
1782.

Other signs of stress followed. In the early stages of the war, though Connecticut's military leaders did not always live in harmony with their Continental counterparts, no discord marred their relations with the state's civil leadership. The two had been closely linked during the late colonial period.[106] Though the war had begun to force a division of labor between the military and civil services, if it had ended in 1778 those functions would soon have regained their compatibility. Men like Samuel Holden Parsons and Gold Selleck Silliman, to name only two, would easily have resumed both their civilian and military roles. Certainly no military function would have precluded the achievement of civil eminence. After 1778, however, the conflict between officer and official steadily increased, with the public on the side of the civilian.

Competition for necessities often started the trouble. That autumn, for instance, Sheldon's men provoked a riot in Norwalk when their filching of grain caused a confrontation with local authorities.[107] Shortages also had something to do with the controversy over quarters for Stephen Moylan's dragoons during the winter of 1779–80. Washington had expressed a preference for housing the dragoons within easy reach of the infantry east of the Hudson, but he had also told Moylan that access to forage came first. If necessary, he said, the horse should move to Colchester where a magazine of forage had been constructed for them.[108] Moylan wanted to quarter the horse in Durham, Wallingford, and Haddam, towns that had already borne the burden of accommodating Continental horse the preceding winter. He quarreled over the matter with deputy quartermaster Nehemiah Hubbard of Middletown, who thought that the job of providing for the horse should not fall on the same small towns twice. Washington tactfully attempted to resolve the controversy by ordering Moylan's horse on to Colchester, but a heavy snow marooned them in Durham on January 14. Their presence led to a confrontation between the townspeople, egged on by James Wadsworth (the town's most prominent resident), and Moylan's men.[109]

Fear that the horse intended to settle down for the winter against the town's will had something to do with the incident, but other elements also entered in. Wadsworth's readiness to take umbrage may have originated in the rudeness shown him by a Continental officer at the Highlands in the preceding June.[110] Wadsworth emerged from the experience with an antipathy for the military that more than matched Moylan's indifference to civilians. And the role that Governor Trumbull now assumed cannot be attributed solely to anxiety over shortages. After Washington had quieted all controversy by ordering Moylan to Colchester, Trumbull gratuitously revived it with a blistering letter in which he told Moylan "not to trample upon, and butcher your *fellow countrymen*, but *their Enemies*." He went on to say that if he heard any further complaint of Moylan's conduct, he, Trumbull, would teach him by some less pacific mode than writing that "the civil authority is superior to the military. That I am Commanding officer—and not you."[111] Trumbull's intemperate letter, completely out of character for him, suggests that, like Wadsworth, he had projected other dissatisfactions onto this dispute.

We know that Trumbull resented Washington's decision on where the army would spend the winter. Now that Connecticut could no longer look for d'Estaing to come, she trembled for her safety. Her leadership still believed that the British concentrations at New York and western Long Island had orders to devastate the coast. In the preceding winter, the Connecticut and New Hampshire lines together with Moses Hazen's Canadian regiment (a total of roughly forty-five hundred men) had been quartered in the Danbury-Ridgefield area to cover the state against attack.[112] This winter, Trumbull wanted more. But though he appealed to Washington for additional support from the Continental army,[113] Washington had sent the entire Connecticut line to the west of the Hudson. He remembered the past year's mutiny and suspected that, left within reach of home, the three-year enlistees might desert. Their departure left less than one thousand men from the New Hampshire line to guard the Connecticut coast. Washington assured Trumbull that, since he meant to keep the enemy at New York under constant pressure from roving parties drawn from the larger force in the Highlands, the coast would have less need of protection;[114] but that was cold comfort.

As it happened, the severe weather that year and the large detachment of British troops that left New York for the South in December removed much of Connecticut's alarm on that score,[115] so that Trumbull's outburst against Moylan did not stem solely from fear. Trumbull, like James Wadsworth, had begun to show a dislike for the military in and for itself. General discontent with the course of the war had produced a hostility to the army which permeated all ranks of Connecticut society. Trumbull was on occasion the victim of it: witness the memorial that complained of the high-handed way in which Lieutenant Colonel Jonathan Dimon, acting under orders from Oliver Wolcott, had treated those who asked William S. Johnson to intercede with the enemy. The memorial, filed by the authorities of Stratford and Fairfield, objected to the power that Dimon claimed "to arrest our fellow Citizens," to detain them without trial, and to place them "under Parole Engagements of a severe and Extraordinary nature." It also denounced the governor and Council of Safety for sanctioning arbitrary procedures which led to the passage of unjust and unlawful judgments.[116] The lower house refused to defend Trumbull's action, which left only the assistants to endorse his reply.[117] The deputies plainly shared the feelings of many of the people that more blame attached to the government and the army than to those charged. If the town of Stratford could have looked confidently to the state for its defense, no one would have sought Johnson's help.[118]

Civilian antimilitarism justified itself on the ground that the army endangered the purity of society. The clergy had pointed the way with their theory that God had prolonged the war to punish sin.[119] Where they saw sin as most manifest in everyday business transactions,[120] the people preferred to blame the military. The profanity of camp language and the indecent behavior of certain officers lent plausibility to their claims. In December 1778, the authority and selectmen of Greenwich complained to the General Assembly that Roger

Enos, commander of a state regiment, had sanctioned the destruction of local property, beaten a town representative to the General Assembly, and conducted an illicit relationship with a woman of dubious loyalty. A similar complaint, filed by sixteen people, protested the election of Michael Grant as captain of Torrington's militia company in 1779. The complaint vilified Grant as a corrupt, profane, lewd man (one deposition cited an occasion when he had threatened to take down his britches in the town meeting) who would corrupt the young.[121] In both cases, the legislature decided to retain the officers accused. But the presence of such men in positions of military authority, together with the steady rise in violent crime that accompanied the prolongation of the war, confirmed (not without reason) the popular prejudice against the army as an agency of brutalization and moral degradation.[122]

Besides the tension building between the civil and military leaderships in 1779, another snag broke the smooth surface of Connecticut's political system. Until then, the deputies and the assistants had avoided being paralyzed by intractable disagreements, always a danger in bicameral government. The Council of Safety, which represented both branches of the legislature, had always adjusted any dispute between them. In the spring of 1779, however, they became locked in long, tedious wrangles over many and various matters. Some of the issues, like that of whether the state should make up her deficiencies in Continental quota by drafting from her troops of horse, revealed social antagonisms inflamed by war weariness. The people regarded the horse as the refuge of the privileged: only the rich could equip themselves with mounts and accoutrements, and because the animals added to the pressure on forage Washington seldom called on them. In 1779, when the upper house wanted a draft law that would fill the 800 deficiencies in the Continental quota, the lower house insisted that 150 of the draftees come from the horse. They could serve either in the militia or in Sheldon's dragoons, but service with the dragoons would require "furnishing their own horses, arms and accoutrements."[123] The upper house at first opposed the proposal, fearing that it would lead to the dissolution of troops of state horse. To judge from the vehement resistance to such a draft in Ashford, it might have done so had not the lower house eventually consented to a compromise that lessened the percentage of horse drafted and raised that of infantry.[124]

An even lengthier dispute arose over who should sit on the Council of Safety and represent the state in Congress. Titus Hosmer's resignation from the congressional delegation in April brought the outgoing House into conflict with the assistants about whether to replace him with Jedediah Strong or with Oliver Wolcott.[125] The issue was still unresolved a month later, when the new House met. By that time the growing antagonism of civilians to the military had apparently produced agreement that members of the Council of Safety would not simultaneously hold high military office.[126] When illness forced Jabez Huntington to resign as first major general,[127] the office should have passed to James Wadsworth of Durham. Though Wadsworth had a place in the Council, everyone expected him to choose the military over the civilian post. Instead Wadsworth chose to resign his commission.[128] The legislature then appointed Joseph Spencer, dropped from the Council, to take Wadsworth's place, with Oliver Wolcott as his second-in-command. Jonathan Trumbull, Jr., now became of the assistants' choice for Hosmer's place in Congress, but he lost to Strong. As clerk of the House, Strong commanded immense influence there. The assistants disliked his election, though, and yielded only when the lower house agreed to a new law providing that in the future the people would choose the congressional delegation.[129]

The lower house did not think the demand unreasonable. The legislative appointment of congressional delegates had been controversial since October 1775, when the Assembly had taken over the job from the Committee of Correspondence.[130] Throughout the first half of 1776, the public prints had energetically debated the proposition that the people themselves should elect their representatives. Popular bodies such as a convention of Litchfield County committees of inspection endorsed the proposition; political insiders like Oliver Wolcott opposed it.[131] By 1779 an influential group of insiders, who had become impatient with the inadequate policies of Congress, had also come to favor popular election. They saw it as the only way to purge the Connecticut delegation of men sponsored by the assistants whose policies jeopardized the war effort. Jeremiah Wadsworth's commissary connection had begun to think and speak of Sherman, Dyer, and Oliver Ellsworth as the "old junto" because Congress's financial policies would soon make procurement impossible.[132]

The new law directed that the freemen at their September meetings should nominate twelve men to represent the state in Congress. In the following April, they would choose seven from the twelve who had received the most nominations. From the seven, the legislature would then choose two to four men as Connecticut's delegates to Congress. The legislature also had the power to fill vacancies in the delegation caused by "death, resignation, refusal, or revocation" or by any delay in executing the established procedures.[133] Wolcott had earlier argued that selection by the Assembly would safeguard the liberties of the people more than their own enfranchisement because the state government could not control representatives once they were invested with the sovereignty of the people.[134] The express declaration in the new arrangement that delegates must account to the legislature for their actions indicated that Wolcott had been heard. And the assistants undoubtedly thought that the procedures which had ensured their tenure in the state's highest offices would now favor their election as delegates to Congress.

In October, the lower house insisted that the freemen no longer vote on candidates in order of seniority, as the Council desired, but in order of votes received. As a result, the two houses of the legislature deadlocked over the order in which to list nominees. For a while it looked as if the power to select the delegates would return to the legislators alone: in other words, as if the new election law would be effectively void. In order to break the deadlock, the upper house even suggested either that the old delegation return unchanged to Congress or that the five men both houses found acceptable, excluding Dyer and Sherman, receive the designation.[135] The lower house would not jettison the new law so casually, and indicated that if the upper house did not cooperate the state might go unrepresented by anyone. The secretary of state also refused to send out nominations on his own authority. Faced with such resistance, the assistants backed down. Their acceptance of the order desired by the lower house led, as everyone had thought it would, to the election in April of the seven top names on the list.[136] Four of the seven delegates remained assistants, and three had previously represented the state in Congress. Once again Connecticut's representation continued with a minimum of change. But the seed of electioneering had been planted and would bear fruit come April. Trumbull failed for the first time in ten years to obtain an electoral majority.[137] And his son-in-law, William Williams, lost the assistantship through the intrigues of an enclave in Windham County that held Trumbull and Williams, both outspoken critics of price-fixing, personally responsible for the misery that followed from the collapse of the currency.[138]

Reviving the Marketplace

Connecticut's political system reached this point of disarray just when she had to confront the consequences of national bankruptcy. Like the other states, Connecticut had to supply the army and also to find replacements for the three-year men of the Connecticut line whose time was almost up; that is, for 48 percent of the long-term enlistees recruited in the spring and summer of 1777 (Table 3). In February Congress decided to reduce the total establishment to 36,211 and, perhaps to balance off its heavy financial demands, to ask Connecticut for only 9 percent or 2,238 men. Congress also offered to credit the states with men whose term of army service ran to September 30, 1780, those in the irregular regiments as well as those in the line,[139] which left Connecticut with only 1,569 men to supply.[140] But the bankruptcy of Congress forced Connecticut to make an unpleasant choice of ways to meet even these reduced obligations. She could employ coercion in the form of taxation and the draft, or she could try to reconstitute the marketplace on her own initiative. Coercion had never yet worked, and the political system was so shaky that the leadership did not want to put any more pressure on it.

When the October legislature adjourned, it had taken the precaution of planning to meet again in January 1780.[141] Though the principal measures enacted that autumn had assumed d'Estaing's arrival, combined operations, and a sudden end to the war, the delegates knew that these hopes were not certainties. Severe weather in early January prevented the collection of a quorum for two weeks, but then the legislature moved at once to make plans for recruitment. Long before Washington announced Connecticut's quota, the legislature called for 1,800 men to be raised by voluntary enlistment. As part of that effort, Colonel John Chandler, armed with $200,000, visited the winter cantonment of the Connecticut line to ask the three-year men to reenlist. The Assembly added $300 to the $200 bounty offered by Congress to those who enlisted for the duration and instructed the treasurer to pay all orders drawn by recruiting officers.[142]

Only if the ranks were not filled by April were recruiters to resort to preemptory detachment, and the legislators devoutly hoped it would never be necessary. They tried every means to avoid it. They empowered the Council of Safety to offer whatever bounty seemed reasonable in order to attract nine-month recruits. They resolved one obstacle to a settling of accounts between the army and the state by agreeing that they owed the Connecticut line some adjustment for depreciation in the last half of 1777. They knew, however, that all these concessions might not suffice to attract volunteers and sought to sweeten the pill of coercion in case they should have to administer it. They decided to extend the offer of wages at guaranteed value not only to volunteers but also to draftees.[143]

Though these measures showed some recognition that the state would have to work at recruitment, they incorporated no new policy but continued to assume that the incentives of the marketplace could be maintained by increasing the sums offered in exchange. Unfortunately, the depreciation of the preceding three months had so eroded people's confidence in the money that the Assembly could not rebuild it by offering more of the same. Nor would it help to put all the blame for the trouble on the Quartermaster and Commissary departments.[144] The crash had come, and only a radical approach could save the marketplace. In the preceding autumn, when the currency had first collapsed, Trumbull and a small circle of friends had sketched one in outline.

Trumbull wanted to retain the currency as "a legal tender to all intents & purposes," provided that nominal value was not allowed "to drown the idea of intrinsic worth." Using "this *substitute* for money as it ought to be used, measuring it by some real standard," it would be possible to "make good all contracts equal to the value contracted" by allowing "the quantity tendered [to] make up the want of quality or value." In other words, real value would be measured on a depreciation scale.[145] The plan had obvious merits. It would reduce the huge nominal debt contracted by Congress, which in itself raised insuperable obstacles to the establishment of public credit. By recognizing the fictitiousness of nominal value, it also offered a way to avoid the perils of appreciation. Thus, it addressed the problems of debtors as well as creditors. Without a stable currency, however, it would never work. If the value of money went on declining, holders would continue to lose; if it appreciated, nonholders would suffer.

The government could stabilize the value of money only by diminishing the quantity. The problem was how to diminish quantity without causing a disastrous appreciation. In January the General Assembly came up with an ingenious scheme to avert appreciation by pegging Continental money to specie. They proposed to issue £40,000 in bills of credit, bearing 5 percent interest from March 1780 and redeemable in specie in March 1784. To support the value of this emission, they levied a sixpenny tax on the list of 1782, payable in specie or the new state emission and due in January 1784. Having provided (as they hoped) a cushion of specie equivalents, the Assembly called in the Continental money by two routes. It opened a loan for $2.3 million in Continental currency at 30:1, paying 6 percent and maturing in six years. Since investors must subscribe to the loan in minimum quantities of $600, which would be exchanged for "bank notes" from the treasury of no less than twenty pounds specie, the Assembly did not expect the bank notes to have wide circulation. And it hoped to draw in all the continental money that remained with a levy of three twelve-shilling taxes on the list of 1778, due in April, June, and November, payable in specie or new state emissions or Continental currency at 30:1.[146]

The three twelve-shilling taxes brought the total in 1780 to thirty-six shillings, eightpence, on the assessed pound, exclusive of town and society rates. Fully collected, they would have yielded $10.75 million. The Assembly raised two hedges against the appreciation that could conceivably follow so massive a withdrawal of currency: all but $3.5 million could be reissued to meet either state or Continental expenses,[147] and people could pay taxes in specie, new state emissions, or state bank notes, if they had no Continental bills. Two currencies pegged to a fixed value at which they were acceptable in payment of taxes meant in theory that if continentals rose above par (defined as 30:1), people would find it cheaper to pay in specie or its equivalents. That would force up the value of specie as it was withdrawn from circulation. If, on the other hand, specie rose higher than Continental currency, people would pay in paper and force its value up. For tax demands to succeed in maintaining the fixed ratio, and therefore the currency, of both media without a drastic appreciation, the government would have to ensure sufficient quantities of both in circulation, each in due proportion to the other. The Assembly could do this by emitting more specie equivalents or reissuing continentals, as the occasion warranted.

Congress also sought to preserve a money economy. The requisition in kind approved on February 25 had merely forgiven the states two-thirds of their obligation in return for supplies.[148] It did not and could not wholly abandon the requirement for money: someone had to pay for transporting supplies from the states to the army. Immediately after it passed the requisition, Congress began to debate various plans to retire Continental money through taxation and to issue a new currency bearing interest at 5 percent, both principal and interest redeemable in specie in seven years. Two-thirds of the new bills would be issued to each loan office at the rate of one for every twenty-five old ones, "to enable [the states] to purchase their quotas of supplies for carrying on the war." The several state legislatures would be asked to raise funds for both the payment of interest and the retirement of the principal through six annual taxes, payable in new bills or specie. This would put the new emissions on a par with specie. To hedge against depreciation, no more than $12 million would circulate.[149]

Such was the plan that Congress adopted on March 18, 1780, though with a few superficial changes. The preamble admitted that the Continental bills had "by common consent" sunk "at least 39-40ths below their nominal value," and in order to arrest the process the states were asked to continue calling them in at $15 million a month until April 1781. By that time, none should remain in circulation. Some features of the plan were designed to prevent an appreciation of the old currency. Specie could pass at a ratio of 1:40 in satisfaction of all claims, and so could the new emission that the states would exchange for the old continentals at 1:20. Other features were designed to protect the new emission from depreciation. Since all Continental money that came into state treasuries after February would be destroyed, the quantity of new bills issued would not exceed $10 million. The "funds provided for their redemption, the shortness of the period, and the payment of annual interest" provided additional safeguards. Congress even pledged "the faith of the United States" as a guarantee for payment of the bills, "in case any State on whose funds they shall be emitted, should, by the events of war, be rendered incapable to redeem them."[150]

The plan as it had evolved by the middle of March had much to recommend it. Though the states were responsible for funding the currency, six-tenths of the total was for their use and the remainder for army wages. The states could implement the plan without excessive taxation by allowing holders of the old money to exchange it for the new. In this way, Congress hoped to provide a stable medium for trade. Of course, to retire the old currency by exchanging it for new would place it in the hands of individuals rather than governments, which would not help the states either collect supplies for the army or raise recruits. Nevertheless, the option to exchange rather than to tax meant that, whatever other obstacles arose, the plan would not founder on its own too harsh demands.[151]

In several respects, the plan drawn up by Congress must have struck the Connecticut legislators as inferior to their own. Congress pegged Continental money lower in March than Connecticut had done in January. In adhering to the quotas set in the October requisition, Congress in effect asked Connecticut to take responsibility for more than her fair share of the total Continental currency. Connecticut had no discretion to adjust the supply of new emissions to Continental bills. The quotas Congress assigned, together with the requirement that the old emission be destroyed, eliminated that possibility. On the other hand, the plan did not differ so much from Connecticut's as to prevent an adjustment of one to the other. Besides, it had the advantage of being national rather than parochial and thus more congruent with wartime patterns of commerce.

In April, the Connecticut legislature reluctantly but dutifully drafted the recommendations of Congress into law. Since Congress had made the state responsible for $22.1 million of the old Continental currency, or $1.1 million of the new emission, the legislature had to lay six sevenpenny taxes, due in specie equivalents at the end of each year from 1781 to 1786, in order to retire her share of the new currency. This was the equivalent of fourteen shillings a year on the pound in old continentals. Mercifully, the taxpayer had a twelve-month grace before that burden would descend upon him. In the immediate future loomed the October requisition, compliance with which required that the state withdraw continentals at the rate of six shillings a month on the pound. The twelve-shilling taxes, due in April, June, and November, would provide for six months of the requisition, but in September an additional twelve-shilling tax had to be collected.[152] And two twelve-shilling levies would be necessary in November and December, bringing the total due in 1780 to sixty shillings, eightpence.

Though the congressional scheme laid burdens on Connecticut, it promised benefits too. For instance, those who had exchanged the old continentals for the new state currency at 30:1 would receive the new emission, worth forty old bills, without paying a premium. It also gave the legislature an excuse to try again to fill the Continental battalions by voluntary enlistment rather than by the draft scheduled for April. During March, there had been virtually no takers for the Assembly's offer of $300 added to the Continental bounty of $200 that would be paid to all who enlisted for the duration. Everyone had known that Congress could not pay $200 in the first place, and furthermore that Connecticut money might have little value outside the state, where the troops would do most of their service. But the creation of a new national currency presumably solved the problem of value elsewhere, and the legislature could compensate for the poverty of Congress by increasing its own bounty.

The legislature therefore proceeded to double its bounty to $600, or £4.10s. in new currency, together with a suit of clothes, and to reduce the time of service to eighteen months, provided a man enlisted before June 1.[153] It no longer guaranteed the value of wages, but theoretically the new scheme rendered that unnecessary. And as the tax burden grew heavier, the exemption from the lists enjoyed by all recruits became in itself a strong, if negative, incentive. Although in May 1779 the Assembly had halved the poll tax on that part of the population from which the army drew most of its men, [154] the majority of the taxes due in 1780 had been assessed on the lists of 1778.

In only one respect did Connecticut refuse to follow the recommendations of Congress, but it was a significant divergence. At the end of 1779, Congress voted to place the commissary and quartermaster's departments, whose administration many held responsible for the collapse of the currency, "under the superintendency and direction of the Board of War."[155] In an effort to cut the costs of procurement by cutting the commissions paid to purchasers, Congress proposed to put the commissary general on salary and to allow the assistant commissaries 2 percent "on twenty fold the prices" that commodities had fetched in 1774.[156] Congress also tried to jettison Wadsworth's tightly centralized system by making the commissary general no more than a coordinator of state-appointed assistant commissaries. Connecticut, however, refused to appoint an assistant commissary because the commission was too small "to make any reasonable compensation for the trouble of business."[157] With the government's approval, Wadsworth and his assistants continued working informally to alleviate recurrent shortages, until at last the April session of the legislature made other arrangements for procuring the rum, meat, salt, and hay that Congress had requisitioned.[158]

Hope Disappointed

In ideal circumstances, even Connecticut's limited implementation of the congressional plan might have helped to remobilize the society's resources. Ideal circumstances, alas, did not exist in the spring of 1780. Though for a time the only military pressure on Connecticut came from loyalist raiders on the southwestern border, she found it a struggle to maintain control on even that small front. In January, the legislature had made an arrangement for the defense of the southwest that looked entirely adequate on paper. It authorized the enlistment of 692 coast guards and two state regiments, each to consist of 544 men, in addition to sending 200 men into Greenwich on rotation.[159] But at the beginning of May, when the legislature hoped to have 600 men stationed there, Colonel John Mead alleged that he still had to sneak about like a fugitive in order to avoid capture, and Gold Selleck Silliman, recently returned from a year of captivity, echoed his complaints.[160] Food shortages presented the major obstacle to recruitment. The men would not serve unless they were fed, and a thriving barter trade was diverting provisions, particularly flour, to the east. The government's inland embargo proved ineffectual despite the resolves of many northern and eastern towns against the illegal exportation of provisions,[161] and the new commissary general's order to break up the Continental depots at New

Haven, Fairfield, Norwalk, and Greenwich only aggravated the shortages. The order was held in abeyance until Connecticut could make independent provision for her coast guards, [162] but this concession meant nothing in a place like Horseneck, for instance, where the Continental store already stood empty.

The measures that Connecticut had instituted in order to recruit replacements for the army produced equally poor results. Between April and June, eighteen persons joined the Connecticut line.[163] On this occasion, the lack of response could not be altogether blamed on the frequent militia alarms or on the competition between state and Continental needs that had interfered with earlier recruitment drives. For once, the legislature had offered sufficient incentives to outweigh any prejudice against the Continental service. True, the decision that only Continental recruits would receive a bounty was not generally known until April, since the legislature only then published the relevant laws, and the General Assembly simultaneously introduced a two-dollar bounty for recruits to state regiments. Nevertheless, the bounty for state service remained less than half the amount offered for Continental service.[164] If competition caused the low recruitment, it was not competition between the state and Continental lines but competition between the attractions of privateering and any kind of military service. In the preceding year, privateers had taken an unusually rich haul, and the Assembly had let them recruit at will up to May.[165] But even privateering had less to do with the failure of recruitment than the widespread knowledge that the army lacked food and clothing.

Washington did not, of course, advertise the hardships his army had suffered during the early months of 1780. The people of Connecticut knew of them through other channels. They could see for themselves, or they could hear firsthand reports about the sorry state of Enoch Poor's New Hampshire brigade in the Ridgefield-Danbury region and how the hunger of his men had driven him to seize flour unlawfully. They also knew that the dragoons wintering at Colchester had refused a government request for a detachment to march west because they had insufficient clothing to fit out the men.[166] These and other harrowing accounts of the army's destitution were spread by many mouths. The recruits for the duration who returned home on winter furlough; discharged three-year men; those who had deserted; the drayers and carters who had traveled to and from the camp during the spring, all helped to carry the tale.

As the weeks passed, and the start of the campaign drew closer, food supplies dwindled still more. Soldiers in the main camp at Morristown had existed for months on one-eighth of their meat ration when, at the end of May, the supply gave out entirely. At that point two regiments of the Connecticut line mutinied.[167] Though the mutiny flickered out and the government tried to smother all report of it, the news nevertheless traveled across the country by the same route as the news that the commissary could not keep the army in food and clothing. And everyone knew that few of the soldiers could buy their necessities themselves, since they had never been paid. As June approached, the desperate condition of the army was so widely known that the most optimistic patriot could not reasonably expect men to join it by voluntary enlistment. Only a draft would fill the ranks now.[168]

At this unpromising moment, Connecticut received a message that a large expeditionary force, on its way from France to America, would arrive in Rhode Island at any moment. The French agent, John Holker, already pestering Connecticut for the grain requisitioned by Congress in December, began to press for additional supplies.[169] Given the unfortunate effect of the French presence on New England's economy in 1778, not to mention the damage that the mere possibility of their return had done in 1779, the leadership might well see the new prospect as a mixed blessing. Any addition to American forces must be welcomed, particularly when the Continental army had lost nearly half its manpower; on the other hand, a French expedition that did not succeed in ending the war could ruin the economy once and for all. This time Congress requisitioned the states from Virginia to New Hampshire for $10 million in Continental money to help support the French, and again it asked Connecticut to bear a proportionately heavier burden than any other state.[170]

Since 1778, however, some auspicious differences had appeared in the economic picture. The French would no longer
be one of four armies making demands on a hard-pressed region
but only one of two. Washington's army, shrunk to a third of
its former size, was now bivouacked mostly to the west of the
Hudson. The region itself enjoyed more comfortable circumstances. In 1780 New England had suffered no recent damage
from the enemy and approached its harvest season with fewer
men absent on army service than at any time since 1776. The
farmers might fail to produce because they lacked incentive but
not because they lacked ability. And the French could provide
them with incentive in the form of specie and bills of exchange
on France.

In earlier years, the preference for French specie and bills
of exchange had raised prices in relation to the domestic currency, which compounded the national economic problem.[171]
The French gave indications, however, that they would try not
to repeat this unfortunate pattern. In a show of support for the
attempts of Congress and the states to introduce currencies
equal to specie, they offered to exchange their specie and bills
for new money, with which they proposed to buy local produce. Thus, Holker accompanied a large requisition for draft
animals, flour, and cider with bills of exchange amounting to
80,000 livres, which Connecticut could use either to pay directly for the commodities desired or to repay herself for the
state currency spent to meet his demands. And Louis de
Corny, the French commissary, asked the state to lend him
$20,000 in state currency with which he could buy local pro-
duce, on the understanding that he would repay the money in
specie when the fleet arrived.[172] Through such gestures, the
French tried to show that this time they intended to put their
procurement on the same footing as American procurement,
not to compete with it as before.

Problems remained, nevertheless. There was no centralized American commissariat with which the French could cooperate, only state commissaries under the nominal direction of a
federal administrator, Ephraim Blaine. The French resolved
that difficulty by appealing to Connecticut while the Assembly

was in session. Wadsworth had won a seat, despite the opposition to him at the April freemen's meeting in Hartford, and had acquired considerable authority among his fellow members. We do not know exactly what happened, since the journals for this meeting of the Assembly have disappeared. But we know that the legislature refused to supply the French, though Wadsworth agreed to act as their agent in procuring the supplies they wanted from the state.[173] He undoubtedly reasoned that, if they were not fed, they might abandon combined operations and perhaps the alliance too. Even so, Wadsworth could not work miracles. The people would have to cooperate, but the people's morale remained low. Just before the arrival of Rochambeau's expeditionary force, Jedediah Huntington wondered whether, when the French perceived the "langour of the Country," they might "stay [only] long enou' to cast a Look of Chagrin and Pity and turn upon their Heals."[174]

In June, however, the fall of Charleston roused the northern states from "langour." The news that five thousand men had surrendered arrived at almost the same time as a report that one hundred ships carrying a large detachment of troops from the South had come in at New York. The latter report proved premature; nevertheless, it raised a fear that Clinton would use any reinforcements he did receive to attack the Highlands. Only two thousand men were there to defend the posts,[175] though a congressional committee formed to assess the state of the army had said that the Highlands must remain in American hands if combined operations with the French were to succeed. How else could the two armies join forces, or the French receive supplies?[176] If the British took the Highlands and divided the allies, the war would continue indefinitely and the people lose heart. The time had come for a supreme effort to end it.[177]

On this occasion, Congress reduced the demand that it placed on Connecticut. Besides filling out her reduced Continental quota, the state had only to raise 2,520 three-month men by July 15.[178] The May legislature responded dutifully. Each militia brigade received a quota. The heaviest demand fell upon the Second and Fourth brigades, probably because the government wanted to spare harvest laborers elsewhere. The state offered any man who enlisted before July 5, if fully equipped, a bounty of £4.10s., or, if not equipped, a bounty of £3. In other words, it offered almost as much for three months of militia service as the April session of the legislature had offered to Continental recruits for eighteen months. If a man could not provide his own equipment, the selectmen in his town must do it for him. If the full complement were not made up by July 5, immediate and preemptory detachment must supply the deficiency. Detachees could still qualify for two-thirds of the bounty by enlisting within three days.[179]

The legislature also ordered preemptory detachments from the Second and Sixth brigades, each of 192 men, to fill out the two state regiments in two-month rotations. To this it added a detachment of one company of dragoons on the same terms. Lastly, the legislature prepared to raise 1,500 six-month men for the army, if not by voluntary enlistment then by preemptory detachment. Of these, 1,274 would come from the infantry according to quotas designed to allow for the number of men from each town already in the army. The remaining 276 would come from the horse. A volunteer would receive ten pounds for six months service if he provided his own blanket, six pounds if he did not; and again, a detachee qualified for a four-pound bounty if he enlisted voluntarily.[180]

To pay these bounties in addition to procuring supplies for both the French and American forces obliged the legislature to find new ways and means. And a delay in the printing and shipping of the new Continental emissions meant that the ways and means would have to include an increase in the state emission. The legislature decided to issue on state credit £150,000 bearing 5 percent interest and redeemable for specie in four to five years. This would raise the total of new state emissions to £190,000 or $632,700. According to the congressional plan, the state should simultaneously withdraw twenty times that sum in continentals, or $12 million, roughly $3 million more than Connecticut owed by congressional requisition from March through July. The legislature decided to make up the difference by overpaying the requisition of May 19 to a corresponding amount. To this end, it ordered immediate collection of a tax at thirteen shillings, fourpence, on the list of 1779, rather than the four shillings, twopence, that would have sufficed. The legislature also forbade the payment of any further warrants on the state treasury for Continental money. This measure both protected the treasury from the massive warrants drawn by Congress and facilitated the substitution of the new emission for Continental bills.[181]

Anyone familiar with the difficulties of raising a military force could see one serious flaw in the Assembly's plan to meet the manpower requisitions of Congress. By granting the three-month men the same bounty as the six-month continentals, the Assembly made the short-term service preferable in every way. Washington found this unacceptable. Combined operations against New York would probably last some time, and he needed the army at full complement more than he needed three-month men. When he heard of the legislature's plan, he sent Parsons to Connecticut at once.

Parsons felt the importance of his errand keenly enough not to linger in the Highlands, though the threat of attack hung over them.[182] Even so, he arrived just after the legislature adjourned. But within a week he had persuaded a reluctant Council of Safety to deviate from the legislature's policy so far as to order that 1,000 more men be detached for the six-month service. The Council obviously felt uneasy about the business. The members insisted that a "full Council" join in making the decision and claimed that Washington, together with the Committee of Congress, had said that 1,000 more six-month men were "indispensably necessary . . . to render successful the operations of the present campaign." In fact Parsons had made that statement, which Washington had only indirectly endorsed. The Council was prepared to stretch its authority to the limit because the members believed that to throw away the opportunity for combined operations would be to throw away the whole revolutionary cause.[183]

How the people would respond to the government's appeal for men and provisions remained to be seen. Clinton's return to New York on June 17 complicated the manpower problem. Washington assumed that Clinton's intelligence would report the weakness of the Highlands to him and that he might attack at any moment. On June 18 Washington told Trumbull to have between two and three thousand militia standing by to relieve West Point in case of attack.[184] On the nineteenth, Major General Robert Howe, then commanding in the Highlands, alarmed by the passage of several British warships to Verplanck's Point, called on Connecticut for assistance.[185]

The Council of Safety immediately detached 3,000 men from the four western brigades and ordered them, together with Levi Wells's state regiment, then stationed on the southwest frontier, to the Highlands.[186] On June 23, however, probably upon hearing that Clinton had invaded New Jersey, the Council called a halt. Apart from other considerations, the Council thought that for so large a force to arrive at the post unnecessarily would increase the drain on its precious store of provisions without any return by way of essential service.[187] But when Howe received word that Washington refused to send him Continental reinforcements, he told the militia to ignore the Council and march on. Not until the twenty-seventh did Washington intervene. Seeing how a detachment of that size would obstruct the completion of the army, he dismissed the men himself. At the same time, since Clinton had just withdrawn from New Jersey, he reinforced Howe with a detachment of continentals.[188]

As the false alarm of June inconvenienced the western brigades, so a similar incident in July threw the eastern brigades into confusion. The First Division of Rochambeau's expeditionary force arrived in Newport on July 10. At almost the same moment, Admiral Arbuthnot received from England a reinforcement of six ships of the line under Samuel Graves, ships with more firepower than the seven commanded by Commodore Ternay. The French troops arrived weak and sickly, not an uncommon response to the long period of close confinement and poor diet entailed in crossing the Atlantic, and Clinton saw his advantage. He promptly positioned a superior naval force in Block Island Sound, assembled transports able to carry seven thousand men at Huntington, and prepared to dislodge the French before they could receive reinforcements.[189]

When news of the impending attack reached William Heath, American commander in the area, he called in all the militia from Rhode Island together with some from Massachusetts. Governor William Greene of Rhode Island went one step further and appealed for reinforcements from Connecticut. On July 27 Connecticut's Council of Safety detached half of the militia in the four eastern brigades for service in Rhode Island.[190] But only Douglas's brigade received their marching orders, and by a mistake at that since the Council had not sanctioned them. At it happened, neither Rochambeau nor Heath had wanted the Connecticut militia at all. They knew that the demand these men would make on the region's dwindling stores of food would probably outweigh any advantage their added numbers would confer. The Council of Safety kept them back more than gladly: after all, Clinton might attack New London instead.[191] The men, however, felt confused and demoralized, a state of mind that did nothing to promote an eager response to the government's latest manpower demands, though it did less harm than the growing fear that service in the army led inevitably to destitution.

The government could no longer offer incentives great enough to overcome the general distaste for all forms of military service. Scarcity of food had made the state organizations as unpopular as the Continental line. Militia commanders in coastal towns could not keep even the coast guards up to the number needed. The men would not stay at their posts with neither provisions nor pay. Those who were stationed too far away for their families to help them simply went home; those better situated hired themselves out in other callings. Between the lack of proper food and the rising incidence of enemy raids, the coast guard, once considered the easiest of services, lost its attraction.[192] So did the state regiments. The General Assembly's draft of 192 men for each regiment implied that in May they were already two-thirds along to completion, yet by the end of June one regiment still had only 133 men or 24 percent of its complement. In August, when the time came to replace the first rotation of two-month men, the government offered a bounty of three pounds to any who would serve out the year. It also ordered a new draft of 250 men for each state regiment, indicating that they had reached at most only half of their complement.[193]

The little information we have suggests that this time the yields on the Continental draft were slightly higher than for the other services. Between July 15 and August 16, Connecticut supplied Washington with 1,356 six-month men. By the end of September, the total exceeded 1,700, reaching almost 70 percent of the goal the Council of Safety had set. Though still 800 men short, the Continental ranks had filled faster than the state regiments.[194] We have less information about the 1,510 three-month men. Trumbull said that by the end of August 800 men detached from the First, Second, Third, and Fifth brigades in the central and eastern parts of the state had collected in the towns on the lower Connecticut River. Since we know that the three-month men drawn from western Connecticut numbered only 412 by late August, we may doubt the precision of this claim. Still, assuming that the number of troops from central and eastern Connecticut did exceed those from the west, the state seems to have mustered at least 60 percent of its quota of three-month men.[195]

The prejudice against the Continental service waned precisely as serious disorders began to plague the militia. In the spring and summer of 1780, the legislature for the first time confronted a rash of insubordination charges against officers who would not execute orders to draft their men. One case, concerning several captains of the horse who had earlier balked at a demand that they contribute to the Continental service, might be dismissed as an isolated protest against the loss of aristocratic privilege,[196] save that by 1780 the same disobedience had infected officers of the foot. A mild example is Captain John Skinner's complaint that a sergeant in his company not only refused to detach a man but sent his command back to him scribbled with the words: "John Skinner Your orders are not worthy of my notice."[197] The refusals of Captain Benjamin Wright and Lieutenant Solomon Bulkley had more serious implications. Bulkley, for instance, said openly that he would not comply because the legislature had set an unfair quota for his town.[198] Nor were charges of insubordination the only ones laid against officers. The legislature also faced an unusually high number of complaints about the election of company officers who were disaffected and about officers who abused their authority.[199]

Considering the circumstances, it is remarkable that Connecticut succeeded in delivering as many men as she did to the Continental service during 1780. The explanation is found in the records of town meetings for the period. They indicate that towns voted, one after another, to offer special bounties for enlistment in the Continental service that summer. Sometimes they appointed committees authorized to borrow all the money they would need in order to hire the town's quota of men for the various services;[200] sometimes they specified the bounties to be paid, grading the sums to correlate with the time served. Milford offered seventy pounds to anyone who enlisted for the duration, six pounds for six months, or three pounds for three months. It considered offering one pound to each man who answered a militia alarm but quickly thought better of that.[201] New Haven offered twelve pounds for a year's service, and £4.10s. for three months.[202] Most of the towns did not have the money in hand to pay the bounties offered and had to lay special rates for their collection. Recruits had to wait and trust in the town's promise. Many towns agreed to pay bounties in kind; that is, in commodities like wheat; others required that recruits pass on to them any bounties received from the state in return for the generous terms offered locally.[203] Nevertheless, the surviving brigade returns of 1780 show that most of the men who did in fact serve had been recruited by their towns.

Only where a town refused to act did the militia receive orders to detach, most notably in the Fourth Brigade of southwestern Connecticut where the towns were either beset by other problems or lukewarm to the cause.[204] Most of the towns still preferred to procure a man's service with his consent, as they had in 1777. But they had begun to concentrate on procurement for short-term service rather than the longer terms that Washington found more valuable. The Third Brigade, for instance, raised 227 men for the six-month service, but only 20 men signed up for three years, and a mere 2 for the duration.[205] The towns were ready enough to do what they could toward ending the war quickly but less ready to face the possibility of its going on for years. Even in raising men for the short term, they took their time. So long as Washington depended on the towns for his men, most of them would not arrive until after the peak of the harvest season. There was also another reason for the delay. The treasury was bare, the state could not afford to pay the bounty it had promised, and the men could not march without it because the army provision stores between their homes and the camp had been broken up.[206]

Nevertheless, the slow assembly of the three-month and six-month men did less damage to combined operations than the deployment of British forces. In July, the British had penned Rochambeau in Newport by threatening an expedition against him. Then they kept him there by maintaining decisive naval superiority in Block Island Sound. Rochambeau dared not try to join Washington for fear that the ships he left behind would fall prey to the enemy's superior strength. In late August, when Washington learned that the British had the Second Division of the French expeditionary force blockaded at Brest in Europe, he saw that his ally almost certainly would not regain supremacy in American waters in time to be useful. His dismissal of the three-month men signaled his opinion that combined operations could not take place that year.[207]

These events put an end to all hope of peace that year too, but they saved Washington from humiliation. Despite the heroic attempts of the various states to finance procurement of supplies for the army, the men had been living from hand to mouth all summer. Matters ought to have improved as the effects of a good harvest made themselves felt. There should have been more grain and more natural grass for fattening cattle and feeding horses to use for overland transport. Instead, Washington found it difficult to concentrate his forces anywhere because of the lack of magazines. He could not obtain forage for the army's draft horses without resorting to coercion. In August he had to cope with a new problem, a shortage of meat that forced him to seize cattle in the no-man's-land of New Jersey.[208] The presence of large numbers of militia could only make this bad situation worse. Washington welcomed the excuse to dismiss them and to have a reason other than the incapacity of his army for the postponement of combined operations.[209]

PART FOUR

Victory

TWO EVENTS toward the end of 1780 convinced the revolutionary leadership that the cause would not survive another campaign as ineffectual as the last. In mid-August, the British defeated Gates's army, hastily raised after the fall of Charleston, a loss which seemed to clear the way for an almost effortless British conquest of the South. Washington could send no reinforcements to prevent it. Not only had his army already fallen well below projected strength, but, because it had proven so hard to obtain long-term recruits that summer, the terms of half his men would expire in December.[1] If Washington could have put pressure on New York, he would have relieved the South at least temporarily. At the time, however, his army threatened no one. During a conference with Rochambeau at Hartford in September, Washington suggested that the French march on New York. Had they done so, they might have saved the day. Rochambeau, however, would not separate his land forces from those at sea until the Second Division arrived.[2]

One hope remained. Either the French expeditionary force under the Count de Guichen, then operating in the West Indies, or the Spanish, who had designs on Florida and might broaden their objectives, could have come to the rescue.[3] But Arnold's attempt to betray West Point to the enemy had cast a doubt on the Revolution's chances for success in the minds of the allies. If the plot had succeeded, the already dispirited army would have suffered a further blow to morale as well as the loss of a vital post, and the French would probably have decided that the alliance was no longer worth supporting. Discovery had averted these misfortunes but not the alarming implications of Arnold's treason. Though the patriots blamed his defection on his own treacherous disposition, they could not wholly conceal either from themselves or from others that the faltering course of the war had contributed. Arnold himself said as much, and invited others to follow his example.[4] He sounded a clear warning that the patriots had better win the war soon or see the cause collapse from lack of support.[5]

Arnold's treason depressed the leadership all the more because they realized that five years of grueling warfare had achieved nothing but the impoverishment of a rich continent and a potentially disastrous stalemate. Without foreign assistance, there would be no more victories like Saratoga. After Burgoyne's surrender, they could not expect the British ever to commit themselves again to a position where the navy could not succor the army. When Cornwallis conducted operations in the interior of South and North Carolina he kept on the move, a strategy which, given the South's pattern of scattered settlement, virtually assured that he would never have to fight save on his own terms. The patriots might win minor victories in remote territory, such as King's Mountain and Cowpens, but they knew that only naval superiority, impossible to achieve without foreign help, could bring the capitulation of a force large enough to make the British acknowledge defeat.[6]

Foreign help seemed equally indispensable to the solution of their economic problems. By September 1780, everyone could see that the scheme propounded in March had failed to stabilize the national currency. To start with, the collapse of the old currency discredited all paper credit instruments.[7] Furthermore, delays in printing and distributing the new currency had obliged those governments directly responsible for financing the campaign to seek other ways and means to pay. Some states had never even tried to follow the plan outlined by Congress.[8] And Congress undermined its own attempt to substitute the new emission for the old by drawing enormous orders for the old emission on the state loan offices. Eventually it stopped the practice, but the huge certificate debt outstanding in New York and New Jersey still obstructed the withdrawal of old currency. Instead of one currency replacing the other, both circulated at once to their mutual detriment.[9] As time went on, the leadership came increasingly to think that paper money would never work unless they made it redeemable on demand in specie, like bank notes.[10] Congress considered asking wealthy citizens to subscribe their specie and plate to a fund for the issuance of such a currency, and in May 1781 it chartered the Bank of North America. But none of these measures could possibly raise a fund large enough to meet the nation's needs without assistance from abroad.[11]

It seemed, indeed, that in every respect the fate of the United States had come to depend on immediate aid of a kind that she had sought for five years, and sought in vain. In the autumn of 1780, however, Congress picked up a new card. When France committed Rochambeau's expeditionary force, she gave a hostage which she could redeem only by investing yet more resource. After the Hartford conference in September, Rochambeau sent his son back to France to plead for more money, more men, and a˙naval reinforcement great enough to establish allied supremacy in American seas.[12] Congress also sent an envoy, Colonel John Laurens, who had instructions to secure a $5 million loan in specie, reinforcements, and supplies of vital clothing.[13] Before he left for Europe, Laurens conferred with both Washington and Rochambeau. Washington told him to think of money as his first objective and naval reinforcements as his second.[14] Rochambeau told him to be frank about the nation's problems, problems dramatized by mutinies in the Pennsylvania and New Jersey lines that January.[15] In the event, Laurens did not have to waste time on excuse or reassurance. New developments at home allowed him to come before the French court as something better than a beggar.

In early January, seeing that the struggle for independence had reached a crisis, Virginia conditionally withdrew her claim to the lands west of the Ohio,[16] whereupon Maryland, though still not satisfied, instructed her delegates to ratify the Articles of Confederation. The national government had at last achieved full constitutional status.[17] Meanwhile, the territorial concessions of the various landed states had set up a unique reserve of national capital with which to pay national debts.[18] Congress had already taken a step in this direction by requesting the authority to lay a 5 percent impost.[19] Congress had also embarked on a thorough reorganization of the executive departments in which the boards and committees that had previously conducted the businesses of war, finance, marine and foreign affairs were replaced with individual secretaries, each having sole responsibility in his area.[20] All these changes gave Laurens a status that no American envoy had had before. He could appear as the representative of a fully legitimate, reconstituted government, presumably able to mount a vigorous campaign in 1781 and to pay the nation's debts if and when she won the day.[21] In other words, he could offer the French, so perilously extended in their commitment, a straw to clutch at.

In spite of these advantages, Laurens met with less than full success. But he did help convince the French of his country's desperate need. And though Laurens played no real part in procuring the naval reinforcements that led to the victory at Yorktown,[22] he did bring back the money. Franklin had already persuaded the court to make a large loan, but on the understanding that the money would be used in Europe.[23] It was Laurens who pried loose 2.5 million livres in specie for shipment to America, and he who saw to its safe arrival.[24] Though the money came too late to finance Washington's march to Virginia directly, the knowledge that it was on its way allowed Robert Morris to borrow specie from Rochambeau's war chest with which to counteract whatever misgivings the troops entertained about the venture.[25] French money, in fact, contributed almost as much to the victory at Yorktown as French naval power. Besides Laurens's supply, Count de Grasse, commander of the French expeditionary force in the West Indies, brought 1.2 million livres in specie with him to the Chesapeake.[26] The allied forces had come together just at the close of an ample harvest; French money meant that the allies could enjoy the fruits of it, and French control of the Chesapeake ensured the safe transmission of supplies along the region's extensive river system. The bounty of nature, together with the contrivances of man, relieved the combined armies and the French navy of all anxiety about food until Cornwallis capitulated.

Good fortune had also played a part, and so large a part that, nature's and man's efforts notwithstanding, many observers then and since have seen an element of the miraculous in the victory at Yorktown.[27] Some have argued that, even if the British had not met defeat then and there, sooner or later, in one place or another, they would have had to give up. But the prostration of the American financial system and the imminent collapse of the French one suggest that the allies might not have had the resource for another vigorous campaign. Some have argued that in the long run Britain would have seen the concession of American independence as promoting her own best interest, a theory which assumes that the revolutionaries had the capacity to carry on a war of attrition indefinitely. A close look at the experience of Connecticut after 1781 casts doubt on that assumption.

CHAPTER SIX

Bankruptcy

JUST as Congress had confessed bankruptcy by shuffling off
the job of maintaining a currency and gathering supplies upon
the states, so Connecticut confessed bankruptcy by shuffling off
the raising of men and supplies upon the towns. In the autumn
of 1780, when Washington and Congress demanded that another permanent army be raised,[1] the state formalized a device
she had previously used informally. For the first time, the legislature explicitly delegated the task of recruiting for the Connecticut line to the towns. Special committees in every town
would divide the population into as many classes as the town
had recruits to procure. Any class that failed to produce its
recruit by February 20, 1781, would pay a fine equal to twice
the cost of hiring a substitute. Each town had to proceed
against its own delinquent classes and individuals, and a town
that did not meet its quota would pay a fine equal to twice the
cost of doing so. On the other hand, each town would receive
thirty pounds in new state emission for every man it did enlist.[2]

The state pursued the same policy in the matter of gathering supplies, whether for her own use or for meeting the congressional requisition. In the autumn of 1780, the legislature ordered each town "to collect . . . and put in good order as
much well fatted beef and pork and wheat flour, as will amount
of six pence on the pound" between December 15 and January
15.[3] In late November, it increased the levy by one and a half

pence.[4] On both occasions, the legislature made the towns as a whole liable to the state for the default of individual inhabitants. Rum and salt were the only items on the congressional requisition of November 4 that the state herself would procure.[5]

The failure of the state emission of 1780 had brought Connecticut to this pass.[6] Yet certain factors peculiar to the state should have maintained her own currency despite the rising mistrust of paper money. Apart from the legislature's vigorous program of taxation, the presence of the French in Rhode Island from July 1780 to June 1781 constituted a windfall for Connecticut. Their willingness to exchange bills on France for currency at par and to buy Connecticut produce with Connecticut currency should have revived the state's economy as well as the state's credit.[7] Instead, the state currency began to depreciate faster than either the new or the old continentals.[8] And because of this depreciation, the state could not withdraw her currency in favor of the new emission even though the legislature repeatedly authorized the exchange.[9] By the time the new emission arrived, state money could not be exchanged for it without either appreciating the one or depreciating the other.

The Decline of the State Currency

The problem that the French encountered in provisioning their army at Rhode Island contributed to the decline in value of Connecticut's money. Anyone familiar with Connecticut's economy could have predicted her inability to supply the French with grain, particularly after a hard winter followed by a dry spring.[10] But no one expected that she would fail to supply sufficient cattle since she specialized in stock and since Wadsworth himself had agreed to act as agent for the French.[11] Wadsworth had not made his commitment until mid-May, however, by which time the task he faced had assumed impossible proportions. He had to gather the necessary provisions on six weeks' notice during the hottest season of the year.[12] Pork was out of the question; the winter's dearth had left all the animals underweight. In any case, they fattened on corn rather than grass, and corn could not be harvested before midsummer. Since pork made better salted meat than beef, and since the armies would need salt meat for winter maneuvers, pigs were best kept for slaughter in the late autumn.[13] Cattle fattened on grass should have provided Rochambeau's main support, but at the time Washington relied largely upon Connecticut beef to feed his own men. Wadsworth certainly did not want to starve the American army in order to feed the French, particularly after the recent rumble of incipient mutiny in the Connecticut line.[14] He did his best to procure for the French in Massachusetts, but the congressional Committee of Cooperation opposed the attempt for reasons that remain obscure:[15] perhaps they wanted the French to have only the best cattle, unquestionably those from Connecticut.

When Wadsworth failed to supply their needs, the French gave up all attempt at joint procurement. They turned instead to private contract, which, while it gave them their best chance of obtaining sufficient food, led also to the very situation everyone had sought to avoid, the provisioning of French soldiers at the expense of the American army. The French saw nothing else to do. After ten weeks at sea, their men were sickly. The prospect of a British attack before they could fortify their position or recoup their health obliged them to supply themselves independently. Since neither Rochambeau's officers nor his men had local or ideological ties to the cause, he could hardly expect them to share the extreme privation endured by the American army.[16] On the eve of the expected attack, Rochambeau agreed to a proposal by Josiah Blakely of Hartford and Gideon Delano of Dartmouth, Massachusetts, that they provision his men by private contract and on terms that would allow them to outbid any state commissary. The French agreed to pay for all supplies delivered on schedule in one-third specie and two-thirds bills of exchange on France. Later they concluded another agreement on the same terms for supplies drawn from outside Connecticut.[17]

Predictably, American producers were less and less willing to sell for anything but the preferred currencies offered by

French agents, while American forces in the North were more and more plagued by shortages.[18] It did not help that in August a Boston convention advised the states to abandon their inland embargoes. When Connecticut complied, the farmers in distant areas began driving their cattle toward the French army.[19] The shortages that threatened the Continental army with dissolution in the late summer derived directly from the French contracts.[20] Connecticut's Council of Safety held several meetings on the problem and appointed commissioners to attend a conference with French officials about how best to provide for both armies.[21] Other states did the same.

As it happened, the French soon grew dissatisfied with Blakely and Delano. In this they had an eye to their own good as well as that of their allies. When the threat of an immediate British attack receded, and when Rochambeau recognized that the Second Division would not come to reinforce him, he became more interested in stretching his limited resource than in making sure of supplies. Blakely and Delano could not help him much in that respect: the mismanagement of their agents had caused a rise in prices, both in hard money and in bills of exchange. And they had only one suggestion for procuring resources when the French had exhausted their specie, a quixotic proposal to barter West Indian produce for provisions.[22] We can be sure, too, that the French received from several quarters the warning that Blakely and Delano were petty adventurers without the power to fulfill all their contracts. Jeremiah Wadsworth, for one, had told them as much when he visited their camp in the early autumn to settle the accounts of his summer agency.[23] In September the French tried to work out an arrangement with Massachusetts.[24] When that failed, they turned back to Wadsworth.

Wadsworth would not be party to a contract. Instead, in partnership with John Carter, the English-born, French-speaking son-in-law of Philip Schuyler, he offered to make contracts for the French on commission. By purchasing with American currency and French bills of exchange as much as possible, he could help them stretch their limited supply of specie.[25] Wadsworth also insisted that he be their sole provisioning agent.

Only if he would buy what purchasers wanted to sell quickly, like beef, could he bargain with them for what they would rather withhold or persuade them to accept part of their payment in the less-desired currencies.[26]

Wadsworth and Carter succeeded in their task despite sundry obstacles, including one raised by the French themselves. They could not immediately break themselves of encouraging competition for contracts, though in the absence of market towns the practice caused the bidding up of prices. Wadsworth had to force Blakely out of the market for beef by persuading the Council of Safety to ban him from buying in Connecticut and by threatening to call in a debt owed to Wadsworth by Champion, on whom Blakely depended.[27] Wildcat buying for the French continued, but Governor Trumbull could control it. The French had agreed always to ask his permission to export grain by water, and Trumbull threatened to withhold it if they received supplies through any person other than Carter or his agents.[28]

No sooner had this problem begun to subside than the dwindling supply of specie raised another. At first, Wadsworth could use bills on France to buy the specie with which he garnished contracts in American currency. Within weeks, however, the value of the bills began to decline, both because their number increased and because the approach of winter diminished opportunities to make remittances on Europe.[29] In December, when Rochambeau ran out of specie, Wadsworth and Carter could still buy some hard money by selling bills of exchange, but at ridiculous discounts.[30] They found it cheaper to promise specie at a future date and to deposit bills of exchange with a seller as collateral.[31] The confidence the French placed in Wadsworth allowed him to pursue this course until relief appeared. In late February, when the *Astrea* arrived with a large supply of specie, he and Carter had no more need to worry about money.[32]

Despite the flow of specie and bills of exchange to Connecticut, and despite Wadsworth's insistence that sellers accept some domestic currency as part of most payments, American currencies continued to depreciate. And the currency of Connecticut

depreciated faster than any other because the French had in effect restructured the southern New England economy. British
naval surveillance in Block Island Sound from August 1780
onward drove most privateering, together with what little commerce existed, to the east. Though it remained possible to ship
provisions to Newport by small, fast-sailing, shallow-draft vessels, prize masters and merchantmen preferred to use ports
north of Cape Cod, with the result that the imports most desired by Connecticut producers had to be purchased from
them. Connecticut currency was useless in such transactions.
No Massachusetts supplier wanted anything from Connecticut
that he could not more advantageously acquire by barter than
by payment in the state's own currency.[33] Continental money,
on the other hand, retained a limited value in these exchanges.
Other jurisdictions besides Connecticut required it for payment
of taxes. The energetic fiscal policy of Massachusetts, for instance, kept the demand for it comparatively high to the east,
where most of the region's commercial transactions took
place.[34]

　　Even so, the presence of the French ought to have represented a resource for Connecticut. Since producers coveted specie and bills of exchange in order to buy foreign goods from
eastern ports, the legislature had one obvious recourse. It could
require payment of taxes in these media, then use them to establish the credit of the state's own currency. The legislature
did attempt some such tactic but defeated its own end by cling-
ing to the fiction that the domestic currencies had a fixed specie
equivalent when everyone knew they were depreciating. Taxpayers given the alternative of paying taxes either in specie or
in the domestic currency at a rate which overvalued it would
naturally choose the latter course.[35] In theory, that choice
should have diminished the supply of domestic currency, particularly the new state currency which was limited both in
amount and in circulation. The decline in the supply of currency should then have caused an appreciation that restored it
to its proper value in relation to specie. This did not happen because disbursements always exceeded receipts. State officials
never succeeded in surmounting the difficulty of meeting current

needs at rising prices in a depreciating medium. The state treasurer no sooner collected money than he reissued it to meet new demands. For the same reason, unpaid orders on the treasury issued by the Committee of the Pay-Table, a legislative committee with responsibility for public accounts, went into circulation in place of currency.[36] To cap all, in the summer of 1780 the state's fiscal mechanism collapsed. The government could no longer collect the money needed to pay for the war effort.

From the earliest days of the Revolution, Connecticut's fiscal system had looked better than it was. The unpleasant truth did not become public knowledge until 1783, when the Committee of the Pay-Table published a report containing a schedule of those taxes for which the state had issued warrants, together with a list of the abatements granted on each.[37] The legislature customarily gave local selectmen the authority to abate 5 percent of all taxes due. Throughout the early war years, however, abatements averaged 20 percent, while in 1778 they jumped to 25 percent. In that particular year, it is true, the increase followed a legislative grant of abatements to all men who enlisted in the army for three years or the duration.[38] But steady abatements averaging 20–25 percent on every tax levied throughout the war invite question because the reasons for abatement should have increased over time. The Pay-Table Committee tacitly raised that question when it attributed the high level of abatement in Connecticut to "devastations made by the enemy" that obliged the legislature to grant the victims generous relief.[39] Furthermore, the legislature's gradual extension of the privilege to most of those in military service should have sent abatements higher still.[40] The Pay-Table came closer to the truth, therefore, when it acknowledged that some of the abatements resulted from "the mistakes of listers." It seems clear that, from the beginning of the war, local authorities had made lavish use of a 1771 law which authorized them to give "proper abatement" to all those who had "been unsuccessful or sustained considerable losses in their trade."[41]

Governor Trumbull and Treasurer Lawrence had known

about "the mistakes of listers" at least since the middle of 1780, and probably much earlier.[42] That the level of abatements remained constant despite a rising tide of reasons for them suggests that the treasurer had initially allowed local authorities more latitude in this respect than the legislature had meant to give. Perhaps he hoped thereby to soften the impact that wartime taxes might otherwise make. The inference receives support from the very absence of the threats against local tax officials that might be expected to follow increasing tax demands. And the one exception proves the rule. The Whig collector in Tory Newtown did complain that he was "menaced with personal abuse and injury," not to mention "something else more dreadful than death," unless he stopped collecting taxes, whereupon the government authorized the local sheriff to collect by force from those who would not pay and even instructed Oliver Wolcott to call out the militia for the purpose if necessary.[43] Yet I know of no other town where such violent hostility existed between townspeople and tax collectors. Where the people elected the officials, and the officials then used their power of abatement to benefit the people, they had no quarrel with each other. The incident at Newtown, such as it was, serves rather to confirm than to destroy the hypothesis that most of those who administered the fiscal system did so with exemplary tact and discretion.

Tact and discretion, however, made the system work only temporarily; in the long run, they eroded its foundations. Abatement softened the tax blow for the poor, but those who received none bore a correspondingly greater burden, which grew still heavier when the increasingly heavy tax demands on Connecticut prompted more and more men to escape them by emigrating. The report of the Pay-Table Committee pointed to "the great emigrations from the State" as the primary cause of the astonishing size of the abatements,[44] and there can be no doubt that these emigrations increased the taxes laid on those left behind to pay them. Even after the reforms of 1779, polls still constituted over 30 percent of the tax base.[45]

Those left behind to pay—that is, those who neither qualified for abatement nor escaped through emigration—sought re-

lief from tax burdens in tax delinquency. Sometimes the treasurer encouraged the delinquents, as when he refused to issue
warrants for the collection of a six-shilling tax, due in January
1780.[46] More often, they acted without official sanction. Delinquency took two forms. There was delay, which, at a time
when the medium of payment depreciated steadily, amounted
to partial default. The Committee of the Pay-Table published a
breakdown of the yield from the four-shilling tax, due in
August 1779, which showed that the state lost 40 percent of its
specie value to depreciation during the time that elapsed between the due date and the date of payment. Then there was
default pure and simple. The Pay-Table report showed that, as
of Jaunary 1783, seventy-one towns remained in arrears of taxes
for Continental money, to the tune of more than $3 million.[47]
It does not say when each town dropped into arrears, but a
schedule of delinquencies appearing in the Jonathan Trumbull
papers, covering the period February 1779 to March 1781,
shows that most of them had fallen behind by the autumn of
1780.[48]

The Towns Go Bankrupt

The tax arrearages do not necessarily mean that all the delinquent towns had exhausted their resources by mid-1780. Since
they coincided with the attempt to recruit three-month and six-
month men for combined operations against New York, they
could mean that many towns had diverted their funds to serve
the other, more pressing purpose. The government certainly assumed as much when it passed the major responsibility for raising and feeding the army to the towns. Between November and
December of 1780, town after town obeyed the General
Aseembly's order to collect sixpence worth of provisions,
usually by levying a town rate to be paid in state currency.
They then appointed committees to procure the provisions with
the money so obtained. Most of the towns gave their inhabitants the alternative of payment in kind,[49] but where people
had money they preferred to use it. Money enabled a more

precise accounting because it allowed the state to give change. Money provided taxpayers with the most efficient way to pay their taxes. And money allowed the committee charged with purchasing to choose the better bargains. All of the evidence indicates that the first requisition made upon the towns met with some success. One or two (Norwich, for instance) defaulted. But we know that the Council of Safety drew on supplies from coastal towns to provision the guard at New London[50] and that in April 1781 the state relieved a shortage for Washington's army by shipping him salted meat mostly procured by the autumn requisitions.[51]

Nevertheless, the strain had begun to tell. Toward the end of 1780, several towns appointed special committees to settle with the recruits raised that summer.[52] The very existence of such committees suggests that the towns had offered more than they could give. And there were other signs of trouble. Few towns levied a tax of more than one shilling to meet the cumulative provisions requisition of seven and a half pence, and some asked as little as ninepence. Given the depreciation of Connecticut's currency, taxes so low would produce nowhere near the amount the state government sought.[53] More ominous yet, the towns responded to the new call for Continental recruits with suspicion and resentment. Gone were the days when they had taken the initiative in offering incentives for enlistment. By autumn of 1780, towns were appointing committees not to fill their quotas but to find out how many men they had sent to the army already. Though few of the town meeting records say why, they probably had the same reason as Hartford, where the selectmen openly expressed suspicion that more of their townsmen were away in the army than appeared in the official returns.[54] In March 1781 the General Assembly passed a law which suggests that this was a common complaint. The law set up an elaborate system for crediting a town with its recruits and established county committees to adjudicate disputes.[55]

Of all their unwelcome tasks, the towns viewed long-term recruitment with the most distaste. The magnitude of the task overwhelmed their diminished resources. At the end of 1780, Congress reduced the number of regiments required of Connecticut from eight to six, five of infantry plus one of horse. At the same time, however, it raised the size of each regiment from 522 to 632,[56] which canceled out much of the concession. Since nearly all the men raised during 1780 had signed for six months, Connecticut needed roughly 2,000 new recruits to bring the state line up to strength in 1781. Because Congress had asked for more long-term recruits, a request backed by an eloquent plea from Washington in which he described the evils that followed from an army in constant flux,[57] the legislature's October requisition specified recruitment for three years or, preferably, for the duration. But if the towns were to do this by providing incentives, the only system that had worked in 1777 and 1780, they would have to offer at least six times the previous summer's bounty. That might prove impossible, considering how hard many towns already found it to deliver on past promises. Some of the more prosperous towns could still raise bounties large enough to let them hire the men to complete their quotas.[58] Others went through the motions of hiring, though they offered bounties so small as to raise doubts that they seriously intended to comply with the law.[59] The majority pursued the course prescribed by the legislature: they resorted to classing.[60]

The new classing law had some advantages over the previous system of raising men. For one thing, it distributed the burden more evenly over the male population. In 1777 the classes were formed on the principle of numerical equality: that is, each class comprised an equal number of men. By the new law, each class would equal the others in the total wealth possessed by their members but not necessarily in the number of their members. And instead of subjecting only eligible men to arbitrary detachment until the fines they paid produced a willing recruit, everyone, including exemptees and those over fifty (sectors of the population likely to be richer than the average),[61] had to contribute to the incentives offered according to their assessments. Besides its greater fairness, the new system of classing was likely to be more effective. Anyone who tried to evade paying his share of the bounty money would find himself subjected to coercion. The classes had the legal power to tax by

distraint and to "doom" delinquents to pay twice the sum originally asked of them. Since everyone had an interest in produc-
ing a recruit to prevent his class from being doomed, strong
social pressure to accept the incentives offered would be
brought to bear on the young men. Yet it was precisely because
classing did encroach on everyone, as no other system had, that
many towns approached it with mixed feelings.

The town of Haddam illustrates the slow and tortuous
road by which most of them came to that pass. On November
20, one week after it levied a one-shilling rate to pay for provisions collected on the Assembly's order, Haddam voted to fill
its quota for the army by classing and appointed a committee to
divide the town as the legislature prescribed. It then betrayed
its dislike for the business by instructing the committee
members to investigate the terms on which the town might still
hire men. On December 4, perhaps in response to their report,
Haddam voted to try other measures first. On January 8 it offered recruits a bounty of ten pounds a year, plus forty shillings
a month and a guarantee of the real value of their wages. Apparently few accepted, since on March 29 the town voted to
revert to classing. At the same meeting it also decided to petition the legislature about the difficulty encountered in meeting
its requisition for supplies.[62] As the order for the towns to contribute supplies had confessed the state's bankruptcy, so Haddam's inability to comply with either this or the demand for
recruits without classing confessed the bankruptcy of the town.
Nor was Haddam alone. Through that winter, one after another, the towns turned to classing, often as the last resort.

The need to recruit men for the state as well as the Continental service certainly accelerated their slide into bankruptcy.
In late 1780, the state confronted the fact that she could no
longer raise state troops by voluntary enlistment. During the
autumn the government heard that the guards along the western frontier were drifting away, largely because they lacked
provisions, and that the enemy meant to exploit the weak spots
they left.[63] In November, the legislature ordered the preemptory detachment of one thousand two-month men to hold the
line. They took this step only after their earlier attempts to

raise troops by voluntary enlistment or by draft had definitely failed. They intended the two-month men to serve only until the state could raise a thousand men for a year. Apparently, the legislature had concluded that the officers of the militia were useless to the procurement of men for any length of time, since it ordered that these troops be raised in the same way as the three-year Continental recruits: that is, the towns would receive quotas that they must fill, by classing if all else failed.[64] The legislature saw no alternative. Silliman, for one, had complained that the officers of the militia hung back from detachment even for the two-month service.[65]

An increase in the tempo of loyalist raids along the coast further complicated the problem of raising men for the critical campaign of 1781. At the end of 1780, the Crown sanctioned the establishment in New York of a paramilitary organization called the Associated Loyalists, which announced its intention to harass and plunder all who had spurned British protection.[66] Loyalist refugees had perpetrated sporadic raids on the coast since 1776, but their official organization threatened to make their activities more systematic and more damaging. On the night of January 21, 1781, Lieutenant Colonel William Hull successfully attacked the loyalist concentration at Morrisania, which relieved the pressure on Greenwich.[67] But the north shore of Long Island remained a safe haven from which the loyalists could launch forays, and during the first few weeks of the year Norwalk, New Haven, and Branford all reported raids.[68] Brigadier Silliman, who had labored throughout the autumn to reach an agreement with his enemy counterpart on Long Island, a Colonel Ludlow, to restrain the piracy that flourished on both sides of the Sound, saw the loyalist association as a threat to all his hopes. As he observed to Trumbull, the "new mode of Warr" gave the British a way to distress the seacoast more with a thousand men than they could have done with an army of ten thousand.[69]

The government's response to the problem only made it worse. Though the legislature did increase the number of state troops, including coast guards, to 150 above the projected 1,780,[70] they tried to cut the cost of coastal defense by leaning more on legal mechanisms. First they passed a measure which instructed the civil authority and selectmen in all vulnerable towns to list their local inimicals. A special committee of the legislature would judge whether or not these persons were justly named, but the burden of proof would rest with the accused. The revised list would then return to the town clerk, and in the event of a raid the authorities could recompense its targets to the full amount of their loss by issuing warrants against the property of the cited inimicals.[71] Far from serving as a deterrent, this act swelled the ranks of those who defected to the enemy because they had nothing left to hope for by staying. Forced to confess its failure, the legislature passed a new law in which any person formerly a "subject of this State or of . . . the United States . . . who shall come into this State, and rob or plunder any person or persons of their goods or effects" would face trial for treason rather than incarceration as a prisoner of war.[72] This time it touched off a series of kidnapping raids in which loyalists carried away patriot citizens to use as hostages if any of their own were ever captured.

Since the war began, both sides had done a certain amount of kidnapping. They usually picked prominent figures on the assumption that, the more important their hostage, the greater their bargaining power. The Associated Loyalists' most notable success in this respect was their capture of Colonel Stephen St. John of Stamford, whom they imprisoned at the Prevost during the hot months, deliberately endangering his life in order to bring the utmost pressure on the state for the release of three ex-Connecticut men held in Hartford on treason charges.[73] Unlike earlier kidnappers, however, the Associated Loyalists did not always discriminate. They also carried off civilians at random, sometimes in large numbers. In July 21, 1781, for instance, they surprised a congregation at worship in Middlesex parish, Stamford, and took away forty-one people, including the pastor, who had been abducted once before. Such nuisances became so common that the legislature had to prescribe compensation for the victims.[74] As the pressure mounted, the coastal towns began to protest all outside demands on their manpower. It was in unpropitious circumstances, then, that in mid-June Washington asked for 2,200 additional three-month men to man the posts in the Highlands and so leave the main army free to concentrate against New York.[75]

Some of the coastal towns, like Norwalk, were willing to supply coast guards at state expense and to make gestures toward filling the state battalions, but they resented the demands of the continent because, as their selectmen put it, they felt that "it is become more hazardous to be an Inhabitant than a soldier in the Continental Army."[76] More often, the towns responded to the simultaneous demand for state and Continental troops without open discrimination between the two, and usually by classing for both. But they let Washington down badly in 1781, for they supplied the line with less than eight hundred men, about 40 percent of the quota, many of whom arrived too late to be much use in that crucial campaign.[77] By contrast, Waterbury's state battalions appear to have reached half strength by the end of July, and the placement of coast guards under his command more than doubled his force by the autumn. Though Waterbury's returns do not show which were guards and which were state troops, it is reasonable to infer that his units achieved 70 percent of their projected strength.[78]

The discrepancy between state and Continental recruitment at first appeared to arise from the longer term of service demanded by the continent. Yet even after Washington had agreed to accept six-month men,[79] at which point the state's requirement became the greater one, the preference for the state continued, suggesting an aversion to the Continental service that no amount of money or social pressure could overcome. Many of those who did sign on for the continent merely took the bounty and absconded.[80] And, to judge from the reluctance of towns to "doom" their delinquent classes, the population at large felt a similar lack of revolutionary fervor.[81] Certain features of the classing laws did undeniably discourage action: no one could know for certain how much it would have cost a class to fill its quota or, by extension, how much the fine of twice that cost would amount to. Even so, the continued inertia of the towns that May, when the legislature called for a preemptory draft as the only way to fill the Continental ranks,[82] indicates a more deeply rooted cause of trouble.

Though by then the civil authorities knew that this was indeed the only way to raise an army, the officers of the militia complained repeatedly of meeting in them a resistance to the measure[83] which undoubtedly originated in the experience of the previous year. The brigade returns for 1780 indicate that, where default had led to detachment, the results were dismal. Of the 158 men detached for the six-month service in the Fourth Brigade, 130 refused or absconded. Of the 135 detached for three months, 83 refused or absconded. In other words, depending on the length of service asked, the yield from detachment was no more than 18 to 33 percent.[84] A substantial decline in the grand list beginning in 1780 (see Table 5) suggests why town authorities resisted the draft. The devastation of the coast during the summer of 1779 contributed something to the decline but does not account for the whole. Though the legislature granted sufferers retroactive abatements on the lists of 1778 and 1779, they show no such drop. Enemy activity along the coast continued to erode the tax base,[85] but emigration was responsible for the greater part of the sustained downward trend beginning in 1780. A shift in the sex ratio of the population from a predominance of men to a predominance of women which took place between 1774 and 1782 confirms the inference.[86] No wonder town authorities hesitated to support a measure that might drive even more young men away.

Similar reasons also kept them from invoking the coercive powers that the classing law bestowed on them. Much as they must have worried about the long-term social implications of the decline in the young male population, they worried more about its immediate economic effects. Polls were taxed because, in a labor-intensive, preindustrial economy, they gave the best measure of economic potential. The last thing local leaders needed in 1781 was any more loss of resource, which might well result if they applied the full range of pressures allowed by classing. Towns with disloyal elements in their midst were not adverse to dooming the disaffected in order to raise men,[87]

TABLE FIVE
CONNECTICUT'S TAXABLE ASSETS
1775–1785
(*In pounds*)

	1 Grand List as Recorded in Colonial and State Records	*2* Decline of Grand List as % of 1775 Grand List	*3* List Used by Treasurer Including Abatements[a]	*4* Yield on Each ld. of tax
1775	1,975,271		1,962,780	8,178.25
1776	1,864,163	5.00	1,855,179	7,729.90
1777	1,934,785	2.00	1,921,670	8,006.75
1778	1,934,315	2.00	1,916,070	7,983.62
1779	1,943,124	1.60	1,929,670	8,040.29
1780	1,845,175	6.00	1,825,680	7,607.00
1781	1,822,122	7.75	1,810,960	7,545.60
1782	1,813,165	8.20		7,554.85[b]
1783	1,774,478	10.20		7,393.65[b]
1784	1,559,624	21.00		6,498.43[b]
1785	1,543,704	21.80		6,432.1[b]

[a] Where known. Last-minute abatements granted by the treasurer probably account for the discrepancy between columns 1 and 3.
[b] Calculated from column 1.

SOURCES: *CR*, vols. 14 and 15.
    SR, vols. 1–6

but it made little sense to pressure loyal inhabitants, either physically or fiscally, to the point where they left the community.

By the time the Council of Safety faced Washington's request for short-term soldiers, it had become clear that the only way to meet it was to sidestep the bankrupt towns and pass to the militia the task of coercion that classing had been designed to accomplish. As for incentives, the Council appealed "to the inhabitants . . . whose circumstances will admit of it, and who are disposed to afford their aid, in the present critical situation of the country, to open their hearts, by advancing a sufficient sum of money," to make up the twenty-shilling bounty promised to men who marched.[88] Though the selectmen in some coastal towns opposed these measures too, enough people supported them for the three-month detachees to reach

70 percent of projected strength. Unfortunately, they did not arrive in the Highlands in force until mid-September, too late to deter Clinton from the attempt to rescue Cornwallis.[89] If nothing else, Connecticut's devolution of the functions of government, first upon the towns and classes, then, when their resources ran out, upon wealthy citizens, had shown that the state could not relinquish responsibility for supporting the war effort without also relinquishing the right to direct it.

The Assembly may have realized this even as it embarked on the policy of devolution. In the autumn of 1780, it had tried to develop another source of funds by liquidating the state's one appreciating asset, the estates of her defectors. Little profit had yet accrued from the loyalist estates, though the provision for confiscation had passed into law by May 1778.[90] Local authorities hesitated to certify "inimicals" for fear of offending their relatives. In the autumn of 1780, the legislature took upon itself to identify the forfeited estates and offered for sale some £50,000 worth of those which had passed through probate. In the following year the government used the device repeatedly, but with poor results. People wanted the goods they had done without since 1775, not real estate. Besides, most of the properties were in the exposed southwest, where they had little appeal for patriots. The government tried to use them to pay off claims against the state made by officers of the line, but they too found the offer unattractive.[91]

The bankruptcy of the towns, added to the legislature's desire to regain direction of the war, led it in May 1781 to relieve them of almost all responsibility for collecting provisions. They were still expected to supervise the collection of a fourpenny provision tax during the coming summer, but otherwise the state resumed her former practice of taxing individuals. The principal tax laid amounted to two shillings, sixpence, on the list of 1781, payable in specie or its equivalents or in provisions.[92] The legislature hoped to use the avails of this tax to pay the second half of the bounty and all the wages of the three-month men, as well as to provide the supplies requisitioned for the Continental army. Collected in full, the tax would have yielded £288,223 in specie. But first abatements up to 20 percent reduced the sum expected to £231,017;[93] then the government actually received only £160,792, £120,260 of which came in as orders on the treasury for goods and services already supplied.[94] The two-and-sixpenny tax showed that, with the bankruptcy of the towns, the state had lost the power to claim even the fruits of future harvests.

The Illicit Trade

The state's bankruptcy opened Pandora's box. As if it were not bad enough that Connecticut could no longer mobilize her resource for the cause, she soon became equally helpless to prevent the passage of that resource, particularly provisions, into enemy hands. Though the illicit trade had existed ever since the British first occupied New York,[95] presumably fostered by loyalists along the Hudson River and in southwestern Connecticut, it caused little concern at first. The revolutionary governments did wish to keep the occupying army dependent on provisions from Europe in the hope that this would make the cost of conquest too high, but in the early days they never doubted their ability to prohibit enemy access to domestic supplies, except where the British were present in force. Washington even sponsored a certain amount of illicit trading because he could use it to gain intelligence of British movements. This cut both ways; he could never be sure that such spies would not give the British more information about the revolutionaries than they gave him about the British. On the other hand, the British would probably learn no more from the traders than from the loyalist refugees who flocked to them from all directions, and the risk seemed worth taking, at least in the first years of the war, in order to obtain otherwise inaccessible information.[96]

The first doubt crept in when the commissaries began to experience difficulty in collecting provisions. When supplies that had always been plentiful suddenly all but vanished from the market, some were ready to assume that the traders had spirited them away to the British and that their greed for British gold had also contributed to the depreciation of the currency.[97] People in general still associated the trade primarily with nonpatriot elements. They attributed it either to pro-British enclaves within the state or to outsiders like the Nantucket traders who secured the privilege of bartering with salt for Connecticut provisions. The prices charged by the Nantucketers, and the amount of provision that they collected (occasionally so great as to provoke the complaint that it had stripped some coastal communities of their resource), gave rise to the suspicion that they were feeding the British as well as the islanders.[98] Yet both forms of illicit trade could be regulated. Embargoes and the Council of Safety's exclusive power to license exportation could cut down the activities of outside traders,[99] while the coast guards could work to put a stop to it in Connecticut. Indeed, the coast guards were better equipped for that purpose than for protecting the coast, given the enemy's ability to concentrate its forces wherever it chose. As soon as the leadership began to feel alarmed about the trade, controlling it became the main mission of the coast guard.[100]

In practice, however, the task proved too much for them. Most of the illicit trade across the Sound took place under cover of darkness and in small whaleboats manned by loyalist refugees who knew how to find obscure inlets where their boats could lie concealed by day. The whaleboats were often supported by larger craft which hovered about the coast constantly, partly to provide artillery cover for any landing party that met opposition but perhaps even more to distract the coast guard.[101] Here again, the remedy suggested itself. The state commissioned her own vessels and whaleboats to sweep coastal waters of enemy craft, which at one stroke relieved the anxieties of shoreline dwellers and stemmed the flow of men and supplies to the British.[102]

Problems remained, nonetheless. There was, for instance, the traffic between the mainland and Long Island, conducted by the numerous refugees who had fled to Connecticut after the British occupation in 1776. These people arrived there virtually destitute, since haste had obliged them to leave most of their property behind. If the war had ended soon afterward, they could probably have lived on what they had succeeded in carrying away, supplemented by the charity of the communities that took them in. But as those communities felt the pinch of a war that dragged on and on, the Long Islanders became burdensome. One way to end the difficulty was to let them return to the island so that they could collect debts, wages, or rents, or even sell their estates and bring off the proceeds.[103] The government did see the possibility for abuse in this procedure and tried to guard against it. In February 1778 the General Assembly passed a law that required anyone who went to Long Island to first obtain a permit from the selectmen, on pain of a $100 fine or, if he could not pay, of compulsory service in the army. The selectmen were to grant permission only if the applicant could post bond for $400 on his promise not to trade with the enemy. Any person who detected the smuggling of unlicensed merchandise could claim it for his own in the state courts.[104] When it became clear that in most places the selectmen would connive at any irregularity in their desire to keep the refugees from becoming a charge on their towns, the legislature transferred the power to grant permits to the Council of Safety.[105] This measure too failed to prevent the trade.

Another problem arose from the changing character of the populations in frontier towns exposed to enemy raiders. At first the raids had stiffened the resistance of the patriotic and encouraged the exodus of those otherwise inclined.[106] Gradually, an insidious change occurred. Because of the law that permitted men detached for the militia to refuse upon payment of a five-pound fine, the defense of the frontier fell most heavily on those loyal to the cause, who soon found themselves exhausted (and impoverished) by the state's continuous demand on their services.[107] They found, too, that their own influence within their local communities began to wane as that of nonpatriot elements increased. In southwestern Connecticut, for instance, James Delancey made deliberate use of his loyalist corps stationed in Westchester to tilt the balance in that direction. He avoided indiscriminate violence of the kind that had characterized the early British cavalry raids and instead employed a network of intelligence, unavailable to regular army officers, which allowed him to single out ardent patriots for attack while showing leniency toward collaborators.[108] As the pressure on the patriots increased, more and more of them migrated, leaving these areas to predominantly neutral or pro-British elements and making it infinitely harder for Connecticut to control them.[109]

The British regarded with equal complaisance both those who collaborated passively—that is, by refusing to fight for the revolutionary movement—and those who gave positive help by supplying information or engaging in illicit trade. But as the currency depreciated and taxes rose, persons not passionately committed to the cause had ever greater incentives to collaborate actively, particularly when it became possible to protect themselves through collusive captures and paroles. Anyone could claim that the British had seized his goods (though he might have just received a handsome payment for them on condition that he would soon supply more). And anyone could submit to a bogus capture followed by a bogus parole: that is, by a release allegedly granted only upon his pledge to take no further part against the British. Since the breaking of parole could bring brutal retaliation on the offender, Connecticut's government had conceded that anyone so bound could excuse himself from military service.[110] This generous gesture gave those who were willing to connive at their own capture the freedom to stay at home and fatten stock for the British.[111]

What could the government do about it? The state might have foraged in these areas, as the Continental army occasionally foraged in Westchester. Or it might have demanded that those who accepted British paroles remain in their jurisdiction instead of returning home.[112] To forage, however, would have further undermined what little political influence the government had there, and it already lacked the power to enforce a decree of exile. The state tried to keep some control over the area, but as long as the British maintained a large force in New York, any concentration of troops around Greenwich would as likely provoke an attack as it would help to defend the frontiers. Though Connecticut retained a precarious military foothold there throughout the war, after 1779 the southwest no longer fully belonged to her in a political sense.[113]

A similar change in the composition of the population took place along the rest of the coast and led almost imperceptibly to a more favorable environment for the illicit trade. But the degree of change varied according to distance from loyalist bases on Long Island and the tempo of enemy operations against the coast. Violent attacks on patriots occurred less often and less systematically the further away they lived, so that British sympathizers had less opportunity to hide behind bogus captures and paroles. Furthermore, the patriots in those parts could take reprisal for loyalist raids with less fear of the consequences.

The state never lacked volunteers to prey on the enemy. On the contrary, the many to whom the Revolution had brought hardship, and particularly the refugees from Long Island, fairly deluged the government with their applications for the job. One group which applied for a commission proposed to name its whaleboat *Retrieve My Losses*. Since the crews of the commissioned vessels received a part of what they seized as booty, this form of service was popular.[114] The commissioned vessels had orders to prey only on enemy shipping in the Sound, but gradually the temptation grew to extend their activities to the island, where, unfortunately, they soon found trade more profitable than plunder.[115] Trading had none of the risks associated with violence; on the contrary, it ensured a continuous flow of supplies as inevitably as violence would ensure their loss. At home, the traders had little to fear from exposure. To intercept a trader, American or British, often cost the accuser more than the value of the goods he received in return.[116] As time went on, the evidence mounted that the commissioned vessels repeatedly abused their trust by visiting Long Island to trade with the enemy.[117]

The government did everything in its power to protect the Long Islanders from forays for plunder, if only because it feared retaliation. At the same time, it strove to make the seizing of illicit traders more attractive than doing business with them. In May 1779 the legislature passed a law reversing the customary presumption of innocence until guilt had been established. Unless the accused could produce incontrovertible proof to the contrary, a libelant established his claim to seized goods merely by showing that it was "probable . . . such wares, goods and merchandize were imported into this State from Long Island."[118] A year later, the legislature passed another law requiring the county to pay the costs of any action a libelant lost, provided he could show reasonable cause for the original seizure. In an attempt to deal with the whaleboat traffic, which brought in small amounts of British goods from each voyage, the law also provided that where the value of goods seized did not exceed thirty pounds, an assistant and a justice of the peace or two justices of the quorum could hear the action instead of the county courts. If either party requested a jury, it would consist of six men rather than twelve, "the cost of . . . summoning and the fees of said jury to be borne and paid by the party requesting the same." The tribunal's decision was final, a provision which protected libelants against costly appeals. The vessels that had transported goods declared illegal were made subject to libel as well as the goods themselves. And to make private citizens as interested in enforcing the law as those commissioned to do so, the legislature agreed that any informant would receive a half share in the value of goods condemned.[119]

Try as it might, the legislature could not weaken the fundamental attraction of the trade, which was that it gave access to the things producers really wanted. The flow of imports and prize goods into Connecticut came nowhere near satisfying that desire, and though larger supplies of both entered the ports of eastern Massachusetts, few Connecticut consumers could obtain them at that distance. Connecticut farmers wanted what they had not seen since the outbreak of war, British dry goods and West Indian produce. To buy them they needed specie, a coveted medium as useful in the illicit trade as in the limited legal commerce that existed. But the supply, particularly before the French arrived, did not equal the demand. Alternatively, the farmer could go through illicit channels and offer his produce in direct exchange for imported goods. Like all illegal activity, it cost heavily, but it did allow him to make a desirable exchange. To sell his produce for currency did little more than enable him to pay his taxes, a poor incentive indeed.

We can obtain no precise knowledge of how much illicit trade went on, any more than officialdom could then. Then as now, however, enough circumstantial evidence existed to suggest that it throve. The evidence ranges from European reports that Connecticut Tories kept the British in both food and information,[120] reports confirmed by the enemy's knack of raiding when the coast was least prepared,[121] to the fact that New York provision markets were clearly impervious to any delay in the receipt of supplies from Europe. For example, in November 1780 Washington wryly observed that, though the Cork fleet arrived two months late, it caused no inconvenience to New York, from which he inferred "that the great number of mouths, which would otherwise be fed from the public Magazines, are now supported upon the fresh meats and flour of the Country."[122] Sometimes the revolutionaries may have jumped too fast to such conclusions. In January 1781 the civil authority of Greenwich blamed a drop in the New York provision prices on the recent withdrawal of a force that had guarded the southwestern frontier, when a more likely explanation lay in the arrival of another Cork fleet just after the British sent large detachments of men southward.[123] But on several crucial occasions the illicit trade did confer upon the enemy a margin for error it would not otherwise have had.

More damaging than this, the trade raised doubts about the loyalty of the people. The government's response to certain events in 1781 illustrates the problem. It began when Captain Joseph Walker, a native of Stratford and Parsons's aide-de-camp, reported a plot in progress among the Tories of Fairfield County. After Arnold's treason, which showed that disaffection had percolated to the upper ranks of leadership, and after the mutinies of the Pennsylvania and New Jersey lines, which raised the possibility that it had filtered down to the common soldier, Washington viewed any such assertion with alarm. He ordered an investigation by Parsons,[124] who somewhat hastily decided that an extensive network of disaffected persons had formed along the lines laid down in a proclamation issued by Sir Henry Clinton and Admiral Arbuthnot in December 1780. The proclamation had invited "any Association of Men" who wished "instantly [to] terminate the Miseries of your Country" and to escape "from the cruel and tyrannical Usurpations which your Leaders are struggling to support for selfish and corrupt Ends, and at your Risk of being delivered over to Popish and arbitrary Nations," to "declare their Abhorrence of the Rebellion, [and] separate from its Councils." All those who did so by July 1, 1781, "and afterwards demean themselves as dutiful and peaceable Subjects of his Majesty's Government" would receive "Pardon for all past Treasons."[125] Parsons, aware how low the general morale had sunk by the winter of 1781, believed that he had stumbled upon a conspiracy inspired by these words.[126] In a letter to Governor Trumbull dated March 3, he outlined the picture he had drawn for himself from his preliminary investigation.

In the first place, "regular channels of conveying dispatches through the States and to and from Canada for the enemy, are settled and their stages as certain as those of post-riders." He knew, he said, of a "register [of those who had subscribed to the disloyal association] kept in the State" which he meant to find and seize. He also claimed to know the objectives of the conspiracy, which included a "general collection of provisions for the use of the enemy and furnishing them under various pretences, purchasing all the fat cattle in their power . . . discrediting and depreciating the currency of the country by counterfeiting and other means," and the intention to "embarass and perplex our affairs by intimidating the weak, encouraging the wicked and enhancing the ideas of expense and misapplications of moneys." Last and worst, the conspirators were enlisting troops for the enemy, with, so Parsons believed, much more success than the patriots.

In his description, the conspiracy touches so unerringly upon the leadership's deepest anxieties as to make us wonder if Parsons's own fear did not induce some of his observations. Equally revealing is his assumption of helplessness to act. He wrote:

To inflict pecuniary penalties and suffer the criminals to continue near our lines, serves only to make them more cautious but not less mischievous. To apprehend and attempt to punish by civil process, will in this case be of no effect, because we cannot develop the witnesses, and the most pernicious characters are probably those against whom no direct proof can be had. To apprehend indiscriminately by military force all those concerned, I do not feel myself at liberty to do without further authority than I have at present. . . . To attempt to procure a law of the kind upon the present exciting emergency, is but defeating a possibility of success in detecting it.

The legislature did not agree that they were doomed, as Parsons put it, "to become spectators of our own destruction."[127] They passed a law declaring it treason to "profess or declare that the King of Great Britain hath or of right ought to have any authority or dominion in or over this State or the inhabitants thereof" or to "seduce or perswade [sic] any inhabitant or inhabitants of this State to renounce his or their allegiance to this State . . . or to acknowledge allegiance or subjection to the King or crown of Great Britain." Persons convicted of having spread treason in writing could receive a death sentence; those who had confined themselves to speech would spend the rest of the war imprisoned in Newgate.[128] The legislature also passed a law temporarily transferring jurisdiction over trials for treason to state and Continental court-martials, though the law applied only to cases tried at Greenwich or cases in which the accused had accepted British protection. Lastly, the governor and Council directed Parsons to continue his investigation.[129]

The legislature and executive responded thus vigorously because, before Parsons ever uttered his alarms, they had already been frightened by reports of a scheme to promote the illicit trade by importing British manufactures from large stockpiles on Long Island.[130] Nothing much came of Parsons's investigation, as it happened: he contracted a serious illness that removed him from the scene of action, besides which the premature arrest of certain suspects may have warned others to retreat.[131] Nevertheless, the government continued to worry about the rumored goods on Long Island. The Council of Safety betrayed its own anxiety when it commissioned vessels to land there and seize British goods, immediately after it had revoked all private commissions on the ground that their holders had used them as a cover for illicit trading or for plundering the people of the island. At first the newly commissioned boats were confined to action against eastern Long Island and placed under the close supervision of William Ledyard. Before long, however, the government extended their scope westward the length of the island,[132] a concession granted in the teeth of strong protest within and without the state. The civil authority and selectmen of several coastal towns petitioned the Council to revoke its action lest they become objects of retaliation.[133] New York's Governor Clinton also protested and said that the inhabitants of Suffolk County had begged him to intervene.[134] But the state continued to issue the commissions, though for only one cruise at a time, apparently in the hope that this restriction would cut down on abuse.

In early August, prompted by the appeals of Clinton and the New York Senate, Congress resolved to censure Connecticut for the raids.[135] Governor Trumbull had attempted to forestall censure with a lengthy defense that began with a disquisition on the implications of the illicit trade:

> The enemy, convinced that they cannot conquer the country by arms, have meditated and are pursuing a different measure, founded on the old maxim, *divide et impera*. For this end the British ministry have sent large quantities of goods to New York; large parcels of them have been brought along the whole length of [Long Island] . . . agreeably to a plan systematically laid, to introduce them on the main to various places on our sea coasts, to the care and disposal of inimical, evil, & artful men, fit tools for their turn, to catch hold of the avarice, luxury, pride and vanity of some persons who are designing and others who are unwary. These pernicious tools, with the allurements furnished them, spread the contagion of corruption, falsehood, unreasonable jealousies, a cry of intolerable taxes, and artfully seduced young men to enlist and join the associated loyalists, and they secretly hand out the declaration of General Clinton and Admiral Arbuthnot offering pardon.

Trumbull described the commissioned vessels as necessary to "counteract the wicked devices of an enemy who leave nothing unessayed by force, seduction, or fraud to destroy us," and the "clamour of inimical and interested persons against the armed boats" as predictable considering "the success these boats have had . . . [against] the dangerous intercourse and trade."[136] The rights of property must yield, he said, to the consideration of how best to further the cause. And the trade threatened the cause in two ways: it prevented the state from procuring her own resource, or from keeping it out of enemy hands, while it undermined that basic trust and willingness to pursue a common objective without which no society at war can function.[137]

Demoralization

In the summer of 1781, Trumbull might well fear the loss of mutual trust. Connecticut's bankruptcy had shattered the public morale. The symptoms of malaise took various forms. A suspicion arose that those in the seats of power abused their position. In the spring of that year, a writer calling himself "A Son of Liberty" attacked the judges of the inferior court, the sheriff, and the state's attorney of New London County in the *Norwich Packet*. "Common fame says," he wrote, "that you, Gentlemen, have declined taking your fees for attending the trial of the capture of goods imported from Long Island, & in the money emitted by this state, and have in lieu, paid yourselves out of the goods when condemned, taking your choice of them, at the appraisal in hard money, and that you have at the same time, refused to dispose of the remainder for this State's money." The writer felt particularly incensed that these officials refused to accept state money themselves at the same time as they accused the Long Island traders of depreciating it.[138]

No less a figure than Benjamin Huntington, one of the state's delegates to Congress, answered "A Son of Liberty." He denied that any court official had refused to accept his fees in the depreciating medium at nominal value, though he did admit that the sheriff who auctioned libeled goods had rejected state money as payment because "the county [had] no present use for [it]." He himself had on occasion accepted goods in lieu of money, but only when all parties agreed to the arrangement and when in fact the money would have had a higher value. The admission only provoked "A Son of Liberty" to renewed fulmination, this time directed against Huntington, who, according to the writer, would have lost his seat in the Assembly if he had published his letter before the freemen's meeting.[139]

Huntington at least escaped the more damaging charge of direct involvement in the illicit trade; Parsons did not. In June 1780, Captain Eliphalet Lockwood had told Silliman that the Long Island traders were using passes given them by Parsons and even alleged to the Council of Safety that both Parsons and General Robert Howe had engaged in the traffic.[140] Parsons evidently learned of the accusation, for in August he sent Lockwood an angry letter pointing out that "there's not a guard on the Coast but is taxed with being concerned in the trade" and none more than those "within the limits of your command." Parsons added furthermore that he was "very sensible many gentlemen would wish the facts you mention were true as to me, and many others would wish to create suspicions of the conduct of other people to serve as a screen to their own transgressions."[141] If this explanation for the rumors of official complicity had any truth to it, the number of "gentlemen" who transgressed had grown great indeed. For by the beginning of 1780 the tide of rumor had risen to engulf the highest personage in the state.

At the end of March, William Williams broke the news to Governor Trumbull that he himself had been accused. A militia subaltern in Mansfield had circulated a rumor that Trumbull connived in the shipping of grain to Long Island, which had helped, perhaps, to erode the once overwhelming majority that elected him to the governorship for ten years in succession.[142] Trumbull responded temperately at first. Undoubtedly, he knew there were other reasons besides the charge of trading for his unpopularity that year.[143] But when he lost his majority again in 1781, he decided to confront the rumor squarely. On January 29, 1782, he sent an address to the legislature declaring that his silence had been construed as an admission of guilt. A committee subsequently appointed to investigate the rumors reported that they originated in calculated enemy attempts to set the people against the government, attempts in which the British had even gone to the trouble of exposing consignments allegedly addressed to Trumbull where Connecticut prisoners in New York could see them. The report appeared in the *Connecticut Courant* in late March,[144] the legislature having timed its publication to allow for maximum effect on the freemen's meetings in April. As a result, Trumbull did regain his majority for a time, but even the legislature's endorsement could not counteract the rumors more than momentarily. The collapse of the economy made them seem all too true.

Trumbull could count himself lucky that the legislature defended his reputation at all. More often than not, such charges of complicity in the trade led the leadership to distrust each other as the people distrusted all of them. Rumor had poisoned the very source of community life. Some hint of its destructive potential appears in the case of William Worthington, a prominent resident of Saybrook. In 1774 he was a rising man, elected to represent the town in the lower house for a fourth consecutive term, honored by an appointment as justice of the peace, and the recipient of a commission as major in the Seventh State Regiment. His military career went on apace. He received the appointment of lieutenant colonel in March 1775 and of colonel in May 1777. In April 1777 he sponsored the presentation to the Council of Safety of David Bushnell's plans for a submarine.[145] He swore the new oath of allegiance in August 1777 and subsequently took part in secret operations against British shipping.[146] Two years later, when the General Assembly authorized an additional guard to patrol the coast from the fort at the mouth of the Connecticut River to Guilford and to watch for illicit traders, Worthington received command of it and also of Captain Shipman's company in the fort.[147]

On November 27, 1779, Sergeant Ephraim Kelsey of Shipman's company seized goods from a vessel operated by Richard Seamans, a Long Island refugee. The goods belonged to another refugee, a Dr. William Lawrence. Seamans had brought them in under a permit issued by Worthington, but

Kelsey seized them because of minor discrepancies between what the permit allowed and what Seamans had carried. In December, when the Council of Safety heard the case, it proposed a compromise in which Kelsey would return the goods to Lawrence and Lawrence would pay him "reasonable expenses" incurred in the seizure. There the matter might have ended. But in January another important Saybrook man, Major William Hart, presented a memorial to the General Assembly accusing Worthington of having helped Seamans to smuggle British goods on occasions preceding the Lawrence affair.[148] The lower house appointed a committee to investigate, which subsequently reported the facts so far as it could discover them. Acting on that report, the upper house resolved that Worthington had been "incautious and imprudent" but nothing worse. A good deal of the "evidence" against him rested on hearsay, besides which the legislators knew that Worthington had done some secret service work and probably decided that any apparently questionable dealings could be explained by reference to that business.[149]

This reasoning failed to satisfy Hart and certain other townsmen. They had not liked the Council of Safety's decision on the Lawrence case, and now Hart complained that Dyer Throop, one of the committee to investigate Worthington, had tried to make Shipman return some other goods his guard had recently seized. Hart said that Throop had gone on to denounce the laws against illicit trading and to declare that "any person that took any property as [Shipman] had . . . and made use of [it] to his private advantage was as bad as a Thief."[150] Hart also repeated a rumor "that Mr. Worthington & his Junto has a plan for the Committee, which is to Report that no proof of any Consequence was to be found against him and that this information and Complaint was sturid [*sic*] up by his Enemies."[151] Armed with these grievances, he rallied the lower house against the upper house. And though he could not have Worthington expelled from the legislature or relieved of military command, he did enough damage for Worthington's name to be removed from the roster of justices.[152]

Worthington then insisted on a trial, which the legislature

appointed for January 30. When the time came, the pressure of other business and a disagreement between the two houses prevented the legislature from taking any further action, which Worthington construed as exoneration. On the strength of that claim, he won election to the General Assembly, though with a bare margin of three votes. It is also possible that most of his support came from the residents of the western parish, generally believed to be traders themselves. Worthington's election provoked a series of angry petitions to the General Assembly, accusing him of "electioneering" and his supporters of giving him their votes because they shared his lawless business interest, while seventeen captains and twenty-four subalterns in his regiment threatened to resign their commissions if the legislature did not remove him from command.[153] Once again the General Assembly resolved to hear the evidence. This time, however, influenced perhaps by the fear that a major coastal regiment would disband, the upper house arrived at a compromise. It passed a resolution that listed the charges, including the charge that said "Worthington associates with persons of inimical characters, and hath frequently and publickly damned and condemned the laws of this State made to restrain illicit trade, and all concerned in executing said laws," invited him to appear before both houses to clear his name, and meanwhile suspended him from command.[154] Though I find no evidence that Worthington accepted the invitation, he won reelection to the legislature in May 1782, again in October 1783, and regained his commission as justice of the peace and quorum in 1785.[155]

Not only did incidents like this set the leadership at odds with one another; in the communities where they originated, they set the people at odds too, and this at a time when the government needed the help of the coastal towns. In Saybrook, the Worthington controversy made a rift between the western parish (modern Westbrook) and the First Society at the mouth of the river. In Branford, a tension arose between the main settlement near Branford Harbor and the eastern part of town opposite the Thimble Islands (modern Stony Creek), a hive of busy traders.[156] In towns with little coastline, division followed the pattern of interior communities pitted against shoreline dwellers.[157] Similar divisions appeared on a larger scale in quarrels between one town and another. Inhabitants of towns in the interior suspected, not without reason, that the authorities in towns vulnerable to attack appeased the enemy by making compromises in their enforcement of the laws against the trade. They heard stories that increased their doubts, like the report that Samuel Whiting had allowed some inimicals to use certain dubious flags.[158] And they knew that the authorities in coastal towns sometimes interceded for persons of questionable character, as when the selectmen and twenty-six leading residents of Norwalk petitioned Parsons to release one Thomas Taylor, a prime suspect in Parsons's conspiracy investigation. When Parsons arrested him, he had cited "clear and convincing proof" that Taylor was "guilty of offences highly injurious to the interests of the country"; yet his fellow townsmen continued to assert their belief in him.[159] The skeptical interpreted these testimonials as evidence that they valued his presence only because his collaboration as a trader won them immunity from British and refugee raids.

The degree to which bankruptcy had demoralized people appeared not only in the rise of the illicit trade but also in the response to Benedict Arnold's attack on Groton and New London. Clinton had conceived the attack as a diversion to keep Washington and Rochambeau from concentrating their troops against Cornwallis in Virginia and also as a way to retake some valuable prizes recently brought into the harbor. Arnold probably hoped to surprise the town by night. But the offshore wind, which so often replaces an evening's southwesterly breeze as the land becomes cooler than the sea, frustrated his design. The town sighted the fleet at first light on September 6, 1781. Though Arnold landed 1,000 men at New London and 800 men at Groton by midmorning, the patriots had already evacuated the women and children and sent the prizes up the river. The small garrison at Fort Trumbull, indefensible because it was not enclosed on all sides, also had time to remove and join Colonel William Ledyard's force at Fort Griswold in Groton, a much stronger position.[160]

Ledyard's men, many of them volunteers, numbered 150 at most. Despite the enemy's vast superiority of numbers, they resolved to defend the fort. They clung to the expectation, a reasonable one in the circumstances, that the militia would soon muster and relieve them.[161] Though the British had scrambled the first alarm signal of two cannon shots by adding a shot of their own to make it sound like three (the victory signal), the continuous firing would warn the countryside of something amiss.[162] And Ledyard had taken the extra precaution of dispatching messengers to appeal for militia relief, as well as messengers to call the seamen from the vessels upriver into the fort.[163] Since the offshore wind delayed Arnold's landing for six hours after the alarm had sounded, the militia could easily have mustered before the attack began. At least one volunteer from Stonington, seven miles away, reached the fort in time for the action.[164] Besides, the attack was not wholly unexpected. Five days before, a deserter from a raiding party at West Haven had warned that the British had bigger things in store for the coast.[165] In any case, the government knew Clinton well enough to guess that, when he heard Washington and Rochambeau were closing in on Cornwallis, he would attack the Connecticut coast.[166] The Council of Safety had already ordered the removal inland of all captured enemy property when word came that Arnold had landed.[167] And though the average militiaman did not know all that the government knew, everyone must have seen that the recent arrival of the prize brig *Hannah*, carrying a cargo estimated at £80,000, invited attack.[168]

With every reason to expect reinforcement, Ledyard found that his small body of men was to receive none. Even so, they almost held out. They would have done, had not their attackers perceived a weak spot in their defense. Forty of the heroic garrison were slaughtered, most of them after Ledyard had surrendered, only to be run through with the sword he presented to the British commander. Almost all the others received wounds.[169] The British took off the walking wounded as prisoners, using them with gratuitous brutality.[170] They tried to take the badly wounded as well, but after they had loaded them on an ammunition wagon, which was then allowed to career down a hill until it crashed into a tree, they left these prisoners, untended, to their fate.[171] During all that time, from eleven in the morning to sundown, the militia made not the slightest attempt either to fight off the British or to help the fort by diverting them. They seem to have spent most of their time extinguishing fires that Arnold's men had set and seizing the opportunity to plunder.[172] Several hours elapsed before anyone discovered and attended to the wounded men.

Yet people who had witnessed events from inside the fort said that they had seen men gathering on hilltops just before the attack began.[173] If we may believe Frances Caulkins, who had heard the personal testimony of people alive at the time, these men had refused at the last moment to commit themselves to a fight against vastly superior numbers in a place from which there was no retreat. Those inside the fort had begged them to enter, but they had answered that the garrison should abandon the position.[174] They might have found the courage to go in if more of them had been there, but, then again, they might not. In April 1782 a group of prominent New Londoners testified that, in their opinion, though a few enthusiasts in outlying towns might respond to an alarm, the majority would always find some excuse.[175] They would never had said so in 1779, when the strong and willing support of neighboring communities had helped to expel the British from East Haven and to press them hard wherever else they landed. A sorry change had come about since then.

Sources of Alienation

The decline in public morale confronted the leadership with an unpleasant choice. Either they must let the people's lack of enthusiasm diminish the vigor with which they pursued the cause or they must resort to force. Many still-passionate patriots favored force. The same New Londoners who had said that they could depend on none but themselves in case of enemy attack also believed that only the harshest coercion would recruit even enough local men to defend New London and Groton. They reasoned that the two towns between them should have mustered at least five hundred men to serve at Fort Griswold and that five hundred men would have made it not only impregnable to attack but strong enough to protect American shipping from British assault. Groton and New London together contained about 1,500 men between sixteen and fifty years of age,[176] not to mention the large number of itinerant seamen who hung about the harbor. "[I]f the late worthy Col. Ledyard . . . had only fifty good men in the Fort under his absolute command, he with them might have empress'd & compelled into its defence two or three hundred seamen & others, which had deserted from Privateers & shipping in order to plunder," they declared, "[b]ut instead of this he was a man without hands, and could get none into the fort only by persuasion [*sic*]." The seamen had disobeyed his orders to come in even though he "fired upon the shiping [*sic*] to stop them from running away . . . [b]ut he was neglected with impunity. He was disobey'd because the laws are not adequate for the punishment of disobedience of orders." They urged that the punishment for disobedience during an alarm take some corporal form since "men will not regard fines when their property is at stake." For, they said, "if men of Spirit who run to the defense of any post in time of danger are to be unsupported and sacrificed by their neighbours (who are at liberty to take care of their effects, keep out of danger and not liable to corporeal punishment), who will run the risque in the future?"[177]

The government's former attempts at coercion had met with small success. Ever since 1779 it had periodically threatened to seize produce if the farmers would not sell it to the army, and the farmers had always responded by secreting their supplies. So it went with recruitment. In 1781 the reluctance of the towns to exploit the coercive aspects of classing for the Continental service, and the open obstructions of detachment by many town officials, had shown that trying to force recruits out of the towns could be as counterproductive as trying to force supplies out of producers. If the legislature that met in January 1782 could have raised its quota of 1,505 for the army by any means other than classing, it would have done so.[178] Like the New London petitioners, it could think of no other means.

Though the legislators had no choice but to revert to classing, they tried to give it a form that would prove more effective. They ordered the towns, acting corporately or in classes, to try to raise recruits by offering monetary inducements. If a town had not hired its men by April 5, the commanding officer of the local militia regiment must make up the deficiency by preemptory detachment. Each recruit would receive an eight-pound bounty whether or not he had enlisted voluntarily, but three-quarters of it would be paid him only after he had completed his eight months of service. If the officer still could not procure men, he must apply to the secretary of state for writs of execution against one or more of the town's principal inhabitants for payment of its fines. The legislature made the same provision for raising 480 state troops, except that in this instance the secretary would issue writs against the selectmen.[179]

Though the legislators intended this measure to give civil authorities and men of property an incentive to cooperate with militia officers, they must have foreseen the equal possibility that it would set them at each other's throats and that in any confrontation the militia would stand at a disadvantage despite the sanction of law. Roger Newberry warned the government that the militia had so sunk in the popular esteem that to use it in pressuring the people would have no other result "than to bring Government into still greater Contempt."[180] And even as the Assembly debated ways to fill the Continental battalions, Trumbull received a report from John Mead that subordinate officers in the militia refused to obey the order to detach. They knew that no penalty under military law would attach to their refusal but that they had much to fear from the people's suspicion of their "thirst after Power and Command."[181] The potential for destructive confrontation could not have escaped the legislature's notice, and perhaps it is not surprising that in May it seized on a minor incident as an excuse to pull the teeth from the law it had passed in January.

When three recruits "who had been received by the Continental Mustering Officers . . . and their bounty paid" were discharged as below the required height, one of them having already served in the army for three years and the others for shorter terms, and all "wanting only an Inch or two of the Standard," [182] the House rebelled. It passed a resolution giving militia colonels the power to certify men as fit recruits and exempting from fines all classes that had furnished men satisfactory to a state recruiting officer. It also refused either to publish the act prescribing execution against the wealthiest members of a delinquent class or to issue blanket executions for the secretary of state to sign. [183] As a result, Connecticut sent only 360 men to the army that year, [184] a contribution almost too small to balance the losses sustained through sickness and desertion in the previous twelve months. Congress might think itself lucky that the autumn of 1782 found the end of the war in sight.

Connecticut's response to congressional requisitions followed the same pattern. Thanks to Robert Morris, director of national finances at last, Congress for once made its requisitions far enough ahead for the states to meet them before the next campaign. Congress hoped to raise $8 million, of which Connecticut owed $747,196 or 9.3 percent, [185] as compared with the 11–12 percent of previous years. The reduction should have allayed the mounting storm of resentment over the former apportionment of burdens, [186] and Connecticut should have found it easier to meet the quota. But the legislature dragged its feet on the collection of money for the continent. The first quarterly payment of approximately $200,000 fell due in April. The legislature proposed a threepenny tax on the list of 1781, payable in specie or the notes issued by the Bank of North America. After abatements, that tax, collected in full, would have yielded only $56,000. To make up the remaining $144,000, the legislature proposed to sell the provisions which they assumed the town collectors had received in lieu of the two-and-sixpenny provision tax due the preceding December. [187] At the beginning of March, the government ordered Jabez Perkins of Norwich and Ebenezer Bernard of Hartford to prepare for sale the provisions gathered in eastern Connecticut.

Those gathered in the western towns they reserved for the use of troops and quartermasters there.[188]

In May, when the new legislature assembled, the Pay-Table reported that the two-and-sixpenny tax had yielded only £26,911 worth of provisions, which, even if all were at hand and in good condition, would yield no more than $90,000.[189] The General Assembly had to lay another tax, this time for one shilling, due on July 1, the date on which the state should also have made her second quarterly payment. After abatements, the tax collected in full would have yielded $226,143, which might have kept the state on time in meeting her obligations until midsummer had collections been punctual.[190] They were not. The collectors did not begin to receive the tax due in April until July, and Robert Morris had yet to receive a penny of the first installment at the beginning of September.[191] When the legislature met in October, it probably recognized the futility of laying more taxes, given the heavy arrearages that were being added to those already accumulated in 1780 and 1781. Instead, it ordered the treasurer to send the towns all balances due on taxes up to October 15, so that they might "use every means in their power" to collect. The legislature also instructed the treasurer to call in all outstanding executions and reduce them to a single one against the property of the town collector. If the town then made provision for settling at least a third of its debt by November 20, the treasurer could stay execution until January 20, 1783, when the whole amount fell due.[192]

Perhaps because people had little to lose, legislative threats and promises had little effect. Where a town bore collective responsibility for certain requisitions, such as those laid for provisions in 1780, a threat of execution that applied to all townspeople equally could produce results. But where individual collectors bore the responsibility, the threat had a hollow ring. The collector's property would not have begun to pay the huge arrearages owed by most towns. In so bankrupt an economy it seemed unlikely that even the forced sale of many properties would have paid them. And the government knew by the experience of Massachusetts that the attempt could rouse violent opposition.[193] The legislature that met in January 1783 authorized the Pay-Table Committee to sue for outstanding debts but exempted "the Collectors of Publick Taxes" from the measure. It took no action to follow up the earlier threat other than ordering the Pay-Table to publish "an Account of all Monies received on any and all Taxes that have been . . . laid."[194] The report, when it appeared, showed that the yield on taxes laid in 1782 had declined almost to the point of total default.[195]

Though bankruptcy played a part in Connecticut's failure to provide either men or money for the continent in 1782, her growing dissatisfaction with the national leadership had just as much to do with it. In the wake of the New London raid, she had asked Congress to put ten companies of state troops on the Continental establishment.[196] The committee that studied the request had favored it, citing Washington's opinion that Connecticut's case was similar to New York's, where militia regiments had been charged to the continent. But the committee also said that the state should receive no Continental aid until she filled her quota for the Continental army. Though Congress admitted that this amounted to refusal, it would not waive the condition.[197] The legislature's willingness to eviscerate its own plan to raise Continental recruits reflected its resentment. And in the autumn, when Congress refused to reduce Connecticut's quota for Continental requisitions from 9.7 percent to 8.3 percent, the delegates gave vent to a vague threat that Connecticut "would do justice to her self" so far as the states were concerned.[198] From foremost supporter of the cause at the start of the war, Connecticut had sunk to the level of "most backward in furnishing [her] quota."[199]

The trouble no longer stemmed just from the general conviction that Congress had asked Connecticut to pay more than her fair share. Two other issues had soured the relations between state and continent. One was the controversy over the Susquehannah lands, which had continued to simmer throughout the war. In 1781, when the states at last ratified the Articles of Confederation, Congress agreed to adjudicate between Pennsylvania and Connecticut. That November, Congress scheduled the hearing for the following June,[200] a date set under pressure from Pennsylvania which had long urged a prompt resolution. Pennsylvania feared that the more Connecticut residents encroached upon the territory, the harder it would be to sort out and settle the matter to another state's advantage. Besides, Pennsylvania wanted to establish her right to as much of the unsettled western territory as possible to use in salvaging her postwar finances.[201] From Connecticut's point of view, an immediate resolution had disadvantages. Many of the documents relevant to her own claim had been sent to England before the war, and it would take time to retrieve them.[202] Once Congress had set a date, however, Connecticut could not refuse to appear without risking forfeiture. She tried to delay the proceedings by questioning the Pennsylvania Council's right to appoint agents, but when Congress indicated that this tactic would not work, she had no recourse left but to plead her case before a tribunal composed of largely unfriendly delegates.[203] Considering the state of her finances, the prospect of losing the Susquehannah lands loomed in the public mind as the prospect of losing the state's last asset.

The other disagreement between state and continent concerned prisoners. The surrender at Yorktown restored to Americans the superiority of numbers they had lost in the fall of Charleston. This made the British anxious to recover what men they could through a general exchange and the American authorities equally anxious to see that any such arrangement also conferred some advantage on them.[204] They wanted compensation in specie for each British prisoner returned, and at a rate which would help restore the nation's finances.[205] The British regarded the figure named as exorbitant and sought to reduce it by bringing a kind of pressure that bore down with cruel force upon the government and people of Connecticut. They had in their custody a large number of naval prisoners taken from the state's privateers, prisoners whom they kept caged in horrifying conditions at New York. Connecticut was not left in comfortable ignorance about the plight of these men. Because of the continuing need to negotiate the release of kidnapped civilians, a good deal of coming and going took place between Connecticut and New York. In the course of it, Connecticut received frequent, heartrending reports about the sufferings of the naval prisoners.[206] Knowing this, the British now saw a way to use those prisoners as a lever to pry loose some of the men they had lost at Yorktown. They demanded that the continent accept naval prisoners in exchange for soldiers.[207]

Simultaneously, sentiment had built up within Connecticut for an immediate, partial exchange of all prisoners held in the state in order to save the Connecticut prisoners at New York.[208] The Connecticut privateers had brought in a great many British prisoners during 1782, but because the state could not provide sufficient guards for them they disappeared at a scandalous rate. When the New London privateers petitioned the Council of Safety for a prison ship, the Council gave them one at once.[209] Since, however, the guard on board consisted mostly of boys, the prisoners soon overpowered them and once again escaped. If the state had so little power to hold her prisoners, why not gain what advantages she could by exchanging them?[210] Washington, of course, had reservations about the proposal. To replenish British manpower in any way might alienate the French and upset the delicate peace negotiations taking place in Europe.[211] Nevertheless, in principle he agreed on the desirability of retrieving the naval prisoners, though he insisted on excluding noncombatants from the exchange and, in the interests of fairness and efficiency, he wanted a central Continental authority to monitor the exchange of prisoners taken by private vessels.[212]

To the government of Connecticut, that authority appeared an unnecessary obstruction,[213] and the government's impatience spread to the people when they read Carleton's letter of August 2 informing Washington that negotiations had begun in Europe and that British delegates had instructions to concede American independence. The letter, published in all the Connecticut newspapers, also proposed a general exchange of naval prisoners for soldiers on the understanding that men recovered by the British could not serve on the continent for a year.[214] Washington had reason to beware even so, since the British might still use the returnees against the French in the West Indies.[215] But the people of Connecticut, anxious for peace and for the release of their relatives from captivity, chafed at his hesitation.

CHAPTER SEVEN

The Perils of Peace

ONE MIGHT expect the approach of peace to have resolved most problems for Connecticut, including that of the naval prisoners. Since the early spring of 1782, Americans had recognized that developments in Europe tended toward a general settlement favorable to their wishes. They drew particular encouragement from the fall of the North ministry and the succession of a new one more inclined to abandon the war.[1] In August, the new British commander in New York, Sir Guy Carleton, announced that American naval prisoners held in Britain would be released along with the peace commissioner, Henry Laurens, a prisoner in the Tower; and that emissaries had left for Paris with power to conclude a general peace. For all their high hopes, Americans hardly dared believe it was true until direct confirmation of Laurens's release, together with a report that Franklin had summoned Jay from Madrid, convinced them that negotiations had begun in earnest.[2] Other good news soon followed: the Netherlands had recognized United States independence and had agreed to make a loan.[3]

Besides the news from abroad, certain developments at home also showed the way the wind blew. The British mounted no new offensive during 1782, or at least none along the Atlantic coast, where most of the fighting had taken place before. British commanders acted in ways that suggested they did not expect to do battle again. In late June, Alexander Leslie proposed a cessation of hostilities in the South,[4] and in October reports that the British were withdrawing from Charleston arrived together with Carleton's proposal for a cease-fire. Though Washington rejected the proposal,[5] in the following January he received news that the British had indeed evacuated Charleston, an act which completed the liberation of the South.[6] The British garrison remained in New York to the end, but quiescent except for a little illicit trading. In Connecticut, as elsewhere, spirits began to rise. It seemed reasonable to suppose that if the state could only tread water she would eventually win free of her difficulties. In December, when Congress at last received official word that the British commissioners had instructions to recognize independence, it came as no surprise.[7] And by the beginning of the year, the Connecticut leadership knew they had not long to wait. Though conflicting rumors kept up some degree of suspense for a few more weeks, most of them pointed in the general direction of peace with independence.

Warning Signals

Peace came but came too late to save Connecticut. Though the worst was over, the last spasms of the war caused her much anguish. Major action had ceased, but the illicit trade made even more trouble than before, not by helping the British to fight on so much as by preventing the Americans from healing their wounds. Many shared Washington's opinion that the trade corrupted "the morals of our people." Certainly it exacerbated shortages by spiriting to Long Island and New York those provisions that rightly belonged to the American army. Certainly it provided the enemy with "regular and perfect intelligence of every thing among us." Even more damaging, the trade increased the difficulty of collecting taxes in hard money by draining off what little specie had entered the economy as a consequence of French purchases and occasional remittances from abroad.[8] And this difficulty obstructed Robert Morris's plan to restore public credit so that the Republic could once more procure with consent rather than by force.[9]

Worst of all, the trade threatened the Franco-American Alliance because it betrayed to the French how much Americans still yearned for the commercial benefits of the British Empire. When the French ambassador finally protested, the leadership took alarm.[10] They saw French support as vital to the achievement of a general European peace treaty that would secure the new nation. They still feared that, should the negotiations end in deadlock, the European powers might make peace on the principle of *uti possedentis*. If this happened, the United States would lack the strength to drive the British from Long Island and New York,[11] and so long as the illicit traffic continued the British would have no incentive to yield them peacefully. Nor would they feel any need to woo Americans for their lucrative trade when they already enjoyed so many of its benefits clandestinely. On the contrary, control of New York would give Britain a base from which to regulate the part of the trade she most wanted. That would hopelessly compromise the results of the Revolution and raise the depressing possibility that all the years of struggle had gone for nothing.[12] If the United States were to keep the support of France, and to keep her own commerce under her own control, the trade must stop.

How to stop it, however, remained a puzzle. Though offensive warfare no longer engrossed the army's time and energy, Washington insisted that his men could not undertake the job. He backed his opinion with sound reasons. At the time, the forces at his command were too weak to seal off British territory from patriot territory. Even if he had had more men, it would be the height of folly to scatter them about New York where the British could pick them off piecemeal.[13] What he did not say, though he probably thought it, was that his own men might succumb to the attractions of the trade as the adventurers commissioned by Connecticut had succumbed before them. Their wages, he well knew, would not keep them from temptation. Since the mutinies of 1781, he could all too easily conceive that his army might end in some such inglorious way. He preferred to have the states deal with the problem by themselves. But he thought they could do so only by making the traffic a capital offense, and no state would pass so Draconian a law.[14] Connecticut refused to increase the penalty by any more than the addition of a prison term to the trader's loss of his goods.[15]

Even if Connecticut had legislated harsher remedies, she lacked the power to apply them. Because Congress had refused to put any state troops on the Continental establishment, Connecticut could afford to deploy only a skeletal force along the coast.[16] That force the government supplemented, as before, with private vessels commissioned to capture traders, which had the advantage of reminding everyone that there was still a war on. But the problem remained that those engaged to suppress the trade too often engaged in it. By the end of 1782, Connecticut had clearly become the center of the traffic with British-occupied New York. At the request of the civil authorities and selectmen of Fairfield, Washington sent Benjamin Talmadge to investigate, who reported to both Washington and Trumbull that the Long Island trade was largely conducted by the state-commissioned vessels.[17]

The Connecticut government responded as best it could. It passed a law requiring that the authorities report any person suspected of abusing his commission and that those convicted, in addition to other penalties, lose the right either to sue in the courts or to vote in elections. The Council of Safety also asked Talmadge to supply the names of the people he suspected.[18] Beyond this, the state could do nothing. Only Washington had sufficient men in arms to suppress the trade by force. And at last he decided that he must overrule his own decision not to use them in that way. He ordered Talmadge to arm and man several vessels to clear the Sound of traders, an order that Talmadge carried out with commendable zeal. In February, for instance, his men captured an eleven-gun enemy vessel off Stratford.[19] Nevertheless, he could not cover the entire coastline.

By the end of the war, Connecticut's principal weapon against the trade remained the law of 1778 that made illegal imports the property of anyone who proved their illegality. Gradual modification of the law had reduced the rigor of the demand for the libelant to show proof at the same time as they increased his protection from the risk that some hastily accused person

would sue him. In return for his greater ease and safety, he had
to share his profits with the state. The legislature had also tried
to seal off the indirect trade via Amsterdam and Saint Eustatius
with a law passed in May 1781 that prohibited "the Importation
from any Country or Place [of] . . . any Goods Wares or Merchandize that have been . . . manufactured within the Dominions or Possessions of the King of England except Goods captured
from the Enemy." The statute instructed the courts to con-
demn goods if the libelant could show even a mere probability
of their illegal status.[20] Laws such as these, which slanted the
judicial process in favor of the libelant, certainly dimmed the
attractions of the trade. But they also encouraged abuses of the
power to search and seize and promoted an atmosphere in
which people grew hardened to preying on one another.[21]

The new state of society had a potential for trouble which
was fulfilled in and demonstrated by two incidents in particular. The first took place in New Haven, where a Long Island
refugee, Ebenezer Dayton, had shown obnoxious assiduity in
the libeling of local vessels. On December 12, 1782, some
New Haven inhabitants held a rump meeting, passed a resolution against the illicit trade, and used it as their license to burn
Dayton's whaleboat.[22] They did have reason to think that he
had done some trading himself, but he was not the only one.
They had probably singled him out for retaliation because he
had violated the bonds of community by accusing fellow townsmen.[23] The Dayton incident had a counterpart in New London. A Groton merchant, Thomas Mumford, had joined with
some Massachusetts investors in a commercial venture on the
brigantine *Thetis*, bound from Amsterdam to Boston with a
cargo of British goods. Bad winter weather drove the *Thetis* into
New London, where the cargo was liable to seizure. Mumford,
who realized his jeopardy, immediately asked the legislature for
an exemption. The legislature agreed, but in the interim two
parties had entered libels against the vessel and a mob had
formed to save the cargo. In the ensuing riot, a local justice of
the peace suffered injury,[24] and only the news that the exemption had been granted prevented worse violence. Both incidents

suggest that the laws passed to stop the illicit trade had more anarchic potential than the trade itself.

One might expect such outbreaks to have multiplied as the war dragged out its last year. In fact, even in 1781–82 when seizures of property rose sharply in number, remarkably little retaliatory violence occurred. Most libelants probably took more care than Dayton to avoid offending their neighbors: that is, they did not libel the goods of those on whom they depended for mutual support and assistance in the everyday course of their lives. Community in this sense did not necessarily follow geographical lines. Marginal members of any neighborhood were vulnerable. Residence in the same town did not guarantee immunity, particularly in coastal towns with large shorelines and bitter internal divisions. But seizure and libel, to be effective, needed effective power behind it. And the power of one man, or even a number of men, would be effective only if backed by the community. So, despite the incentives to seize and the large number of takers (to judge from the admiralty court advertisements in the newspapers), the barriers erected against the trade still had holes in them.

Some patriots, disgusted with the apparent inability of the government to control the trade and driven by the fear that it would negate their many sacrifices for the cause, began to urge a reversion to the desperate remedies adopted during the showdown with Britain in 1774 and the collapse of the currency in 1779. They sought to revive the network of popular committees and conventions which had mobilized the people in the past and might do so again, in order to achieve vital objectives that eluded the state. The movement started in the summer of 1782 with a call from Farmington for a county convention of town delegates at Hartford.[25] The convention took place and on August 13 issued a pledge of all-out exertion against the trade which called on the several towns to form associations.[26] Few complied with the convention's explicit recommendations, though some took independent action to ensure that the laws against illicit trading were enforced. New Haven and Fairfield County conventions followed the lead of the Hartford group, but the New Haven convention resolved to continue working through established channels. The only action taken in New London County appears to have been an association of sixty-eight Norwich residents against the trade.[27]

The proponents of the convention movement probably thought that popular initiatives to achieve good ends would enjoy the approval of all patriots.[28] Yet both the convention movement and the associations drew considerable public criticism. Some of the critics felt that the laws against the trade had already tipped the scales of justice so heavily in favor of the libelants as to threaten the liberties of individuals. And some laid the serious charge that it threatened legitimate government too. A writer signed "Pacificus" described Farmington's call for a county convention as "well calculated to excite the *populace* to . . . unjustifiable measures to suppress the Illicit Trade, who by some cooler heads may perhaps be thought already too much influenced to conduct themselves agreeable to the true spirit and meaning of our laws to suppress it." He warned his readers against the "jealousies and suspicions of men of irreproachable characters" being "excited by some *low dirty fellows*, who set themselves up as *patriots*."[29] Governor Trumbull echoed his concern. In October 1782 he harangued the General Assembly on the "danger of running into extream [*sic*] equality—when each citizen would fain be upon a level with those he has chosen to govern him—then the people, incapable of bearing the very power they have delegated, want to manage every thing for themselves—to debate for the senate—to execute for the magistrates—and to decide for the judges." And several anonymous newspaper writers expressed the same fears.[30]

Why, when all the signs pointed to peace, did so many people act as if the state tottered on the brink of catastrophe? The answer is that peace would bring, not the day of redemption from bankruptcy, but the day of reckoning. Already there were ominous indications that the tensions generated both by financial problems and by any attempt to solve them would strain Connecticut's institutions to the limit. For one thing, more and more people blamed the state's bankruptcy on the maladministration of her officials. What else could explain why the army went unpaid and the debt increased at a time when taxation had risen to unprecedented heights?[31] The suspicion led Benjamin Gale to demand a public accounting for all receipts and expenditures of the treasury and to revive proposals that dated from the beginning of the war for full publication of the Assembly's debates and of all roll call votes,[32] measures that would inevitably render the government more responsive to popular pressure.

The most threatening of all the people's demands, however, was that for tax reform. Ever since the burdens of the war had begun to weigh heavily, the system of assessment had come under attack for favoring merchants over farmers. For a long time the controversy had simmered discreetly, confined within the walls of the legislature. In 1781 it boiled over. The whole subject burst on the public that autumn by way of a piece entitled "Strictures on the present mode of Taxation in the State of Connecticut; in a series of Letters from a Gentleman in the northern Part of the state, to one in the southern Part of the same." The "Gentleman" was none other than Erastus Wolcott, who sought to prove the inequities of the system by showing how the lists discriminated against the stock raisers of the interior and in favor of the plowland owners and merchants along the coast.[33] In the following spring, a series published in the *Gazette*, entitled "Upon our present Mode of Taxation and our Practice thereon" and signed "S.M.," restated his arguments. "S.M." did differ from Wolcott in one respect: he charged that the rural towns along the coast received higher assessments than the commercial towns even though they were poorer. But he agreed that the system discriminated against the farmer.[34]

Wolcott had sufficient stature in Connecticut for his "Strictures" to go unchallenged. Not so "S.M." A writer signed "A Lover of Order," who accused him of kindling sedition,[35] spoke for all those who realized that the agrarian interest constituted the majority and feared what would happen if that majority became convinced of the tax system's injustice. Farmers might either engage in tax resistance or seek to assess the mercantile interest so punitively as to cripple the economy. Either course would obstruct the establishment of public credit. Nor could a government that had failed to stop the illicit trade entertain much hope of its ability to negotiate these hazards. In the circumstances, Trumbull and those who shared his views had real reason to fear that a people aroused and organized to support the government might turn round and use their power against it when the time came to pay the debt.

The First Test

The capacity of Connecticut's government to survive the perils of peace received its first serious challenge from a wholly unexpected quarter. The trouble began when Richard Smith, a former Massachusetts merchant who owned substantial property in Connecticut, applied for permission to resettle in the state. Smith had sailed from Boston to Great Britain in July 1775 and stayed there. In 1778 the Massachusetts legislature had proscribed him as a Tory and forbidden him to return. In 1781 Connecticut also appointed a committee to investigate him. His property included the Salisbury foundry, which the state had worked for her own benefit throughout the war, and extensive timber lands, which she had stripped. When the committee (predictably) found that Smith had "voluntarily gone over to and put himself under the protection of the enemy," the legislature ordered him to appear by the following May to defend his estate from forfeiture.[36] Since he did not respond, most people assumed that it would become public property once it had passed the formality of probate.

Smith had some explaining to do when he unexpectedly appeared on November 25, 1782, to plead his case before the Council of Safety. He claimed that he had planned his visit to Europe long before 1775, intending to liquidate his mercantile interests there and in the West Indies. On return, he had expected to settle in Connecticut. But his departure and return were both delayed by circumstances beyond his control, circumstances resulting from the imperial crisis and the revolutionary war. His present request to settle in the state and bring in with him "his goods Furniture & Effects, being chiefly French & Spanish Goods," thus followed a design he had conceived ten years earlier. The Council seems to have believed him but to have fought shy of indulging a suspected loyalist with state citizenship. It referred the issue to the legislature, which met in January 1783.[37] On January 13, Smith petitioned the General Assembly to hear him speak. The Assembly granted the request, Smith spoke both for himself and through counsel, and Erastus Wolcott, who had conversed with Smith during his mission to Gage in 1775, testified in his favor.

Though the legislature submitted Smith to a grueling examination, he somehow managed to persuade a large majority of the House to readmit him.[38] When his case came before the upper house, he met more opposition. He forestalled the non-concurrence of the assistants with a memorial in which he waived all claims against the state for her use of his property,[39] but in the interim new members had arrived in the House who insisted on rehearing the case.[40] This brought a third memorial from Smith. He offered to pay whatever sum the legislature thought he should contribute to the war effort; to lend the government £1,000 from the sale of his goods, as proof of his intention "to mix his Interests with theirs"; and to make no remittances to New York or Britain so long as the war continued. Smith concluded his memorial by reminding the House that he had received prior encouragement to appeal, that he had burned his bridges with the British in doing so, and that for the state to refuse him citizenship now would leave him destitute.[41]

With this, the Assembly yielded. By a large majority the members voted to allow Smith to enter Connecticut with his goods provided that he took the oath of allegiance and released the state from all claims. The Assembly placed only one restriction on his right to bring in goods: he had to swear they had been "his own Property before the passing of this Grant, and not that of any other Persons."[42] This was more than generous in view of the recent law excluding all British goods from Connecticut except those taken as prizes. For Smith alone to receive such a privilege aroused suspicion and resentment. Even before the House made the concession, Moses Seymour had circulated a rumor "that His Excellency Governor Trumbull has during the Session of this Assembly received a Bribe of One Hundred Guineas from one Mr. Richard Smith a Petitioner." The legislature charged Seymour with scandalous insinuations intended "to Injure the reputation and Influence of His Excellency" and "to wound and destroy the Honour and Dignity of the Legislative Body of this State,"[43] which silenced him, but not the controversy over Smith.

On January 19, 1783, just after the legislature allowed Smith's request, a Hartford town meeting, held right under the legislature's nose, appointed a committee to draft a memorial in protest. The memorial accused the legislature of conferring "an exclusive claim to all the Emoluments of the British trade" on a man who had contributed nothing to the Revolution. "[A]t a time, when the Legislature of this State have used every exersion [sic], & imposed the severest penalties to prevent the importation of a single article of British Goods into the Country," they wrote, "We cannot but Be surprised to find liberty granted, to Men, who have nothing to plead in their favour, to double at once the whole amount of their property by bringing into the State, any quantity of British goods they may think proper to call their own." They also suggested that the legislature had negated its own laws.

> The inconsistency between such Grants & the laws in force against Illicit Trade, are so manifest, that we beg leave to offer it as our Opinion, that those laws can never, without the utmost difficulty, be supported & inforced against our own Subjects, if such privileges are granted to those, who have never risqued any thing in our favour, 'till our Independence was established.

The memorial warned the legislators that in opening so advantageous a trade to "our Enemies" while denying it to loyal citizens they had "kindled a flame in this State, which may give birth to such confusions & changes in the Government, as must greatly weaken the strength of the legislation, & fill every part of the Commonwealth with faction & disorder."[44]

The Hartford memorial of January 19 drew answering fire from twenty-two prominent residents. They addressed the legislature, regretting that some people had taken upon themselves the right to criticize the government, and said that they hoped it would "not be considered, as the deliberate Act of the Town, but only the ebullition of intemperate zeal, inspired by design & ambition." Though "it may be the right of the Citizens of a free state to Present decent Addresses upon some occasion," they wrote, "yet we cannot consider it prudent for any, to review or determine, without the knowledge of facts, upon the Acts or doings of a Legislative body, after full enquiry made, & where every one is fully represented. The consequences of such undue measures, are, in our opinion, truly alarming, & in their tendency must terminate in confusion, & the Subversion of order & good Government." They urged the legislature to "suspend any consideration upon the Address that May be presented, as the Supposed act of this Town, until the cool deliberate sentiments of the People may be had."[45] And that august body obliged them by suspending consideration, not only of the Hartford protest but also of a letter that Governor Trumbull had received from a group of New Londoners who opposed the admission of Smith's effects through their port.[46]

On February 1 the privateer *Hampton Packet* seized the sloop *Polly* as she brought Smith's belongings from Long Island to New London and carried her into Rhode Island waters. Four residents of Norwich owned the *Packet*, the most prominent of them Thomas Mumford. Mumford had lived at Groton before moving to Norwich in September 1781. He had married Silas Deane's sister and thanks to that connection had served as an agent for the French. In 1780 the legislature had named him a member of the Council of Safety. He had then suffered a series of reverses. On September 7, 1781, Arnold's men burned his house.[47] The following May, the assistants nominated him to serve again on the Council of Safety, but the lower house rejected him.[48] His standing with them had not been improved by the unfortunate letters Silas Deane had written from Europe the previous spring to several prominent Americans, including Mumford. The British had intercepted the letters and printed them in Rivington's *Gazette* during the autumn. Deane had painted the picture of an undaunted Britain facing an exhausted France, and had counseled his countrymen to abandon the French alliance for reconciliation with the former mother country.[49] But whatever the Assembly's reason for rejecting him, it is plain that Mumford resented the action; that the burning of Groton had left him in need; and that, between alienation and desperation, he was not in a mood to consider his means too scrupulously. We know that he instructed his agents to send a brig named the *Marquis* "into the Sound after said goods."[50]. But his agents, suspecting that Samuel McClellan, the local commander at New London, might refuse the *Marquis* a pass, applied instead for one that would allow the lightly armed *Packet* to take in freight in Stonington.

On the evening of the day that they received the pass, Mumford's men transferred cannon from the *Marquis* to the *Packet* and made off before McClellan could detect the ruse. When Smith told him what had happened, McClellan issued a warrant to a Mr. Angell, commander of a privateer brig, to retake the *Polly*. Angell and Smith pursued and caught her off Narragansett Bay. Mumford's men then applied to the civil authority of Rhode Island demanding the return of the sloop, which bad weather had forced into the bay. Angell threatened to fight if anyone tried to take the *Polly* back and soon afterward succeeded in returning her to New London.[51]

The governor of Rhode Island, incensed by this invasion of his jurisdiction, asked Governor Trumbull to give the vessel up. He made the request at the same time as Mumford and his partners had asked the Connecticut Council of Safety to give her to them.[52] The Council of Safety decided that the General Assembly alone could resolve the issue, which had the dual advantage of postponing action while serving notice that the party to any appeal would be the state itself, not its executive. The Council also took the opportunity to present the issues to the Assembly in language that made clear its disapproval of Mumford.[53] And Trumbull briefed Connecticut's delegates to Congress on the dispute so that if Mumford or Rhode Island did try to carry it before a congressional forum they would be ready to put up opposition.[54]

Mumford saw at once how the land lay, but he bided his time till the end of March. The freemen's meetings would take place at the beginning of April, and the part Governor Trumbull had taken in the controversy gave Mumford's group reason to remove him from office if they could. The people's dissatisfaction over Smith's victory, exemplified in the resolve adopted by the Hartford town meeting, encouraged them to try.[55] On March 28 Mumford, Daniel Rodman, Joshua Huntington, and Giles Mumford published a statement in the *Connecticut Gazette*. In it they purported only to defend themselves from representations of their conduct that showed them "as refractory and disorderly subjects of the State," but in fact they used the statement as a vehicle for an attack on the governor and the Council of Safety. They took care to inform the public that the *Polly* had carried £200 worth of unlicensed goods. They stressed that the *Hampton Packet* had seized her outside Connecticut's jurisdiction and that Captain Angell had retaken her in Rhode Island waters where she was their lawful prize. "Thus while the authority of this state, vested in the hands of Governor Trumbull, is improved as a protection to Mr. Smith, even where it cannot be supposed to extend," they concluded, "we apply to that authority, and apply in vain for our undoubted right."[56]

They had picked a vulnerable adversary in Trumbull. Other damaging rumors were already in circulation about him. He was said to have misapplied various moneys that Congress had sent the state, as well as to have engaged in the illicit trade under cover of his office.[57] As the election drew closer, more rumors arose: for instance, Moses Holmes told William Williams of a report that Trumbull had demanded seventy dollars "for granting a permit Relative to Exchange of a prisoner."[58] The people, made miserable by economic woes, were in the mood to think ill of any authority. "Philanthropus," writing in the *Connecticut Gazette*, lamented that, though the Tories had lost the war, they would soon achieve by innuendo what they had failed to achieve by force. He found it alarming that so many people in western Connecticut, a nest of Tories during the war, had for the first time taken freemen's oaths to qualify in the next election.[59] John Chester also saw signs that the government stood in jeopardy, though he, as an embittered kinsman of Silas Deane in whose official disgrace Trumbull had taken a hand, approved. He looked forward to seeing the Smith controversy "jolt some folks out of the Saddle."[60]

The governor's supporters soon challenged Mumford. Writing under the name "A Spectator," Samuel McClellan justified Smith's reseizure of his goods on the grounds that Mumford and his friends were themselves subject to the very state laws they sought to subvert. He pointed out the inconsistency in Mumford's actions: when he asked and received exemption for the *Thetis*, he invoked the state's authority; when he seized the *Polly*, he defied it.[61] And in April a writer signed "Blunt" argued that since all states assumed the right to regulate the conduct of their citizens on the high seas, Mumford's capture of a ship under the protection of the state to which he owed allegiance amounted to piracy.[62] By that time, however, a new development had compounded the problems of the governor's party.

In the last week of March, the newspapers had published an account of the preliminary treaty between the United States and Britain. Article 5 of the treaty required that Congress "earnestly recommend it to the Legislature of the respective States, to provide for the Restitution of all Estates, Rights, and Properties of Persons . . . residents in Districts in the Possession of his Majesty's Arms; and who have not borne Arms against the said United States."[63] The prospect that this raised of Tories returning in large numbers threw the people into ferment. Feelings ran higher in Massachusetts and New York than in Connecticut because more wealthy Tories had once lived in those states and might come back. But even in Connecticut a strong aversion to the idea appeared, especially in those towns which had suffered attacks led by loyalist defectors. When Stephen Jarvis, a Danbury Tory, returned to the town in the summer of 1783 in order to marry the daughter of a suspected loyalist, a party of armed men threatened his life.[64] When Solomon Ferris of Greenwich, who had deserted to the British in 1777, returned to take his family to Nova Scotia, a mob seized him from his father's house and carried him before a local justice of the peace, who bound him over to trial.[65] Many of the towns in the southwest, including Danbury, Norwalk, Fairfield, Stamford, and Stratford, discouraged the return of loyalists.[66]

The furor over readmitting Tories found a convenient focus in the Smith case, which boded ill for Trumbull. Along with the other charges against him, his role in Smith's readmission might add the name of "Tory lover" to the list of his alleged offenses. It is not surprising, then, that in May, when the votes for the governorship were counted, Trumbull again lacked the necessary majority. Yet the Smith case by itself did not, as the Hartford petitioners had threatened, "give birth to . . . changes in the Government, as must greatly weaken" it.[67] Lieutenant Governor Matthew Griswold won reelection, the twelve councilors of the preceding year retained their seats, and the new legislature chose Trumbull as governor.[68] Though the wartime turnover rates continued to prevail in the house, the Tory issue did not cause them. The new house refused to act on a report from a committee of the preceding legislature which had advocated harsh treatment of loyalists, and some observers had even begun to see that the state might recoup some of her losses by offering sanctuary to rich returnees who found New York and Massachusetts inhospitable.[69] Instead of harassing them, therefore, the legislature repealed most laws against loyalists, except for those which confiscated their estates. The towns followed suit, as more and more people recognized the economic gains they might derive from welcoming back the refugees.[70]

Commutation

The government of Connecticut survived the Smith controversy, though not without loss of face. But peace brought to the surface another, less tractable problem, the problem of pay for army officers. In 1778, when the issue of half pay for officers first arose in Congress, Connecticut's opposition had helped to force a compromise whereby both officers and men would receive compensation comparable in value to their wages.[71] The arrangement assumed that the government would soon bring depreciation under control and that the war would soon end. By 1780, when the continent declared bankruptcy, it was clear that both assumptions were wrong. Congress now had no choice but to reduce expenses by reducing the number of officers. At the same time, it had to promise those whom it hoped to retain some token reward in lieu of the wages it could not immediately pay. Washington felt that half pay for life would suffice as an incentive but that it must be offered to those who had involuntarily retired as well as to those who remained. And by the autumn of 1780, Congress had grown desperate enough to concur, despite opposition.[72]

Connecticut opposed it, for one. Half pay for life seemed to most of her residents to exceed by far the wages and rations originally promised. Their government had already agreed to make good the specie value of wages and rations, forced into that concession by the mutinies of 1779 and 1780; now the new dispensation of Congress threatened to compensate the officers twice over while the people suffered on. Samuel Huntington, the president of Congress, smelled trouble brewing. "[T]his resolution will give general satisfaction to the officers, and those [in Congress] who oppose it will incur their disesteem, and perhaps censure; but I am much more concerned on account of its consequences among the people," he wrote. "What effects it will have with them time will best discover."[73]

Both the legislature and the people of Connecticut had some excuse, then, to lose interest in meeting their guarantee of wages and rations for officers. But they could hardly abandon the men. The mutinies in the Pennsylvania and New Jersey lines during January 1781 dramatized the need to do something for the rank and file. Even as Washington used the Connecticut line to suppress the mutiny of the New Jersey line, he knew that the inability of Congress and the states to pay the men their due raised the danger of contagion. At the first sign of trouble, he had written urging the New England states "to furnish at least three Months pay to the Troops, in Money that

will be of some value to them." He had also sent Henry Knox
on a special mission to impress the New England governments
with the importance of a prompt, effective response,[74] and
Knox had told them that the immediate threat came from long-
term recruits for the war who "are held . . . without any extra
reward while new and short levies receive large rewards."[75]

The Council of Safety toyed with the idea of asking that
towns raise twenty dollars specie for each recruit enlisted for
the duration but decided instead to let the legislature debate the
problem in spite of the delay that would entail.[76] The Council
had its reasons: the half-pay measure had evoked much hostility
toward the army, and Parsons reported to Trumbull that the
soldiers returning from winter furlough had warned their
officers to expect very little from Connecticut since "your influence in the State is at an end, and we constantly hear you
traduced and treated with the greatest disrespect in the country."[77] Indeed, the legislature showed no enthusiasm for Washington's request. The state had enough fiscal problems without
trying to raise three months' pay in specie for the army, especially when it seemed that some of her officers might receive a
further reward in the form of half pay. On the other hand, the
legislature saw the need to maintain morale, especially since the
approaching campaign would almost certainly decide the out-
come of the war.

At the end of February, the state of Connecticut reluctantly levied a twopenny tax in specie, due on May 1, "for the
sole purpose of making payment in part to the officers and
soldiers of the Connecticut Line."[78] To exclude the officers
from the measure might have defeated its intention, which was
the appeasement of the army. The legislature also conceded the
justice of a complaint from the Committee of the Army that a
two-and-a-halfpenny tax, levied to pay the interest on securities
given the men to compensate them for depreciation, had itself
been paid in depreciating state money. Therefore, they ordered
that the tax be collected again, this time in specie.[79] And in
May the new legislature laid a third twopenny tax for the army,
again to be paid in specie.[80] To levy a tax was not necessarily to

collect it, of course; nevertheless, the legislature had at least shown the will to pledge the state's last, best resources to meet the emergency.

When it came time to honor the guarantee of all rations and other promised emoluments at specie value, however, that will began to weaken. No one expected the state to produce all the money at once, only to commit herself to the payment of specific sums in the future by tendering securities. But in the spring of 1781 a deadlock between the Committee of the Army and the Assembly over the question of officers' retained rations led to an exchange between Parsons, speaking for the officers, and Trumbull, speaking for the government, that left both parties convinced of the other's ill will.[81] The government felt that the officers had taken advantage of the state's need for their services and her fear of the "fatal consequences, if denied," to ask for "more than justice." Trumbull spoke for many when he reminded Parsons that the legislature had already given the army no small advantage of the civilian population. "The whole Line knows, and ought to consider, their pay and wages are secured in full," he wrote, "while depreciation operates as a heavy tax upon the rest of the people."[82] The officers, on the other hand, felt more grievance than gratitude. A memorial signed by sixty-seven of them gave an eloquent account of an army reduced to poverty by the denial of wages, to rags by the denial of clothing, and to sickness by the rigors of campaigns they had fought while their countrymen remained "at home in ease and luxury." For themselves, these officers expressed no confidence in the government's intentions to honor its promises, given its unwillingness to compensate for the retained rations and its inability to pay interest on the depreciation certificates or to give a farthing toward the wages promised the line.[83]

A common concern for the critical campaign underway, together with the government's realization that some show of good faith was absolutely necessary, momentarily eased the tensions that had arisen between civil and military leaders. In September, after descending to threats of execution against the property of tax collectors who did not do their job, the government at last delivered $4,100 in specie to the army.[84] This amounted to only one month's wages for the Connecticut troops, but it soothed their tempers. Though the Assembly held firm on the issue of retained rations, it did reach an agreement with the Committee of the Army on how to make up other arrearages due for 1781. The line agreed to accept securities bearing 6 percent interest in specie from June 1, 1782, redeemable in equal portions in 1788 and 1789. The legislature laid an annual twopenny tax to pay the yearly interest on these securities and provided also for retiring the principal.[85] Subsequently, the legislature also agreed to consider any extra rations received by the officers between November 1780 and January 1782 as a gratuity.[86]

Even so, the attempt to improve relations between the state and her line ultimately depended on the assumption that the army would agree to accept the original stipulation. Half pay and further gratuities were out of the question; the Assembly made that plain in May 1782, in a grant to Congress of the power to collect a Continental impost which contained the reservation "that no part of said Monies be used and applied for the Payment of any Pension or half Pay to discharged Officers, or to any Person or Persons whatsoever as a Pension Gratuity."[87] The army might have agreed if it had indeed received pay according to the original terms. But though the state continued to tax for the army, hardly any of the proceeds found their way to camp. In 1783, the report of the Pay-Table Committee reinforced the growing suspicion of something amiss. The tax delinquency schedules printed there showed that the state had collected a greater proportion of the army taxes than of the others; yet the army had seen little of it.[88] The fault probably lay with the willingness of tax collectors to accept orders on the treasury rather than holding out for specie. Whatever the explanation, the state's continued inability to give the army anything but promises revived the demand for half pay.

In other states besides Connecticut, relations between the government and the line had soured as the war progressed. At the end of 1782, the whole northern army, afraid of being left in the lurch when peace came, chose a committee to request compensation from Congress for deficiencies in pay, retained rations, and undelivered clothing. The committee eventually presented a petition stating that though some states had "made settlements and given securities for the pay due for part of that time" the securities had turned out "to be worth but little indeed," and "many have been under the sad necessity of parting with them, to prevent their families from actually starving." The petitioners pointed out that men entitled to half pay by resolution of Congress were "not only destitute of any effectual provision, but are become the objects of obloquy," though they themselves could imagine no one "so hardened in the sin of ingratitude, as to deny the justice of the reward." On the assumption "that the objection generally, is against the mode only," they suggested that Congress commute half pay into "full pay for a certain number of years, or for a sum in gross." [89]

On February 8, 1783, Alexander McDougall and Matthias Ogden reported for the committee from Philadelphia that the army could expect no more immediate restitution than one month's current pay in notes. This communication produced a call for a meeting of the officers at Newburgh about "what measures (if any) should be adopted to obtain that redress of grievances which they seem to have solicited in vain." The call was accompanied by a fierce exhortation to "[c]hange the milk and water stile [*sic*] of your last memorial," or in other words to change the course of their appeal "from the justice to the fears of government." The address continued:

> Tell them . . . That in any political event, the Army has its alternative.—If peace, that nothing shall separate you from your arms but death.—If war, that courting the auspices, and inviting the direction of your illustrious leader, you will retire to some yet unsettled country, smile in your turn, and mock when their fear cometh on. [90]

The threat that the army would not lay down arms until Congress had rendered what the officers considered their due had the intended effect. It scared Eliphalet Dyer, who had obstructed the passage of commutation on March 10, into reopening the question on March 20. Madison observed in his journal of the proceedings in Congress that the action "seemed to be extorted from him by the critical state of our affairs."[91]

Fortunately, Congress received Washington's dispatches of March 18, with copies of his speech to the meeting of officers and of their resolutions on it, just before the committee considering Dyer's motion reported on March 22.[92] Washington had condemned the "dreadful alternative, of either deserting our country, in the extremest hour of distress, or turning our arms against it . . . (unless Congress can be compelled into instant compliance)" as something "so shocking . . . that humanity revolts at the idea." He assured the officers that Congress entertained "exalted sentiments of the services of the Army, and from a full conviction of its merits and sufferings, will do it compleat justice." And he pledged his "services to the utmost extent of [his] abilities" to obtain that justice. The officers had responded warmly. They resolved unanimously to "reject with disdain, the infamous proposition contained in the late anonymous address" and expressed "unshaken confidence in the justice of Congress and their country." Nevertheless, they did expect the army to remain in arms "until their accounts are liquidated, the balances accurately ascertained, and adequate funds established for payment."[93]

Madison recorded that Washington's dispatches swept away "the cloud which seemed to have been gathering" and "afforded great pleasure on the whole to Congress."[94] The officers' request that any settlement comprehend either half pay or commutation now elicited a prompt response: Congress immediately agreed to commutation in the form of five years' full pay in securities "such as shall be given to other creditors of the United States." The law provided "that it be at the option of the lines of the respective states, and not of the officers individually in those lines, to accept or refuse the same."[95] Needless to say, the Connecticut officers accepted. Not only did they doubt their government's intentions toward them; they also saw that federal securities would give them a surer foundation for the future than patient attendance upon a vague hope that someday the state would pay up.

Turmoil

To the people of Connecticut, commutation represented the betrayal of what they had thought an implicit agreement that the officers would renounce half pay in return for the state's generosity to them. Congress knew it would be unpopular and attempted to excuse it in an address to the states on April 26. The writers of the address concentrated on itemizing the consolidated debt of the United States and justifying the proposal to finance interest charges through a Continental impost as well as through requisitions on the states. Since commutation would increase the debt by 14 percent, they appended documents relating to the negotiations with the army in February and March and to the so-called Newburgh conspiracy. Congress described the Newburgh documents as a "fresh and lively" illustration of the army's "superiority to every species of seduction from the paths of virtue and honor."[96] But the public, which had already seen most of them in the newspapers, had a different interpretation. Many people saw the sudden and hasty adoption of commutation as the central government's admission of weakness in the face of the officers' threat not to disband the army till Congress met their demands. And, already exhausted from bearing the burden of war for so long, they saw commutation as the straw that could break their backs.[97]

Massachusetts and Connecticut had vied with one another since 1780 in the effort to provide for their fighting men; now, in return for their pains, Congress saddled them with new debts. Both rejected the address. Massachusetts led the way with a long letter to the president of Congress denouncing commutation as "in our Opinion a Grant of more than adequate reward for their Services, and inconsistent with the Equality which ought to subsist among Citizens of free and Republican States . . . a measure [which] appears to be calculated to raise and exalt some Citizens in wealth and Granduer [*sic*], to the injury and oppression of others." In conclusion the letter attributed the General Court's failure to pass favorably on Congress's request for an impost to the people's resentment of commutation and hinted that the measure, if persisted in, might eventually provoke the dissolution of the Union.[98]

Superficially, at least, Connecticut showed more complaisance. Though the Connecticut legislature neither said nor did anything in open opposition to commutation, its inactivity was more apparent than real. The Journal of Proceedings of the House shows that it had drafted a letter of protest to Congress which received majority approval. Since the Council wanted to postpone a final decision to the next meeting of the legislature, however, no letter went to Congress at that point, and the House had to settle for blocking the impost.[99] Trumbull had evidently warned Washington that this might happen, for only one day after the vote he received and read to the House the circular letter in which Washington defended commutation and urged the adoption of an impost.[100] The House, unmoved, refused to change its mind.

The legislature paid a price for the official silence it maintained on the subject of commutation. On July 15 the town of Torrington voted to make an elaborate address, which began by reminding the people how the Revolution had originated in the fear that Britain would saddle them with privileged officials and an unpayable debt. Since then, the towns had made great sacrifices to supply the army at a time when both Congress and the state legislature had lacked the means. Torrington agreed that the army had also made sacrifices. When both were cast into the balance, however, the army and the citizens had earned equal title to recompense. No one had deserved a measure which ignored the citizens and soldiers while heaping riches on the officers. Torrington charged that most officers had owned no more property than their fellow citizens to begin with but had profited during the war from high wages and the state's measures to protect them from depreciation. As a consequence, many who left home indigent had returned affluent. Why, then, did the members of Congress seek to increase the debt of an already impoverished country by $7 million in payments to officers? Was it their intention to create a class of government pensioners who would then impose a tyranny on the people? The British had attempted no worse.

So far, Torrington had said nothing that other complainants had not said before. But the address passed from criticism of the officers and Congress into a tirade against Connecticut's government. The members of the General Assembly had paid not the slightest attention to the "equitable petitions . . . of so many towns and a part of the legislature itself" against commutation. "Their doors are shut," the townsfolk declared, "and nothing transpires but imposts, excises, restrictions on trade, embargoes and calls for taxes." They complained of the taxes and accused the legislature of keeping the people in ignorance about matters of public finance. They hinted at sinsister reasons for the reticence of public officials and suggested that "confederacies are forming by individuals . . . that will, unless immediately checked, prove the destruction of American Liberty." And they concluded that the proper remedy for these abuses was that which the nation had applied in 1774. Once again, they said, the people must establish conventions, frame petitions and remonstrances, and set up committees of correspondence. The Torrington address ended with a call for a convention of towns in Litchfield County to demand redress from a legislature that had willfully ignored the public.[101]

Ordinarily, the actions of a town like Torrington, which boasted no prominent citizens and had acquired a slightly unsavory reputation during the war, would have drawn little attention. But, to the dismay of those who thought that Connecticut's interests were best served by cooperation with Congress, Torrington's extremism found support in one of the oldest and largest towns in the state. On August 4, the townsfolk of Farmington had met to censure Captain William Judd, recently deputed by the officers of the Connecticut line to pick up their commutation securities in Philadelphia. They went on to criticize the General Assembly for failing to oppose that measure effectively, and to advocate the exclusion of commutation certificates from the funded debt in order to give their holders "a perpetual evidence of their folly in attempting to invade the rights of a people determined to be free." The town argued that "Nothing . . . but an attack upon the vital principles of the constitution can rouse the great body of the people" and called for the legislature and the people to join in preventing such a calamity. To that end it set up a committee of correspondence, as Torrington had suggested, and promised to attend a general convention if other towns followed suit.[102]

Acting on the suggestion, a Hartford town meeting held on August 31 appointed a committee of five to draft an appeal to the legislature for relief from public burdens, particularly commutation. The committee also received instructions to correspond with other town committees as they formed.[103] Shortly afterward the following notice appeared in the *Courant*, signed by the Hartford Town Committee and endorsed by members of the Wethersfield and Glastonbury committees:

> It being the desire of many respectable towns in the counties of Hartford, New-Haven, Fairfield and Litchfield, signified by their committees, already chosen for the purpose, that there should be a GENERAL CONVENTION of the several towns in this State, at Middletown, on the first Wednesday of September next . . . to consider what ought to be done upon the subject of COMMUTATION, in order to some [*sic*] Constitutional Mode of Redress, etc., etc. This therefore is to notify the several towns in this state, then are there to meet by their Delegates duly chosen, for the purposes aforesaid.[104]

The allowance of only eight days for the summons to spread throughout the state meant that the outlying towns could not send representatives. Delegates who did not want to pay their own expenses would have no time to hold town meetings to vote funds. But there was a reason for this haste.

The first Wednesday in September preceded by thirteen days the meeting at which the freemen would vote on nominees for the Council and for delegates to Congress. The town committees all agreed that the composition of the Council would decide the success or failure of any opposition to commutation. They hoped that the Middletown convention would allow the populous towns along the Connecticut River and the seacoast to choose as nominees to the Council men who shared the popular feeling. They hoped that through these nominees they could first intimidate the upper house and then force the election of one they liked better. Since only twenty-eight towns sent delegates to Middletown on September 3, they limited their public actions to two recommendations: that the towns instruct the legislature to oppose the inclusion of commutation in the public debt, and that the newspapers publish any roll call taken in the Assembly which touched upon the issue.[105] Their moderation deceived no one. Everyone knew that the convention's true purpose was to turn "out of the Legislature such men as are supposed to approve the measures of Congress, and appoint others of opposite sentiment."[106] That objective received particularly strong support from the address of the town of Killingworth, published in the *Courant* just before the convention met, then carried back to the towns by returning delegates.

The Killingworth address claimed that most of the officers had joined the army "for the want of more lucrative employments at home" and that their "estates had been doubled since they entered the service, exclusive of the monies they hope to receive by the act of commutation." The writers charged that the officers had misrepresented their original circumstances in order to gain Washington's approval of their request for half pay and had no real right to cry poverty. Besides other evidence, they cited the recent formation of the Society of the Cincinnati with a permanent fund of $200,000. The townsfolk of Killingworth entertained profound suspicions of this fund, not only because it showed that the officers were far from destitute but also because they feared that the society might use it to influence Congress. In their resolves, they explored more thoroughly than any previous critics the sequence of events leading to commutation. They dwelt upon the suggestion in the letter written by McDougall and Ogden that Congress had not referred the army's demands to the states because it hoped to use those demands to obtain a revenue for itself. And they pointed out that Congress had adopted commutation just after the Newburgh incident, a piece of timing they adduced as further proof of their suspicions.[107]

The popular conventions of 1782 and their self-appointed crusaders against the illicit trade had caused anxiety; the inflammatory addresses that proliferated with the Middletown convention fomented hysteria. The movement drew a barrage of criticism in the newspapers well beyond anything that the Farmington resolves had provoked in 1782.[108] Its leading opponent, Noah Webster, Jr., writing under the name "Honorius," declared that the constitution itself stood in danger from these malcontents who would not rest until they had purged the upper house of its best men. He said that incendiaries were whipping the people into such frenzy that "should God Almighty place Gabriel at the head of our affairs, they would find fault with his administration, especially if it were rigourously just." In his opinion, "the resolves of some towns in this State according to our own laws, amount to high treason against the United States and render the leaders liable to an impeachment." The present popular measures, he said, if carried to extremes, would produce "the confusions of anarchy or the convulsions . . . of civil war," either of which would breed despotism.[109]

At first glance, the anticonvention pieces read like the exaggerated responses of overwrought imaginations. Surely a refusal to fund commutation and a change in the composition of the Council, no matter how much a person deplored them, did not portend anarchy and civil war. But a closer look at the general state of Connecticut society in the autumn of 1783 suggests the reason for the uproar. The leadership had at last realized the full extent of the political and economic problem confronting them. Connecticut received an early warning of the trouble to come in the repercussions felt there when Massachusetts took the first steps toward paying her wartime debt. The attempt had generated a wave of tax resistance whose ringleaders, according to rumor, received considerable support from their Connecticut neighbors along the border.[110] If Connecticut were to avoid a repetition when she provided for her own debt, her economy would have to improve, and no one saw any hope for improvement on the horizon. Peace had inspired an orgy of importation from Europe, particularly Britain, without expanding the means of payment. Though Americans did not know until September that the British would definitely exclude American shipping from their West Indies,[111] they had known since June that some elements in Britain favored such a step and that peace would not necessarily bring commercial opportunity.[112] Now that the worst had happened, it seemed likely to sustain a level of private indebtedness high enough to make people unwilling or unable to deal with the state's huge debt.

The government's first attempt to blaze a trail back to solvency met a discouraging response. In January 1783, the legislature had yielded to the pressure for a redistribution of the tax burden by levying a heavy excise tax on retail sales. Any merchant who retailed excisable commodities beyond a certain low limit had to apply for a license and put up £200 as surety that he would pay the tax.[113] This measure redressed the inequities in assessment that Erastus Wolcott and "S.M." had assailed. It also seemed to offer a way of raising a revenue that would not drive people to emigrate, as taxation during the last years of the war had done. It did nothing, however, to revive economic activity. The merchants and retailers opposed it with a vigor and by a means that augured ill. They began to organize a statewide network of associations which reached sufficient strength by August to hold a convention at Middletown in protest against the increased taxes.[114] Their resistance failed to achieve a revision of the law but raised a disturbing question about the strength of Connecticut's political system. Could it continue to withstand the pressure of special interests?

The repercussions of the Smith affair, no less than the convention movement, had helped to render those who identified with authority almost morbidly sensitive to attacks upon it and inclined to see anarchists everywhere. Webster, for instance, bitterly complained that "several insurrections and riots, a resistance of the execution of law, and a trampling upon the executive authority of this State, have already passed unnoticed, and the perpetrators of such crimes walk the roads with as much security and respectability as the best citizens."[115] For more than a year the issues of illicit trade and returning loyalists had given comparative upstarts an unprecedented opportunity to climb the ladder of government: now the issue of commutation arose to excite popular passions more violently than ever, and hence to open an even broader road to power for ambitious and unscrupulous men to travel. So said the critics of the Torrington, Farmington, and Killingworth addresses, at least.[116]

To this day, a certain mystery shrouds the question of exactly who did promote the convention movement. The Middletown convention published only a fragmentary journal in addition to its resolutions. Nevertheless, the fifteen names that do appear in published documents offer clues to the character of its leadership. Some of them, like Elkanah Tisdale of Lebanon, were new to Connecticut politics. Most of them had embarked on their political careers before the Revolution. For instance, Colonel Street Hall and Hugh Ledlie had emerged during the Stamp Act controversy as the advocates of radical resistance.[117] Then, for reasons which remain unclear, they receded into the background during the war. They hoped to use the convention movement to reestablish their political fortunes. The same was true of William Worthington, clerk at three of the four convention meetings, the same man who had been accused of complicity in the illicit trade. Worthington's brother-in-law, Aaron Eliot, presided over two meetings of the convention. The Eliot family, of which Benjamin Gale was a member by marriage, had gone into eclipse after the death of Aaron's father, Jared, in 1763. Revolutionary society had failed to accord the cultural accomplishments of the Eliots those honors to which they felt entitled.[118] Another member of the convention, Thomas Seymour, who had commanded the state horse throughout the war, had experienced a similar loss of status as a direct consequence of the Revolution. His personal reputation had suffered when his troops, unwilling to serve on foot, had tried to exempt themselves from the draft. He and another conventioneer, Leonard Chester, had also cut poor figures during the New Haven alarm, in which they bore partial responsibility for the shamefully late responses of Hartford and Wethersfield.[119]

Besides men with reputations to regild, the Convention attracted an even less desirable category of persons: men of dubious loyalty to the cause. People suspected the Eliot clan of Tory sympathies, and Chester's patriotism had been compromised by the apostasy of his kinsman, Silas Deane.[120] Two

members of the committee of correspondence, Ephraim Carpenter and Elisha Fitch, had raised a similar suspicion when
they resigned their commissions during the early, most unpromising days of the war. Carpenter had resigned at the end
of 1776, when the patriot cause looked particularly bleak.[121]
Fitch had resigned a year later, along with fifteen other officers,
in protest against the legislature's appointment of Joshua Huntington as major of the Twentieth Militia Regiment, which the
dissidents ascribed to improper influence.[122] But the most sinister figure among the conventioneers was a Dr. Samuel Woodward. Woodward enrolled as a student at Yale in 1776. Shortly
afterward, when the college moved to Glastonbury, he abandoned academic education for medical training. In the early
1780s he settled in Torrington, where he drafted the address of
1783 which led directly to the Middletown convention. Some
of the leadership doubted his loyalty to the Revolution because
of his Anglican faith and because he avoided military service.
They saw him as the vanguard of a Tory element that would
seek to reassert itself in state politics.[123]

Certainly such men as these would not stop at tampering
with nominations, and with Connecticut's economy *in extremis*
they would find it all too easy to bring pressure against paying
the debt. Jedediah Huntington had heard that "some have been
so much off their Guard as to say that now is the Time to ex-
punge all publick debts."[124] Refusal to pay the debt at its true
value (as determined by the depreciation tables) was precisely
the kind of injustice that Webster had warned would lead to
anarchy or civil war. And it would threaten the achievements
of the Revolution in other, more dangerous ways. The war had
shown that coercion was no substitute for consent when it came
to mobilizing resource. Until the Republic established public
credit, it would remain vulnerable to challenges from abroad.
Indeed, the lack of public credit might eventually tempt Britain
to reopen hostilities or foreign creditors to intervene in American affairs.[125] Men in ruthless pursuit of political rehabilitation
would not stop to consider these factors before they exploited
the pains of paying the debt. Nor would they hesitate to use
the ferment over commutation as a weapon in their battle to

prevent a national impost, though most of the leadership realized that public credit could not be achieved without one.[126]

The results of the September elections enhanced the leadership's anxiety. Not only had those who voted against the impost won reelection more often than those who voted yes,[127] but the convention cut an even deeper swathe through the ranks of nominees to the upper house and Congress. Six of the twenty nominated as assistants in 1783, including the governor, the lieutenant governor, and Eliphalet Dyer, the man most responsible for the passage of commutation, lost their places in the nominations of 1784. Only two of those nominated to Congress in 1783 reappeared in the nominations for 1784.[128] The convention's electioneering did seem to have had its effect. And in October 1783 the convention increased its pressure on the General Assembly with a public petition denouncing the "GRATUITY made by the honorable American Congress to the Officers of the Army, for services not to be performed," and "the undue and Artful manner" in which the officers had persuaded Congress to bestow it. The petitioners claimed that "ample justice had been done" the officers of the line. They cited the "many repeated stipulations for wages and pay made on the part of this state . . . for actual service . . . the liquidation of the same upon a fair and equitable scale, assented to by all parties," and the "exemption from taxes and other emoluments allowed."[129]

The lower house responded to the petition by setting up a committee to collaborate with another that they hoped the upper house would appoint to draft a remonstrance against commutation.[130] When the assistants declined to join in any such committee, the House decided to remonstrate with Congress independently. The remonstrance, when framed, questioned that the Articles of Confederation gave Congress the power to make such a grant, especially when it offended so many Americans with an "Establishment of Pensioners and Placemen" that struck them as "incompatible with the Principles of Liberty" on which the states had formed their constitutions. Even if Congress did have that power, was the grant a just one? The House could see no reason to promise the officers half pay or commutation as part of the settlement already granted and told Congress that this made it "impracticable to execute any measures to raise its *quota*." [131] With the best will in the world, the Council alone could not move a House in this mood to adopt an impost.

Incomplete Recovery

During late 1783 and early 1784, the context in which anticommutation sentiment grew underwent a change. The response of Congress to the Massachusetts remonstrance began the process. In a series of resolutions adopted on September 25, Congress first reiterated the reasons for granting half pay, then delivered an exhortation on the duty of minorities to submit to majorities. Congress pointed out that "a perfect compliance with the wishes of every part [of their constituents] will often be found . . . impractical," and "that if a State every way so important as Massachusetts, should withhold her solid support to constitutional measures of the Confederacy, the result must be a dissolution of the union; and then she must hold herself as alone responsible for the anarchy and domestic confusion that may succeed, and for exposing all these confederated states . . . an easy prey to the machinations of their enemies, and the sport of European politics." The resolutions ended with a reminder that Congress had adopted commutation in part out of a "desire to give satisfaction to such of the states as expressed a dislike to the half-pay establishment" and "that if the objections against the commutation were ever so valid, yet it is not now under the arbitration of Congress, but an act finally adopted, and the national faith pledged to carry it into effect." [132] In other words, Congress did not mean to budge.

Congress was heard. Later that autumn, a majority of the Massachusetts lower house voted to empower Congress to raise an impost, with no restrictions on its right to use the funds for commutation. [133] After this response from Massachusetts, the lower house in Connecticut saw that their remonstrance could have no possible effect. The message from Congress may also have affected attendance at the December meeting of the Mid-

dletown convention, to which only ten towns sent representatives. Bad weather had something to do with it too. But there
is no doubt that the convention's feeble attempt to keep the
public up in arms by switching the focus of dissent from commutation to the Cincinnati smacked of desperation. After
recommending "to the notice and perusal of the people at large"
a recent attack on the organization by Aedanus Burke, entitled
Considerations on the Society or Order of Cincinnati, they adjourned
until March without further action or debate.[134]

The opponents of the convention drew the correct inference. So far they had felt obliged to stand on the defensive;
now they felt sufficiently confident to attack the convention by
making fun of it. A verse parody published in the *Courant* at
the end of December expressed their new assertiveness:

> We then resolv'd with skill no less,
> In this Convention's next recess,
> That every person, great or small
> Shall read a pamphlet which they call
> Chief Justice Burke's considerations
> On these new-fangled Cincinnations.

The verses went on to describe what the convention hoped to
achieve by this:

> Now Burke's declaring his suspicions
> Develops what we all are wishing;
> Which plainer will appear you'll find,
> By strictures on the powers combin'd;
> These will disclose as plain as day,
> What artful schemes we tories lay,
> How every member of Convention,
> Tortures his brain and wracks invention,
> To blast good men, and in their place
> Foist knaves and fools with better grace;
> O'erturn our happy constitution,
> Reduce all order to confusion,
> With want of law make mankind groan,
> And on their miseries raise a throne.[135]

The taunt of toryism, formerly avoided for fear of reviving the
storm that had accompanied Richard Smith's return, came to

the surface in this and other pieces against the convention now that the agitation over returning loyalists had subsided.[136]

Oddly enough, Connecticut's declining economy offered convention critics a still more promising line of approach. Commentators measured the decline less in terms of increasing private indebtedness than in terms of visibly shrinking resource, and the tax base provided the most accurate gauge of that. In 1778–79 the grand list stood at slightly more than £1.9 million; by 1784 it had dwindled to £1,559,624, or almost 20 percent (see Table 5). Since that list was not completed until May 1785, in 1784 neither the authorities nor the people could have known just how fast the tax base was shrinking. They would find out eventually that it had dropped about 12 percent in the one year. But the authorities did know by early 1784 that their principal hope for increasing the tax base had failed them. The legislature had put too much stock in the 1782 tax reform which provided for the assessment of the "faculty" of commercial and professional people by assigning fixed values for these intangibles. In January 1783 it even went to the trouble of inspecting the lists and citing the errors of individual listers. Yet a year later, when the new system had been fully implemented, assessments added only £44,776, or less than 3 percent, to the grand list.[137] At the same time, the legislature knew that a massive emigration was underway, which had already depressed the value of real estate.

The general economic picture gave the proponents of a federal impost strong arguments with which to woo those whose opposition had originated in hostility to commutation. Though Noah Webster's "Honorius" essays had already argued the case for an impost,[138] it took a series of restatements to drive the point home. The most influential of these was an essay entitled "Policy of Connecticut," whose writer argued that neither the claims of the army nor the demands of Congress had caused the state's money troubles; rather, the cause was the powerlessness of the central government. In the absence of an impost, he said, Connecticut virtually subsidized the other states. He pointed out that since most of Connecticut's imports came through New York, Rhode Island, and Massachusetts, the farmers of Connecticut paid their taxes to the governments of those states rather than to their own. Of the £400,000 in foreign commodities consumed by Connecticut each year, only £50,000 were imported directly. If each state laid an impost of 5 percent, Connecticut would net only £2,500. Her neighbors would deprive her of £17,500 in revenue. A national debt serviced by a national impost would allow Connecticut to receive credit for money contributed to a common fund rather than poured into the ever-open coffers of other states.[139]

The supporters of an impost also succeeded in turning the debate on the equity of the tax laws to advantage. A series signed "C.H." appeared in the *Courant* in early 1784 arguing that present modes of taxation would never bring sufficient yields to pay the debt. "C.H." blamed the enormous tax arrearages of the poor and middle classes on the failure of the tax lists to discriminate between the intrinsic quality of land, its fertility or infertility.[140] To those who saw this as the problem, the advocates of the impost could offer a solution. They did not pretend that it would pay all Connecticut's share of the debt, but they did say that it could make a big enough dent in it to lighten the load of the remaining payments. They pointed out two other advantages as well: the ease of collection and the lack of coercion. For, as one enthusiast wrote, "no one is obliged to pay it; no person pays a farthing of it, unless he does it voluntarily."[141] Such a tax would fall only on those able and presumably willing to pay. If the farmers and mechanics found their taxes insupportable, they should back the governor and Council and elect an Assembly that would grant Congress the power to raise an impost.

Some advocates also claimed that an impost would end emigration from the state and raise the value of real estate.[142] Others argued that Connecticut would suffer in different ways if she continued to oppose a national revenue. For instance, the state could not then hope to receive any compensation from Congress for the loss of the western lands. She also wanted Congress to make certain financial concessions, such as the assumption of extraordinary expenses incurred by the state in

defending her coastline and southwestern frontier and in providing for her line between 1780 and 1782.[143] In the course of
settling the state's accounts, other areas of dispute would undoubtedly arise, and Congress would be more likely to grant
the state her due if she in turn conceded the right of Congress
to collect an impost.[144]

These economic arguments appealed to the very people
who had supported the convention movement. In its May session, the legslature quietly agreed to an impost. Though only
forty-two of the ninety-three representatives, or 45 percent, who
voted for the impost in May 1783 had won seats in the next
House, thirty-two of the thirty-seven, or 86 percent, who voted
for the impost in January 1784 were reelected.[145] These figures
suggest that during the spring of 1784 the people of Connecticut had come to understand that a federal impost would serve
their economic interests. Whether for this reason or because the
electoral procedures for the assistants continued to favor incumbents, the assault on the upper house also failed. The convention had hoped that six of the seven new names on the convention's list would be elected.[146] None were, even though one of
the convention candidates, James Wadsworth, stood higher in
the lists by virtue of seniority than a successful rival named
Stephen Mitchell (perhaps the author of the "S.M." series). Of
all the nominees who shared the convention's goals, only William Williams took a seat.[147]

The political system had weathered the immediate crisis. But
Connecticut's assent to the impost failed to achieve the desired
ends because of the recalcitrance of several other states.[148] Only
two alternatives for paying the federal debt remained. The state
could either comply with congressional requisitions for this
purpose or anticipate the final settlement of accounts between
the states by assuming the federal obligations of their citizens.
Connecticut did not favor assumption, for several reasons. The
state's debt alone would strain her dwindling resources. And
people still resented the addition of commutation costs to the
federal debt, besides which most of them thought that any fair
final settlement of accounts between the states would show

Connecticut as already a major creditor of the others. Connecticut did not follow the lead of New Jersey, which openly refused to comply with the requisitions of Congress.[149] After all, the state government had not abandoned hope of compensation for the loss of the western lands. But she made no provision to comply with the requisition beyond allowing the revenue from a state impost to be paid in indents, which the government then appropriated to satisfy congressional demands.[150]

Instead, the state began to put her own financial house in order, an endeavor in which she labored under considerable difficulties because of the huge tax arrearages that had accumulated. She could not proclaim a general tax forgiveness and start afresh because the arrearages left her in debt to many of her own citizens who held unpaid orders on the treasury. A tax forgiveness that repudiated this debt would demoralize the society beyond hope. The most eligible solution to the problem was to consolidate the unpaid orders, together with the other claims against the treasury, into a liquidated state debt. In May 1783 the Assembly had opened a loan for £609,572 and had invited the state's creditors to subscribe their debts at a liquidated specie value. The state then laid an annual sixpenny tax in gold and silver to pay interest on the principal until it could be retired, presumably after a final settlement of accounts.[151] In the following May the Assembly resolved "that the Treasurer be . . . directed to suspend Issuing his Warrants for any Taxes not now in Collection except the Annual December 6d Tax for Interest and such as it may be necessary to grant for the support of Civil Government."

The taxes most affected by the suspension of warrants happened to be those levied to redeem the depreciation certificates issued to the army and to retire the state currency. According to the Assembly, compliance with the sixpenny tax "would be more beneficial to the Public Creditors than attempts at this Time to discharge the principal of their Debts further than is provided for by the Taxes already collecting."[152] The legislators probably assumed that some of the army debt had been previously subscribed to the consolidated debt and that the state currency, like the Continental, should be abandoned for similar reasons. Punctual interest payment on the consolidated debt, on the other hand, would raise its value to par and create a fund of capital that could serve as a medium of exchange. The economy would then recover what it most needed—its liquidity—and be able to pay its remaining debts. In the autumn of 1783, Webster had touted this as one of the benefits that would ensue from funding the federal debt.[153] Though circumstances had forced the abandonment of that effort, Connecticut could still look forward to the benefits of funding her own debt. To ensure collection of the sixpenny tax on time, the government ordered the authority and selectmen of the towns to put pressure on their collectors, promising to suspend interest on all back accounts brought up to date at once.[154]

The legislature realized that to pressure collectors and the people would only partly solve the problem of paying the state's debt. They must also find ways to revitalize the state's economy. In an attempt to enhance the value of the state's exports, the government standardized the weight and construction of containers for salted provisons. To increase the production of staples, it removed certain items from the tax lists; for instance, swine, to increase the production of salt pork. To encourage the production of new commodities, such as silk and wool, the state exempted shorn sheep from the lists and offered bounties. All manufactures of the state received exemption from the excise.[155] And the central sections of the principal maritime towns received charters of incorporation, making them "cities" which administered their affairs through mayors, aldermen, and common councils empowered to make bylaws. A mayor and two aldermen of a city constituted a court, with the same jurisdiction as the county courts in settling disputes between inhabitants. The legislature hoped that the port cities would use their new power to increase the flow of commerce locally and to develop a direct trade with Europe.[156] As another step in that direction, the legislature declared both New Haven and New London free ports.[157] Interior towns with no pretensions to the status of "cities" received liberal privileges to hold fairs. Lastly, the legislature authorized the establishment of a mint to produce copper coinage.[158]

At the same time, the government attempted certain political reforms. The most important innovation was the effort to professionalize the administration of justice by codifying the laws and by separating the legislative and judicial powers, both formerly exercised by the assistants. When the government barred the assistants from sitting on the state's highest court, it forced the best legal minds to focus their energies on the law rather than on political concerns.[159] The state also sought to reorganize its administrative machinery by creating two new counties, Middlesex and Tolland,[160] and by breaking some of the larger towns into several small ones. The impulse to divide almost always came from within, usually because some hitherto subordinate group desired autonomy. But the rash of divisions that appeared during the war years and immediately thereafter broke out primarily because of the difficulty that all the towns had experienced in coping with successive devolutions upon their heads of central government functions.[161] The tendency to multiply local institutions worked against the restoration of public finances in one respect, since the increased number of officers cost the state more money. Attempts to economize by reducing the representation allowed each town met with rejection by one legislature after another.[162] Nevertheless, to limit the newly incorporated towns to one representative each did help to keep down the size of that body. And as a concession to popular demand, the government reformed itself to the extent of publishing its roll calls and a journal.[163]

None of these political or economic reforms addressed the heart of the state's economic ills, her continued dependence on the markets of the West Indies and, to a lesser extent, on the southern states for the earnings with which to pay for her consumption of European goods. Welcoming New York loyalists to the newly incorporated cities and granting certain cities the status of free ports did not remove the obstacles to direct trade with Europe. The state alone could produce nothing that Europe wanted, and her patterns of settlement precluded the use of any Connecticut port as a central distribution point.[164] Though politically independent, the state remained a colonial economy whose postwar prosperity was threatened by the unsettled market for southern staples and the exclusion of American shipping from the British West Indies.[165] To add to her problems, the French decided to limit American access to their islands.[166] A series of devastating hurricanes in the Caribbean during the mid-1780s caused a momentary distress that gave American captains an occasional chance to circumvent restrictions on trade, but the luck of a skipper here and a skipper there would not rescue the state's fortunes.[167]

Desperate for some truly efficacious way to revive the economy, Connecticut tried still harder than before to convert her public debt from a liability to an asset. In May 1785 the legislature enlarged the power of the treasurer to pressure communities that fell behind in their payments. Heretofore he had had no remedy except to imprison the collector and sell his property. Now the legislature made the selectmen's property a hostage for any delinquency that remained after the collector's property had been sold and even permitted the indiscriminate attachment of other properties if necessary to make up the full amount owed.[168] The legislature also forestalled individual attempts to escape tax liabilities by the timely conveyance of real estate with a law that retained the property of any tax delinquent as hostage, regardless of sale, until he met his liability. Lastly, the legislature created the new office of comptroller with summary powers over the state's debts and accounts.[169] Beginning in 1786 the reader encounters numerous advertisements placed in newspapers announcing the forced sale of property for tax delinquencies.

These measures only aggravated the postwar liquidity crisis because they led private creditors to press as hard for the prompt payment of private debts as the state pressed for the payment of public ones.[170] From 1785 on, there appeared repeated complaints of economic oppression. Some focused upon the high cost of legal procedures, which the state had begun to tax in 1783. The volume of litigation and the laws prescribing imprisonment for debt also came in for criticism.[171] Both the complaints and the measures that provoked them reflected the strain of the effort to pay both public and private debts in an economy that lacked a stable medium of exchange. The consolidated state debt failed to supply that lack. Connecticut never persuaded all her creditors to subscribe the outstanding debt in warrants, certificates, and notes to the loan of 1783, and just as well, since the principal sum as it was had grown too large to be serviced in specie. In 1785 one commentator complained that the economy did not contain hard money enough for even those with good estates to pay a twopenny tax.[172] It seemed cheaper to let taxpayers cancel their liabilities to the state by setting state liabilities against them.

This method of tax gathering, or nongathering, began in 1783 when the Assembly had authorized the receipt of orders on the treasury for all taxes due in state bills. As money became tighter, the practice expanded. In 1784, certificates of interest for moneys loaned to the state, issued in lieu of specie, became receivable for the sixpenny tax. Eventually, soldiers' notes, most of which had found their way into civilian hands, were also admitted in payment for the sixpenny tax.[173] The practice of canceling one obligation with another caused the consolidated state debt to depreciate so that it remained a claim against the future resources of society at face value but did not provide the economy with the needed capital and liquidity.[174] The people continued to labor under demands they could not meet, and the public creditors remained uncompensated.

The policy was not a total failure, of course; presumably, the legislature did not intend to repudiate the principal, and a gradual liquidation of arrearages, even if it did compromise payment of interest and thus the value of the debt as a source of capital, would benefit creditors in the long run. But in general the economic picture looked grim. "Modern Whig" declared in March 1786 that "unless some better measures be taken to support public credit, than has ever yet taken place in New England, so that a plentiful current medium may be held in our domestic commerce, either in bills that will hold in full value, in full plenty, or in money that will abide our trade in full plenty, the whole public debts of this State will never be lessened more than what is paid by the sale of state lands and wronging State creditors."[175] His warning rang true. The state had not been able to pay her notes and certificates of interest without some forced sale of lands, and even then she had wronged her creditors. There seemed to be no way for the state to retire the principal of her debt without becoming ever more hopelessly enmeshed in a policy that left everyone dissatisfied.

CHAPTER EIGHT

Epilogue

CONNECTICUT'S postwar problems were not unique: all the states had them to some extent,[1] and the New England states in particular. Rhode Island had suffered as much if not more. The British had destroyed many of her coastal towns despite exhausting and expensive efforts to defend them; her population had declined not relatively but absolutely; and when peace came, Rhode Island too contended with a decrease in resources paralleled by an increase in demands.[2] She also opposed a federal impost at first but came around to it after wrestling for a while with postwar problems.[3] And 1786 found Rhode Island in much the same financial mess as Connecticut.

Rhode Island, however, tried to extricate herself by way of injustice to creditors. A debtor majority from the countryside seized control of the legislature and issued paper money which they dignified as legal tender. When it depreciated at wartime rates, they blamed their merchant creditors. They passed a series of Draconian laws that forced creditors to accept the money at par or pay crushing penalties. Those who tried to resist found themselves subjected to summary judicial process without the benefit of a jury.[4] Rhode Island's legislation is now remembered chiefly because it provoked the state's superior court to rule one law unconstitutional, an early attempt to exercise the power of judicial review.[5] But at the time, as the people watched merchants and farmers exchanging threats to withhold

goods or produce, the laws appeared noteworthy chiefly for
their tendency to incite anarchy.[6]

Massachusetts followed the opposite course. In 1781 the
creditor interest, concentrated in the east, used its control of
the legislature to fund a large state debt payable in specie.[7] A
wave of violent opposition ensued but subsided when the government postponed payment of the principal and charged the
interest to state impost and excise taxes that fell largely upon
the east. The debt-ridden west received further relief from a law
passed in July 1782 which provided that the value of property
taken in execution for private debts should be estimated by a
panel of assessors rather than by reference only to the going
market rate.[8] Nevertheless, the creditor interest kept so strong
a hold on the Senate that the debtor majority was powerless to
influence the state's fiscal policy. In 1786, furthermore, the creditor interest persuaded the lower house to lay a heavy direct
tax in specie that would maintain interest payments on the
Massachusetts debt, in arrears because of declining yields on
the impost and excise, and help pay the state's share of the
Continental requisition. For large parts of the interior, given
the dearth of money, this amounted to paying the debt by a
forced sale of assets, and a rebellion broke out. The government
suppressed it, of course, but only with a mighty effort that left
the state's finances in chaos.[9] Thus, both the weakness of the
public creditors in Rhode Island and the strong policies of their
counterparts in Massachusetts turned out to be nothing but alternative routes to the same destination.

In 1786, Connecticut stood in a position to pursue either
course. Early in the year, a grass-roots movement in the towns
along the Rhode Island border had agitated for an emergency
meeting of the legislature to relieve the distress that the shortage of money had brought upon people all over the state.
Though the petitioners did not say so outright, they wanted a
large issue of paper money with which to pay their debts.[10]
And several pieces appeared in the *Middlesex Gazette* arguing
that the public debt should be paid not at nominal value
but at depreciated value, an idea also current in western
Massachusetts.[11] As the year wore on, and Massachusetts

erupted in the violence of Shays's Rebellion, the Connecticut government heard that an association to support the Shaysites had formed in the eastern town of Preston. Though the government easily dispersed it, the incident showed that Connecticut too contained the raw material for such a challenge to authority. " 'Tis by no means to be wondered at," wrote one correspondent to the newspapers, "that such an infection should take effect in this state, when . . . some of our rulers and leading men . . . afford their council and personal assistance to have this most horrid distemper become universal." He had in mind men like William Williams, who adjourned the Windham County Court because of events in Massachusetts.[12]

In the end Connecticut avoided either of the extremes on which Rhode Island and Massachusetts had foundered, though only because the government embarked on an appealing but misguided plan to establish public credit without taxation. In 1786, Congress had implicitly recognized Connecticut's claim to a tract of land west of Pennsylvania. When Connecticut had ceded other western claims to the nation in 1784, she had reserved one part for the officers and men of her line.[13] Congress found the original stipulation unacceptable, but another act passed by the state in October 1785 was more favorably received because it made only implicit reference to the Reserve. Besides, Congress undoubtedly knew of the growing support in Connecticut's General Assembly for the assertion of a claim to *all* her western lands if Congress rejected the present offer.[14] Yet Congress still objected that the state had not renounced jurisdiction along with title. On May 26, 1786, William S. Johnson at last persuaded Congress to accept the ceded land as soon as Connecticut relinquished "right, title, interest, jurisdiction, and claim." On the assumption that Congress had confirmed the state's right to the land reserved, the Connecticut legislature immediately made the suggested concession.[15]

This windfall, the first for a long time, opened the prospect of relief for public creditors without oppression of public debtors. Now, however, the leadership divided over the question of how best to use it. One group advocated the fastest possible divestiture. They wanted to sell the land at half the price that Congress was asking, and without waiting for surveys, to anyone who would pay in federal and state securities at par. Since federal securities had depreciated far more than state securities, the offer would have the most appeal for federal creditors and would attract out-of-state speculators as well as Continental veterans. Some saw this as a positive advantage. Small holders would not buy land in the Reserve unless they had an assurance that wealthy, powerful men shared their interest in defending title. And a quick sale to veterans allowing payment in federal securities minimized the risk that Congress would withdraw its tacit assent to Connecticut's claim. In any case, there was probably enough land to go around for all interested creditors, both state and federal.

The opposite view, espoused by a group of which William Williams took the lead, held that the benefits from the Reserve should be kept within the state. This faction believed that even without the retirement of any more federal certificates Connecticut would emerge as a creditor in the final settlement of accounts. In the continued absence of that settlement, on the other hand, she could expect to receive no recompense whatever for any further exertion she made. She should therefore use the Reserve as an asset in settling with her own creditors. To make the most of it, she should divide the land according to mathematical survey into regular townships, of 22,000 acres each, in tiers from east to west across the Reserve. Indiscriminate location might cause confusion and would almost certainly leave large tracts of less desirable land impossible to sell, or salable only at a miniscule price. Williams argued that to accept payment in federal securities would exclude the possibility of any payment in state securities because the one was so much cheaper than the other. It would also give outside speculators a monopoly of the best lands and discourage Connecticut migrants. In other words, it would keep the state from providing for her own surplus population at the same time as it took away her one opportunity to retire the state debt without overburdening her taxpayers.[16]

The legislators settled the controversy by choosing the state-centered policy. They restricted the sale of the Reserve to the state's creditors, insisted that survey precede sale, and asked for the full congressional price.[17] They also refused to take any action in support of federal credit. On August 2 Congress had sent each state a requisition for specie with which to pay the first installment of principal on the Dutch and French loans, a transaction on which the nation's foreign credit absolutely depended. The Assembly's only response was a letter to the president of Congress excusing the state's delinquency as having been caused by economic distress rather than by lack of support for the Confederation.[18]

The antifederalist tack taken by Connecticut's government drew sharp criticism from the author of "Political Paragraphs, Connecticut," an essay which appeared in most of the state's newspapers in late November. At the time, commissioners from Massachusetts and New York were meeting at Hartford to discuss their conflicting claims to land in western New York. The imminence of an agreement, which would open the rich Genesee lands to settlement, undercut the legislature's hope of quick returns on the Western Reserve.[19] The author underscored the point, accusing the legislature of squandering the windfall by restricting sales to state creditors. But for "that insect policy—that selfish narrow system of measures which now disgrace this state," he wrote, the legislature might have sold the western lands for Continental and state securities. Events bore him out.[20] No one rushed to buy land in the Reserve. No one could before a survey had been made, and the October legislature had neglected to arrange one.[21] He warned that "the system of measures now pursuing by the majority of the legislature would, if carried through, inevitably bring disgrace, poverty and ruin upon the state."

The writer of "Political Paragraphs" went on to draw some equally grim conclusions about republicanism in general. The division of the leadership into federalists and antifederalists had, in effect, made the people the arbiters of public business. "But people in general are too ignorant to manage affairs which require great reading and an extensive knowledge of foreign nations," he wrote. The recent defeat of the proposal to reduce the size of the legislature made him wonder if they were fit to manage anything. The *"howling state"* of Connecticut politics, where some howled for fear of losing their influence and some for fear of paying their debts, had led him, once a staunch proponent of republican government, to change his mind about it.

> *Now,* a republican is among the last kinds of governments I should choose. I should infinitely prefer a limited monarchy, for I would sooner be subjected to the caprice of one man, than to the ignorance and passions of a multitude. I believe men as individuals enjoy more security, more peace and more *real liberty* under a limited monarch, take princes as they rise, than in republics, where people sometimes get furious and make laws destructive of all peace and liberty.

For example, he pointed out that "[s]ome of the late laws of Rhode Island are greater stretches of tyranny than have been tolerated in the despotic governments of Europe; and life and property are less secure in Massachusetts, than in Turkish dominions." An anonymous writer in the *New Haven Gazette* shared his disenchantment and warned that Connecticut's blustering patriots could plunge her into war again, either foreign or civil.[22]

Subsequent events appeared to confirm these misgivings. In late February 1787 the town of Sharon openly proposed that the Assembly free the people from their debts by enacting a paper money law like that of Rhode Island, supplemented with a tendery law like that of Massachusetts.[23] The proposal elicited some strong criticisms of paper money, and the Assembly never seriously considered it.[24] But proposals for a tendery law, and a law barring the sale of land to pay taxes, did gain a hearing. And though they were summarily rejected, so was the proposal to comply with the most recent requisition from Congress.[25] The town of Sharon greeted the rebuff of its proposal by trying to raise an insurrection, soon suppressed but useful to those who wished to obstruct all further attempts to pay the state debt. The Assembly took it as the excuse to instruct that no warrants be issued for the eightpenny tax due in March 1788.[26]

Though Connecticut's public creditors faced a bleak land-scape at home, salvation had appeared on the horizon. The intractable problem of debt, and the violence it had caused in Massachusetts and Rhode Island, had at last convinced the rest of the states that if they wanted to make the achievements of the Revolution secure they would have to revise the Articles of Confederation. Throughout the winter and spring, the Federalists of Connecticut rejoiced to see one state after another answer the call for delegates to a constitutional convention in Philadelphia. Though Governor Huntington's reluctance to summon an emergency session of the legislature made Connecticut almost the last state to act, very few voices then opposed the sending of a delegation. If Connecticut had not sent one, she would have forfeited all right to take part in the deliberations. Even those who rejected the Federalist view that Connecticut's political system could support neither her own credit nor that of the nation, and that her one hope was a stronger federal government, understood this.[27]

A struggle ensued, however, over whom to send. Erastus Wolcott, one of the first men named, had in the past upheld discrimination against federal creditors because a final settlement would show that the nation owed Connecticut money. He had also said that equalization of the tax burden, at present disproportionately borne by the agrarian majority, should stand higher in order of priority than payment of the debt.[28] But Wolcott resigned, and Roger Sherman, who replaced him, held a more federal view.[29] Sherman, together with William S. Johnson and Oliver Ellsworth, gave the state outstandingly able representation at the Convention, in which, indeed, they played a vital part. They sponsored the so-called Connecticut Compromise, which prevented a deadlock between the large and small states by allowing proportional representation in one branch of the federal legislature and equal representation in the other.[30]

At home, the General Assembly made up for its reluctance to send delegates by being one of the first states to call a ratifying convention. In its October session, the Assembly authorized the election of delegates to meet in Hartford on the first Thursday in January. Those who attended were promised the same compensation as delegates to the Assembly itself. Connecticut's ratifying convention took only six days to do its job, and, to judge from the few reports that survive, the antifederalists had little to say. The record suggests that James Wadsworth alone spoke against ratification and that the Federalists easily overbore him. When the votes were counted on January 9, the yeas had a majority of eighty-eight. Even some of the foremost antifederalists, like William Williams, Erastus Wolcott, and Joseph Hopkins, had voted to ratify the Constitution.[31] Apparently any expedient that might free the state from financial embarrassment was worth a try.

It took three years for Hamilton's program of funding and assumption to restore solvency, but since the antifederalists had no alternative to suggest they could hardly complain of the delay. During the interval, it became clear that the Western Reserve would be worthless until the federal government persuaded or pressured the British to evacuate their posts in the Northwest. Only one sale of 24,000 acres took place under the Assembly's plan of 1786, to a syndicate led by Samuel H. Parsons, who drowned soon afterward in a river accident.[31] In 1792 the state gave away 500,000 acres to the inhabitants of towns devastated by the British[32] but sold no more until 1795 when a large syndicate of Connecticut investors, known as the Connecticut Land Company, purchased the remainder for $1 million. The land was not settled until after 1800.[33]

This experience, offset by the stunning success of Hamilton's fiscal program in restoring prosperity, convinced almost everyone that Connecticut stood to gain by a strong central government. The funding of the federal debt and the assumption of most of the state debt made possible the establishment of the state's first banks between 1792 and 1796.[34] These institutions protected the economy from any recurrence of the money shortages that had plagued Connecticut throughout the colonial and postwar periods, and from depreciation, while they also helped to build up the capital that supported the transformation of her economy in the early nineteenth century.[35]

Yet the foundation of the new prosperity looked shaky. Too much of it rested on the revival of a trade that British restrictions had crippled twice before. In the mid-1790s, the upheavals of the French Revolution prompted the British to encroach upon France's rich West Indian possessions, and they bought most of the provisions for the attempt from the United States. Connecticut suppliers met a sizable portion of the demand, and between 1795 and 1796 the state's exports almost doubled.[36] In 1796, however, the French began to retaliate upon American commerce, with devastating effect. Though Britain responded by opening more and more of her islands to American skippers and by convoying their ships to the West Indies,[37] everyone suspected that her friendship would last no longer than the war, after which she would most likely revert to discrimination against them.

Connecticut's merchants fully understood the danger of remaining a colonial economy. They made every effort to cultivate new, diversified trades to give them immunity from the caprice of British imperial policies and the vagaries of war. Some tried to gain a foothold in the Far Eastern trade; others explored the possibilities burgeoning in South America with the collapse of the Spanish Empire.[38] Many renewed their perennial struggle to enter the direct trade with Europe, though none succeeded who did not first take the step of removal to New York.[39] The best way to transcend the limitations of a colonial economy would be to develop a product with appeal for many markets, particularly the national market, fast-growing and safe from political disruption. But most of Connecticut's agricultural products could not compete with local suppliers in other states, and, aside from timber and stone, Connecticut had few natural resources to draw on. She did have some success with sheep farming and dairying for the domestic market, but both required the conversion of land from intensive cultivation to pasture, which drove increasing numbers of farmers either into the towns or to the west.[40] One solution remained that would give Connecticut a sound economic role she could play without depleting her resource: the development of manufactures.

One might have thought that the displacement of people from the land would so swell the pool of cheap labor as to improve the prospects for industry. But scarcity of capital, and incomplete development of the domestic market, continued to hinder large-scale industrial growth. Some of the landless farmers found a niche in the smaller enterprises that mushroomed all over the state.[41] The majority preferred to continue their old calling, even if that meant going elsewhere. During the 1790s as many as a hundred thousand people, by some estimates, left Connecticut. Their departure brought the state's population growth almost to a halt.[42] So massive an emigration, at a time of relative prosperity, gave a silent but sharp reminder that Connecticut's political system still could not solve the various economic problems that had plagued her since prerevolutionary days.[43]

The Revolution had inflicted wounds on Connecticut that would not heal during the lifetime of those who had passed through it. The leadership, bruised by the experience of war and by Connecticut's inability to recover from it fully, never showed the enterprise in politics that they brought to economic ventures. The threat of another war with Britain in 1794 and 1795 left them in no doubt that they had best accommodate to her wishes, and support for the Jay Treaty increased in proportion to the benefits that accrued from British military contracts.[44] Connecticut's federalist tendencies became more pronounced as her commerce groaned under the increasing pressure applied by France. And the spectacle of anarchy then raging in that unhappy country seemed to many a fate that Connecticut herself had barely avoided.

The harsh trial of the Revolution and the hardship of the postwar years gave most of Connecticut's Federalist leadership a passion for order and a horror of republican heresy that equaled all their former apprehensions of Tory conspiracy. Fortunately for them, dissidents who found no place in the political structure had strong incentives to go where the sun of economic opportunity shone brighter, with the result that the Federalists maintained their power until after the close of the War of 1812.[45] Connecticut had embarked upon the Revolution as one of the most republican-minded of all the colonies, but the crucible of war had traumatized without transforming her society. Not until a new generation of leaders emerged, men who proved able to rebuild the state's economy on an industrial base, would Connecticut integrate with the fast-growing national economy. Not until then would her society acquire confidence in the new order and, with the rest of the nation, salute the rising star of the Republic.

Abbreviations

PCC   Papers of the Continental Congress. National Archives, Washington, D.C. (Microfilm ed.)

SFC   Silliman Family Correspondence. Sterling Memorial Library, Yale University, New Haven.

WP   Washington Papers. Library of Congress, Washington, D.C. (Microfilm ed.)

WW   William Williams Papers. Connecticut Historical Society, Hartford.

PUBLISHED SOURCES

AA   Peter Force, ed. *American Archives: . . . A Documentary History of . . . the North American colonies; of the causes and accomplishment of the American revolution. . . .* 4th ser., 6 vols.; 5th ser., 3 vols. Washington, D.C., 1837–53.

AHR   *American Historical Review.*

AR   Henry Clinton. *American Rebellion; Narrative of Campaigns, 1775–1782.* Edited by William B. Willcox. Hamden, Conn. 1971.

ARC   *Address and recommendations to the States, by the United States in Congress assembled.* Philadelphia; reprinted Hartford, 1783.

ASP,F   *American State Papers: Documents, Legislative and Executive, of the Congress of the United States. Financial Series.* 5 vols. Washington, D.C., 1832–61.

CC   *Connecticut Courant.*

CG   *Connecticut Gazette.*

CHSC   Connecticut Historical Society. *Collections.* 31 vols. 1860–1932.

CJ   *Connecticut Journal.*

CR   J. H. Trumbull and C. J. Hoadley, eds. *Public Records of the Colony of Connecticut, 1636–1776.* 15 vols. Hartford, 1850–90.

DAR   K. G. Davies. *Documents of the American Revolution 1770–1783.* 21 vols. Shannon and Dublin, 1972–78.

HPF	Henri Doniol. *Histoire de la participation de la France à l'établissement des Etats-Unis d'Amérique.* 5 vols. Paris, 1886–92.
JCC	Worthington C. Ford, ed. *Journals of the Continental Congress, 1774–1789.* 34 vols. Washington, D.C., 1904–37.
JEH	*Journal of Economic History.*
LDC	Paul H. Smith, ed. *Letters of Delegates to Congress 1774–1789.* Washington, D.C., 1976–.
LMCC	Edmund C. Burnett, ed. *Letters of Members of the Continental Congress.* 8 vols. Washington, D.C., 1921–38.
LOA	*The Last official Address, of his excellency General Washington . . . To which is annexed, A Collection of papers relative to half-pay, and commutation of half-pay . . .* Hartford, 1783.
MG	*Middlesex Gazette.*
MHSC	Massachusetts Historical Society. *Collections,* 1792–.
ND	William B. Clark and William J. Morgan, eds. *Naval Documents of the American Revolution.* Washington, D.C., 1964–.
NEQ	*New England Quarterly.*
NGP	Richard K. Showman, ed. *The Papers of General Nathanael Greene.* Chapel Hill, N.C., 1976–.
NP	*Norwich Packet.*
PMHB	*Pennsylvania Magazine of History and Biography.*
PRM	E. James Ferguson, ed. *The Papers of Robert Morris, 1781–1784.* Pittsburgh, 1973–.
RCM	Henry P. Johnston, ed. *Record of Service of Connecticut Men in the War of the Revolution . . .* Hartford, 1889.
RDC	Francis Wharton, ed. *The Revolutionary Diplomatic Correspondence of the United States.* 6 vols. Washington, D.C., 1889.
SBW	Worthington C. Ford, ed. *Correspondence and Journals of Samuel Blachley Webb.* 3 vols. New York, 1966.

SCP   Julian P. Boyd and Robert J. Taylor, eds. *Susque-
             hannah Company Papers.* 11 vols. Wilkes-Barre, Pa.,
             1930–33, and Ithaca, N.Y., 1968–71.

SHP   Charles S. Hall. *Life and Letters of Samuel Holden Par-
             sons, Major General in the Continental Army and Chief
             Judge of the Northwestern Territory.* New York, 1968.

SOI   Charles H. Lesser, ed. *The Sinews of Independence*
             . . . Chicago, 1976.

SR   C. J. Hoadley et al., eds. *Public Records of the State of
             Connecticut.* Hartford, 1894–.

WGW   John C. Fitzpatrick, ed. *The Writings of George Wash-
             ington.* 39 vols. Washington, D.C., 1931–44.

WHM   William Heath. *Memoirs.* New York, 1968.

WMQ   *William and Mary Quarterly.*

WR   Christopher Ward. *The War of the Revolution.* 2 vols.
             New York, 1952.

Notes

PREFACE

1. See Howard H. Peckham, *The Toll of Independence: Engagements &*
Battle Casualties of the American Revolution (Chicago, 1974). The figures exclude
Westmoreland County.

PART ONE: INTRODUCTION
CHAPTER ONE: REVOLUTIONARY POTENTIAL

1. East Apthorp, *The Felicity of the times* . . . (Boston, 1763), p. 19 and
passim; James Lockwood, *A Sermon preached at Wethersfield, July 6, 1763* . . .
(New Haven, 1763), p. 14ff.; James Horrocks, *Upon the peace. A Sermon* (Wil-
liamsburgh, Va., 1763), p. 9; Samuel Haven, *Joy and salvation by Christ* . . . *A*
Sermon preached . . . *in Portsmouth* (Portsmouth, N.H., 1763), passim; Thomas
Balch, *A Sermon preached to the Ancient and Honourable Artillery Company* . . .
(Boston, 1763), p. 31.
2. Henry Caner, *The Great blessings of stable times* . . . (Boston, 1763), p.
8ff.; Horrocks, *Upon the peace*, p. 10ff.; Lockwood, *A Sermon*, p. 20ff.
3. See the suggestive typology developed by Philip Greven, *The Protes-*
tant Temperament . . . (New York, 1977), especially pp. 146–48; also Alan
Heimert, *Religion and the American Mind* . . . (Cambridge, Mass., 1966), passim.
4. The absence of an executive veto remained a peculiarity of Connecticut's constitution in the early national period; Zephaniel Swift, *A System of the*
Laws of the State of Connecticut (Windham, Conn., 1795), 1: 63, 65–66.
5. Oscar Zeichner, *Connecticut's Years of Controversy, 1750–1776* (Chapel
Hill, N.C., 1949), p. 8; Charles S. Grant, *Democracy in the Connecticut Frontier*
Town of Kent (New York, 1961), pp. 109–12; Bruce P. Stark, "Lebanon, Connecticut: A Study of Society and Politics in the Eighteenth Century" (Ph.D.
thesis, University of Connecticut, 1970), pp. 203, 218.

6. Bruce C. Daniels, *The Connecticut Town* . . . (Middletown, Conn., 1779), pp. 134–35. The two full-scale studies of the militia are Richard H. Marcus, "The Militia of Colonial Connecticut, 1639–1775: An Institutional Study" (Ph.D. thesis, University of Colorado, 1965) and Stewart L. Gates, "Disorder and Social Organization: The Militia in Connecticut Public Life, 1660–1860" (Ph.D. thesis, University of Connecticut, 1975).

7. The rapid expansion took place despite a dispute over title to the Mohegan lands. See Richard Bushman, *From Puritan to Yankee* . . . (Cambridge, Mass., 1967), pp. 82, 93ff., 122, 170–72.

8. See *CHSC*, vols. 17–18, passim; Bernard Knollenberg, *Origin of the American Revolution, 1759–1766* (New York, 1960), passim; Alan Rogers, *Empire and Liberty* . . . (Berkeley, Calif., 1974), passim.

9. See James A. Henretta, "Economic Development and Social Structure in Colonial Boston," *WMQ*, 3rd ser. 33 (1965): 75ff.; Stark, "Lebanon," p. 172; Gary B. Nash, "Urban Wealth and Poverty in Pre-Revolutionary America," *Journal of Interdisciplinary History* 6 (1975–76): 550–74; Jackson T. Main, "The Distribution of Property in Colonial Connecticut," in James K. Martin, ed., *The Human Dimensions of Nation Making* . . . (Madison, Wis., 1976), p. 71.

10. Leonard W. Labaree, *Conservatism in Early American History* (New York, 1948), pp. 21–23. My point is compatible with Main's central argument that wealth distributed itself unevenly; see "Distribution of Property," p. 60ff.

11. Daniels, *Connecticut Town*, p. 164; Harold E. Selesky, "Patterns of Officeholding in the Connecticut General Assembly, 1725–1774," in George J. Willauer, Jr., ed., *A Lyme Miscellany, 1776–1976* (Middletown, Conn., 1977), pp. 172–74.

12. Ibid., pp. 174–76. The point is developed in greater detail in Selesky, "Connecticut Goes to War: The Evolution of the Leadership Structure, 1740–1785" (Wesleyan University Honors Essay, 1972), chap. 2. The pattern of plural officeholding also reached down into the towns; see William F. Willingham, "Deference Democracy and Town Government in Windham, Connecticut, 1755–1786," *WMQ*, 3rd ser. 30 (1973): 407ff.

13. *CR*, 14: 498; Gaspare J. Saladino, "The Economic Revolution in Late Eighteenth Century Connecticut" (Ph.D. thesis, University of Wisconsin, 1964), p. 2; Max G. Schumacher, *The Northern Farmer and His Markets during the Late Colonial Period* (New York, 1975), pp. 30, 33.

14. Saladino, "Economic Revolution," p. 5; Albert E. Van Dusen, "The Trade of Revolutionary Connecticut" (Ph.D. thesis, University of Pennsylvania, 1948), p. 145ff.; Glen Weaver, *Jonathan Trumbull* . . . (Hartford, 1956), pp. 33–34.

15. Bushman, pp. 292–93; Grant, p. 10.

16. Benjamin Trumbull, *A Complete History of Connecticut* . . . (New London, 1898), 2: 233–35, 245–46.

17. Henry Bronson, "A Historical Account of Connecticut Currency . . . ," *Papers of the New Haven Colony Historical Society* 1 (1865): 63–69; Weaver, p. 41.

18. Weaver, p. 70; Joseph A. Ernst, *Money and Politics in America, 1755–1775* (Chapel Hill, N.C., 1973), pp. 37–41.

19. *SCP*, 1: 1–28.

20. See Rog. Wolcott to Jas. Hamilton, Mar. 13, 1754, in ibid., pp. 60–62.

21. Edith A. Bailey, "Influences toward Radicalism in Connecticut, 1754–1775," *Smith College Studies in History* 4 (1920): 195.

22. *CR*, 10: 378.

23. Grant, p. 21; Neil A. McNall, *An Agricultural History of the Genesee Valley, 1790–1860* (Philadelphia, 1952), p. 27; see also Silas Deane to Pat. Henry, Jan. 2, 1775, in New York Historical Society, *Collections* 19 (1887): 36.

24. *SCP*, 2: xviii–xix, xxv.

25. Ibid., p. viff.

26. Bailey, "Influences," pp. 200–202.

27. Lawrence H. Gipson, "Connecticut Taxation and Parliamentary Aid Preceding the Revolutionary War," *AHR* 36 (1930–31): 731–32.

28. Very little has been written on this subject. See Weaver, pp. 76–90; Zeichner, p. 41.

29. *SCP*, 2: xviii–xxxv; Jeff. Amherst to Thos. Fitch, May 17, 1761, and Wm. Johnson to Fitch, Mar. 30, 1763, in ibid., pp. 95–96, 122–23.

30. Earl of Egremont to Thos. Fitch, Jan. 27, 1763; Minutes of the Susquehannah Co., May 18; Fitch to Wm. Johnson, May 30, in ibid., pp. 194–95, 219, 235.

31. Ibid., pp. 255–56.

32. See Clarence W. Alvord, *The Mississippi Valley in British Politics . . .* (Cleveland, 1917), 1: 151–82.

33. Charles E. Clark, *The Eastern Frontier . . .* (New York, 1970), pp. 344–45; Matt B. Jones, *Vermont in the Making, 1750–1777* (Cambridge, Mass., 1939), p. 116 and n. 18; Philip M. Zea, "A New Hampshire Grant Town, 1760–1815" (Wesleyan University Honors Essay, 1974), p. 7; Lois K. M. Rosenberry, "Migrations from Connecticut Prior to 1800," in Tercentenary Commission of the State of Connecticut, *Publications* 28 (1934): 9.

34. Zeichner, pp. 47–48, 81.

35. Bushman, p. 116; Guy Trégault, *Canada: The War of Conquest* (Toronto, 1969), p. 204.

36. Zeichner, pp. 143–44. Various contemporary estimates form the basis for this conclusion; see Franklin B. Dexter, ed., *The Literary Diary of Ezra Stiles . . .* (New York, 1901), 1: 439, 444; Silas Deane to Pat. Henry, Jan. 2, 1775, in New York Historical Society, *Collections* 19 (1887): 35. See also Rosenberry, "Migrations from Connecticut."

37. Main, "Distribution of Property," p. 90.

38. Aside from the requirement that the colony quarter 150 troops during the winter of 1766–67; Zeichner, p. 80.

39. Egremont to Thos. Fitch, July 9, 1763, in *CHCS*, 18: 247; Knollenberg, pp. 176–80; Zeichner, p. 47; Weaver, p. 115.

40. Gipson, "Connecticut Taxation," pp. 732–35; also his *Jared Ingersoll . . .* (New Haven, 1920), p. 252; Wm. Pitkin to Rich. Jackson, Feb. 14, 1767, and to the earl of Hillsborough, n.d., in *CHSC*, 19: 75. The government tried to cushion the impact of these developments by abating taxes, Gipson, "Connecticut Taxation," p. 734, and by emitting small amounts of currency, *SR*, 12: 338.

41. Richard Buel, Jr., "Democracy and the American Revolution . . ."

WMQ, 3rd ser. 21 (1964): 182ff.; also Wm. Pitkin to Wm. S. Johnson, June 6, 1768, in 5*MHSC*, 9: 279.

42. The best statement of the colonists' position was made by Daniel Dulany, *Considerations of the propriety of imposing taxes in the British Colonies* (1765), in Bernard Bailyn, ed., *Pamphlets of the American Revolution* (Cambridge, Mass., 1965), 1: especially 611–16, 623, 627, 652–58.

43. Gipson, *Ingersoll*, p. 125; Bailyn, *Pamphlets*, pp. 381–83.

44. *CR*, 12: 299.

45. Gipson, *Ingersoll*, p. 168ff.

46. See Jon. Trumbull to Thos. Fitch, n.d., in *CHSC*, 18: 355; Fitch to Wm. Pitkin, Sept. 12, 1765, in ibid., p. 356.

47. Gipson, *Ingersoll*, p. 177ff.; Bushman, pp. 285–86.

48. *CR*, 12: 411. The emergency session also appointed delegates to the Stamp Act Congress but instructed them to "form no such junction with the other Commissioners as will subject you to the majority vote"; ibid., p. 410.

49. Ibid., pp. 421–25; Jar. Ingersoll to Commissioners of Stamps, Nov. 2, 1765, in *Mr. Ingersoll's Letters relating to the Stamp-Act* (New Haven, 1766), p. 51. Gipson got this wrong; see *Ingersoll*, pp. 193, 204.

50. His official instructions didn't arrive until Dec. 18 and made no mention of the oath; Chas. Lowndes to Thos. Fitch, Sept. 14, 1765, in *CHSC*, 18: 257.

51. Zeichner, p. 57; Franklin B. Dexter, *Extracts from the Itineraries and other miscellanies of Ezra Stiles . . .* (New Haven, 1916), pp. 63–64.

52. Jones, *Vermont*, chap. 3.

53. See Patricia Bonomi, *A Factious People . . .* (New York, 1971), p. 10.

54. Zeichner, pp. 73–75; Bushman, chap. 8.

55. C. C. Goen, *Revivalism and Separatism in New England, 1740–1800* (New Haven, 1962), pp. 186–87; Bruce E. Steiner, "Anglican Officeholding in Pre-Revolutionary Connecticut: The Parameters of New England Community," *WMQ*, 3rd ser. 31 (1974): 374–75, insert.

56. Bushman, p. 259.

57. Grant, p. 98ff.; Daniels, chaps. 1, 2, 6. See also Ebenezer Baldwin, *An Appendix, stating the heavy grievances the Colonies labour under . . .* , in Samuel Sherwood, *A Sermon . . .* (New Haven, 1774), p. 44.

58. Grant, pp. 125–26.

59. Zeichner, pp. 73–74.

60. See "Plaind Facts," in *CC*, Jan. 12, 1767; quote from "Justice," in ibid., Mar. 9; "General Plan," in ibid., Apr. 6.

61. Parity on the Council does not seem to have been left to chance; see Zeichner, pp. 72–74; Christopher Collier, *Roger Sherman's Connecticut . . .* (Middletown, Conn., 1971), p. 57.

62. "Senex Quondam Senatorius" and "A.Z.," in *CC*, Mar. 9, 1767.

63. See Sung Bok Kim, *Landlord and Tenant in Colonial New York* (Chapel Hill, N.C., 1978), p. 401ff.

64. John Dickinson, "The Farmer's Letters to the Inhabitants of the British Colonies," in *Political Writings of John Dickinson, Esquire . . .* (Wilmington, Del., 1801), 1: 155.

65. Oliver M. Dickerson, *The Navigation Acts and the American Revolution* (Philadelphia, 1951), pp. 184–86, 189 n. 34; Thomas C. Barrow, *Trade and*

Empire . . . (Cambridge, Mass., 1967), p. 214. Connecticut accounted for only a modest portion of the whole; see *CHSC*, 19:147, 155–58.

66. See *CC*, Aug. 17, 1767.

67. Dickinson, *Political Writings*, 1: 143–284, passim.

68. *CC*, May 9, 1768; Zeichner, p. 85; *CR*, 13: 82–90.

69. Zeichner, pp. 85–86; also New York Merchants to New Haven Merchants, July 27, 1769, in *CHSC*, 19: 163.

70. *CC*, June 11, 1770.

71. Committee of Connecticut Merchants to New York Merchants, June 19, 1770, in *CC*, July 23, 1770; also *CC*, Aug. 6, 13 and Sept. 17, 1770.

72. Zeichner, pp. 87–88; "Issachar," in *CC*, Jan. 18, 1771; also Willauer, ed., *Lyme*, pp. 230–35.

73. Wm. S. Johnson to Wm. Pitkin, May 25 and Sept. 18, 1769, in *5MHSC*, 9: 346–47, 357–58.

74. Richard Buel, Jr., "The Freedom of the Press in Revolutionary America," in Bernard Bailyn and John B. Hench, eds., *The Press and the American Revolution* (Worcester, Mass., 1980), pp. 76–79.

75. Hiller B. Zobel, *The Boston Massacre* (New York, 1970), passim. See also Wm. S. Johnson to Wm. Pitkin, Sept. 18, 1769, in *5MHSC*, 9: 360–61; Johnson to Pitkin, Mar. 6, 1770, in ibid., p. 424, and Jon. Trumbull to Johnson, Jan. 29, in ibid., p. 403.

76. Ernst, *Money and Politics*, p. 277.

77. See Wm. S. Johnson to Wm. Pitkin, Jan. 3 and Feb. 9, 1769, and Feb. 3, 1770, in *5MHSC*, 9: 308–10, 316–17, 406.

78. See Wm. S. Johnson's letters to Connecticut correspondents during this period, in *5MHSC*, 9: 303, 314, 321, 324–25, 335–39, 354, 366.

79. For the seeds of this notion, see Dickerson, *Navigation Acts*, pp. 239ff., 248; Wm. Pitkin to Wm. S. Johnson, June 10, 1768, and Feb. 15, 1769, in *5MHSC*, 19: 128, 129. It took longer for the idea to receive popular currency; see *CC*, June 2, Sept. 15, 1772. I follow Pauline S. Maier, *From Resistance to Revolution* . . . (New York, 1972), in seeing the agitation over the Townshend duties as crucial to a transition to colonial attitudes, though for slightly different reasons.

80. Benjamin W. Labaree, *The Boston Tea Party* (New York, 1964), pp. 52–56.

81. *SCP*, 2: xxi, xxxvi, xxxix–xli; the company was still taxing its members for this purpose in the spring of 1768, ibid., 3: 14–15.

82. See Wm. S. Johnson to Wm. Pitkin, July 23, 1768, in *5MHSC*, 9: 291–92.

83. *SCP*, 3: iv, ix, xiv.

84. Ibid., pp. 43–47.

85. Ibid., p. 234.

86. Ibid., p. xxvii.

87. Ibid., pp. 93, 96–97.

88. Ibid., p. 234.

89. Ibid., 3: 278; 4: 346–48, 358–59.

90. Ibid., 3: 170–73; Durkee had petitioned the Council in July on the same subject, ibid., pp. 147—48.

91. See "A Son of Liberty," Feb. 20, 1770, in ibid., 4: 64.

92. Ibid., 3: 279.

93. Benjamin Gale, *Doct. Gale's Letter to J.W. esquire* . . . (Hartford, 1769), in ibid., p. 237; also Gale's *Observations, on a pamphlet, entitled Remarks on Dr. Gale's Letter to J.W. esq.* . . . (Hartford, 1769), in ibid., pp. 277–78; *The State of the lands said to be once within the bounds of the Charter of the Colony of Connecticut West of the Province of New-York, considered* (New York, 1770), in ibid., 4:346–48, 358–59.

94. [Thomas Fitch], "Some Remarks and Observations . . . ," in ibid., 3: 292–330, is wholly devoted to this subject; also ibid., pp. 236–37, 269–77; 4: 349–54.

95. Ibid., 4: 65, 355–56; 3:287.

96. Ibid., 3: 191–92.

97. Ibid., pp. xxiv, 200–202.

98. Ibid., 4: i–xv.

99. Ibid., p. 147.

100. See ibid., 6: 179–80.

101. Ibid., 4: 215; "To the Candid Public," in ibid., 6: 152, gives a slightly distorted view of the Assembly's action here, though referral of the company's case to English counsel was undoubtedly regarded as a disappointment by many company supporters.

102. Ibid., 6: xxii–xxiv; 5: xxii–xxiii.

103. Ibid., 6: 179–80, also 4: 201.

104. See ibid., 5: 130–32.

105. Jones, *Vermont*, chaps. 12–13.

106. *SCP*, 5: 174–80, 248–50, 268.

107. Ibid., pp. 299–301, 332–34, 345–49, 353, 359–61.

108. Ibid., 6: 148–49.

109. Ibid., pp. 168, 219.

110. Ibid., pp. 264–67.

111. Richard D. Brown, *Revolutionary Politics in Massachusetts* . . . (Cambridge, Mass., 1970), pp. 51–55, 80–81, 99–100, 129–30, 140–41; *CC*, June 23 and Sept. 15, 1772, and Jan. 5, 1773; *CR*, 14: 156. For another gauge of how these events affected public opinion, see Benjamin Trumbull, *A Discourse, delivered at the anniversary meeting of the freemen . . . of New Haven, April 12, 1773* (New Haven, 1773), pp. 23–24.

112. Baldwin, *An Appendix*, pp. 54–55, 61–64; Labaree, *Boston Tea Party*, chap. 7.

113. Baldwin, *An Appendix*, pp. 56–60, 65–67, 69.

114. *CR*, 14: 347–50, quote 348; *CC*, June 21, 1774.

115. *CC*, June 14, 21, 28 and July 5, 19, 1774; 4*AA*, pp. 390, 445; also Francis O. Allen, *The History of Enfield* . . . (Lancaster, Pa., 1900), 1: 455–56. Canterbury, *Ex*, June 27, 1774; Colchester, *Ex*, July 5; Bolton, *Ex*, July 12; Farmington Town Records, 1: 427.

116. 4*AA*, 1: 336. The iconographical significance of the pole's height is explained in Pauline Maier, "John Wilkes and American Disillusionment with Britain," *WMQ*, 3rd ser. 20 (1963): 379–80.

117. 4*AA*, 1: 629–33, quote 632.

118. Ibid., pp. 724–25; also Gipson, *Ingersoll*, p. 333.

119. 4*AA*, 1: 711–18, quote 711. Peters subsequently wrote a history of

Connecticut in a similar vein, which has recently been republished in Kenneth W. Cameron, ed., *The Works of Samuel Peters* . . . (Hartford, 1967), pp. 7–84. Peters claimed in this history that he had drawn the enmity of the mob by obstructing a collection for the people of Boston (see pp. 81–84); a provocative letter written by Peters to his mother expressing the hope that "Hanging work will go on" appeared in *CJ*, Oct. 21, 1774.

120. *4AA*, 1: 731–32.

121. Ibid., p. 787. The town took further action against him on Jan. 5, 1775; see East Haddam Town Records, 1766–1822, p. 43.

122. *4AA*, 1: 304.

123. Ibid., pp. 788–89, also 826–27.

124. Samuel Sherwood and Ebenezer Baldwin in their joint publication, n.57 above. Receipt of the Quebec Act just before a colony fast helped inspire the clergy to action; see Gurd. Saltonstall to Silas Deane, Aug. 29, 1774, in New York Historical Society, *Collections* 19 (1887): 4.

125. Israel Holly, *God brings about His holy and wise purpose or decree* . . . (Hartford, 1774), pp. 15–19; Levi Hart, *Liberty described and recommended* . . . (Hartford, 1775).

126. *4AA*, 1: 1227.

127. See *CC*, Oct. 10, 1774; also *CJ*, Oct. 28, 1774.

128. For an exaggerated account of the incident, see *CC*, Sept. 15, 1774. Documentation about precise numbers is hard to find, but Israel Putnam to Aaron Cleveland, Sept. 3, 1774, in *4AA*, 1: 325, shows that there was an alarm. See John H. Scheide, "The Lexington Alarm," *Proceedings of the American Antiquarian Society*, n.s. 50 (1940): 54–57, for a balanced discussion of the incident.

129. See *Heads of inquiry relative to the present state and condition of his majesty's Colony of Connecticut, signified by his majesty's secretary of state . . . with the answers thereto* (New London, 1775), reproduced in *CR*, 14: 493–507, especially 499, for Connecticut's share. The General Assembly ordered *Heads of inquiry* published in pamphlet form during its October 1774 session to give the people a sense of the colony's military potential. The document claimed that Connecticut's population had increased 52,266 since 1762 and that 26,620 names appeared on its militia rolls. Don Higginbotham, *The War of American Independence* . . . (New York, 1971), pp. 18–23; John W. Shy, "Thomas Gage: Weak Link of Empire," in George A. Billias, ed., *George Washington's Opponents* (New York, 1969), pp. 4–9.

130. *CR*, 14: 261, 264, 296, 308–9.

131. In *4AA*, 1: 787–88.

132. *CR*, 14: 327–28, 346.

133. Orlando W. Stephenson, "The Supply of Gunpowder in 1776," *AHR* 30 (1925): 271–72: Ellen Chase, *The Beginnings of the American Revolution* (Port Washington, N.Y., 1970), 2: 40, 50, 60–61, 147, 151–53.

134. *CR*, 14: 346.

135. Ibid., pp. 386–87n.; Jos. Trumbull to Jon. Trumbull, Dec. 30, 1774, in *4AA*, 1: 1077. See also Nath. Shaw, Jr., to Jon. Trumbull, Apr. 25, 1775; to a friend, Dec. 14, 1774; and to Peter Vandervoort & Co., Dec. 15, Jan. 15, Jan. 24, 1775, in Ernst E. Rogers, *Connecticut's Naval Office at New London*, in New London County Historical Society, *Collections* 2 (1933): 26,

262–63, 265–66; 4*AA*, 1: 1139. Efforts to keep the government's actions a secret were unsuccessful; 4*AA*, 1: 1177. Some towns took independent action; see Colchester, Ex, Sept. 12, 1774; Ashford, Ex, Sept. 13; Bolton, Ex, Jan. 16, 1775.

136. 4*AA*, 1: 1038, 1075; see, for example, Saybrook Town Records, Dec. 1, 1774; Guilford Town Records, 2: 259–60; Branford Town Records, 1691–1788, pp. 361–60 (numbered backward); Middletown Town Records, 2: 342–43; Milford Town Records, p. 78; New Haven Town Records, 1769–1807, p. 46; Hartford Town Votes, 2: 250; Farmington Town Records, 1: 430.

137. 4*AA*, 1: 1202, 1215, 1258–60, 1270. A minority in Ridgefield dissented; ibid., p. 1210.

138. Ibid., pp. 1236–38.

139. Ibid., p. 1236.

140. *CR*, 14: 391ff.

Part Two: War

1. See *Massachusetts Spy*, Jan. 14, 1775; Gurd. Saltonstall to Silas Deane, Aug. 29, 1774, in New York Historical Society, *Collections* 19 (1887): 4–5.

2. *Massachusetts Spy*, Feb. 2, 1775; 4*AA*, 1: 1466, 1468–69, 1474–75.

3. *Massachusetts Spy*, Apr. 6, 1775; 4*AA*, 1: 1541–42, 1566.

4. Ellen Chase, *The Beginnings of the American Revolution* (Port Washington, N.Y., 1970), 2: 148; Sam. Graves to Phil. Stephens, Dec. 15, 1774, in *ND*, 1:23.

5. 4*AA*, 1: 1323ff.

6. Ibid., p. 1345.

7. Chase, *Beginnings*, 2: 250–58.

8. Allen French, *The Day of Concord and Lexington* (Boston, 1925), pp. 61–62.

Chapter Two: Commitment

1. Franklin B. Dexter, ed., *The Literary Diary of Ezra Stiles* (New York, 1901), 1: 535–36.

2. Elizabeth Merritt, "The Lexington Alarm, April 19, 1775: Messages Sent to the Southward after the Battle," *Maryland Historical Magazine* 41 (1946): 978; J. H. Scheide, "The Lexington Alarm," *Proceedings of the American Antiquarian Society*, n.s. 50 (1940): 62–65.

3. Scheide, "Lexington Alarm," pp. 76–78; see also "Interesting Intelligence, Norwich, April 22, 1775," listed in Charles Evans, *American Bibliography: A Chronological Dictionary of all Books Pamphlets and Periodical Publications Printed in the United States of America . . .* 14 vols. (Chicago, 1903–59), 42848, hereafter cited as Evans; Connecticut Committee of Correspondence to John Hancock, Apr. 21, 1775, in 4*AA*, 2: 372–73.

4. William Cutler, *The Life of Israel Putnam . . .* , 5th ed. (Boston, 1846), p. 151; George C. Hill, *General Israel Putnam . . .* (Boston, 1858), p. 130.

5. Connecticut Committee of Correspondence to John Hancock, Apr. 21, 1775, in 4*AA*, 2: 373.

6. The figures are derived from *RCM*, pp. 5–28.

7. James Lockwood to ?, Apr. 24, 1775, in 4*AA*, 2: 365.

8. *RCM*, pp. 10–12, 22; see also 4*AA*, 2: 480.

9. *CR*, 14: 439.

10. Isaac Lee to Jon. Trumbull, Apr. 27, 1775, in 4*AA*, 2: 423.

11. "Heads of inquiry relative to the present state and condition of his majesty's Colony of Connecticut," in *CR*, 14: 499, also 417.

12. Allen French, *The First Year of the American Revolution* (Boston, 1934), pp. 40, 56–57. See also Canterbury, *Ex*, Mar. 27, 1777.

13. Reenlistment rates were assessed by comparing the muster rolls of sixteen companies in the seven-month army whose provenance was confined to one or two towns with Lexington Alarm lists for those towns as printed in *RCM*. Cf also Jed. Huntington to Jos. Trumbull, May 10, 1775, in JosT.

14. *RCM*, pp. 37–38.

15. *CG*, Dec. 30, 1774.

16. 4*AA*, 2: 472; Douglas E. Leach, *Arms for Empire* . . . (New York, 1973), pp. 428–32.

17. Cf. Benj. Trumbull to his wife, June 28, 1775, in BT; John W. Shy, *Toward Lexington* . . . (Princeton, N.J., 1965), pp. 358ff.

18. "Americanus," in *CG*, Dec. 30, 1774.

19. 4*AA*, 1: 1550, 1570, 1622–23, also 2: 377.

20. In November 1776 the General Assembly enacted a price regulation measure which fixed peak wages at three shillings per diem "and so in the usual proportions at other seasons of the year"; *SR*, 1: 62. Cf. also Kenneth W. Cameron, ed., *The Works of Samuel Peters of Hebron, Connecticut* (Hartford, 1967), p. 57.

21. The wages and bounties are in *CR*, 14: 417–18; see also 15: 16, for the liberal rations promised by the Assembly in its May session.

22. Ibid., 14: 432.

23. Joel A. Cohen, "Lexington and Concord: Rhode Island Reacts," *Rhode Island History* 26 (1967): 100; see also the broadsides issued by Governor Wanton and by Darius Sessions, Evans 42978, 42936–37.

24. 4*AA*, 2: 373, also 391–93.

25. *CR*, 14: 416, 440–41, 442–44; 4*AA*, 2: 473–74. Governor Trumbull also wrote Joseph Warren on May 4, 1775, to reassure the Massachusetts Congress; see 4*AA*, 2: 506.

26. *WR*, 1: 52; Willard M. Wallace, *Traitorous Hero* . . . (New York, 1954), p. 38; Sam. H. Parsons to Jos. Trumbull, June 5, 1775, in *CHSC*, 1: 181n.

27. 4*AA*, 2: 450, 455.

28. *RCM*, p. 29.

29. Ethan Allen to the Massachusetts Congress, May 11, 1775; Ben. Arnold to the Massachusetts Committee of Safety, May 11; Edw. Mott to the Massachusetts Congress, May 11, in 4*AA*, 2: 556–60.

30. Ben. Arnold to the Massachusetts Committee of Safety, May 4, 1775, in ibid., pp. 584–85.

31. See Committee of War for the Expedition against Ticonderoga and

Crown Point to the Massachusetts Congress, May 10, 1775, and Ben. Arnold to the Massachusetts Committee of Safety, May 11, in ibid., pp. 556, 557; Wallace, *Traitorous Hero*, chap. 5.

32. *4AA*, 2: 4, 44–50; Carl L. Becker, *The History of Political Parties in the Province of New York, 1760–1776* (Madison, Wisc., 1909), chap. 8.

33. Becker, p. 194; Declaration of the New York Committee, Apr. 26, 1775, in *4AA*, 2: 400, also 459.

34. *JCC*, 2: 56. The relief of Connecticut's leadership at this development can be seen in Wm. Williams to the Connecticut Congressional delegates, May 23, 1775, in *ND*, 1: 510–11.

35. Jon. Trumbull to Connecticut Congressional delegates, May 25, 1775, in JTP; Nath. Wales, Jr., to the Speaker of the Assembly of Connecticut, May 23, 1775, in *4AA*, 2: 685; see also pp. 843–44, 1247, 1250.

36. Jon. Trumbull to Connecticut Congressional delegates, May 27, 1775, in JTP; Ben. Arnold to Massachusetts Committee of Safety, May 23, in *4AA*, 2: 693–94.

37. Jon. Trumbull to Connecticut Congressional delegates, May 29 and June 5, 1775, in JTP; Connecticut Congressional delegates to Wm. Williams, May 31, in *LDC*, 1: 423.

38. *4AA*, 2: 1257, 1274, 1285.

39. I simplify a complicated sequence of events here. For a full discussion of the episode see Jonathan G. Rossie, *The Politics of Command* . . . (Syracuse, N.Y., 1975), 46–48.

40. *RCM*, pp. 45, 53; *CR*, 15: 84–85. For the constitution of the Council of Safety, ibid., p. 39.

41. *ND*, 1: 47, 222, 785; Dexter, *Diary of Stiles*, 1: 539—40.

42. *RCM*, p. 22.

43. *ND*, 1: 291, 256–57.

44. Ibid., pp. 343–44, 361, 596.

45. *CR*, 15: 87, 89.

46. Massachusetts Congress to Jon. Trumbull, June 25, 1775, in *4AA*, 2: 1090–91.

47. Jon. Trumbull to the Massachusetts Congress, June 27, 1775, in ibid., p. 1116; *CR*, 15: 92–93; Connecticut Congressional Delegates to Trumbull, July 10, in *LDC*, 1: 619.

48. See Washington's comments on these problems in *WGW*, 3: 385, 394–95, 421, 442–43; also Orlando W. Stephenson, "The Supply of Gunpowder in 1776," *AHR* 30 (1925): 271–78; Douglas S. Freeman, *George Washington* . . . (New York, 1948–57), 3: 510ff.

49. See Chas. Lee to Benj. Rush, Sept. 19, 1775, in New York Historical Society, *Collections* 4 (1871): 206.

50. Washington to the President of Congress, July 10, 1775; to Rich. H. Lee, July 10; and to John A. Washington, July 27, in *WGW*, 3: 321–22, 330, 372.

51. Washington to the major and brigadier generals, Sept. 8, 1775, in ibid., pp. 483–84.

52. Council of War, Sept. 11, 1775, in *4AA*, 3: 768.

53. See Washington to Jon. Trumbull, Aug. 9, 14, 1775, in *WGW*, 3: 411–12, 419; also Washington to Phil. Schuyler, July 10, in ibid., p. 332.

54. See Edw. and Wm. Ledyard to Jos. Trumbull, July 31 and Aug. 10, 1775, in JosT. The Council of Safety ordered a partial mobilization of the militia in response to the British appearance off New London; see Jon. Trumbull to Washington, Aug. 7, in 4*AA*, 3: 58; also Trumbull to Chris. Leffingwell, July 28, in JTP.

55. *JCC*, 2: 186.

56. Ibid., pp. 109–10.

57. Schuyler's growing enthusiasm for entering Canada can be traced in Phil. Schuyler to Jon. Trumbull, July 4, 31, 1775, in 4*AA*, 2: 1704, 1762; see also Trumbull to Schuyler, July 17, 24, in ibid., pp. 1676, 1721.

58. Washington to the President of Congress, Aug. 4 and Sept. 5, 1775; to Phil. Schuyler, Aug. 20; and General Orders, Sept. 5, in *WGW*, 3: 393, 437, 473, 511.

59. Washington to Jon. Trumbull, Sept. 2, 1775, in ibid., p. 470.

60. Gurd. Saltonstall to Jon. Trumbull, Aug. 30, 31, 1775, and to Jabez Huntington, Aug. 31, in 4*AA*, 3: 461, 469–71; also *ND*, 1: 1261–63.

61. Jos. Fish to Mary Silliman, Sept. 5, 1775, in SFC, box 1.

62. Matt. Griswold to Jon. Trumbull, Sept. 2, 1775, in *ND*, 1: 1294; Gurd. Saltonstall to the Committee of Lyme, Aug. 31, in 4*AA*, 3: 472; *CR*, 15: 123–24.

63. Jon. Trumbull to Washington, Sept. 5, 1775, in 4*AA*, 3: 647; Washington to Jon. Trumbull, Sept. 8, 1775, in *WGW*, 3: 486–87; *CR*, 15: 128.

64. Dav. Wooster to Jon. Trumbull, June 15, 1775, in *ND*, 1: 687.

65. *CR*, 15: 110.

66. Sam. Graves to Phil. Stephens, May 18, 1775, in *ND*, 1: 355–56; Jack Coggins, *Ships and Seamen of the American Revolution . . .* (Harrisburg, Pa., 1969).

67. *CR*, 15: 117, 120.

68. Ibid., pp. 99–100, 176, 177, 201–2; Giles Hall to Jon. Trumbull, Dec. 13, 1775, in *ND*, 3: 88.

69. *CR*, 15: 201–2; Jon. Trumbull to John Hancock, Oct. 17, 1775, in *ND*, 2: 496.

70. *CR*, 14: 432, 15: 14, 101; Henry Bronson, "A Historical Account of Connecticut Currency . . . ," *Papers of the New Haven Colony Historical Society* (1865): 85; Jon. Trumbull to Phil. Schuyler, Aug. 21, 1775, in 4*AA*, 3: 225. For a complete schedule of state emissions of paper money during the Revolution, see Ralph V. Harlow, "Aspects of Revolutionary Finance, 1775–1783," *AHR* 35 (1929–30): 50–51, insert.

71. Cf. Lawrence H. Gipson, "Connecticut Taxation and Parliamentary Aid Preceding the Revolutionary War," *AHR* 36(1930–31): 723.

72. *JCC*, 2: 236, 3: 263; Eliph. Dyer to Jon. Trumbull, July 18, 1775, in *LDC*, 1: 634; also pp. 618–19.

73. See Matt. Griswold to Jon. Trumbull, Oct. 20, 1775, in *ND*, 2: 536; New Haven Memorial, Oct. 31, in JTP.

74. Sam. Graves. to Jas. Wallace, Nov. 4, 1775, in *ND*, 2: 881–82.

75. For an estimate of the stock on the island, see ibid., p. 521; for Wallace's orders, see Sam. Graves to Jas. Wallace, Nov. 4, 5, 1775, in ibid., pp. 881–82, 894.

76. Ibid., pp. 1023, 1034–35, 1044–45; Dexter, *Diary of Stiles*, 1: 633.

77. *CR*, 15: 178, 180–81.
78. Phil. Schuyler to the Continental Congress, July 21, 1775, and to the New York Congress, July 31 and Aug. 30, in *4AA*, 2: 1702, 1760, 3: 212.
79. *CR*, 15: 100 and n.; *JCC*, 2: 186, 256. Congress had authorized Connecticut to supply Schuyler at the end of June; *JCC*, 2: 110. See also Phil. Schuyler to Jon. Trumbull, June 20, 1775, and Trumbull to Schuyler, July 6, in *4AA*, 2: 1139, 1594.
80. Washington detailed his strategy for imposing discipline on the New England troops in various letters to be found in *WGW*, 3: 445, 448, 472–73, 490, 496, 4: 19–20, 22, 28, 95, 112. An insight into some of the problems he encountered can be gained from Washington to John Hancock, July 20, 1775, to Lund Washington, Aug. 20, and to Rich. H. Lee, Aug. 30, in ibid., 3: 348, 433, 450.
81. See David Wooster to Washington, Aug. 29, 1775, in ibid., 3: 465n.; Jer. Wadsworth to Jos. Trumbull, May 9, and Jon. Trumbull, Jr., to Wadsworth, Aug. 30, in JW, box 123; Rossie, *Politics of Command*, p. 21.
82. *JCC*, 2: 237.
83. Phil. Schuyler to the Continental Congress, July 11, 21, 31, 1775, in *4AA*, 2: 1646, 1703, 1760; Benson J. Lossing, *The Life and Times of Philip Schuyler* (New York, 1872; rpt. 1973), 1: 371–75; also Benj. Hinman to Schuyler, July 7, 1775, in *4AA*, 2: 1606.
84. Phil. Schuyler to Washington, Aug. 6, 1775, in *4AA*, 3: 50.
85. Washington to the President of Congress, Sept. 21, 1775, in *WGW*, 3: 505–6. Jed. Huntington to Jon. Trumbull, Sept. 21, in *4AA*, 3: 771; General Orders, Sept. 27, in *WGW*, 3: 524.
86. Phil. Schuyler to John Hancock, Oct. 14, 1775, and to David Wooster, Oct. 19, in *4AA*, 3: 1065–66, 1107. See also Benj. Hinman to Jon. Trumbull, Oct. 12, in JTP.
87. Phil. Schuyler to David Wooster, Oct. 23, 1775, in *4AA*, 4: 1008.
88. See David Wooster to John Hancock, Feb. 11, 1776, with enclosures, in ibid., pp. 1001–8.
89. See Rich. Montgomery to Phil. Schuyler, Sept. 10, 24, Oct. 6, 9, 13, Nov. 13, and Dec. 5, 1775, in ibid., 3: 741–42, 840–41, 1095–98, 1603, 4: 189.
90. See Return of sick discharged at Ticonderoga, Oct. 12, 1775, in JTP. The outbreak of sickness among the Connecticut units coincided with the reduction in their rations.
91. Phil. Schuyler to John Hancock, Nov. 20, 1775, in ibid., p. 1617; also, Schuyler to Jon. Trumbull, Oct. 12, in ibid., p. 1034.
92. Lt. Warnham Gibbs to Jon. Trumbull, Oct. 10, 1775; Nath. Taylor and others to Trumbull, Oct. 15; J. Young to Trumbull, Oct. 16, in ibid., pp. 1006, 1068, 1074.
93. *WR*, 1: 195.
94. *JCC*, 4: 39, 64, 70–71.
95. *4AA*, 4: 931–32; *CR*, 15: 231.
96. *4AA*, 4: 933–35; *CR*, 15: 232.
97. Phil. Schuyler to John Hancock, Mar. 6, 1776, in *ND*, 4: 193; cf. Return of the Northern Army, May 11, 1776, in *4AA*, 6: 411–12.
98. *CR*, 15: 275–76.

99. See Jon. Trumbull to Jon. Trumbull, Jr., Feb. 14, 1776, in JTjr, 1: 22.

100. Washington to Jon. Trumbull, Jan. 16, 1776, in *WGW*, 4: 248–49.

101. See Washington to Jon. Trumbull, Jan. 21, 1776, in ibid., p. 265.

102. See *JCC*, 4: 157; Oliver Wolcott to Samuel Lyman, Feb. 19, 1776, in *LMCC*, 1: 355; Jon. Trumbull to Connecticut Congressional delegates, Dec. 9, 1775, in JTP.

103. *JCC*, 3: 321–26, for Congress's blueprint for the new army.

104. See General Orders, Oct. 26, 28, 1775, in *WGW*, 4: 44, 49.

105. For letting the rear division abandon Arnold on his march to Quebec, Enos was court-martialed and acquitted, though wholly on the basis of the testimony of his subordinates, who were parties to the crime.

106. Jon. Trumbull to Washington, Dec. 7, 1775, in *4AA*, 4: 213; *CR*, 15: 235; Washington to John Hancock, Dec. 15, in *WGW*, 4: 183.

107. Washington to Jon. Trumbull, Dec. 2, 1775, in *WGW*, 4: 137–38.

108. Washington to John Hancock, Dec. 4, 11, 1775, in ibid., pp. 142, 157. The men lacked winter clothing; see Jon. Trumbull to Connecticut Congressional delegates, Oct. 18, in JTP.

109. Washington to Jos. Reed, Nov. 28, 1775, in ibid., 124.

110. Eliph. Dyer to Jos. Trumbull, Dec. 16, 1775, in *LMCC*, 1: 279.

111. See Returns of Nov. 18 and Dec. 30, 1775, in *4AA*, 3:611–12, 4: 491–92.

112. Washington to Nich. Cooke, Dec. 5, and to Jos. Reed, Dec. 15, 25, 1775, in *WGW*, 4: 146, 166, 185.

113. J. Steven Watson, *The Reign of George III, 1760–1815* (Oxford, 1960), pp. 139–40.

114. Jon. Trumbull to Connecticut Congressional delegates, Oct. 18, 1775, in JTP. See also *LDC*, 2: 14–15, 92, 98. The petitions and addresses against the colonies far outnumbered those in their behalf; see *4AA*, 3: 1969—72.

115. Cf. *Plain Truth; addressed to the inhabitants of America* . . . (Philadelphia, 1776), p. 19.

116. David Klingman, "Food Surpluses and Deficits in the American Colonies, 1768–1772," *JEH* 31 (1971): 558, 563–65.

117. Jon. Trumbull, Jr., to Jer. Wadsworth, Aug. 30, 1775, in JW, box 123; see also *ND*, 2: 40–41.

118. See *4AA*, 2: 1459. New York reacted in a different way; see ibid., pp. 1262–64.

119. Jos. Trumbull to Jer. Wadsworth, July 27, 1775, in JW, box 123; Jer. Wadsworth to Jos. Trumbull, July 2, 1775, in ibid.; Washington to the President of Congress, July 10, 1775, in *WGW*, 3: 324; *JCC*, 2: 190.

120. *JCC*, 2: 103.

121. "Cato," in *CG*, Feb. 2, 1776.

122. Jon. Trumbull to Washington, Dec. 7, 1775, in *4AA*, 4: 213.

123. *CR*, 15: 196–97, 187–89, 192–95, 200, 202.

124. Washington to Nich. Cooke, Jan. 6, 1776, in *WGW*, 4: 215–16.

125. Returns of Dec. 30, 1775, and Jan. 8, 1776, in *4AA*, 4: 491–92, 631; *SOI*, pp. 15–17.

126. Washington to the Massachusetts legislature, to Jon. Trumbull, and to the New Hampshire legislature, Jan. 16, 1776, in *WGW*, 4: 246–51.

127. See *CR*, 15: 229.

128. Jon. Trumbull to Washington, Feb. 2, 5, 12, 1776, in 4*AA*, 4: 917, 945, quote 1017–18.

129. See Returns of Mar. 3, 1776, in ibid., 5: 117–18.

130. Ibid., 3: 1318–19, 1322.

131. Ibid., 4: 401; Otto Hufeland, *Westchester County during the American Revolution, 1775–1783* (n.p., 1926), pp. 94–95.

132. Cf. Samuel Seabury, *An Alarm to the legislature* . . . (New York, 1775), p. 8; [Thomas B. Chandler], *What think ye of the Congress now?* . . . (New York, 1775), p. 40, tried to associate the New Englanders with the extremism of the seventeenth-century Presbyterians during the English Civil War. *Plain Truth* picked up on this theme after the November disturbance, pp. 64–65, 77–78.

133. 4*AA*, 4: 434.

134. Ibid., pp. 435–36; also Jon. Trumbull to Washington, Jan. 15, 1776, in ibid., p. 683.

135. Washington to Chas. Lee, Jan. 8, 1776, in *WGW*, 4: 221.

136. Ibid., pp. 221–22.

137. *JCC*, 3: 463, 4: 22, 47–48; see also 4*AA*, 4: 859.

138. See Declaration signed by sundry inhabitants of Queen's County, Jan. 19, 1776, in 4*AA*, 4: 858–61.

139. *CR*, 15: 225 n.; also Chas. Lee to Washington, Jan. 16, 1776, in 4*AA*, 4: 694; Jon. Trumbull to the President of Congress, Jan. 20, in ibid., p. 789.

140. New York Committee of Safety to Chas. Lee, Jan. 21, 1776, in 4*AA*, 4: 807–8.

141. Washington to Chas. Lee, Jan. 23, 1776, in *WGW*, 4: 266–67.

142. *JCC*, 4: 92; Proceedings of the New York Committee of Safety, Jan. 31, 1776, in 4*AA*, 4: 1095–96.

143. Washington to Jos. Reed, Mar. 25, 1776, in *WGW*, 4: 431; Washington to the commanding officer at New York, and to Jon. Trumbull, Mar. 14, 1776, in ibid., pp. 395, 399; See *ND*, 4: 506, 577–78.

144. Washington to Jon. Trumbull, Mar. 14, and to the commanding officer at New York, Mar. 14, 1776, in *WGW*, 4: 396, 399.

145 *CR*, 15: 249–51, 253.

146. Ibid., p. 252; Gold S. Silliman to Ebenezer Silliman, Apr. 1, 1776, in SFC, box 1. See also Jon. Trumbull to Washington, Mar. 18, in 4*AA*, 5: 406–7; *CR*, 15: 326–27.

147. Cf. Nich. Cooke to Washington, Mar. 31, 1776, and Washington to John Hancock, Apr. 15, 1776, in *ND*, 4: 593, 836.

148. Developments in Rhode Island are best traced in ibid., pp. 751, 767, 784, 808–09, 835, 902, 937–38, 1158–59.

149. *CR*, 15: 224, 227–28, 234.

150. Ibid., pp. 222–23, 227, 229–30, 233, 236, 237, 239.

151. Sam. Mott to Jon. Trumbull, Feb. 14, 1776, in 4*AA*, 4: 1146–47.

152. See Ira D. Gruber, *The Howe Brothers and the American Revolution* (New York, 1972), p. 201ff.

153. Cf. Gurd. Saltonstall to Washington, Apr. 8, 1776, and Jas. Wallace to Molyneux Shuldham, Apr. 10, in *ND*, 4: 710, 746.

154. Ezek Hopkins to Jon. Trumbull, Apr. 8, 1776, in ibid., p. 711; *CR*, 15: 262; Washington to John Hancock, Apr. 15, 1776, in *WGW*, 47: 481.

155. *JCC*, 4: 333, 406; see also Ezek Hopkins to Jon. Trumbull, May 21, 1776, and to John Hancock, May 22, in *ND*, 5: 185, 199; Hollingsworth and Richardson to the Pennsylvania Committee of Safety, May 21, in ibid., p. 186; Trumbull to Hancock, May 27, in *4AA*, 6: 600.

156. Jon. Trumbull to John Hancock, June 17, 1776, in *4AA*, 6: 944.

157. *JCC*, 5: 485–86; also Oliver Wolcott to Matt. Griswold, July 1, 1776, in *LMCC*, 1: 520; *ND*, 5: 925.

158. *CR*, 15: 256–57.

159. Capt. John Ely to Jon. Trumbull, Apr. 19, 1776, in *4AA*, 5: 992.

160. Washington to John A. Washington, Apr. 29, 1776, in *WGW*, 4: 530.

161. Washington to Jon. Trumbull, Apr. 26, 1776, in ibid., p. 523.

162. *CR*, 15: 295–96, 286.

163. *JCC*, 4: 347, 355, 357, 360.

164. Thos. Cushing to John Hancock, May 7, 1776, with enclosures, in *4AA*, 5: 1184–85; see also Washington to the Committee of the Massachusetts legislature, May 9, 1776, in *WGW*, 5: 27.

165. *JCC*, 4: 360.

166. *CR*, 15: 296–97.

167. See Evans 14784–89; also Eliph. Dyer to Jos. Trumbull, Jan. 15, 1776, in *LDC*, 3: 95. Parliamentary proceedings relating to America between October 1775 and March 1776 can be found in *4AA*, 6: 1–388.

168. Art, Lee to Benj. Franklin, Feb. 13, 1776, in *4AA*, 6: 1125–28; Washington to John Hancock, May 18, in *WGW*, 5: 56–72, 68 n.; for a text of the treaties, see *4AA*, 6: 271–77.

169. See *CC*, June 10, 1776.

170. "Armatus," in ibid., June 17, 1776; see Nath. Greene to Sam. Ward, Sr., Dec. 18, 1775, in *NGP*, 1: 165, for the prevailing assumption about Britain's capabilities up until May.

171. Letter from a correspondent in London, in *CC*, July 8, 1776.

172. *CR*, 15: 280–83, 297–301.

173. Oliver Wolcott to Matt. Griswold, Mar. 9, 1776, and to Sam. Lyman, Mar. 16, in *LMCC*, 1: 384, 397.

174. Continental troops got twelve shillings for their blankets but were supplied with firearms by the continent. The state bounty was twelve shillings for a blanket and ten shillings for a musket; *CR*, 15: 299; also 306.

175. Ibid., pp. 399–400.

176. See the clergy's development of this theme in Enoch Huntington, *A Sermon, delivered at Middletown, July 20th*, A.D. *1775* . . . (Hartford, 1775) and *The Happy effects of union* . . . (Hartford, 1776); Andrew Lee, *Sin destructive of temporal and eternal happiness* . . . (Norwich, 1776); also, Izrahiah Wetmore, *A Sermon* . . . (Norwich, 1775), p. 15ff.

177. *JCC*, 4: 410, 412–13.

178. See Oliver Wolcott to Roger Newberry, June 4, 1776, and to Laura Wolcott, June 11, in *LDC*, 4: 143, 195; Wolcott to Matt. Griswold, July 1, 1776, in *LMCC*, 1: 520; Jon. Trumbull to John Hancock, June 17, in *4AA*, 6: 945; Hancock to Trumbull, June 19, in *LDC*, 4: 268. The two northern bat-

talions were authorized at 1,633 and the seven New York ones at 5,712; see *CR*, 15: 416–18.

179. Jon. Trumbull to John Hancock, July 5, 1776, in *5AA*, 1: 28–29; *CR*, 15: 418–19, 422, 436.

180. *CR*, 15: 440, 414–16.

181. Seth Harding to Jon. Trumbull, May 15, 1776, in James L. Howard, *Seth Harding, Mariner: A Naval Picture of the Revolution* (New Haven, 1930), pp. 16–17, also 20.

182. Ibid., p. 23; Howard's paraphrase of their confession.

183. See Trumbull's tone in his letter to Seth Harding, May 18, 1776, in ibid., p. 24; also Justin Mills's deposition, Nov. 22, in JT, 5: 266a.

184. William to Gold S. Silliman, May 27, 1776, in SFC, box 1; *CR*, 15: 486–87.

185. Returns of July 13, July 20, 27, Aug. 3, 1776, in *5AA*, 1: 331–33, 507–8, 639–40, 763–64.

186. See ibid., pp. 1199–200.

187. And. Ward to Jon. Trumbull, Aug. 7, 8, 1776, in ibid., pp. 830, 858.

188. Jon. Trumbull to John Hancock, July 5, 1776, in ibid., p. 29.

189. Jon. Trumbull to Phil. Schuyler, July 9, 17, 1776, in ibid., pp. 145, 400; see also *CG*, July 5, 1776.

190. Jon. Trumbull to Phil. Schuyler, July 29, 1776, in *5AA*, 1: 660.

191. Washington to the President of Congress, July 11, 1776, in *WGW*, 5: 254.

192. Washington to the Massachusetts legislature or . . . Committee of Safety, June 28, 1776 in *WGW*, 5: 187–88.

193. *CR*, 15: 460–62; Washington to Thos. Seymour, July 8, 1776, in *WGW*, 5: 236–37; Seymour to Jon. Trumbull, July 22, in *5AA*, 1: 513–14.

194. Jon. Trumbull to Jas. Wadsworth, Aug. 6, 1776, in JT, 5: 131; Washington to John Hancock, July 10, in *WGW*, 5: 249.

195. See *CJ*, July 17, 1776; also Dutchess County Committee to Nathaniel Woodhull, July 12, in *5AA*, 1: 1408 n.

196. And. Ward to Jon. Trumbull, Aug. 7, 1776, in *5AA*, 1: 830.

197. Thos. Seymour to Jon. Trumbull, July 22, 1776, in ibid., p. 514.

198. *CR*, 15: 493. A copy of Trumbull's circular dated Aug. 1, 1776, is in JTP.

199. Thos. Mumford to Jon. Trumbull, Aug. 8, 1776, in *5AA*, 1: 858–59; also Wm. Pitkin to Trumbull, Aug. 5, in JT, 5: 133a.

200. Washington to Jon. Fitch, to Jon. Trumbull, and to Jesse Root, Aug. 7, 1776, in *WGW*, 5: 387–88, 389–90, 391. Washington exaggerated the size of Howe's force. It was closer to 20,000 men; see Freeman, *Washington*, 4: 148 n.

201. *CR*, 15: 497–98. The only western regiments excluded from these orders were the Seventh and Fourteenth.

202. Ibid., p. 499. The state was disappointed in its efforts to recruit new levies out of the militia; see Jer. Wadsworth to Jon. Trumbull, Oct. 11, 1776, in JT, 5: 205a.

203. See John MacKay to Washington, Aug. 20, 1776, in *5AA*, 1: 1086.

204. Thos. Seymour to Jon. Trumbull, Aug. 19, 1776, in ibid., p. 1074.

205. See Chas. Chandler to Jon. Trumbull, Aug. 8, 1776; Jon. Fitch to Trumbull, Aug. 13; and Arch. Lewis to Trumbull, Aug. 15, in JT, 5: 138*a*, 144*a*, 148*a–b*; also Jos. Cooke to Jon. Trumbull, Aug. 9, 23, in ibid., pp. 139*a*, 156*a*.

206. Jer. Wadsworth to Jos. Trumbull, Sept. 4, 1776, in JW, box 123.

207. *RCM*, pp. 454–59, 466–74; Washington to Lund Washington, Aug. 19, 1776, in *WGW*, 5: 457–58.

208. Washington to John Hancock, Aug. 26, 1776, in ibid., p. 491. The Council of Safety advanced marching money to most of the regiments on the assumption they would contain 400 men each; see *CR*, 15: 498.

209. Washington to the President of Congress, Sept. 8, 1776, in *WGW*, 6: 32.

210. See General Orders, Aug. 24, 1776, in ibid., 5: 482.

211. Washington to Jon. Trumbull, Aug. 24, 1776, in ibid., p. 486.

212. *CR*, 15: 510 n.

213. New York Convention to Jon. Trumbull and to the committees of Horseneck, Stamford, Norwalk, Fairfield, Stratford, Milford, New Haven, Guilford, Saybrook, Lyme, Groton, New London, and Stonington, Aug. 28, 1776, in 5*AA*, 1: 1196–97.

214. *CR*, 15: 511, 512.

215. See Samuel Buel to Jon. Trumbull, Aug. 30, 31 and Sept. 7, 1776; the petitions of Southold and the Hamptons, Aug. 31; and Henry Livingston to Trumbull, Aug. 30 and Sept. 1, 5, in JT, 5: 162*a–c*, 163*a–b*, 164, 165, 166*a*, 167*a–b*, 171*a–b*, 174*a*.

216. See *CR*, 15: 514.

217. Ibid., pp. 514, 515.

218. See General Orders, Sept. 4, 1776; Jos. Trumbull to Jon. Trumbull, Sept. 1, and Jon. Trumbull to Sam. Abbott, Sept. 6, in JTP; Washington to John Hancock, Sept. 8, and to Jon. Trumbull, Sept. 9, in *WGW*, 6: 16, 32, 39; also Benj. Trumbull to his wife, Sept. 10, in BT. The anxiety about being enveloped by the British was shared by the whole army; see Nath. Greene to Washington, Sept. 5, 1776, in *NGP*, 1: 295; Gold S. Silliman to his wife, Sept. 20, in SFC, box 1.

219. New York Convention to Washington, July 16, 1776, in 5*AA*, 1: 1409.

220. Washington to Jon. Trumbull and to the New York Convention, July 19, 1776, in *WGW*, 5: 308, 309.

221. *CR*, 15: 516.

222. Ibid., 14: 499.

223. See JT, 24: 34, 37, 39, 44, 65, 67, 94, 123–24, 137, 154, 167.

224. A smaller sample of returns suggests that the state had sufficient arms to equip only 60 percent of her able-bodied men; ibid., pp. 34, 39, 119, 155, 160. The census of 1774, alas, gives figures for the male cohorts of 10–20 and 20–70. The census of 1782 gives figures for the male cohorts 0–16, 16–50, and over 50. One can extrapolate an estimate for the 16–50 cohort of the 1774 population by computing the percentage of total population comprised by the first and last cohorts in 1782 and applying it to the 1774 total. For the census of 1782, see JT, 24: 178, and Evans 44184; for the census of 1774, *CR*, 14: 491.

225. Jer. Wadsworth to Jos. Trumbull, Sept. 21, 1776, and Peter Colt to Wadsworth, Oct. 3, in JW, boxes 123, 124; also Wm. Williams to Jon. Trumbull, Sept. 20, in JT, 5: 194*a–c;* and Benj. Trumbull to his wife, Sept. 10, in BT.

CHAPTER THREE: EXERTION

1. *JCC*, 5: 762. The military advantages of a standing army were summarized by "Agricola Americanus," in *CG*, Jan. 10, 1777.

2. Jer. Wadsworth to Jos. Trumbull, Dec. 17, 1775, in JW, box 123; also, Sam. Squire to Jos. Trumbull, Oct. 23, in JosT.

3. Jer. Wadsworth to Jos. Trumbull, Sept. 4, 1776, in JW, box 123; also Peter Colt to Wadsworth, Sept. 28 and Oct. 3, 30, in ibid., boxes 123, 124; "Publicola," in *CJ*, Mar. 5, 1777.

4. Quote from Jer. Wadsworth to Jos. Trumbull, Sept. 4, 1776, in JW, box 123; also Isaac Miles to Wadsworth, Oct. 9, in ibid., box 124.

5. Peter Colt to Jer. Wadsworth, Oct. 3, 1776; Gurdon Starr to Wadsworth, Oct. 11; Humphrey Lyons to Wadsworth, Oct. 14; And. Huntington to Wadsworth, Oct. 21; and Wm. Hart, Jr., to Wadsworth, Nov. 10, all in ibid., box 124.

6. Hen. Champion to Jer. Wadsworth, Oct. 8, 1776; And. Huntington to Wadsworth, Oct. 26; and Chris. Leffingwell to Wadsworth, Oct. 27, all in ibid.

7. Cf. *ND*, 1: 406–9 and n.

8. *JCC*, 4: 290, 5: 831; also, Jos. Trumbull to John Hancock, Oct. 7, 9, 1776, in 5*AA*, 2: 920, 963.

9. *CR*, 15: 529; also John Lloyd to Jer. Wadsworth, Oct. 28, 1776, in JW, box 124.

10. *CJ*, Oct. 23, 1776. The loss led to the movement of salt supplies along the coast inland; see Dan. Gray to Jer. Wadsworth, Oct. 23, 1776, in JW, box 124.

11. Peter Colt to Jer. Wadsworth, Sept. 24, 28, 1776, in JW, box 123.

12. Jer. Wadsworth to Jos. Trumbull, Sept. 9, 1775, in ibid.; see also Peter Bulkley's attempt in November 1775 to challenge the manner in which the commissariat was being run, in CARW, 1st ser., 4: 193–216.

13. Jer. Wadsworth to Barnabas Deane, Oct. 9, 1776, in JW, box 124; *ND*, 6: 1178–83. The action in which the row galleys were captured did not reflect credit on Connecticut; Jos. Reed to Jon. Trumbull, Oct. 18, in *ND*, 6: 1317–18.

14. Barn. Deane to Jer. Wadsworth, Oct. 3, 1776, and Jos. Trumbull to Wadsworth, Oct. 22, in JW, box 124.

15. Cf. "A.Z.," in *CC*, Dec. 23, 1776.

16. E. James Ferguson, *The Power of the Purse* (Chapel Hill, N.C., 1961), pp. 26–27, 31, attaches greater importance to the quantity of money issued than to the other factors influencing its credit.

17. *SR*, 1: 5–6, 9.

18. Ibid., pp. 62–65, 72.

19. Ibid., pp. 585, 590, 592–95.

20. Ibid., pp. 100, 105, 111, 139.

21. *JCC*, 7: 124.

22. *SR*, 1: 230–31.

23. Hen. Livingston to Jon. Trumbull, Sept. 8, 11, 14, 1776; Chris. Leffingwell to Trumbull, Sept. 14, 30; Trumbull to Livingston, Sept. 9, in JT, 5: 181, 190, 197, 189, 196, 178; Trumbull to Livingston, Sept. 15, in 5*AA*, 2: 344.

24. David Gelston to the Committee for New London, Sept. 6, 1776, and Hen. Livingston to Washington, Sept. 11, in 5*AA*, 2: 207, 296.

25. The Long Islanders did not want a patriot force on the island; see the Easthampton petition to Jon. Trumbull, Sept. 7, 1776, and anonymous (probably Sam. Buel) to Trumbull, Sept. 22, in JT, 5: 174, 195.

26. Hen. Livingston to Jon. Trumbull, Sept. 15, 1776, and Washington to Trumbull, Sept. 20, 30, in 5*AA*, 2: 344–45, quote 416, 609–10; also Examination of prisoners, Sept. 29, in ibid., pp. 597–99.

27. Jon. Trumbull to Washington, Oct. 13, 1776, with enclosure of J. Cable to Hezekiah Jarvis, Sept. 27, and Trumbull to Hen. Livingston, Oct. 13, in 5*AA*, 2: 128–30.

28. Washington to Jon. Trumbull, Oct. 15, 1776, in *WGW*, 6: 209–10; Wm. Heath to Gurd. Saltonstall, Oct. 1; Saltonstall to Heath, Oct. 1; and Heath to Maj. Eben Backus, Oct. 2, in 5*AA*, 2: 828, 845.

29. Robt. H. Harrison to John Hancock, Oct. 17, 1776, in *WGW*, 6: 215 n.

30. Robt. H. Harrison to John Hancock, Oct. 14, 1776, in ibid., pp. 204–5 n.

31. Cf. Geo. Clinton to John M'Kesson, Oct. 31, 1776, in 5*AA*, 2: 1312.

32. Washington to John Hancock, Oct. 12, 1776, and to Jon. Trumbull, Oct. 15, in *WGW*, 11: 196–97, 209–10; *SR*, 1: 20.

33. Robt. H. Harrison to Jon. Trumbull, Oct. 22, 1776, in 5*AA*, 2: 1187–88, also 1172.

34. Washington to Wm. McIntosh and to Zabdiel Rogers, Oct. 31, 1776, in *WGW*, 6: 219–20, 221. Returns of Rogers's and Cogswell's militia for Nov. 1 are in 5*AA*, 2: 475.

35. *SR*, 1: 16–17, 25; Trumbull's Proclamations of Oct. 21, 24, 1776, in 5*AA*, 2: 1171, 1225–26.

36. In 5*AA*, 2: 1315.

37. David Wooster to Jon. Trumbull, Nov. 18, 1776, in ibid., p. 755.

38. *SHP*, p. 74.

39. *SR*, 1: 8, 27–28; for the New Haven petition of Sept. 16, 1776, see 5*AA*, 2: 374–75.

40. Washington to John Hancock, Nov. 6, 1776, in *WGW*, 6: 249.

41. Cf. Return of Nath. Greene's troops, Sept. 29, 1776, in 5*AA*, 2: 607. Washington to Wm. Heath, Sept. 17, in *WGW*, 6: 59; extract from the Journal of the chaplain to Durkee's regiment in 5*AA*, 2: 461.

42. Return of Wm. Heath's division, Nov. 9, 1776, in 5*AA*, 3: 621–22; Heath to Jed. Huntington, Nov. 13, in ibid., p. 664; *WHM*, pp. 75–76.

43. Return of Chas. Lee's division, Nov. 16, 1776, in 5*AA*, 3: 709–10; Washington to Lee, Nov. 10, in *WGW*, 6: 265.

44. *WGW*, 6: 266.

45. *RCM*, pp. 414–23.

46. *WHM*, p. 90.

47. See Returns of the Army, Dec. 22, 1776, in *5AA*, 3: 1401–2.

48. *CJ*, Nov. 6, 1776; see also *5AA*, 3: 551; *CC*, Nov. 18, 1776.

49. Jon. Trumbull to Washington, Oct. 11, 1776, in *5AA*, 2: 1001–2; also, Trumbull to Ezek Hopkins, Sept. 12, in ibid., pp. 304–5.

50. *SR*, 1: 16, 25–27.

51. *CJ*, Nov. 20 and Dec. 4, 1776; *CG*, Nov. 22.

52. *SR*, 1: 39.

53. See Reports dated Nov. 2, 1776, in *5AA*, 3: 484; Washington to John Hancock, Nov. 6, in *WGW*, 6: 249.

54. See Nich. Cooke to Massachusetts Assembly, Dec. 2, 1776, and Jos. Trumbull to Jon. Trumbull, Dec. 4, in *5AA*, 3: 1032, 1072–74. Governor Trumbull received garbled intelligence, judging from his letter to Cooke, Dec. 5, in ibid., pp. 1086–87, but it was clarified that evening; see Trumbull to Jas. Bowdoin, ibid., pp. 1087.

55. Piers Mackesy, *The War for America, 1775–1783* (Cambridge, Mass., 1965), pp. 53, 110; Ira D. Gruber, *The Howe Brothers and the American Revolution* (New York, 1972), pp. 135–36; Wm. Howe to Geo. Germain, Nov. 30, 1776, in *5AA*, 3: 926.

56. Jon. Trumbull to Jas. Bowdoin, Dec. 5, 1776, and to Washington, Dec. 7, 8, in *5AA*, 3: 1087, 1111–12; *SR*, 1: 83, 84.

57. *CC*, May 6, 1776. Burgoyne seriously considered the plan in 1777; see Mackesy, *War*, pp. 114.

58. Committee for Superintending Prisoners to Jon. Trumbull, Oct. 27, 1776, in JT, 5: 210; Trumbull to Joh. Trumbull, Jr., Oct. 30, in JT jr, 2: 11.

59. See JT, 5: 346*a*–*c*.

60. *5AA*, 3: 864, 1139. "Inimicals" like Ralph Isaacs took advantage of winter shortages in ways that were difficult to control; see *SR*, 1: 85–86, 160–61, 166; JT, 6: 19, 25, 27, 28, 29.

61. Jon. Trumbull, Jr., to Jon. Trumbull, Dec. 5, 1776, in *5AA*, 3: 1086; Matthews's letter is in JT, 5: 347*a*–*c*; *SR*, 1: 84, 87, 152, 154, 158.

62. "Philo Patriae," "A Soldier," and "A.Z.," in *CC*, Nov. 18 and Dec. 16, 23, 1776; "A Militia Man," in ibid., Oct. 14, 1776; "Perseverance," in ibid., Dec. 23, 1776.

63. David Trumbull to Jos. Trumbull, Jr., Nov. 26, 1776, in JTjr, 2: 35.

64. Jon. Trumbull to Jas. Bowdoin, Dec. 9, 1776, in *5AA*, 3: 1143. Howe's proclamation is in ibid., pp. 927–28. Offers of clemency caused the leadership as much anxiety as British victories; see "A Watchman," in *CC*, Nov. 4, 1776, and "Philo Patriae," in *CG*, Dec. 27; see also Jos. Fish to Gold S. Silliman, Jan. 11, 1777, in SFC, box 2; and a verse parody of Howe's proclamation, *The second edition of Lord Howes & General Howes proclamation with notes and emendations . . .* (Norwich, 1777). For Carleton's clemency, see Larry G. Bowman, *Captive Americans: Prisoners during the American Revolution* (Athens, Ohio, 1977), p. 98.

65. "A Militia Man," in *CC*, Oct. 14, 1776; Jer. Wadsworth to Jon. Trumbull, Jr., July 29, in JTjr, 1: 117; Jos. Trumbull to Jon. Trumbull, Dec. 4, in *5AA*, 3: 1073–74.

66. *SR*, 1: 91–97, quotes 92, 95.

67. Ibid., pp. 4–5, 94.

68. "Freeman" and "A Plain Dealer," in *CJ*, Mar. 19, 1777; "Julius," in ibid., Mar. 26; also, "A Freeman," in ibid., Apr. 4, and in *CG*, Apr. 4; unsigned in *CJ*, Apr. 8.

69. See John W. Shy, "Charles Lee: The Soldier as Radical," in George A. Billias, ed., *George Washington's Generals* (New York, 1964), pp. 36–40; *WHM*, pp. 79–88.

70. New York Committee of Safety to Jon. Trumbull, Dec. 8, 1776, in *5AA*, 3: 1125–26.

71. *SR*, 1: 589, 65–66.

72. Ibid., pp. 108–10. The Providence convention had agreed that the three-month regiments should replace the new levies, as Washington had recommended; ibid., p. 589; Washington to Jon. Trumbull, Dec. 12, 1776, in *WGW*, 6: 353.

73. Jos. Trumbull to Jon. Trumbull, Dec. 16, 1776, in *JT*, 5: 282*a–b*. We can infer the volunteers achieved only regimental strength from the manner in which the legislature designated field officers, though Trumbull insisted they comprised sixteen companies at battalion strength; see *SR*, 1: 115; Jon. Trumbull to Washington, Jan. 23, 1777, in *5MHSC*, 10: 28.

74. *SR*, 1: 591.

75. Jon. Trumbull to Washington, Dec. 6, 1776, in *5AA*, 3: 1103; Washington to Trumbull and to Jos. Spencer, Dec. 14, in *WGW*, 6: 366, 373–74.

76. *SR*, 1: 591.

77. Ibid., pp. 126–27 and n.

78. Ibid., pp. 120, 123, 162–63.

79. Ibid., p. 127 n. The three-month men were ordered to march once companies had reached a strength of twenty; ibid., p. 124.

80. *WHM*, pp. 94–95.

81. See Washington to John Hancock, Sept. 25 and Dec. 5, 1776, in *WGM*, 6: 117–18, 332–33; also, Washington to Lund Washington, Sept. 30; to Pat. Henry and to Sam. Washington, Oct. 5; to Phil. Schuyler, Oct. 22, in ibid., pp. 137, 160, 169, 223–24.

82. *SR*, 1: 207–8; also, Jos. Trumbull to Phil. Schuyler, Feb. 11, 1777, in *7MHSC*, 2: 20.

83. *JCC*, 5: 753, 854–55.

84. Eliph. Dyer to Jos. Trumbull, Nov. 26, 1776, in *JosT*.

85. Washington to John Hancock, Nov. 6, 1776, and to Jos. Trumbull, Nov. 10, and General Orders, Nov. 10, in *WGW*, 6: 250, 270, 262–63.

86. See Washington's concern about deserters in General Orders, Oct. 1, 3, 24, 31, 1776, and Washington to the President of Congress, Oct. 4, in ibid., pp. 145–46, 181, 227, 234, 154.

87. See Washington to Chas. Lee, Nov. 21, 1776, and to Wm. Livingston and John Hancock, Nov. 30, in ibid., pp. 298, 313, 316.

88. *JCC*, 5: 855; Jos. Trumbull to Jon. Trumbull, Dec. 21, 1776, in *5AA*, 3: 1352.

89. Cf. *JCC*, 6: 1019; *CJ*, Jan. 1, 8, 1777; Jon. Trumbull to Washington, Feb. 7, in *5MHSC*, 10: 35–36.

90. Harry E. Brown, *Medical Department of the Army, from 1773 to 1873* (Washington, D.C., 1875), pp. 29–31.

91. *JCC*, 5: 762–63.

92. *SR*, 1: 12.

93. Washington to Jon. Trumbull, Nov. 10, 1776, in *WGW*, 6: 271; *SR*, 1: 66.

94. *JCC*, 6: 971; *SR*, 1: 66.

95. *SR*, 1: 596.

96. Jos. Trumbull to Washington, Feb. 11, 1777, in WP; Washington to Jon. Trumbull, Mar. 3, 1777, in *WGW*, 7: 229; *SR*, 1: 592–96; cf. "A.Z.," in *CC*, Jan. 13, 1777.

97. *SR*, 1: 139; Lawrence H. Gipson, "Connecticut Taxation and Parliamentary Aid Preceding the Revolutionary War," *AHR* 36 (1930–31): 724–27, especially 724 n., 731–32; for criticism of the legislature's timidity, cf. n. 68, above.

98. *JCC*, 5: 845–46.

99. *SR*, 1: 10, 107, 111.

100. Ibid., p. 133; Washington to Jon. Trumbull, Dec. 16, 1776, in *WGW*, 6: 384.

101. *SR*, 1: 105; see also Jon. Trumbull to Washington, Jan. 23, 1777, in 5*MHSC*, 10: 27–28; Washington to Trumbull, Feb. 9, 11, in *WGW*, 7: 122, 135. The expedient was condemned in Congress; Rog. Sherman to Trumbull, Mar. 4, in 7*MHSC*, 2: 26.

102. Washington to Robt. H. Harrison, Jan. 10, 1777, and to Hor. Gates, Jan. 28, in *WGW*, 7: 38, 72, 73. Inoculation also meant that militia could not be used to support continentals in case of attack because of the danger of infection; see Jos. Spencer to Jon. Trumbull, Mar. 5, in JTP.

103. Washington to the President of Congress, Feb. 5, 14, 1777, in ibid., pp. 105, 149.

104. *SR*, 1: 198.

105. Ibid., pp. 165, 180, 183, 198; Mary Silliman to her parents, Apr. 11, 1777, in SFC, box 2.

106. *SR*, 1: 119–20. For enemy pressure along the coast, see Norwalk Committee to the Council of Safety, Feb. 20, 1777; Thaddeus Burr to Jon. Trumbull, Mar. 21, in JT, 6: 47, 64; John Davenport to Jer. Wadsworth, Mar. 22, in JW, box 124; Mary Silliman to her parents, Apr. 11, and Gold S. Silliman to Jos. Fish, Apr. 13, in SFC, box 2.

107. *SR*, 1: 174–75, 187.

108. Ibid., pp. 189–90, 191, 196; see also Jos. Spencer to Jon. Trumbull, Mar. 15, 1777, in JTP.

109. See *SHP*, p. 90.

110. Washington to Jon. Trumbull, Mar. 23, 1777, in *WGW*, 7: 316. Some February enlistees must have been omitted from the returns; see Table 2.

111. *SR*, 1: 181; Washington to Jon. Trumbull and to the Massachusetts legislature, Feb. 1, 1777, in *WGW*, 7: 85–87.

112. See Washington to Jon. Trumbull, Oct. 29, 1775, and to Jos. Reed, Nov. 20, in *WGW*, 4: 51, 105; Trumbull to Washington, Nov. 6, in JTP.

113. He was accused of creating unnecessary brevet officers to cover discrepancies between the weekly returns and the provision returns; see Jos. Trumbull to Jon. Trumbull, Dec. 4, 1776, in 5*AA*, 3: 1073–74. He also

imbued his men with quixotic expectations; see Wooster to Trumbull, Jan. 9, 1777, in JTP.

114. Gold S. Silliman to Mary Silliman, Oct. 31 and Nov. 16, 1776, in SFC, boxes 1, 2.

115. Cf. n. 68, above.

116. *SR*, 1: 193–94.

117. Ibid., pp. 196–97; Alex. McDougall to Washington, Mar. 29, 1777, in *WGW*, 7: 328–29 n.; *WR*, 1: 323.

118. See, for example, Canaan, Ex, Mar. 26, 1777; Colchester and Bolton, Ex, Mar. 31; Goshen and Waterbury, Ex, Apr. 1.

119. Washington to Jon. Trumbull, Mar. 23, 1777, in *WGW*, 7: 316; see also Sam. H. Parsons to Trumbull, Apr. 9, in JT, 6: 74.

120. *SR*, 1: 167.

121. See Washington to Jon. Trumbull, Apr. 21, 1777, and to the President of Congress, Apr. 28, in *WGW*, 7: 450, 491.

122. *SR*, 1: 207–9.

123. Ibid., p. 209.

124. Ibid., p. 207; excerpt from Sam. H. Parsons to Washington, Apr. 23, 1777, in *SHP*, p. 93; Washington to Parsons, Apr. 23, in *WGW*, 7: 459–60.

125. Cf. Thos. Mifflin to Jer. Wadsworth, Feb. 6, 1777, in JW, box 124.

126. Washington to Sam. H. Parson, Apr. 23, 1777, in *WGW*, 7: 460; cf. also Gold S. Silliman's General Orders, Apr. 25, and Jed. Huntington to Alex. McDougall, Apr. 27, as quoted in Robert McDevitt, *Connecticut Attacked . . .* (Chester, Conn., 1974), pp. 35, 36.

127. *CC*, Mar. 24, 1777; Nathan Strong, *The Reasons and designs of public punishments . . .* (Hartford, 1777); also *The last speech and dying words of Moses Dunbar . . .* (n.p., 1777).

128. Washington to Jon. Trumbull, Apr. 12, 1777, in *WGW*, 7: 402–3. The Connecticut delegation in Congress challenged these reports; see Rog. Sherman to Trumbull, May 14, in *7MHSC*, 2: 47–48.

129. Gold S. Silliman to Jos. Fish, Mar. 1, 1777, and Mary Silliman to her parents, Apr. 11, in SFC, box 2.

130. James R. Case, *An Account of Tryon's Raid on Danbury . . .* (Danbury, Conn., 1927), pp. 15–20; McDevitt, *Connecticut Attacked*, pp. 32–34.

131. Washington to Geo. Clinton, Apr. 26, 1777, and to Alex. McDougall, Apr. 26, 28, in *WGW*, 7: 474, 477, 487. James M. Bailey, *History of Danbury, Conn., 1684–1896* (New York, 1896), pp. 62–63.

132. McDevitt, *Connecticut Attacked*, pp. 32, 40, 48–57; cf. also *WGW*, 7: 487 n.

133. McDevitt, *Connecticut Attacked*, p. 50, though the author argues the British were unaware of their danger, p. 51.

134. Ibid., pp. 59–62; Gold S. Silliman to Adam Babcock, Apr. 29, 1777, in JT, 6: 87.

135. There is considerable dispute as to how many men the British did lose. Under the circumstances, we are probably closest to the truth in relying on the highest British estimate of twenty-four killed, ninety-two wounded, and twenty-eight missing in "Journals of Lieut.-Col. Stephen Kemble," in New York Historical Society, *Collections* 16 (1884): 115; for the stores de-

stroyed, see McDevitt, *Connecticut Attacked*, pp. 46–47; for the impact of the raids on the location of magazines, *JCC*, 7: 315–16; Washington to Alex. McDougall and Geo. Clinton, May 2, 1777, in *WGW*, 8: 4–5; Jos. Trumbull to Jer. Wadsworth, May 7, in JW, box 124.

136. See Returns of the Fourth Brigade in JT, 24: 119, 155, 162. Regiments from the Second Brigade had been ordered by Wooster to cover the coast; see Jas. Wadsworth to Jon. Trumbull, May 1, 1777, in JT, 6: 94.

137. *CC*, May 12, 1777.

138. Cf. Washington to John Hancock, Dec. 5, 1776, in *WGW*, 6: 332.

139. See Washington to the President of Congress, Apr. 28, 1777, in *WGW*, 7: 490. For Silliman's orders, see McDevitt, *Connecticut Attacked*, p. 35; also, Charles B. Todd, *History of Redding, Conn* . . . (New York, 1880), p. 51; Silvio A. Bedini, *Ridgefield in Review* . . . (Ridgefield, Conn., 1958), p. 62.

140. In *5MHSC*, 10: 60.

141. Eliph. Dyer and Nath. Wales, Jr., to Jon. Trumbull, Apr. 30, 1777; Ebenezer Huntington to Trumbull, May 1; and Benj. Henshaw to Trumbull, May 5, in JT, 6: 92*a*, 95, 101*a–c*; the Authority and Selectmen of Stamford to Trumbull, May 2, in JTP.

142. Jon. Trumbull to Washington, May 4, 1777, in *5MHSC*, 10: 60.

143. *SR*, 1: 216, 218.

144. Jon. Trumbull to Washington, May 4, 1777, in *7MHSC*, 2: 60; also, Sam. H. Parsons to Washington, May 11, 1777, in *SHP*, p. 94.

145. Washington to Jon. Trumbull, May 11, 1777, in *WGW*, 8: 42–44.

146. Washington to Jon. Trumbull, May 23, 1777, in ibid., p. 104.

147. Ibid., p. 105.

148. Mary Silliman to her parents, May 11, 1777, in SFC, box 2; *CG*, May 16, 23, 1777; Jon. Trumbull to Washington, May 19, 22, 1777, in *5MHSC*, 10: 63, 64.

149. *SR*, 1: 240.

150. Ibid., pp. 241–42.

151. See Petition of South Farms militia, Apr. 25, 1777, in JT, 7: 85*a–b*; Petition of fifty-four draughted men from Salisbury, May 1, 1778, in CARW, 1st ser., 10: 254.

152. See Return in JT, 24: 36. Some towns waited until after the Council of Safety's orders to class the militia before offering bounties to recruits; see Haddam Town Records, 2: 112; also Middletown Town Votes, 2: 353; Hartford Town Votes, 2: 260. See also Stratford Memorial, July 21, 1777, in JT, 6: 188, and Voluntown Memorial, Jan. 20, 1779, in ibid., 8: 50*a–c*.

153. Washington to Sam. B. Webb, July 15, 1777, in *WGW*, 7: 411–12.

154. Washington to Wm. Heath, May 19, 1777, and to Jas. Warren, May 23, in *WGW*, 8: 86, 102.

155. *SR*, 1: 242–44, 254–55; also, Jon. Trumbull to Washington, May 18, 1777, in *5MHSC*, 10: 62.

156. The five-pound bounty for a fully equipped soldier was well below the combined congressional, state, and town bounties offered a Continental recruit.

157. Sam. H. Parsons to Washington, May 25, 1777, in *SHP*, pp. 97–98; also *CG*, May 20.

158. *JCC*, 8: 580.

159. Washington to Phil. Schuyler, June 16, 1777, in *WGW*, 8: 253.

160. Washington to Isr. Putnam, June 12, 1777, in ibid., p. 235.

161. Isr. Putnam to Jon. Trumbull, June 13, 1777, in JT, 6: 143*a*.

162. *CJ*, June 11, 18, 1777; Gold S. Silliman to Jos. Fish, July 1, in SFC, box 2.

163. *SR*, 1: 320–21, 340, 335, 344, 352–53.

164. Oliver Wolcott to Jon. Trumbull, July 14, 1777, in 7*MHSC*, 2: 79.

165. Jon. Trumbull to Washington, July 25, 1777, in 5*MHSC*, 10: 85–87; *SR*, 1: 124.

166. Washington to the President of Congress, July 2, 1777, in *WGW*, 8: 330; *SR*, 1: 344.

167. Washington to Isr. Putnam, July 24, 31, 1777, in *WGW*, 8: 460, 503.

168. Washington to Isr. Putnam, Aug. 1, 1777, in ibid., 9: 1–2. Washington also called on George Clinton, governor of New York, "to lend speedy" aid; see Washington to Clinton, Aug. 1, in ibid., p. 5.

169. Jesse Root to Jon. Trumbull, July 28, 1777, in JT, 6: 202*a–d*; Trumbull to Phil. Schuyler, Aug. 11, in 7*MHSC*, 2: 95.

170. Phil. Schuyler to Jon. Trumbull, July 21, 1777, in 7*MHSC*, 2: 85; Trumbull to Washington, July 25, 28, in 5*MHSC*, 10: 88–90.

171. Jon. Trumbull, Jr., to Jon. Trumbull, July 22, 24, 1777, in 7*MHSC*, 2: 87–89.

172. *SR*, 1: 360, 361, 362.

173. Isr. Putnam to Jon. Trumbull, Aug. 3, 1777, in JT, 7: 5.

174. *SR*, 1: 362–63; Gold S. Silliman to his parents-in-law, Aug. 15, 1777, in SFC, box 2; Oliver Wolcott to Jon. Trumbull, Aug. 5, 1777, in JT, 7: 9.

175. Jon. Trumbull to Washington, Aug. 7, 1777, in 5*MHSC*, 10: 93; Trumbull to Phil. Schuyler, Aug. 9, in 7*MHSC*, 2: 108.

176. Oliver Wolcott to Jon. Trumbull, Sept. 25, 1777, in JT, 7: 64*a*; Israel Knapp, Jr., to Jer. Wadsworth, Aug. 7, 1777, in JW, box 125.

177. Isr. Putnam to Washington, Aug. 15, 1777, in WP; also Jer. Wadsworth to Jos. Trumbull, Aug. 10, in JW, box 125.

178. Washington to Isr. Putnam, Aug. 18, 1777, in *WGW*, 9: 91.

179. General Orders, Aug. 14–20, 1777, in *SBW*, 1: 271–75.

180. Isr. Putnam to Sam. H. Parsons, Aug. 16, 1777, in *SHP*, pp. 108, 109–10; see also General Orders, Aug. 25, 1777, in *SBW*, 1: 278.

181. Isr. Putnam to Jon. Trumbull, Sept. 15, 1777, in 7*MHSC*, 2: 145; Sam. H. Parsons to Putnam, Sept. 20, in *SHP*, pp. 113–14.

182. *JCC*, 8: 720.

183. Isr. Putnam to Jon. Trumbull, Sept. 15, 1777, in 7*MHSC*, 2: 145–46.

184. *AR*, p. 72.

185. Isr. Putnam to Jon. Trumbull, Sept. 27, 1777, in JT, 7: 66*a–b*.

186. Sam. H. Parsons to Gold S. Silliman, Sept. 27, 1777, in ibid., p. 67*a*; also, Jed. Huntington to Jon. Trumbull, Sept. 27, in ibid., pp. 69*a–b*.

187. *SR*, 1: 405–6; Jon. Trumbull to Isr. Putnam, Sept. 30, 1777, in JT, 7: 74*a*.

188. See Nich. Cooke to Jon. Trumbull, Sept. 11, 1777, in JT, 7: 44.

189. See Jos. Spencer to Jon. Trumbull, Aug. 5, 1777, and Nich. Cooke to Trumbull, Aug. 7, in ibid., pp. 8, 14.

190. *SR*, 1: 399–400, 403; also Governor Trumbull's draft of a Proclamation, Sept. 23, 1777, calling for volunteers in JT, 7: 61.

191. *SR*, 1: 401, 404, 405, 406; also, Jos. Spencer to Jon. Trumbull, Sept. 20, 1777, in JT, 7: 56.

192. See Jon. Trumbull to Jos. Spencer, Sept. 29, 1777, in JT, 7: 70.

193. Hor. Gates to Jon. Trumbull, Aug. 6, 1777, in 7*MHSC*, 2: 105; Trumbull to David Trumbull, Aug. 14, in JTP. They did so at some cost, as can be seen from Trumbull to Gates, Aug. 21, in 7*MHSC*, 2: 124–25.

194. Jon. Trumbull, Jr., to Jon. Trumbull, Aug. 6, 8, 11, 1777, in ibid., pp. 103–5, 107–8, 109–12.

195. *SR*, 1: 371–72, 373.

196. Ibid., p. 375.

197. Estimates derived from data in *RCM*, pp. 504–9.

198. See Thos. Seymour to Jon. Trumbull, Sept. 20, 1777, in JT, 7: 57*a–b*; also *WR*, 2: 521–31, for an account of the battle.

199. Chas. Burrall to Jon. Trumbull, Aug. 18, 21, 1777, in 7*MHSC*, 2: 121–24.

200. Oliver Wolcott to Jon. Trumbull, Sept. 25, 1777, with enclosure, in JT, 7: 64*a–c*, 65*a–b*.

201. Oliver Wolcott to Jon. Trumbull, Oct. 10, 1777, in 7*MHSC*, 2: 159–62.

202. *SR*, 1: 407.

203. Jon. Trumbull to Gold S. Silliman, Oct. 7, 1777, in JT, 7: 79*a*; Jas. Wadsworth to Jon. Trumbull, Oct. 5, 1777, in ibid., p. 85. See also Putnam's circular to Col. Thaddeus Cook and other colonels of the western regiments, Oct. 4, 1777, in ibid., p. 81; cf. also Roger Enos to Jon. Trumbull, Oct. 25, in ibid., p. 143.

204. Gold S. Silliman to Mary Silliman, Oct. 9, 1777, in SFC, box 2; also, Isr. Putnam to Jon. Trumbull, Oct. 8, in JT, 7: 94; Sam. H. Parsons to Trumbull, Oct. 7, in 7*MHSC*, 2: 154.

205. Chas. Burrall to Jon. Trumbull, Oct. 7, 1777, in JT, 7: 88*a–b*; also, Sam. Whiting to Trumbull, Oct. 7, in ibid., p. 87*a*, and John Mead to Trumbull, Oct. 24, in ibid., p. 150.

206. Gold S. Silliman to Mary Silliman, Oct. 10, 12, 14, 16, 1777, in SFC, box 2.

207. Gold S. Silliman to Mary Silliman, postscript, Oct. 17 to Oct. 16, 1777, in ibid.

208. Isr. Putnam to Jon. Trumbull, Oct. 15, 1777, in 7*MHSC*, 2: 166; Chas. Burrall to Jon. Trumbull, Oct. 16, 1777, and Royal Flint to Jon. Trumbull, Oct. 20, in JT, 7: 126, 128; Isr. Putnam to Washington, Oct. 16, in *SHP*, p. 122; Gold S. Silliman to Mary Silliman, Oct. 12, in SFC, box 2.

209. *JCC*, 11: 804.

210. Isr. Putnam to Washington, Oct. 16, 1777, in PCC, item 159, 1: 107.

211. Washington to Isr. Putnam, Oct. 25, 1777, and Putnam to Washington, Oct. 25, in *SBW*, 1: 369–70, 372; Washington to Alex. Hamilton and to Isr. Putnam, Oct. 30, 1777, in ibid., pp. 374–77.

212. Alex. Hamilton to Washington, Nov. 6, 1777, and to Isr. Putnam,

Nov. 9, in Harold C. Syrett, ed., *The Papers of Alexander Hamilton* (New York, 1961–), 1: 353–60.

213. Council of War, Oct. 31, 1777, in *SBW*, 1: 379–80.

214. Alex. Hamilton to Washington, Nov. 10, 1777, in Syrett, ed., *Papers of Hamilton*, 1: 359; Washington to Isr. Putnam, Nov. 4, in *WGW*, 10: 3.

215. Jesse Root to Jon. Trumbull, Nov. 7, 1777, in *7MHSC*, 2: 187; also, Root to Trumbull, Nov. 11, in JT, 7: 184; Isr. Putnam to Washington, Oct. 27, 1777, in PCC, item 159, 1: 115.

216. Isr. Putnam to Washington, Nov. 7, 1777, in ibid., pp. 111–12; Alex. Hamilton to Washington, Nov. 10, in Syrett, ed., *Papers of Hamilton*, 1: 358.

217. Alex. Hamilton to Washington, Nov. 15, 1777, in Syrett, ed., 364; Isr. Putnam to Washington, Nov. 14, in *SBW*, 1: 389–90.

218. Isr. Putnam to Jon. Trumbull, Nov. 12, 1777, in JT, 7: 186*a–c*.

219. See Jon. Trumbull to Hor. Gates, Sept. 16, 1777, in *7MHSC*, 2: 147; Jos. Spencer to Trumbull, Sept. 23, in JT, 7: 62.

220. Jos. Spencer to Jon. Trumbull, Sept. 28, 1777, in JT, 7: 70*a*.

221. Jon. Trumbull to Hor. Gates, Sept. 29, 1777, in *7MHSC*, 2:151; also Jabez Brown and Nich. Cooke to Trumbull, Oct. 3; John Douglas to Trumbull, Oct. 4, 13; and Sam. McClellan to Trumbull, Oct. 10, in JT, 7: 78, 83, 90, 115, 123.

222. Jos. Spencer to Jon. Trumbull, Oct. 15, 1777, in JT, 7: 122; John Douglas to Trumbull, Oct. 28, in *7MHSC*, 2: 177–78; and Jos. Spencer to John Hancock, Dec. 20, in PCC, item 161, 2: 356, claimed that a deserter had alerted the British on the sixteenth.

223. *SR*, 1: 458.

224. Oliver Wolcott to Jon. Trumbull, Dec. 9, 1777, in JT, 7: 277.

225. John Ely to Jon. Trumbull, Nov. 21, 1777, in ibid., p. 197.

226. Gold S. Silliman to his parents-in-law, Dec. 7, 1777, in SFC, box 2; *SHP*, p. 125. Public expectation was allowed to run well ahead of what Putnam accomplished; see *CG*, Dec. 12, 26, 1777.

227. Sam. H. Parsons to Jon. Trumbull, Dec. 4, 1777, in JT, 7: 214; also Parsons to Washington, Dec. 29, in *SHP*, p. 135.

228. Sam. B. Webb to Wm. Heath, Dec. 16, 1777, in *SBW*, 1: 399; Sam. H. Parsons to Washington, Dec. 29, in *SHP*, pp. 135–37.

229. Washington to Isr. Putnam, Dec. 2, 1777, in *WGW*, 10: 129–30.

230. Isr. Putnam to Washington, Dec. 16, 1777, in *SBW*, 1: 401–2; Putnam to Sam. H. Parsons, Dec. 20, in *SHP*, p. 127.

231. Washington to Isr. Putnam, Dec. 27, 1777, in *WGW*, 10: 212–13.

232. Washington to Isr. Putnam, Mar. 16, 1778, in *WGW*, 11: 95; cf. also ibid., p. 69 n.; General Orders, Aug. 24, in ibid., 12: 353; *JCC*, 11: 807–8.

233. Jos. Spencer to the President of Congress, Dec. 20, 1777, in PCC, item 161, 2: 358; also, *CG*, Dec. 19, 1777.

PART (TWO): ATTRITION

1. See *CC*, Feb. 24, 1778, also Apr. 7; *CJ*, Dec. 24, 1777, also Jan. 7, 1778, Mar. 4, and Apr. 15; *NP*, Jan. 5, 1778; *CG*, Dec. 5, 12, 1777, also Jan. 30, 1778, Feb. 6, and Mar. 6.

2. *JCC*, 11: 477. The alliance was ratified May 4, 1778; ibid., p. 462. Congress's address bears the date May 8.

3. Ibid., p. 478.

4. Ibid., and pp. 480–81.

5. Piers Mackesy, *The War for America* (Cambridge, Mass., 1964), p. 187.

6. Eric Robson, *The American Revolution . . .* (London, 1955), p. 113ff.

7. Mackesy, *War for America*, p. 183ff.; see also Silas Deane to Jon. Trumbull, Feb. 13, 1779, in *7MHSC*, 2: 350.

8. Piers Mackesy, "British Strategy in the War of American Independence," *Yale Review* 52 (1963): 550ff.; *War for America*, p. 156ff.

9. *AR*, p. xxxff.

10. See Adrian C. Leiby, *The Revolutionary War in the Hackensack Valley . . .* (New Brunswick, N.J., 1962), for an account of Clinton's impact on New Jersey.

CHAPTER FOUR: SIGNS OF STRAIN

1. Wm. Tryon to Jon. Trumbull, Apr. 17, 1778, with enclosures, in *7MHSC*, 2: 222–27.

2. News of the ministry's conciliatory proposals became public at the end of the month; see *CG*, Apr. 24, 1778.

3. Jon. Trumbull to Wm. Tryon, Apr. 23, 1778, in *7MHSC*, 2: 228–29.

4. Ibid., p. 229; see also *CC*, May 5, 1778; *CG*, May 1.

5. See Jas. Duane to Phil. Schuyler, June 19, 1777, in *LMCC*, 2: 383; also Jed. Huntington to Jon. Trumbull, Sept. 10, in *JT*, 6: 42.

6. At least according to the official depreciation schedule, which probably understated the rate of depreciation in New England; see E. James Ferguson, *The Power of the Purse . . .* (Chapel Hill, N.C., 1961), p. 32.

7. *JCC*, 7: 266–67.

8. See ibid., 8: 499–500.

9. Ibid., 7: 70, 8: 501; Rog. Sherman to Oliver Wolcott, May 13, 1777, in *LMCC*, 2: 361; also, Sherman to Jos. Trumbull, Apr. 2, in ibid., p. 315.

10. *JCC*, 8: 267.

11. Ibid., pp. 434–48.

12. See Jos. Trumbull to Jer. Wadsworth, May 17, 1777, in *LMCC*, 2: 364 n. for his terms; *JCC*, 8: 469–70 for the regulations. See also Trumbull to John Hancock, June 15, 1777, in *LMCC*, 2: 393 n.; Trumbull to Chas. Stewart, June 30, and to Hancock, June 30 and July 9, 19, in PCC, item 78, 22: 241–42, 245–46, 255–57, 259–60, 265–67.

13. Rog. Sherman to Jos. Trumbull, Apr. 2, 1777, in *LMCC*, 2: 315; *JCC*, 7: 134. Buchanan was not the first to suggest provisioning by contract; see *LDC*, 2: 491; 4: 315.

14. Wm. Buchanan to Hen. Laurens, Oct. 20 and Nov. 21, 1777, in PCC, item 29, pp. 97–98; *JCC*, 9: 960–61.

15. *JCC*, 8: 477, 627; Isr. Putnam to Wm. Buchanan, Sept. 7, 1777, in PCC, item 159, p. 87; Peter Colt to Buchanan, Sept. 2, in ibid., pp. 91–94; Colt to Jer. Wadsworth, Sept. 7, in JW, box 125.

16. *JCC*, 9: 766–68.

17. Isr. Putnam to Jer. Wadsworth, Oct. 9, 10, 1777, and Jesse Root to [unidentified], Oct. 24, in JW, box 125.

18. Jer. Wadsworth to Eliph. Dyer, Jan. 20, 1778, in ibid.; also, Wadsworth to Wm. Williams, Nov. 26, 1777, in *LMCC*, 2: 543 n.

19. *SR*, 1: 457, 459.

20. See Peter Colt to Jer. Wadsworth, Nov. 27, 1777, in JW, box 125.

21. John Canfield to Jer. Wadsworth, Oct. 27, 1777, in ibid.; Jos. Trumbull to Wadsworth, May 17, in *LMCC*, 2: 364 n.; Eliph. Dyer to Trumbull, July 15, in ibid., p. 414; Theodore Sizer, ed., *The Autobiography of Colonel John Trumbull* . . . (New Haven, 1953), pp. 36–39; Jos. Trumbull to Jon. Trumbull, Aug. 21, 1777, in JT, 7:24.

22. Washington to Isr. Putnam, Oct. 8, 1777, and to Rich. H. Lee, Nov. 18, in *WGW*, 9: 336, 10: 82; Washington to Jon. Trumbull, Feb. 6, 1778, in *5MHSC*, 10: 110–11.

23. *JCC*, 9: 858.

24. *SR*, 1: 512.

25. Wm. Williams to Jos. Trumbull, Nov. 28, 1777, and Eliph. Dyer to Trumbull, Dec. 8, 15, in *LMCC*, 2: 573, 584, 588–89; Jas. Lovell to Trumbull, Jan. 27, 1778, and Eliph. Dyer to Trumbull, Feb. 8, in ibid., 3: 53, 77–78.

26. Hen. Laurens to Jos. Trumbull, Jan. 5 and Feb. 9, 1778, in ibid., pp. 73–74, 79. The protocol issue involved the failure to address Governor Trumbull with the title "Your Excellency," as the legislature had prescribed the preceding summer; *SR*, 1: 229. The family had misgivings about the title; see Jos. Trumbull to Jon. Trumbull, July 6, 1777, in *7MHSC*, 2: 72. The congressional circular can be found in *JCC*, 9: 1046–47.

27. *JCC*, 10: 91–92.

28. Ibid., p. 327; Eliph. Dyer to Wm. Williams, Feb. 17, 1778, and to Jer. Wadsworth, Mar. 10, in *LMCC*, 3: 88, 121.

29. See Ferguson, *Power of Purse*, p. 32.

30. See ibid., n. 19; and Wm. Williams to Jon. Trumbull, Sept. 30, 1777, in *LMCC*, 2: 505.

31. Hen. Laurens to John Rutledge, Sept. 10, 1777, in *LMCC*, 2: 491; *JCC*, 9: 956; Nicholas Street, *The American States acting over the part of the children of Israel in the Wilderness* . . . (New Haven, 1777), pp. 24, 26.

32. Calculations derived from data in Ralph V. Harlow, "Aspects of Revolutionary Finance, 1775–1783," *AHR* 35 (1929–30): 50–51, insert.

33. *SR*, 1: 606, for a table of Connecticut currency outstanding in Aug. 1777.

34. Cornelius Harnett to Thos. Burke, Dec. 8, 1777, in *LMCC*, 2: 583; also Hen. Laurens to Robt. T. Paine, Dec. 3, in ibid., p. 580.

35. See petitions from eastern New England for permission to purchase provisions in Connecticut, in JT, 7: 229, 8: 155, 231; and complaints from New York against the operation of Connecticut's embargo laws, Jos. Livingston to Jon. Trumbull, Jan. 14, 1777, in *7MHSC*, 2: 8–9.

36. *JCC*, 9: 956.

37. See Connecticut's attempt to accommodate to the different values of state and Continental currency, in *SR*, 1: 122.

38. Ibid., p. 603.

39. Steph. Hopkins to John Hancock, Aug. 6, 1777, in ibid., p. 606.

40. *JCC*, 8: 731, 9: 955–56.

41. Congress saw confiscation as an integral part of its other strategy, to borrow $20 million, as can be seen from its recommendation that the proceeds be invested "in loan office certificates"; ibid., 9: 971. See also Hen. Laurens to John Rutledge, Sept. 10, 1777, in *LMCC*, 2: 488.

42. In October 1777 Connecticut had sequestered the estates of "inimicals;" *SR*, 1: 412, but it did not order them into probate preparatory to sale until May 1778, ibid., 2: 9–12.

43. *SR*, 1: 530.

44. Ibid., p. 531. Connecticut funded only $782,550 of her own currency. Much of it had flowed out to neighboring jurisdictions where it died.

45. See Ferguson, *Power of Purse*, p. 38; *JCC*, 6: 102–3 n., 138, 158.

46. Benj. Franklin, Silas Deane, and Art. Lee to the Committee of Secret Correspondence, Jan. 17, 1777, in *RDC*, 2: 248–51; *JCC*, 8: 724–25, 730, 743, 778.

47. Depending on when one subscribed; Ferguson, *Power of Purse*, p. 37.

48. Eliph. Dyer to Jos. Trumbull, Sept. 7, 1777, in *LMCC*, 2: 485–86; also Jas. Lovell to Oliver Wolcott, Aug. 21, and to Wm. Whipple, Aug. 18, in ibid., pp. 461, 454.

49. See Jared Tracy to Jer. Wadsworth, May 7, 1778, in JW, box 126.

50. Jas. Lovell to Oliver Wolcott, Aug. 21, 1777, in *LMCC*, 2: 461; Hen. Laurens to John Rutledge, Sept. 10, in ibid., p. 489. Congress attempted to borrow additional funds in Europe shortly afterward; *JCC*, 9: 989.

51. *JCC*, 9: 856–57.

52. *SR*, 1: 603–4; Jon. Trumbull to Connecticut Congressional delegates, Sept. 24, 1777, in JTP; Jos. Spencer to the President of Congress, Dec. 20, in PCC, item 161, 1: 351–52; John Lloyd to Jer. Wadsworth, Sept. 17, 21, and Oct. 1; and Peter Anspach to Wadsworth, Dec. 18, in JW, box 125.

53. Rich. H. Lee to Sam. Adams, Nov. 23, 1777, in *LMCC*, 2: 568–69.

54. Cf. *CC*, June 7, 1778. Governor Trumbull was critical of the exorbitant interest rates offered by the new loan office scheme for the same reason; see Trumbull to Connecticut Congressional delegates, Sept. 24, 1777, in JTP.

55. *SR*, 1: 613–18, quotes 614–15.

56. Ibid., pp. 413–15, 417.

57. Ibid., pp. 524–28.

58. See Peter Colt to Jer. Wadsworth, Feb. 19, 1778, in JW, box 125.

59. Jer. Wadsworth to Eliph. Dyer, Feb. 28, 1778, in ibid.; also, Jar. Tracy to Wadsworth, Feb. 6, in ibid.; William M. Dabney, *After Saratoga: The Story of the Convention Army* (Albuquerque, N.M., 1954), pp. 27, 35.

60. *SR*, 1: 522; Jon. Trumbull to Connecticut Congressional delegates, April 3, 1778, in JTP. See also Hen. Champion to Jer. Wadsworth, Mar. 15; Jos. Trumbull to Wadsworth, Mar. 25; Peter Colt to Wadsworth, Apr. 3; John Canfield to Wadsworth, Apr. 14; Wadsworth to Hen. Laurens and Sam. Huntington, May 27, in JW, box 126. It was still possible to procure for cash, though not on contract; see John Canfield to Wadsworth, Apr. 31, in ibid.

61. Jon. Trumbull to Jer. Wadsworth, Mar. 25, 1778, in ibid.; Wadsworth to Sam. Huntington, May 23, in ibid. A delegation also went to Rhode Island; see Wm. Greene to Trumbull, May 31, in JTP.

62. Jar. Tracy to Jer. Wadsworth, June 4, 1778, in ibid., and Wads-

worth to the Board of War, June 4, in ibid. The measure was sufficiently popular in Connecticut that some towns like Groton began to implement the recommendations of the New Haven convention before the legislature acted; see Evans 15846.

63. *JCC*, 11: 569; *SR*, 2: 12–13; Kenneth Scott, "Price Control in New England during the Revolution," *NEQ* 19 (1946): 464–65.

64. *JCC*, 10: 235; Hen. Champion to Jer. Wadsworth, Mar. 15, 1778, in JW, box 126.

65. John Hughes to Jer. Wadsworth, Jan. 1, 1778, in JW, box 125. The Connecticut loan office was described by Wadsworth as being rich in the middle of February—see his letter to Thos. Mifflin, Feb. 10—but a month later it had been drained by demands of $235,000; see John Jeffery to Wadsworth, Mar. 20, in JW, boxes 125–26.

66. *JCC*, 10: 322–24; also, Oliver Wolcott to his wife, Apr. 25, 1778, in *LMCC*, 3: 186.

67. *JCC*, 11: 480.

68. Jar. Tracy to Jer. Wadsworth, May 7, 1778, and Wm. Stewart to Wadsworth, May 11, in JW, box 126; Ferguson, *Power of Purse*, p. 32 and n. 19.

69. Jer. Wadsworth to Hen. Laurens, May 27, 1778, and Wadsworth to Washington, June 4, in JW, box 126.

70. The sentiments articulated in Jed. Huntington to Jer. Wadsworth, Jan. 7, 1778, and Eliph. Dyer to Wadsworth, Mar. 10, in ibid., boxes 125, 126, still applied.

71. *JCC*, 9: 869 n., 873, 993, 10: 78, 82, 174–75, 223.

72. Undated memo in Jer. Wadsworth's hand, probably written around Mar. 30, 1778, and Wadsworth to Thos. Mumford, June 7, in JW, box 126.

73. *JCC*, 11: 524, 627, 731, 12: 884, 902, 1100, 1218.

74. Ibid., 11: 479.

75. *CC*, Apr. 10, 1778.

76. William B. Willcox, "British Strategy in America, 1778," *Journal of Modern History* 19 (1947): 105–6.

77. *AR*, pp. 89–90.

78. Danske Dandridge, *American Prisoners of the Revolution* (Charlottesville, Va., 1911), pp. 17–19, 25–32, 48ff.; Washington to Col. Samuel Atlee, Nov. 27, 1776, in *WGW*, 6: 297; Washington to Wm. Howe, Jan. 13, 1777, in ibid., 7: 4; *CJ*, Jan. 30, 1777; *JCC*, 5: 708–9; Washington to Howe, July 30, 1776, in *WGW*, 5: 356–57; Howe to Washington, Aug. 1, in *5AA*, 1: 711.

79. See Washington to Wm. Howe, Dec. 12, 17, 1776; Washington to Jos. Trumbull, Dec. 21; Washington to the Massachusetts legislature, Dec. 21, in *WGW*, 6: 359, 390, 410, 414; Washington to Wm. Livingston, Feb. 14, 1777, in ibid., 7: 152.

80. Washington to Wm. Howe, Apr. 9, 1777, in ibid., p. 376.

81. Washington to the President of Congress, May 28, 1777, in ibid., 8: 133; also, the slightly different report in *CC*, Apr. 14, 1777.

82. *SR*, 1: 125.

83. Benj. Payne to Jon. Trumbull, Feb. 22, 1777, in JT, 6: 49*a–b*.

84. Jon. Trumbull to Washington, Jan. 23, 1777, in *5MHSC*, 10: 28–29; *SR*, 1: 160.

85. Richard H. Amerman, "Treatment of American Prisoners during

the Revolution," *Proceedings of the New Jersey Historical Society* 78 (1960): 260; Larry G. Bowman, *Captive Americans: Prisoners during the American Revolution* (Athens, Ohio, 1977), p. 107.

86. *JCC*, 10: 197, quotes Washington's account of Howe's overture.

87. Adrian C. Leiby, *The Revolutionary War in the Hackensack Valley . . .* (New Brunswick, N.J., 1962), p. 143. See also David L. Sterling, ed., "American Prisoners of War in New York: A Report by Elias Boudinot," *WMQ*, 3rd ser. 13 (1956): 382; Charles H. Metzger, *The Prisoner in the American Revolution* (Chicago, 1971), pp. 204–5; *CC*, Mar. 15, 1778.

88. *SR*, 1: 510. See also Joseph Nourse to Jon. Trumbull, Dec. 22, 1777, in JTP.

89. See *JCC*, 9: 1036–37, 1069, 10: 330–31.

90. Washington to the President of Congress, Mar. 8, 1778, in *WGW*, 11: 40–41.

91. John Beatty to Washington, July 18, 1778, in WP. I infer the number of continentals from information in George A. Boyd, *Elias Boudinot: Patriot and Statesman, 1740–1821* (Princeton, N.J., 1952), p. 46, and Sterling, "American Prisoners," p. 382.

92. Willcox, "British Strategy," p. 112.

93. *WR*, 2: 588.

94. *SR*, 2: 100–104, and Jon. Trumbull to Connecticut Congressional delegates, Aug. 26, 1778, in JTP, for Connecticut's slow response.

95. Willcox, "British Strategy," p. 115; *WR*, 2: 590; Ira D. Gruber, *The Howe Brothers and the American Revolution* (New York, 1972), pp. 314–17.

96. *WR*, 2: 588.

97. Louis Gottschalk, *Lafayette Joins the American Army* (Chicago, 1937), pp. 262–63.

98. Willcox, "British Strategy," pp. 117–18.

99. *AR*, pp. 103–4.

100. Ibid., pp. 106–7. Governor Trumbull articulated Connecticut's disappointment in a letter to Washington, Aug. 27, 1778, in JTP.

101. Evans 15832.

102. *CC*, Oct. 6, 1778.

103. Sam. Buel to Jon. Trumbull, n.d. (probably early Oct.), in JT, 8: 202.

104. Ephraim Blaine to Jer. Wadsworth, July 14, 1778; Solomon Southwick to Wadsworth, July 27; Peter Colt to Royal Flint, Aug. 8, in JW, box 126. It was even feared for a while that the French fleet would be joined by the Spanish, requiring provisions for as many as 20,000 additional men; Wadsworth to Hen. Champion, Aug. 16, 1778, in ibid.; see also *SOI*, p. 76ff.

105. Washington to Wm. Heath, Oct. 18, 1778, in *WGW*, 13: 99; *SOI*, pp. 88–89.

106. See Congress's resolutions on the subject in *JCC*, 12: 906; also Nehemiah Hubbard to Jer. Wadsworth, July 4, 1778; Peter Colt to Wadsworth, Sept. 1; Colt to Royal Flint, Sept. 18, 26, 29 and Oct. 5, in JW, boxes 126, 127.

107. *WHM*, p. 179.

108. *AR*, p. 104; Peter Colt to Jer. Wadsworth, Sept. 6, 1778, in JW, box 126.

109. Peter Colt to Jer. Wadsworth, Aug. 16, 1778; Jacob Cuyler to Wadsworth, Oct. 8; also Colt to Royal Flint, Aug. 5 and Sept. 18, 26; and Colt to Washington, Oct. 12, in ibid., boxes 126, 127. The scarcity of forage didn't begin to obstruct carting until the end of September; see Chas. Stewart to Wadsworth, Sept. 21; Colt to Flint, Oct. 26, in ibid., box 127.

110. Jacob Cuyler to Royal Flint, Sept. 15, 1778, in ibid., box 126; Jer. Wadsworth to Thos. Johnson, Sept. 9, 1778, in ibid., box 153.

111. Peter Colt to Jer. Wadsworth, July 15, 1778, in ibid., box 126.

112. *JCC*, 10: 45, 49, 52.

113. Ephr. Blaine to Jer. Wadsworth, June 10, 1778, and Wadsworth to Hen. Champion, June 11; Jar. Tracy to Wadsworth, July 21 and Aug. 1, in JW, box 126; also Pat. Henry to the Virginia Delegates in Congress, Jan. 20, 1777, in Henry R. McIlwaine, ed., *The Official Letters of the Governors of the State of Virginia* (Richmond, 1926), 1: 231–32.

114. *JCC*, 11: 687.

115. Peter Colt to Jon. Trumbull, July 16, 1778, in JTP; Colt to Jer. Wadsworth, Oct. 24, 1778; Colt to David Van Ness, Nov. 4; Trumbull to Wadsworth, Mar. 29, 1779, in JW, box 127.

116. Jer. Wadsworth to Hen. Laurens, Aug. 24, 1778, in ibid., box 153; *JCC*, 11: 831.

117. Jer. Wadsworth to the Marine Committee, Sept. 1, 1778, in JW, box 153.

118. Jer. Wadsworth to Hen. Laurens, Sept. 6, 1778, in ibid.

119. Jer. Wadsworth to Wm. Aylett, Sept. 25, 1778, and to the Board of Treasury, Oct. 8, in ibid.

120. *JCC*, 12: 974–78; Jer. Wadsworth to Ephr. Blaine, Oct. 5, 1778, in JW, box 153.

121. Sol. Southwick to Peter Colt, Nov. 23, 1778, and Colt to Southwick, Dec. 5; Chaloner and White to Jer. Wadsworth, Nov. 16 and Dec. 11, 19; Colt to Wadsworth, Jan. 2, 1779, in ibid., box 127; also John Davenport to Wadsworth, Nov. 4, 1778 in ibid.

122. Conradt Elmendorph to Jer. Wadsworth, Aug. 11, 1778; Jacob Cuyler to Wadsworth, Aug. 6, 10 and Sept. 4, 18; Thomas J. Douglass to Wadsworth, Aug. 10; Wm. Heath to Peter Colt, Aug. 11; Colt to Wadsworth, Aug. 23; Jos. Reed to Wadsworth, Sept. 12; Jacob Bayley to Wadsworth, Sept. 22; and Colt to Royal Flint, Sept. 23, in ibid., box 126. For the disbursements of the Convention army, Robert Pigot to Wm. Howe, Apr. 10, and Howe to John Robinson, Mar. 16, in Great Britain, Historical Manuscripts Commission, *Report on American Manuscripts in the Royal Institute of Great Britain* (London, 1904), 1: 229, 210.

123. Peter Colt to Royal Flint, Sept. 29 and Oct. 3, 1778, in JW, box 127; also Hen. Champion to Jer. Wadsworth, June 18, in ibid., box 126. The shortage of money began to be felt immediately after the repeal of the Regulatory Act; see Colt to Wadsworth, June 21, 30, July 15, and Sept. 15; John Moore to Wadsworth, July 7; Miller and Tracy to Wadsworth, July 14; Wadsworth to Elbridge Gerry, Aug. 13, in ibid.; Wadsworth to the Board of Treasury, Oct. 8, in ibid., box 127.

124. Jer. Wadsworth to Royal Flint, Aug. 12, 1777, in ibid., box 126.

125. Peter Colt to Geo. Clinton, Sept. 25, 1778, and to Royal Flint,

Sept. 29, in ibid.; Colt to Flint, Oct. 5 and David Van Ness to Colt, Oct. 25, in ibid., box 127.

126. See Peter Colt to Thomas Fanning, Oct. 30, 1778, in ibid., box 127.

127. *SR*, 2: 132–33. For commissary dissatisfaction with the legislature's actions, see Peter Colt to Royal Flint, Nov. 3, 1778, in JW, box 127.

128. See Peter Colt to Hen. Schenk, Sept. 16, 1778, in JW, box 126.

129. Peter Colt to Jer. Wadsworth, Sept. 6, 1778; Colt to Royal Flint, Sept. 20, 23, 26; Jacob Cuyler to Colt, Sept. 28, and to Wadsworth, Sept. 18, 20, in ibid.; Wadsworth to Conrad A. Gerald, Oct. 10, and to Chevalier Anne-César de la Luzerne, Oct. 15, in ibid., box 153; Cuyler to Flint, Oct. 1; Colt to Flint, Oct. 17; David Van Ness to Wadsworth, Oct. 20, in ibid., box 127.

130. Peter Van Ness to Jacob Cuyler, Oct. 6, 1778; Van Ness to Jer. Wadsworth, Oct. 14; Cuyler to Royal Flint, Oct. 19; Peter Colt to Van Ness, Oct. 25; Colt to Wm. Heath, Oct. 30; Colt to Jos. Reed, Oct. 25; Colt to Wadsworth, Nov. 3; Colt to Flint, Nov. 8, in ibid., box 127.

131. Peter Colt to Asa Waterman, Oct. 31, 1778; Colt to Roy. Flint, Nov. 1, in ibid.

132. Sol. Southwick to Peter Colt, Oct. 31, 1778; Colt to Roy. Flint, Nov. 8, 9; Colt to Thos. Fanning, Nov. 9; Hen. Champion to Jer. Wadsworth, Nov. 19; Jas. Sullivan to Washington, Nov. 20, in ibid.

133. Peter Colt to Royal Flint, Nov. 1, 1778, in ibid.

134. Jer. Wadsworth to Ephr. Blaine, Oct. 15, 1778; also, Wadsworth to Royal Flint, Oct. 6, in ibid.

135. *JCC*, 12: 861; Peter Colt to Peter Van Ness, Nov. 3, 1778; Maj. Robert Burnet to Van Ness, Nov. 14; Jacob Cuyler to Jer. Wadsworth, Dec. 3, in JW, box 127.

136. Peter Colt to Jer. Wadsworth, Nov. 19, 1778; Colt to Sol. Southwick, Dec. 1, 5, in JW, box 127.

137. John Fitch to Jer. Wadsworth, Jan. 2, 1779, and Sam. H. Parsons to Wadsworth, Jan. 7, in ibid.

138. Peter Colt to Jer. Wadsworth, Nov. 24, 1778; Colt to Royal Flint, Nov. 16; Wadsworth to Sol. Southwick, Mar. 19, in ibid.

139. Ephr. Blaine to Royal Flint, Jan. 14, 1779, in ibid.; see also Jer. Wadsworth to Jacob Cuyler, Mar. 3; Abraham Livingston to Wadsworth, Feb. 10, in ibid.

140. Peter Colt to Jer. Wadsworth, Jan. 2, 11, 1779; Sol. Southwick to Colt, Nov. 27 and Dec. 2; Southwick to Wadsworth, Dec. 18; Colt to Southwick, Dec. 5; Colt to Royal Flint, Nov. 16; Colt to Miller and Tracy, Dec. 13; Colt to Wadsworth, Dec. 16 and Feb. 12, 1779; Asa Waterman to Wadsworth, Dec. 19, in ibid.

141. Connecticut received the first requests for assistance in the autumn; see Wm. Greene to Jon. Trumbull, Oct. 31, 1778, and Jan. 21, 1779, in JT, 8: 236, 9: 16; see also Selectmen of Plymouth to Trumbull, Feb. 22; Peleg Clarke and Nath. Mumford to the General Assembly of Connecticut, Jan. 23; Nath. Coffin to Trumbull, Jan. 26, in 7*MHSC*, 2: 334–37; the government's response can be traced in *SR*, 2: 166ff.

142. See Jer. Wadsworth to the Suffield selectmen, Mar. 2, 1779, in JW, box 127.

143. Jer. Wadsworth to the Committee of Congress, Mar. 27, 1779; Wm. Ledyard to Wadsworth, Mar. 16, in ibid.; Nath. Shaw to Jon. Trumbull, Feb. 24, in JT, 9: 53.

144. Ephr. Blaine to Jer. Wadsworth, Mar. 17 and Apr. 19, 29, 1779, in JW, boxes 127, 128; Board of War to Wadsworth, May 18, and Wadsworth to Board of War, May 22, in ibid.; see also Max G. Schumacher, *The Northern Farmer and His Markets during the Late Colonial Period* (New York, 1975), chap. 1.

145. See Jas. Forbes to Thos. Johnson, Feb. 13, 1778; John Henry, Jr., to Johnson, Feb. 14; Rich. H. Lee to John Adams, May 13 and June 20; Committee of Foreign Affairs to Commissioners of Paris, Apr. 30; Robert Morris to Jas. Duane, Sept. 8, in *LMCC*, 3: 84, 85, 233, 308, 208, 405.

146. Josiah Bartlett to Wm. Whipple, July 27, 1778, and to John Langdon, Aug. 18; Titus Hosmer to Jon. Trumbull, Aug. 11, in ibid., pp. 351, 379, 366.

147. See And. Adams to Oliver Wolcott, July 22, 1778, in ibid., p. 347; also, Adams to Sam. Lyman, Aug. 17, and Josiah Bartlett to Wm. Whipple, Aug. 18, in ibid., pp. 378, 379; *JCC*, 11: 776–77.

148. Silas Deane to Jon. Trumbull, Oct. 20, 1778, in *7MHSC*, 2: 297; also, Committee of Foreign Affairs to Benj. Franklin, Dec. 8, in *LMCC*, 3: 523.

149. The figures are derived from Rich. H. Lee to John Adams, Oct. 29, 1778, in *LMCC*, 3: 472; Ferguson, *Power of Purse*, p. 38.

150. See *JCC*, 12: 930.

151. Connecticut delegates to Jon. Trumbull, Nov. 10, 1778, in *LMCC*, 3: 486–87; also Rog. Sherman to Trumbull, Oct. 6, in ibid., p. 443; the plan is in *JCC*, 12: 929–33; for its adoption, see ibid., 13: 20–23. The Lee-Deane controversy is discussed on pp. 178–79.

152. The original proposal for a forced loan encountered considerable opposition in Congress; Thos. Burke to the governor of North Carolina, Dec. 20, 1778, and North Carolina delegates to the governor, Dec. 22, in *LMCC*, 3: 542–43, 547. This led Congress to give possessors of the bills options; *JCC*, 12: 1224, 1231–34, 1235–38, 1256–58.

153. *JCC*, 13: 21; Francis Lewis to Geo. Clinton, Dec. 31, 1778, in *LMCC*, 3: 554.

154. By the summer of 1778 the leadership was aware that the issue could become more explosive, though; see And. Adams to Sam. Lyman, Aug. 17, in *LMCC*, 3: 378.

155. See "Honestus," in *CC*, Dec. 29, 1778.

156. The official depreciation was 8:1—see Ferguson, *Power of Purse*, p. 32—but a more accurate though complex picture of the currency's value can be derived from Peter Colt to Royal Flint, Jan. 7, 1779; Chaloner and White to Jer. Wadsworth, Jan. 21; Ephr. Blaine to Wadsworth, Mar. 17, in JW, box 127. For Connecticut's reaction to the official depreciation schedule, see *CJ*, May 24, 1781.

157. James Watson to Jer. Wadsworth, Jan. 4, 1779, in JW, box 127; also, Peter Colt to Royal Flint, Nov. 3; John Chester to Wadsworth, Nov. 24; and John Lloyd to Wadsworth, Dec. 1, in ibid.; Tim. Dwight to Sam. H. Parsons, Apr. 23, 1779, in *SHP*, p. 237.

158. Congressmen continued to talk about appreciating the currency throughout the autumn; Sam. Adams to Jas. Warren, Nov. 3, 1778; Hen.

Laurens to Jon. Trumbull, Nov. 10; John Penn to Wm. Woodford, Dec. 6, in *LMCC*, 3: 476, 486, 520. But other councils began to prevail; Thos. Burke to the governor of North Carolina, Dec. 20; Jas. Duane to Geo. Clinton, Jan. 3, 1779; Francis L. Lee to Rich. H. Lee, Jan. 5, in ibid., 3: 543, 4: 2–3, 10. By the following spring appreciation had ceased to be a serious objective; Rog. Sherman to Benj. Trumbull, May 20, in ibid., 4: 221. Congress considered mentioning the tendency taxation would have to appreciate the currency in its address to the people of May 26, 1779, but decided against it; *JCC*, 14: 657, also 13: 60.

159. *JCC*, 13: 139, 209.

160. Jer. Wadsworth to Scudder, Morris, and Whipple, Mar. 4, 1779, and to Royal Flint, Mar. 5, in JW, box 127; Board of War to Wadsworth, May 18; Hen. Champion to Wadsworth, June 22, in ibid., box 128.

161. Peter Colt to Royal Flint, Feb. 17, 1779; Ephr. Blaine to Jer. Wadsworth, Mar. 17, in ibid., box 127; Colt to Wadsworth, June 6, in ibid.

162. See Jer. Wadsworth to Royal Flint, May 7, 1779; Sam. Leonard to Wadsworth, May 1; Peter Colt to Wadsworth, May 2; Wadsworth to Hor. Gates, May 3; Colt to Flint, May 18, in ibid.

163. Jas. Watson to Wadsworth, May 11, 1779, in ibid.

164. See Wadsworth's account dated Apr. 2, 1779, in ibid.; for background, Wadsworth to the Suffield selectmen, Mar. 2, and their reply, Apr. 7, in ibid., boxes 127–28.

165. See Benj. Brooks to Edw. Hallam, Jan. 22, 1779; John Sullivan to Jon. Trumbull, Feb. 13; complaint of Wm. Sharp against Amasa Sessions, Feb. 13; and Sam. McClellan to Jon. Trumbull Mar. 27; New York order to Capt. Merely, Mar. 2; Alex. McDougall to Trumbull, Mar. 12, in JT, 11: 19*a*–*b*, 46*a*, 61*a*–*b*, 116, 75, 100.

166. Thos. Fanning to Jer. Wadsworth, Apr. 13, 1779, and Jacob Cuyler to Wadsworth, Apr. 12, 22, 1779, in JW, box 128.

167. *SR*, 2: 224–27; see Jas. Watson to Jer. Wadsworth, May 7, 1779, and Wadsworth to Royal Flint, May 7, in JW, box 128.

168. See Jon. Trumbull to Jer. Wadsworth, Mar. 27, 1779, in ibid., box 127; Jon. Stevens to Wadsworth, May 3, in ibid., box 128.

169. Jer. Wadsworth to Morris and Whipple, May 5, 1779, in ibid., box 128.

170. Chaloner and White to Jer. Wadsworth, May 24, 1779, in ibid.; also, Frederick D. Stone, "Philadelphia Society One Hundred Years Ago; or, The Reign of Continental Money," *PMHB* 3 (1879): 384; John K. Alexander, "The Fort Wilson Incident of 1779: A Case Study of the Revolutionary Crowd," *WMQ*, 3rd ser. 31 (1974): 595ff.; Gouverneur Morris to Robert R. Livingston, May 20, 1779, in *LMCC*, 4: 238; also Chas. Carroll to Wm. Carmichael, May 31, in ibid., pp. 239–40.

171. Jas. Duane to Geo. Clinton, Mar. 21, 1779, and Jas. Lovell to Hor. Gates, Mar. 23, in *LMCC*, 4: 110, 115–16.

172. *JCC*, 14: 561.

173. Ibid., p. 626; Wm. Whipple to Josiah Bartlett, May 21, 1779, in *LMCC*, 4: 223.

174. See Wm. Flemming to Thos. Jefferson, May 22, 1779, and Samuel Holten to the President of the Massachusetts Council, July 13, in *LMCC*, 4: 226, 313.

175. Rich. H. Lee to John Adams, Apr. 24, 1779, and Wm. Whipple to John Langdon, June 12, in ibid., p. 260.

176. Jas. Lovell to Jas. Warren, June 15, 1779, in ibid., pp. 268–69.

177. *JCC*, 14: 783–85; John Armstrong to Hor. Gates, July 12, 1779, in *LMCC*, 4: 311; for a more optimistic view, see Sam. Huntington to Jer. Wadsworth, July 22, 1779, in JW, box 128.

178. Peter Colt to Jer. Wadsworth, June 3, 1779, in JW, box 128.

179. *SR*, 1: 365–66, 377.

180. Dated Sept. 8, 1778, in CARW, 1st ser., 13: 46.

181. Dated Oct. 1, 1778, in ibid., p. 45.

182. *SR*, 2: 172–73.

183. Ibid., p. 135.

184. Unsigned to Benj. Huntington, May 21, 1779, in JT, 9: 210. Norwich was not the only eastern town that indicated its dislike for the tax system; see Canterbury, Ex, Apr. 19, 1779.

185. See Matthew Talcott to Jer. Wadsworth, June 26, 1779, and Peter Colt to Wadsworth, June 3, 16, in JW, box 128.

186. Cf. Jon. Trumbull to Connecticut delegates in Congress, Dec. 8, 1778, in 7*MHSC*, 2: 319, with Rich. H. Lee to George Mason, June 9, 1779, in *LMCC*, 4: 255.

187. Matt. Talcott to Jer. Wadsworth, June 26, 1779, in JW, box 128; *SR*, 2: 258–61.

188. Washington to Jon. Trumbull, Dec. 15, 1777, in 5*MHSC*, 10: 103–4; also, Isr. Putnam to Trumbull, Jan. 6, 1778, in 7*MHSC*, 2: 210.

189. *SR*, 1: 474–75, also 241.

190. Isr. Putnam to Jon. Trumbull, Mar. 27 and Apr. 27, 1778, and Erastus Wolcott to Trumbull, Apr. 5, in JT, 8: 112, 119, 114.

191. Chas. Burrall to Jon. Trumbull, May 1, 1778, and Gold S. Silliman to Trumbull, May 1, in ibid., pp. 127, 125.

192. *SR*, 1: 533–34.

193. Ibid., pp. 577, 579–80.

194. Hor. Gates to Jon. Trumbull, May 15, 1778, in 5*MHSC*, 10: 318; Trumbull to Gates, May 30, in 7*MHSC*, 2: 235; also, Washington to Gates, May 17, in *WGW*, 11: 402; *SR*, 2: 15–16.

195. *SR*, 2: 89, 91, 116.

196. See Silas Deane to Jon. Trumbull, Feb. 13, 1779, in 7*MHSC*, 2: 352.

197. Jon. Trumbull to Hor. Gates, August 18, 1778, in JTP; Trumbull to Hen. Laurens, Oct. 5, in ibid., p. 274; also Jon. Trumbull, Jr., to Congress, Apr. 23, 1779, in JT, 10: 185*a–b*.

198. Jon. Trumbull, Jr., to Jon. Trumbull, Apr. 20, 1779, and Jon. Trumbull to Connecticut Congressional delegates, May 27, in JT, 10: 179*c*, 216.

199. See Richard Buel, Jr., "Time: Friend or Foe of the Revolution?" in Don C. Higginbotham, ed., *Reconsiderations on the Revolutionary War* (Westport, Conn., 1978), p. 138.

200. See Jon. Trumbull to John Jay, Apr. 15 and June 22, 1779, in PCC, item 66, 2: 9, 19; *SR*, 2: 234, 285.

201. *JCC*, 9: 946–47; Silas Deane, "To the Free and Virtuous Citizens of America," in New York Historical Society, *Collections* 21 (1889): 66–76.

202. Documents relating to the public controversy are to be found in New York Historical Society, *Collections*, vol. 21, passim. Deane's address appeared in the Connecticut papers, Dec.-Jan. 1778–79: *CC*, Dec. 22; *CJ*, Dec. 29; *CG*, Jan. 1. Other items are to be found in *CC*, Jan. 12, 26, Feb. 2, 9, 23, and Mar. 2; *CJ*, Jan. 6 and Feb. 10; *CG*, Jan. 15, 22, 29 and Feb. 19, 26; *NP*, Jan. 11.

203. Christopher Collier, *Roger Sherman's Connecticut . . .* (Middletown, Conn., 1971), pp. 130–35.

204. Deane's influential connections might have spoken for him, but they were preoccupied with other problems; see *SBW*, 2: 136ff.

205. See, for instance, CARW, 1st ser., 30: 20, 80, 81, for Haddam's claims.

206. See Return J. Meigs to Jon. Trumbull, Dec. 26, 1778, in 7*MHSC*, 2: 327; also CARW, 1st ser., 13: 345; John Shy, *A People Numerous and Armed* (New York, 1976), p. 172; David O. White, *Connecticut's Black Soldiers* (Chester, Conn., 1973), passim.

207. Memorial of the officers in the Connecticut line in behalf of themselves and the soldiers, Oct. 2, 1778, in PCC, item 66, 1: 443.

208. Jon. Trumbull to Washington, Oct. 28, 1778, in 5*MHSC*, 10: 129.

209. Sam. H. Parsons to Washington, Oct. 17, 1778, in *SHP*, p. 197.

210. See Washington to Jon. Trumbull, Nov. 7 and Dec. 19, 1778, in *WGW*, 13: 212, 434–35; also, Washington to Isr. Putnam, Nov. 20, 25; Washington to the President of Congress, Nov. 27, in ibid., pp. 289, 324, 339–43, 351.

211. Half pay was initially suggested by the field officers to quiet discontent among the officers over the reorganization of the army during the winter of 1777–78. Washington quickly endorsed the proposal; see Remarks on Plan of Field Officers for Remodeling the Army, Nov. 1777; Committee of Congress to Washington, Dec. 10; Washington to the President of Congress, Dec. 23; Washington to the Committee of Congress with the Army, Jan. 29, 1778, in ibid., 10: 125, 144 n., 196–97, 363–65; Washington to the President of Congress, Apr. 10, in ibid., 11: 237–40; *LOA*, pp. 13–16.

212. *SR*, 1: 480.

213. *JCC*, 10: 396.

214. Connecticut Congressional delegates to Jon. Trumbull, May 18, 1778, in 7*MHSC*, 2: 232–33. They had misled Trumbull slightly as to Congress's pledge; *JCC*, 11: 502.

215. *SR*, 2: 136–37; Memorial of Oct. 3, 1778, in PCC, item 66, 1: 443–45.

216. Jon. Trumbull to Connecticut's Congressional delegates, Dec. 8, 1778, in PCC, item 66, 1: 438.

217. Return J. Meigs to Jon. Trumbull, Dec. 28, 1778, in 7*MHSC*, 2: 325–27, quote 327.

218. Isr. Putnam to Jon. Trumbull, Jan.?, 1779, in JT, 9: 30*a–d*; Sam. H. Parsons to Jer. Wadsworth, Jan. 7, in JW, box 127; *SHP*, pp. 213–15. Putnam subsequently executed in an especially grisly manner two men accused of spying; see John W. Barber, *Connecticut Historical Collections . . .* (New Haven, 1838), p. 399.

219. *SR*, 2: 180.

220. See Ferguson, *Power of Purse*, p. 32. Parsons's General Orders, Feb. 9, 1779, in *SHP*, p. 215, stressed the token nature of the action.

221. See Jon. Trumbull to Connecticut Congressional delegates, Feb. 22, 1779, in 7*MHSC*, 2: 361–62.

222. *SR*, 2: 234; Jon. Trumbull to John Jay, Apr. 15, 1779, in PCC, item 66, 2: 9.

223. *SR*, 2: 229.

224. Sam. H. Parsons to Jon. Trumbull, Apr. 10, 1779, in JT, 9: 171*a–b*; Parsons to Trumbull, Apr. 30, in *SHP*, p. 240.

225. *SR*, 2: 285–86; Jon. Trumbull to John Jay, June 22, 1779, in PCC, item 66, 2: 24; *JCC*, 14: 629–30.

226. See *AR*, p. 117; Isr. Putnam to Washington, Mar. 2, 1779, in WP; also Jed. Huntington to Jon. Trumbull, Mar. 3, and Putnam to Trumbull, Mar. 4, in JT, 9: 76*a–b*, 78; Spencer P. Mead, *Ye Historie of ye Town of Greenwich* . . . (New York, 1911), pp. 160–71.

227. Putnam's General Orders, Feb. 3, 1779, in *SHP*, p. 213; *CG*, Feb. 19, 1779.

228. Sam. H. Parsons to Jon. Trumbull, Mar. 1, 1779, in JT, 9: 67; *SR*, 2: 216–17.

229. Isr. Putnam to Jon. Trumbull, Mar. 4, 1779, in JT, 9: 78*a–b*.

230. Sam. H. Parsons to Jon. Trumbull, Mar. 12, 13, 1779, in *SHP*, pp. 220, 221–22; Trumbull to Parsons, Mar. 16, in JT, 9: 91; Isr. Putnam to Jon. Trumbull, Mar. 23, 1779, in JT, 9: 123; Putnam to Washington, Mar. 22, in WP.

231. Isr. Putnam to Washington, Mar. 28, 1779, in WP; Alex. McDougall to Jon. Trumbull, Mar. 20; Stephen Johnson to Trumbull, Mar. 25; Jon. Shipman to Sam. H. Parsons, Mar. 27; Parsons to Putnam, Mar. 28; Parsons to Jab. Huntington, Mar. 28, in JT, 9: 111*a–c*, 127*b–c*, 128, 131, 134; Parsons to Trumbull, Mar. 26, in 7*MHSC*, 2: 376–77; *CG*, Mar. 25, 1779.

232. See the Council of Safety's mobilization orders in *SR*, 2: 220–21. Putnam was reluctant to take decisive measures on his own; see his letter to Washington, Mar. 28, 1779, in WP. But he did move 300 of the 600 on the western coast eastward; see his letter to Washington, Mar. 30, in ibid.

233. See *SHP*, p. 223.

234. Sam. H. Parsons to Jon. Trumbull, Apr. 6, 8, 1779; John Tyler to Trumbull, Apr. 20, in ibid., pp. 165, 170; Jas. Wadsworth to Trumbull, Apr. 6, 1779, in 7*MHSC*, 2: 383.

235. Sam. H. Parsons to Jon. Trumbull, Mar. 21, 1779; Isr. Putnam to Trumbull, Mar. 23, in JT, 9: 113, 123.

236. Washington to Isr. Putnam, Apr. 17, 19, 23, 28, 1779, in *WGW*, 14: 397, 410, 433–34, 456.

237. Washington to Hor. Gates, Apr. 17, 1779, in ibid., p. 398; Gates to Jon. Trumbull, Apr. 28, 1779, in JT, 9: 193.

238. Washington to Jon. Trumbull et al., Mar. 24, 1779, in *WGW*, 14: 290.

239. Report of the Committee of the General Assembly to draft a reply to Washington's letter of Mar. 24, 1779, in JT, 9: 122*b–c*; Jon. Trumbull to Washington, Apr. 27, in 5*MHSC*, 10: 135.

240. Jon. Trumbull to Hor. Gates, May 1, 1779, in JT, 9: 198.

241. *JCC*, 11: 538–39.
242. CARW, 1st ser., 14: 28.
243. Ibid., p. 29; *SR*, 2: 229–30, 234.
244. Alex. McDougall to Jon. Trumbull, May 29, 1779, in JT, 9: 219; *SR*, 2: 288–89.
245. John Mead to Jon. Trumbull, June 17, 1779, in JT, 9: 244; *SR*, 2: 292.
246. *SR*, 2: 280–81; Jon. Trumbull to John Jay, June 22, 1779, in PCC, item 66, 2: 24.
247. *SR*, 2: 281–82, 291.
248. See ibid., pp. 280, 282.

CHAPTER FIVE: EXHAUSTION

1. See "To the Inhabitants of the United States of America," May 26, 1779, in *JCC*, 14: 656.
2. See Wm. H. Drayton's Memorandum of Conference with the Minister of France, Feb. 15, 1779, in *LMCC*, 4: 69–71.
3. *NP*, Mar. 15, 1779; also, *CJ*, Mar. 17; *CC*, Mar. 30.
4. *JCC*, 14: 655.
5. Daniel of St. Thomas Jennifer to Thos. Johnson, Jr., May 24, 1779, in *LMCC*, 4: 232.
6. John Armstrong to Washington, June 25, 1779, in ibid., p. 284.
7. *JCC*, 14; 653, 657.
8. John Lloyd to Jer. Wadsworth, July 4, 1779, in JW, box 128.
9. *SR*, 2: 286–87.
10. Wayne E. Verry, "The Connecticut Privateers and Their Prizes: A Comparative Study" (Master's thesis, Wesleyan University, 1976), p. 64; Peter Colt to Jer. Wadsworth, July 5, 1779, in JW, box 128; also, Washington to Edm. Pendleton, Nov. 1, in *WGW*, 17: 53. For the balance of naval forces see Piers Mackesy, *The War for America* (Cambridge, Mass., 1964), p. 211; Jonathan R. Dull, *The French Navy and American Independence . . .* (Princeton, N.J., 1975), pp. 160–61.
11. Royal Flint to Jer. Wadsworth, July 6, 1779, in JW, box 128.
12. *AR*, p. 130.
13. The tide was on the flood, making it plausible that the anchored vessels were bound eastward; see Charles H. Townshend, *The British Invasion at New Haven, Connecticut* (New Haven, 1879), p. 29; Chauncy Goodrich, "Invasion of New Haven by the British Troops, July 5, 1779," *Papers of the New Haven Colony Historical Society* 11 (1877): 37.
14. Townshend, *British Invasion*, pp. 7–16, 35–36, 63–65; Goodrich, "Invasion," p. 37ff.; *CJ*, July 7, 1779; Peter Colt to Jon. Trumbull, July 8, 1779, in 7*MHSC*, 2: 401–2; Franklin B. Dexter, ed., *The Literary Diary of Ezra Stiles* (New York, 1901), 2: 353–55.
15. *CC*, July 13, 1779; *SR*, 2: 545–53; Peter Colt to Jon. Trumbull, July 8, 1779, in 7*MHSC*, 2: 403.
16. Chas. Garth to Wm. Tryon, July 5, 1779, as quoted in Townshend, *British Invasion*, p. 40.
17. Wm. Tryon's Report, July 20, 1779, in *DAR*, 17: 163; Dexter, *Diary*

of Stiles, 2: 355. Goodrich, relying on the oral tradition of the town, suggests that Garth's detachment was incapacitated with drink. His vulnerability found expression in his threat to burn the town if his men were fired on during the evacuation; "Invasion," pp. 49, 92. See also Rollin G. Osterweis, *Three Centuries of New Haven, 1638–1938* (New Haven, 1953), pp. 147–48.

18. And. Ward to Jon. Trumbull, July 7, 1779, in *7MHSC*, 2: 400; Peter Colt to Jer. Wadsworth, July 8 (fragment), in JW, box 128; Dexter, *Diary of Stiles*, 2: 364.

19. See *CC*, July 13, 1779.

20. Peter Colt to Jon. Trumbull, July 8, 1779, in *7MHSC*, 2: 403–4.

21. Wm. Tryon's Report, July 20, 1779, in *DAR*, 17: 163; Journal of Wm. Wheeler in Cornelia P. Lathrop, *Black Rock Seaport of Old Fairfield, Connecticut, 1644–1870* (New Haven, 1930), pp. 29–30; Elizabeth H. Schenck, *The History of Fairfield . . .* (New York, 1905), 2: 386–93.

22. *CC*, May 11, 1779; Sam. Whiting to Jon. Trumbull, July 22, 1779, in JTP.

23. See JT, 9: 267; Wm. Tryon's Report, July 20, 1779, in *DAR*, 17: 163; Sam. Whiting to Jon. Trumbull, July 9, in *7MHSC*, 2: 405.

24. Dexter, *Diary of Stiles*, 2: 364.

25. Sam. Whiting to Oliver Wolcott, July 9, 1779, in OW, vol. 2.

26. Washington to Jon. Trumbull, July 7, 1779, in *WGW*, 15: 379.

27. Wm. Ledyard to Jon. Trumbull, July 5, 1779, in JT, 9: 263; Peter Colt to Trumbull, July 8, in *7MHSC*, 2: 404; *SR*, 2: 355–57; Trumbull to Wolcott, July 9, 12, in OW, vol. 2; Colt to Jer. Wadsworth, July 10, in JW, box 128.

28. Washington to Jon. Trumbull, July 8, 1779, and to John Glover, July 8, 9, in *WGW*, 15: 379–80, 383–93; *SR*, 2: 359; Trumbull to Wolcott, July 12, in OW, vol. 2.

29. Abraham Davenport to Sam. Whiting, July 8, 1779, and Jonathan Dimon to Oliver Wolcott, July 9, in OW, vol. 2; *SR*, 2: 358–59.

30. Washington to Sam. H. Parsons, July 8, 1779, to Jon. Trumbull, July 9, and to Wm. Heath, July 10, in *WGW*, 15: 382–85.

31. See Henry Clinton to Geo. Germain, June 18 and July 25, 1779, in *DAR*, 17: 146, 168; *AR*, p. 130; Washington to Jon. Trumbull, July 7, in *WGW*, 15: 379.

32. See And. Ward to Jon. Trumbull, July 7, 1779, in *7MHSC*, 2: 401; John Tyler to Trumbull, July 7, in JT, 9: 268.

33. Wolcott's letter has been lost, but it is referred to in Jon. Trumbull to Wolcott, July 12, 1779, in OW, vol. 2; see also *SR*, 2: 359.

34. *SR*, 2: 360; Jon. Trumbull to Wolcott, July 12, 1779, in OW, vol. 2.

35. Oliver Wolcott to Washington, July 17, 1779, in OW, vol. 2; Wm. Tryon's Report, July 20, in *DAR*, 17: 164.

36. See *SR*, 2: 545–61.

37. Ibid.; Sam. H. Parsons to Jon. Trumbull, July 17, 1779, in *7MHSC*, 2: 411–12. Stiles gives a slightly higher estimate of the damage in Dexter. *Diary of Stiles*, 2: 364.

38. *AR*, p. 131; Wm. Tryon's Report, July 20, 1779, in *DAR*, 17: 164. Washington to Sam. H. Parsons, July 11, in *WGW*, 15: 407–8; *WHM*, pp. 191–92.

39. *WR*, 2: 596–610.

40. *AR*, p. 132.

41. Otto Hufeland, *Westchester County during the American Revolution, 1775–1783* (n.p., 1926), p. 303; Washington to Wm. Heath, July 16, 1779, in *WGW*, 15: 427–28; also, Jon. Trumbull to Oliver Wolcott, July 19, in OW, vol. 3; John Glover to Trumbull, July 18, 19, in JT, 10: 35, 36; *WHM*, pp. 194–95.

42. Oliver Wolcott to Jon. Trumbull, July 22, 25, 30, 1779, in OW, vol. 3; also, Wolcott to John Glover, July 30, in ibid.; And. Ward to Trumbull, July 21, in JT, 10: 42; Wolcott to Trumbull, July 24, in JTP.

43. John Jeffery to Jer. Wadsworth, July 8, 13, 1779, in JW, box 128; also, Neh. Hubbard to Wadsworth, July 15, in ibid.; Art. Lee to Jon. Trumbull, Apr. 6, and Joshua Jonston and Wm. Carmichael to Trumbull, Apr. 11, in JT, 9: 166, 172; Ezekiel Cheevers to Trumbull, July 11, and Titus Hosmer to Trumbull, July 12, in ibid., 10: 13, 15; Thos. Seymour to Trumbull, July 10, in ibid., 9: 281; Wethersfield gentlemen to Trumbull, July 10, in ibid., 10: 6; *SR*, 2: 358–60; Nath. Peabody to Meshech Weare, July 20, in *LMCC*, 4: 332; cf. Trumbull to Wallingford Selectmen, Aug. 5, 1779, in JTP.

44. *SR*, 2: 361–62; 363–64; Jon. Trumbull to Jeremiah Powell, July 16, 1779, in JT, 20: 203.

45. *NP*, Aug. 10, 1779; Jon. Trumbull to Oliver Wolcott, July 19, 1779, Wolcott to Wm. Heath, July 26, and Stephen St. John to Wolcott, July 22, in OW, vol. 3; Wm. Ledyard to Trumbull, July 13, and John Tyler to Trumbull, July 18, in JT, 10: 20, 31; also, Petition of Stonington, July 17, in ibid., p. 28; *WHM*, p. 196.

46. Washington to Wm. Heath, July 19, 1779, to John Glover, July 23, to Oliver Wolcott, July 24, and to Robert Howe, July 28 and Aug. 4, in *WGW*, 15: 438, 468, quote 496–97; 16: 49–50; Glover to Jon. Trumbull, July 15, in JT, 10: 24; Heath to Wolcott, July 10, and Wolcott to Trumbull, Aug. 15, 20, in OW, vol. 3.

47. Massachusetts Council to Jon. Trumbull, July 13, 1779, in JT, 10: 19; *SR*, 3: 359, 366.

48. *SR*, 3: 379; And. Ward to Oliver Wolcott, July 27, 1779, in OW, vol. 3.

49. *SR*, 2: 358, 374, 375; Jon. Dimon to Oliver Wolcott, July 17, 1779, in OW, vol. 3; George C. Croce, Jr., *William Samuel Johnson: A Maker of the Constitution* (New York, 1937), pp. 108–11. A copy of the interrogation of Stratford residents by military authorities can also be found in the William Samuel Johnson Papers; Connecticut Historical Society.

50. Oliver Wolcott to Jon. Trumbull, Aug. 29, 1779, in OW, vol. 3.

51. *SR*, 2: 379.

52. Steph. St. John to Oliver Wolcott, July 13, 1779; Ezra Starr to Wolcott, July 15; Wolcott to Jon. Trumbull, July 22; And. Ward to Wolcott, July 22; Comfort Sage to Wolcott, July 23, in OW, vols. 1, 3.

53. And. Ward to Oliver Wolcott, July 27, 1779, in OW, vol. 3; Ward to Jon. Trumbull, Sept. 1, in JT, 10: 136; Selah Hart to Trumbull, Sept. 5, in ibid., p. 138; Wolcott to Trumbull, Oct. 2, in ibid., p. 174.

54. And. Ward to Jon. Trumbull, Sept. 1, 1779, in JT, 10: 136.

55. Oliver Wolcott to Jon. Trumbull, Aug. 29, 1779, in OW, vol. 3.

56. *SR*, 2: 392–93; Wm. Worthington to Jon. Trumbull, Aug. 30, 1779, in 7*MHSC*, 2: 431; John Lloyd to Jer. Wadsworth, Sept. 1, in JW, box 129; also, Peter Colt to Wadsworth, Aug. 31, in ibid.

57. Jer. Wadsworth to Jon. Trumbull, Jr., Sept. 7, 1779, in JW, box 129; Jabez Fitch to Oliver Wolcott, Sept. 8, in OW, vol. 3. Calculations as to the strength of the state regiments are inferred from *SR*, 2: 399–401, 405–8.

58. Aar. Cleveland to Jon. Trumbull, Aug. 20, 1779, in JT, 10: 106. The initial attempt to secure volunteers for the Continental service had failed; see Wm. Bull to Trumbull, July 10, in ibid., p. *7a;* also Amasa Keyes to Jer. Wadsworth, Aug. 3, in JW, box 129; John Ripley to Trumbull, July 10, and Cleveland to Trumbull, July 13, in 7*MHSC*, 2: 408–9, 410–11. Estimates as to the manpower Connecticut actually supplied the continental army come from *SOI*, pp. 124–36¡

59. Quote from the Report of a Court of Inquiry, July 30, 1779, in JT, 10: 60. See also Gustavus Erkelens to Jon. Trumbull, June 3, in JTP. For the progress of the depreciation, during the summer, see Peter Colt to Jer. Wadsworth, July 13 and Aug. 3, 10, 1779; Royal Flint to Wadsworth, July 20; Chaloner and White to Wadsworth, Aug. 21 and Sept. 8; Wadsworth to Jon. Trumbull, Nov. 1, in JW, boxes 128, 129.

60. Jacob Cuyler to Jer. Wadsworth, Sept. 7, 8, 1779; David Van Ness to Royal Flint, Sept. 29; and Hendrick Wyckoff to Flint, Sept. 15 and Oct. 21, in JW, box 129. New York tried to force the farmers to thresh by law; see Melancton Smith to Flint, Sept. 8, in ibid.

61. Hen. Champion to Jer. Wadsworth, Sept. 10, 1779, in ibid.

62. This may briefly have happened in Connecticut during the summer; see Royal Flint to Jer. Wadsworth, July 20, 1779, in ibid., box 128.

63. Hen. Laurens's Notes on Proceedings, June 12, 1779, in *LMCC*, 4: 259.

64. W. W. Hening, ed., *The Statutes at Large, Being a Collection of All the Laws of Virginia* (Richmond, 1809–23), 10: 50–55, 148; Instructions of the General Assembly of Maryland to Geo. Plater, Wm. Paca, Wm. Carmichael, and John Henry, in *JCC*, 14: 619–22; see also Jas. Forbes to Thos. S. Lee, Sept. 21, 1779, and Nath. Scudder to Nath. Peabody, Dec. 6, in *LMCC*, 4: 428, 533.

65. *SR*, 2: 413–14; Jon. Trumbull to Sam. Huntington, Nov. 2, 1779, in PCC, item 66, 2: 33–35.

66. Rog. Sherman to Jon. Trumbull, Dec. 30, 1779, in 7*MHSC*, 2: 463–64; *JCC*, 15: 1416; see also *ARC*, table 1.

67. *JCC*, 14: 650–51, 812.

68. Ibid., p. 1013. Sentiment for this action had been growing for some time; see Sam. Huntington to Oliver Wolcott, July 7, 1779, in *LMCC*, 4: 301.

69. *JCC*, 15: 1200, 1326, 1349.

70. Jer. Wadsworth to Jon. Trumbull, Nov. 1, 1779, in JW, box 129.

71. See *JCC*, 14: 561, 15: 1150; Hen. Laurens to Jon. Trumbull, Oct. 19, 1779, in 7*MHSC*, 2: 445.

72. Royal Flint to Jer. Wadsworth, July 30, 1779, and John Trumbull to Wadsworth, Sept. 16, in JW, boxes 128, 129.

73. *Boston Gazette*, Aug. 2, 1779; see also Evans 10228–29 and *SR*, 2: 568.

74. *NP*, June 22, 1779; *CJ*, Aug. 25 and Sept. 22; *CG*, July 28, Aug. 4,

and Sept. 8, 15; Peter Colt to Jer. Wadsworth, Sept. 16, 1779, in JW, box 129; Fairfield, Ex, July 1; Danbury, Ex, Aug. 9; Canterbury, Ex, Aug. 12; Norwalk, Ex, Aug. 16; Ashford, Ex, Sept. 14.

75. The Windham County Convention did call for a statewide convention to meet at Hartford in October; *CG*, Sept. 15, 1779, and Hartford finally chose delegates—*CC*, Sept. 28, and Hartford Town Votes, 2: 272—but attendance was so light that no action was taken; *CC*, Oct. 20.

76. Washington to the governors of New York, New Jersey, Pennsylvania, Connecticut, and Massachusetts, Oct. 14, 1779, in *WGW*, 16: 403–6; *JCC*, 15: 1108.

77. See Washington to d'Estaing, Sept. 13 and Oct. 14, 1779, in ibid., pp. 272–74, 409–14.

78. John Jeffery to Jer. Wadsworth, Oct. 5, 1779, in JW, box 129. Congress was considering a scheme to import foreign merchandise on public account; see *JCC*, 16: 1174–77.

79. *JCC*, 15: 1150.

80. *SR*, 2: 563–65, 568.

81. Ibid., p. 568 n.

82. Peter Colt to Jer. Wadsworth, Oct. 25, 28, 1779, in JW, box 129; de Valnais to Jon. Trumbull, Oct. 19, and Trumbull to de Valnais, Oct. 25, in 7*MHSC*, 2: 446, 448.

83. Peter Colt to Jer. Wadsworth, Oct. 4, 8, 14, 23, 1779, in JW, box 129.

84. *SR*, 2: 405–10.

85. John Chester to Jer. Wadsworth, Nov. 7, 1779, in JW, box 129; And. Ward to Jon. Trumbull, Nov. 24, in JT, 10: 244; *SR*, 2: 443.

86. See Peter Colt to Jer. Wadsworth, Nov. 21, 1779, in JW, box 129, and Colt to Jon. Trumbull, Dec. 19, in JT, 10: 287.

87. Ephr. Blaine to Jer. Wadsworth, Nov. 2, 1779, and Royal Flint to Wadsworth, Nov. 7, in JW, box 129.

88. See John Jeffery to Jer. Wadsworth, Aug. 19, 1779, and Peter Colt to Wadsworth, Sept. 23, 30, in ibid.; also, Nath. Greene to Wadsworth, Dec. 19, in ibid., box 130.

89. Peter Colt to Jer. Wadsworth, Sept. 4 and Oct. 12, 1779; Chaloner and White to Wadsworth, Sept. 17; Moses Hazen to Wadsworth, Sept. 18; John Jeffery to Wadsworth, Oct. 5; Royal Flint to Wadsworth, Nov. 7; Robt. L. Hooper to Wadsworth, Nov. 10 (copy); Wadsworth to Flint, Dec. 24, in ibid., boxes 129, 130.

90. Jer. Wadsworth to Jon. Trumbull, Nov. 1, 1779, and Peter Colt to Wadsworth, Nov. 21, in ibid., box 129.

91. See Washington to d'Estaing, Oct. 4, 1779, in *WGW*, 16: 410.

92. John Tyler to Jon. Trumbull, Oct. 28, 1779, in JT, 10: 196. It was clear in advance that the British were evacuating Newport; *CJ*, Oct. 13; Washington to the President of Congress, Oct. 21, in *WGW*, 17: 2; *CC*, Nov. 2. The British had begun fortifying New York in mid-August; see John Lloyd to Jer. Wadsworth, Aug. 18, 1779, in JW, box 129.

93. See Washington to d'Estaing, Sept. 13 and Oct. 4, 1779, in *WGW*, 16: 273, 411.

94. See Washington to d'Estaing, Oct. 4, 1779, and to Du Portail, Oct. 18, 1779, in ibid., pp. 412, 483.

95. Peter Colt to Jer. Wadsworth, Nov. 18, 24, 1779, in JW, box 129; also, John Tyler to Jon. Trumbull, Nov. 24, in JT, 10: 241.

96. Peter Colt to Jer. Wadsworth, Nov. 30, 1779, in JW, box 129; also, John Lloyd, Jr., to Wadsworth, Dec. 1, in ibid., box 130.

97. *SR*, 2: 562–63; Jon. Trumbull to Sam. Huntington, Dec. 13, 1779, in 7*MHSC*, 2: 458.

98. See Barn. Deane to Jer. Wadsworth, Dec. 2, 8, 1779, in JW, box 130.

99. Connecticut learned of Congress's scheme from Rog. Sherman to Jon. Trumbull, Dec. 20, 1779, in 7*MHSC*, 2: 464.

100. Hen. Champion to Jer. Wadsworth, Nov. 22 and Dec. 2, 1779, in JW, boxes 129, 130; also, Isaac Tichnor to Jacob Cuyler, Nov. 22 (enclosure in Cuyler to Wadsworth, Dec. 1); Wadsworth to Sam. Huntington, Dec. 31; Robt. Hoops to Royal Flint, Jan. 1, 1780, in ibid., box 130; Peter Colt to Jon. Trumbull, Dec. 19, in JT, 10:287.

101. Hen. Champion to Royal Flint, Dec. 27, 1779, and Jan. 13, 23, 1780, in JW, box 130; Rog. Sherman to Jon. Trumbull, Jan. 11, 1780, in 7*MHSC*, 3: 8.

102. *JCC*, 15: 1299–300; Jer. Wadsworth to Royal Flint, Dec. 14, 1779, in JW, box 130; also Robt. Throup to Wadsworth and John Chaloner to Wadsworth, Jan. 24 and Feb. 15, in ibid.

103. *JCC*, 8: 611, 690, 9: 809, 893, 964, 1044, 15: 1371–72.

104. Ibid., 16: 196–201.

105. See also Harold E. Selesky, "Patterns of Officeholding in the Connecticut General Assembly, 1725–1774," in George J. Willauer, Jr., ed., *A Lyme Miscellany, 1776–1976* (Middletown, Conn., 1977), pp. 179–83. Selesky notes that turnover rates varied from county to county and that some counties experienced considerably higher turnover rates than the general average; ibid., pp. 183–92.

106. Selesky, "Patterns of Officeholding," pp. 174–75, and his "Connecticut Goes to War: The Evolution of the Leadership Structure, 1740–1785" (Wesleyan University Honors Essay, 1972), passim, especially p. 24.

107. The relevant documents can be found in CARW, 1st ser., 13: 51–52.

108. Washington to Stephen Moylan, Nov. 27, 1779, in *WGW*, 17: 199–200.

109. Steph. Moylan to Washington, Jan. 17, 1780, in WP; Moylan to Jon. Trumbull, Jan. 26, in JT, 11: 44; Washington to Moylan, Dec. 20, 25, 1779, in *WGW*, 17: 291–92, 318. See also Washington to Trumbull, Dec. 17, 1780, in 5*MHSC*, 10: 219.

110. See Peter Colt to Jer. Wadsworth, June 16, 1779, in JW, box 128.

111. Jon. Trumbull to Steph. Moylan, n.d., in JT, 11: 33.

112. See *SOI*, pp. 92–109.

113. Jon. Trumbull to Washington, Nov. 5, 16, 1779, in JT, 10: 208, 227.

114. Washington to Jon. Trumbull, Nov. 20, 1779, and Washington to the President of Congress, Nov. 24, in *WGW*, 17: 146–47, 177–80; Oliver Wolcott to Trumbull, Nov. 30, 1779, in JT, 10: 252.

115. See John Mead to Jon. Trumbull, Dec. 27, 1779, and Jan. 6, 1780, in JT, 10: 241, 11: 6; also Wm. Ledyard to Trumbull, Apr. 19, in ibid., 11: 147; C. T. Atkinson, "British Forces in North America, 1774–1781: Their Distribution and Strength," *Journal for the Society of Army Historical Research* 16 (1937): 18–19.

116. Memorial dated Jan. 26, 1780, in CGAP. Samuel Whiting, a resident of the town, thought only a small minority had been involved in the plan to "treat" with Tryon, and that the incident's significance had been "much exaggerated." See Whiting to Jon. Trumbull, July 22, 1779, in JTP.

117. Jon. Trumbull to the memorialists of Stratford, n.d., in JT, 20: 229.

118. So strong had antimilitarism become that one state commissary even tried to use it in an attempt to protect a butcher from court-martial for embezzling the by-products of the slaughter. See New London Selectmen and Civil Authority to Jon. Trumbull, Nov. 19, 1779, and Edw. Hallam to Trumbull, Nov. 24, in ibid., 10: 230, 244; *SR*, 2: 442–43.

119. *A Discourse on the times* (Norwich, 1776), passim; Isaac Foster, *A discourse upon extortion* . . . (Hartford, 1777); Timothy Dwight, *A Sermon, preached at Stamford* . . . (Hartford, 1778), p. 15; Anonymous, *A Discourse on Daniel* vii 27 . . . (Norwich, 1777), p. 21; David Avery, *The Lord is to be praised* . . . (Norwich, 1778), pp. 12, 25, 37–40; Cyprian Strong, *God's care of the New England Colonies* . . . (Hartford, 1777), p. 16; Nicholas Street, *The American States acting over the part of the children of Israel in the Wilderness* . . . (New Haven, 1777), passim.

120. Street, *American States*, pp. 22, 24–25; Avery, *The Lord*, p. 36 n.; also, *CJ*, Aug. 3, 1780.

121. Documents relating to these incidents are in CARW, 1st ser., 14: 181–88, 19: 119–29. See also the case of Capt. David Barber, Lt. Silvanus Griswold, and Ens. Joab Griswold in ibid., 21: 186–212.

122. Street, *American States*, p. 28; Strong, *God's care*, p. 17; Avery, *The Lord*, p. 44; see also *CJ*, Sept. 16, 1778. On the rising incidence of violent crime, see *CJ*, Jan. 21, 1778, June 2, 1779, Apr. 20, 1780, Apr. 24, 1782.

123. *SR*, 2: 280–81; also CARW, 1st ser., 14: 110, 28, 29.

124. See CARW, 1st ser., 19: 111–18, 14: 110*b–c*.

125. Ibid., 14: 64.

126. See ibid., p. 148.

127. *SR*, 3: 5 n.

128. Peter Colt to Jer. Wadsworth, June 16, 1779, in JW, box 128. Wadsworth was subsequently reelected to the Council of Safety; *SR*, 2: 292.

129. *SR*, 2: 292, 294; CARW, 1st ser., 14: 149.

130. *CR*, 15: 136–37.

131. "A Freeman," in *CC*, Apr. 1 and May 20, 1776; Litchfield County Committees of Inspection, May 15, in 4*AA*, 6: 471–72, and *CC*, May 27; also, ibid., June 10; and "Marcus Brutus," in ibid., June 17. See also n. 134, below, and *CC*, Sept. 29, 1777.

132. Peter Colt to Jer. Wadsworth, Sept. 6, 1779, in JW, box 129. For the response of Wadsworth's group to Oliver Ellsworth's efforts at defending

Congress from criticism, see Colt to Wadsworth, Sept. 23, in ibid.; also, "A Friend to Truth and Fair Play," in *LMCC*, 4: 408–11; *CC*, Sept. 7, 1779. For Wadsworth's opinion of Roger Sherman, see his letter to Royal Flint, Jan. 4, 1780, in JW, box 130.

133. *SR*, 2: 264.

134. *CC*, June 17, 1776. A manuscript version dated Apr. 17, 1776, is in OW, vol. 1.

135. See CARW, 1st ser., 15: 39; John Chester to Jer. Wadsworth, Nov. 7, 1779, in JW, box 129.

136. *SR*, 3: 5; also CARW, 1st ser., 15: 329–31.

137. *SR*, 3: 5–6 n.

138. See David Humphreys to Jer. Wadsworth, Apr. 5, 1780, and Wadsworth to Jon. Trumbull, Mar. 30, in JW, box 130; Philip H. Jordan, Jr., "Connecticut Politics during the Revolution and Confederation, 1776–1789" (Ph.D. thesis, Yale University, 1962), pp. 109–10; Christopher Collier, *Roger Sherman's Connecticut* . . . (Middletown, Conn., 1971), pp. 179–80.

139. *JCC*, 16: 150; Sam. Huntington to Jon. Trumbull, Feb. 10, 1780, in JT, 11: 58.

140. Washington to Jon. Trumbull, Feb. 20, 1780, in *5MHSC*, 10: 155–57. The state government expected to be asked for more men; see CARW, 1st ser., 15: 295.

141. *SR*, 2: 435.

142. Ibid., pp. 452–53.

143. Ibid., pp. 453–55.

144. Ibid., pp. 473–77.

145. Jon. Trumbull to Hen. Laurens, Nov. 1, 1779, in *7MHSC*, 2: 450–51; also, Trumbull to Sam. Huntington, Dec. 13, in ibid., pp. 459–60; cf. Jon. Trumbull, Jr., to Huntington, Dec. 10, in JTjr, 2: 162.

146. *SR*, 2: 477–81.

147. Ibid., pp. 465–66.

148. *JCC*, 16: 200.

149. Ibid., pp. 206–7.

150. Ibid., pp. 262–66, quotes 263, 264; and from Rog. Sherman and Oliver Ellsworth to Jon. Trumbull, Mar. 20, 1780, in *7MHSC*, 3: 26. The plan seems to have originated with the New England members of Congress; John Collins to Nath. Greene, Mar. 21, in *LMCC*, 5: 90.

151. Rog. Sherman and Oliver Ellsworth to Jon. Trumbull, Mar. 20, 1780, in *7MHSC*, 2: 27.

152. *SR*, 2: 516–20. In addition, the £1 million loan was abandoned; ibid., p. 521.

153. Ibid., pp. 526–27.

154. Ibid., pp. 257–58.

155. *JCC*, 15: 1312.

156. Ibid., 16: 5.

157. Jon. Trumbull to the Connecticut Congressional delegates, Mar. 10, 1780, in *7MHSC*, 3: 18; Ephr. Blaine to Trumbull, Feb. 15, in JT, 11: 63.

158. See *SR*, 2: 521–26.

159. Ibid., pp. 456–58.

160. John Mead to Jon. Trumbull, May 9, 1780, and Gold S. Silliman to Trumbull, May 12, in JT, 11: 177, 183.

161. Peter Colt to Jon. Trumbull, Feb. 11, 1780, in JT, 11: 59; also Samuel Bishop to Trumbull, Mar. 28, in ibid., p. 120. See, for instance, the actions of Goshen, Ex, Mar. 23, 1780; East Windsor, Ex, Mar. 6; Canaan, Ex, Mar. 6; Bolton, Ex, Mar. 13; Canterbury, Ex, Mar. 14.

162. John Fitch to Jon. Trumbull, Apr. 10, 1780, in JT, 11: 133; Andrew Johnson's circular, May 8, and Johnson to Trumbull, May 12, in ibid., pp. 133, 174, 178.

163. *SOI*, pp. 160–70. During the same interval, thrity-three enlisted in the dragoons and artificers; *RCM*, pp. 273–94.

164. *SR*, 2: 452–54, 526–27; David Humphreys to Jer. Wadsworth, May 13, 1780, in JW, box 130. Recruits into the state regiments who equipped themselves were entitled to an encouragement amounting to one-third the bounty offered Continental recruits, but only Continental recruits received the congressional bounty.

165. *SR*, 3: 13; Jed. Huntington to Jon. Trumbull, Mar. 20, 1780, in JT, 11: 102.

166. Enoch Poor to Jon. Trumbull, Feb. 11, 1780, and Steph. Moylan to Trumbull, Feb. 24, in JT, 11: 60, 70.

167. Washington to Jon. Trumbull, May 26, 1780, in *5MHSC*, 10: 165–66.

168. Circular of the Committee of Congress, May 25, 1780, in JT, 11: 203.

169. Luzerne to Jon. Trumbull, May 17, 1780, and John Holker to Trumbull, May 17, in *7MHSC*, 3: 41–44, 44–46; Holker to Trumbull, Mar. 21 and May 12, in JT, 11: 107, 155; *JCC*, 15: 1372; Wm. Ledyard to Trumbull, May 16, in JT, 11: 187.

170. *JCC*, 17: 437.

171. See Jon. Trumbull to de Valnais, Oct. 25, 1779, in *7MHSC*, 2: 448.

172. Luzerne to Jon. Trumbull and John Holker to Trumbull, May 17, 1780, in ibid., 3: 43–44, 45; de Corny to Trumbull, June 19, in JT, 12: 29; Sam. Huntington to Trumbull, June 5, 10, in ibid., 11: 240, 266; *JCC*, 15: 11, 467, 496–97; *SR*, 3: 110.

173. Jer. Wadsworth to Nath. Greene, July 3, 1780, in JW, FC; the first entry in Wadsworth's letter book relating to the French contract is June 23. Agreement had been reached by June 21; see Wadsworth to Lafayette, June 21, in ibid., box 151, letter book J. Noah Webster, Jr., alluded to the Assembly's refusal to supply the French in an essay signed "Honorius," in *CC*, Sept. 2, 1783.

174. Jed. Huntington to Jer. Wadsworth, May 5, 1780, in *CHSC*, 20: 150.

175. *SOI*, pp. 164–65.

176. Circular of the Committee of Congress, June 1, 1780, in JT, 11: 237.

177. See Washington to Jos. Reed, May 28, 1780, in *WGW*, 18: 434–35.

178. Washington to Jon. Trumbull, June 2, 1780, in *5MHSC*, 10: 168–70.

179. *SR*, 3: 27–28.

180. Ibid., pp. 29–31.

181. Ibid., pp. 24–25, 39.
182. See *SHP*, p. 292; also Washington to Jon. Trumbull, June 20, 1780, in *5MHSC*, 10: 177–78.
183. Sam. H. Parsons to the Committee of Congress, June 24, 1780, in *SHP*, pp. 292–95; Washington to Parsons, June 29, in *WGW*, 19: 94; *SR*, 3: 117, 119–21. The exhortations of Congress and the commander-in-chief seem to have had the necessary effect; see Sam. Huntington circular, June 15, 1780, in *JT*, 12: 15; Washington to Jon. Trumbull, June 27, 30, in *5MHSC*, 10: 180–82.
184. In *5MHSC*, 10: 177.
185. Robt. Howe to Jon. Trumbull, June 19, 1780, in *JT*, 12: 24.
186. *SR*, 3: 109–10; Welles's men were to be replaced by detachments from Bezaleel Beebe's state regiment.
187. Ibid., p. 112.
188. Robt. Howe to Jon. Trumbull, June 23, 24, 1780, in *JT*, 12: 38, 43; Washington to Trumbull, June 27, in *5MHSC*, 10: 180; also, Gold S. Silliman to Trumbull, June 28, in *JT*, 12: 58.
189. See Washington to Nath. Greene, July 19, 1780, in *WGW*, 19: 211–12; *AR*, p. 201 and n. American intelligence exaggerated the threat; Wm. Ledyard to Jon. Trumbull and Trumbull to Wm. Greene, July 24, in *JT*, 12: 128, 129.
190. Wm. Heath to Jon. Trumbull, July 26, 1780, and Wm. Greene to Trumbull, July 26, in *JT*, 12: 115, 147; *SR*, 3: 138–139.
191. John Douglas to Jon. Trumbull, Aug. 3, 1780; Nath. Greene to Trumbull, Aug. 1; also, Rochambeau to Trumbull, July 30; and Wm. Heath to Trumbull, Aug. 11, in *JT*, 12: 188, 185, 170, 212.
192. See Eliphalet Lockwood to Gold S. Silliman, June 13, 15, 1780; Silliman to Jon. Trumbull, June 30 and July 13; Matt. Griswold to Trumbull, Aug. 9, in ibid., pp. 9, 13, 90, 204; see also Silliman to Trumbull, June 4 and Sept. 23, in ibid., 11: 239, 13: 28. At some posts the provision problem went back to 1779; see Matt. Mead to Jon. Trumbull, Oct. 24, in *JTP*.
193. *SR*, 3: 29, 149; Gold S. Silliman to Jon. Trumbull, June 26, 1780, in *JT*, 12: 50; also Bez. Beebe to Trumbull, June 25, in ibid., p. 46. Lesser's figures show Beebe's regiment at 248 or 45 percent of authorized strength and Welles's at 192 or 35 percent at the end of August; *SOI*, p. 176.
194. *SOI*, pp. 172–76; see also Gold S. Silliman to Jon. Trumbull, July 7, 1780, and Oliver Wolcott to Trumbull, Aug. 17, in *JT*, 12: 78, 231. Late enlistments account for the discrepancy between the numbers used here and those appearing in Table 4.
195. John Trumbull to Washington, Aug. 31, 1780, in *5MHSC*, 10: 202; *SOI*, p. 177. Evidence that the Connecticut River contingent was more substantial than that ordered to the westward is in *SR*, 3: 127, 131; see also ibid., p. 135, and Hez. Wyllys to Trumbull, Aug. 5, in *JT*, 12: 191.
196. *CARW*, 1st ser., 19: 108–18.
197. See memo in *JT*, 13: 82.
198. *CARW*, 1st ser., 19: 134–40.
199. Ibid., pp. 100–104, 130–32, 145.
200. Middletown Town Votes and Proprietors' Records, 2: 390; Guilford Town Records: Town Meetings, 2: 305–6.
201. Milford Town Records, 2: 95–96.

202. New Haven 'Town Records, 1769–1807, pp. 112–13.

203. Hartford Town Votes, 2: 277–78; Haddam Town Records, 2: 119.

204. Cf. Returns in JT, 24: 127*a–v*, with 135*a–g*.

205. Ibid., p. 140.

206. Wm. Worthington to Jon. Trumbull, July 2, 1780, and Sam. H. Parsons to Trumbull, July 3, in JT, 12: 67, 71; see also Hen. Champion to Trumbull, July 30, in ibid., p. 172. Parsons complained bitterly at the delays encountered in assembling the six-month men; Parsons to Trumbull, July 14, and to Gold S. Silliman, July 25, in ibid., pp. 91, 142. See also Silliman to the colonels of the Fourth Brigade, July 15, in ibid., p. 93.

207. Washington to Lafayette, Aug. 3, 1780; to Luzerne, Aug. 4; to the President of Congress, Aug. 20; to Rochambeau, Aug. 21; to Jos. Reed, Aug. 26; and to Jas. Bowdoin, Aug. 28, in WGW, 19: 314, 320, 398–99, 403, 441, 454–55; also, Wm. Ledyard to Jon. Trumbull, Aug. 5, 8, in JT, 12: 190, 196.

208. Washington to the Committee of Cooperation, Aug. 17, 1780; to Jos. Reed, Aug. 20; to the President of Congress, Aug. 20, 24, 26, in WGW, 19: 393, 399, 403–4, 437, 450; also, Washington to Jon. Trumbull, Aug. 22, in ibid., p. 427.

209. Washington to the President of Congress, Aug. 20, 1780, in ibid., p. 404; Circular to the States, Aug. 27, in ibid., p. 462.

PART IV: VICTORY

1. Cf. Washington to the President of Congress, Sept. 8, 15, 1780, in WGW, 20: 15, 22.

2. "Summary of a Conversation between His Excellency General Washington, the Count de Rochambeau, and the Chevalier de Ternay," Sept. 22, 1780, in ibid., p. 80; also, "Copie de l'instruction secrete pour le sr. comte de Rochambeau," Mar. 9, in HPF, 5: 327.

3. Washington to the comte de Guichen, Sept. 12, 1780, in WGW, 20: 39–43; also Washington to Lafayette, Dec. 14, and to the comte de Rochambeau and chevalier de Ternay, Dec. 15, in HPF, 5: 473–74, 480–84.

4. Ben. Arnold, "Address to the Inhabitants of America," Oct. 7, 1780, and Proclamation, Oct. 20, in Evans 16701, 16789.

5. Washington first discounted the threat Arnold posed—see his letter to the President of Congress, Oct. 15, 1780, in WGW, 20: 189—but he changed his mind after the January mutinies; see Washington to John Laurens, Jan. 15, 1781, in ibid., 21: 107. British intelligence suggested popular dissatisfaction with the French alliance was almost as great as the discontent of the army; see DAR, 16: 2542*i*.

6. Cf. "Answers to Queries of Comte de Rochambeau and Chevalier de Ternay," Sept. 22, 1780, in WGW, 20: 77.

7. Washington to John Laurens, Jan. 15, 1781, in ibid., 21: 106.

8. Oliver Ellsworth to Jon. Trumbull, June 6, 1780; Trumbull to Sam. Huntington, July 10; Rog. Sherman to Trumbull, July 22; and Huntington to Trumbull, July 22, in 7*MHSC*, 3: 46–47, 60, 79, 82.

9. For a schedule of the larger orders, see ASP,F, 1: 59–62; see also Jas. Madison to Joseph Jones, Nov. 21, 1780, and Jas. Duane to Washington, Dec. 9, in LMCC, 5: 453, 478.

10. Washington to John Laurens, Jan. 15, 1781, in *WGW*, 21: 106; John Sullivan's Proposal for a Bank, Nov. 1780, in *LMCC*, 5: 467–72; also, Sullivan to Washington, Jan. 29, 1781, in ibid., p. 548.

11. *JCC*, 20: 545–48. The bank was not successfully capitalized until a specie subsidy was received from France; see *PRM*, 1: 67, 2: 244n., 262 n.

12. Arnold Witridge, *Rochambeau* (New York, 1965), p. 103.

13. *JCC*, 18: 1138, 1141; instructions to John Laurens, Dec. 23, 1780, and additional instructions, Dec. 27, in *RDC*, 4: 205–6, 212–3.

14. Washington to John Laurens, Jan. 15, 1781, in *WGW*, 21: 107–8.

15. Edward S. Corwin, *French Policy and the American Alliance of 1778* (Princeton, N.J., 1916), p. 292.

16. Congress helped arrange the compromise; cf. *JCC*, 17: 806–8; cf. also Jos. Jones to Washington, Sept. 6, 1780, and Jas. Madison to Jones, Dec. 19, in *LMCC*, 5: 364, 491, xxxii–xl; Thos. Jefferson to Sam. Huntington, Jan. 17, 1781, in Julian P. Boyd, ed., *The Papers of Thomas Jefferson* (Princeton, N.J., 1950–), 4: 386–88.

17. *JCC*, 19: 138–39, 186. The Confederation was formally implemented on Mar. 1, 1781; see ibid., pp. 208–23.

18. Jas. Duane to Washington, Jan. 29, 1781, in *LMCC*, 5: 552; also, John Matthews to Washington, Jan. 30, and Thos. McKean to Thomas Collins, Feb. 3, in ibid., pp. 554, 557.

19. *JCC*, 19: 102–3, 105, 112, 124–25.

20. Ibid., pp. 51, 71, 126; Jas. Duane to Washington, Jan. 29, 1781, in *LMCC*, 5: 551; also Ezekiel Cornell to Wm. Greene, Jan. 29, in ibid., p. 549 n.

21. John Laurens to the President of Congress, Sept. 2, 1781, in *RDC*, 4: 687.

22. Laurens is not mentioned in Jonathan R. Dull's canvass of those most responsibile for Yorktown; cf. *The French Navy and American Independence* (Princeton, N.J., 1975), pp. 247–48.

23. See John Laurens to Washington, Mar. 24, 1781, in *RDC*, 4: 327.

24. Laurens acted according to the instructions of Dec. 27, 1780, in ibid., p. 212. The task proved to be a difficult one; see John Laurens to the President of Congress, Sept. 2, 1781, in ibid., pp. 687–89.

25. Robt. Morris Diary, Sept. 1–5, 1781, and Morris to Philip Audibert, Sept. 6, in *PRM*, 2: 172–73, 175 n., 196–97.

26. Corwin, *French Policy*, p. 312; William C. Stinchcombe, *The American Revolution and the French Alliance* (Syracuse, N.Y., 1969), p. 140.

27. Dull, *French Navy*, p. 247; see also Jer. Wadsworth to Moses Talcott, Dec. 16, 1781, in JW, box 132.

CHAPTER SIX: BANKRUPTCY

1. See Washington to the President of Congress, Sept. 15, 1780; Washington to John Matthews and to Jas. Duane, Oct. 4; Washington to John Cadwaladar, Oct. 5; Washington's Circular to the States, Oct. 18, in *WGW*, 20: 49–50, 113–16, 117–18, 120–23, 204–11; *JCC*, 17: 895. The Convention of the New England States and New York, meeting at Hartford in November 1780, also endorsed the raising of a permanent army; *SR*, 3: 567–70.

2. *SR*, 3: 174–75.

3. Ibid., p. 176; *JCC*, 17: 1011–18. Wheat was not part of Congress's requisition, but it was needed for the state troops.

4. *SR*, 3: 238–39, erroneously republishes the sixpenny requisition of October as the November requisition. The error can be detected by reference to ibid., p. 522. The towns complying with the tax refer to it as the one-and-a-half penny tax; see Branford Town Records, 1691–1788, p. 338; Milford Town Records, 2: 100; New Haven Town Records, 1769–1807, p. 119; Hartford Town Votes, 2: 282.

5. *SR*, 3: 248. The legislature did appoint an agent to "purchase salt pork" from the towns.

6. See Gold S. Silliman to Jon. Trumbull, June 4, 1780; Eliph. Lockwood to Silliman, June 13; Hen. Champion to Trumbull, July 30; Wm. Ledyard to Trumbull, Aug. 11, in JT, 11: 239, 12: 9, 172, 210; Memorial of Levi Welles and Bez. Beebe, Nov. ?, in CARW, 1st ser., 19: 302; Hen. Champion to Jer. Wadsworth, Aug. 4, in JW, box 130.

7. See Royal Flint to Jer. Wadsworth, July 4, 1780, in JW, box 130.

8. Hen. Champion to Jon. Trumbull, July 30, 1780, in JT, 12: 172; Chauncey Whittelsey to Trumbull, Nov. 18, in ibid., 13: 142, reported state currency had depreciated to 6.7:1 nominal value. New emission continentals had a value of 1:2.5 in relation to old continentals at this time; see Trumbull to Robt. Morris, Nov. 7, 1781, in ibid., 15: 242. Trumbull was referring back to the autumn of 1780; see *SR*, 3: 179, 189.

9. Jon. Trumbull to Robt. Morris, Nov. 7, 1781, in JT, 15: 242; Resolution of the General Assembly, May 1782, in CARW, 1st ser., 22: 259; *ASP*, *F*, 1: 58.

10. See Jer. Wadsworth to de Corny, July 15, 1780, in JW,FC; also, Jon. Trumbull to John Holker, Aug. 21, in JT, 20: 269*a–b*.

11. Royal Flint to Jon. Trumbull, July 17, 1780, in 7*MHSC*, 3: 65–67.

12. See *SR*, 3: 114; the first entry in Jer. Wadsworth's letter book relating to the French contract is dated June 23 in JW,FC.

13. Jon. Trumbull to John Holker, Aug. 21, 1780, in JT; 20: 269*a–b*.

14. For the mutiny and Washington's dependence on Connecticut for meat, see Washington to Jon. Trumbull, May 16, 1780, and to Hen. Champion, May 26, in 5*MHSC*, 10: 165–66. For the difficulties encountered by Wadsworth, see Jer. Wadsworth to Nath. Greene, July 3; Wadsworth to Royal Flint, July 6; Wadsworth to Hen. Champion, July 12, 15, in JW, FC; also, Benj. Talmadge to Wadsworth, July 14, in JW, box 130.

15. Jer. Wadsworth to Nath. Greene, July 3, 1780; Wadsworth to Oliver Phelps, July 8, 15; Wadsworth to de Corny, July 16, and to the Massachusetts Council, July 20, in JW, FC.

16. Royal Flint to Jer. Wadsworth, July 17, 1780, in 7*MHSC*, 3: 66.

17. The contract is dated July 23, 1780, in JT, 12: 126; see also the contract between Benoît de Tarlé and John Baptiste, Arthur Vermonet, and Thomas Walker, July 29, in ibid., p. 164. For background material on Blakely and Delano, see *SR*, 1: 15, 2: 152, 533.

18. The reluctance of American producers to sell predated the contracts because the French were purchasing in neighboring jurisdictions with hard money; see Jer. Wadsworth to Nath. Greene, July 11, 1780, in JW,FC; Royal

Flint to Wadsworth, July 21, in JW, box 130; also, Oliver Phelps to Wadsworth, July 17, in ibid. For the shortages see Ephr. Blaine to Sam. Huntington, Oct. 17, in JT, 13: 81.

19. *SR*, 3: 150, 562; Governor Trumbull's Proclamation of Aug. 25, 1780, in Evans 43782; Jer. Wadsworth to John Carter, Nov. 4, in JW,FC.

20. Washington's Circular to the States, Aug. 27, 1780, in *WGW*, 19: 449.

21. *SR*, 3: 157, 162, 163.

22. See Blakely's proposal, probably of mid-August, in JT, 12: 222.

23. Jer. Wadsworth to Jon. Trumbull, Oct. 7, 1780, in JW,FC; also, Wadsworth to Trumbull, Oct. 29, in JW, box 131.

24. Tarlé to Thos. Cushing and Robt. T. Paine, Aug. 12, 1780, in JT, 12: 230; Jas. Bowdoin to Jon. Trumbull, Sept. 30, in ibid., 13: 44.

25. Jer. Wadsworth to Jon. Trumbull, Oct. 7, 1780, in JW,FC; also Wadsworth and John Carter to de Corny, Aug. 12, and Wadsworth to de Corny, Oct. 16, in ibid. A short sketch of Carter can be found in Robert A. East, *Business Enterprise in the American Revolutionary Era* (New York, 1938), pp. 90–91. See also Wadsworth's orders to Wm. Hooker and Thos. Lewis, Oct. 23, 1780, in JW, box 131.

26. Jer. Wadsworth and John Carter to Tarlé, Oct. 14, 1780, and Wadsworth to Carter, Nov. 3, 4, in JW,FC; Carter to Wadsworth, Nov. 25, in JW, box 131.

27. Jer. Wadsworth to Jon. Trumbull, Oct. 29, 1780, in JW, box 131; *SR*, 3: 221. The French were reluctant to break contracts that were being observed; see Tarlé to Carter and Wadsworth, Oct. 12, in JW, box 131.

28. Jer. Wadsworth to John Carter, Oct. 29 and Nov. 4, 20, 1780, in JW,FC; Royal Flint to Wadsworth, Nov. 4, in JW, box 131.

29. See Thos. Russell to Jer. Wadsworth, Aug. 21, 1780, in JW, box 130; Wadsworth to John Carter, Feb. 14, 1781, in JW,FC; John Chaloner to Wadsworth, Feb. 10, in JW, box 131.

30. Jer. Wadsworth to John Carter, Dec. 1, 1780, in JW,FC.

31. Jer. Wadsworth to Joshua(?) Huntington, Oct. 21, 1780, in JW, box 131, and the contract between Wadsworth and Carter and Morgan Lewis and Dan Parker, Feb. 9, in ibid.

32. John Carter to Jer. Wadsworth, Feb. 28, 1781, in JW,FC.

33. See Nathaniel Gorham to Jon. Trumbull, Aug. 15, 1780, in JT, 12: 226. The seizure of part of the Quebec fleet in the late summer of 1780 produced an influx of coveted European goods in eastern Massachusetts; see the exaggerated report in ibid., 13: 18; Washington to the President of Congress, Sept. 9, 10, and to Jas. Bowdoin, Sept. 12, in *WGW*, 20: 21, 23–24, 35. Geo. Germain to Hen. Clinton, Sept. 22, and to the Lords of Treasury, Nov. 1, in *DAR*, 18: 174–75, 223. See also *SR*, 3: 310.

34. See Peter Colt to Jer. Wadsworth, Feb. 22, 1781, in JW, box 131. Massachusetts withdrew $29 million of Continental money during this period; see 7*MHSC*, 3: 345 n. See also William B. Norton, "Paper Currency in Massachusetts during the Revolution," *NEQ* 7 (1934): 60.

35. Collectors seem to have permitted this even after the legislature forbade it; see *ARC*, p. 48.

36. The legislature authorized the reissue of the state currency during its

October 1780 session; see *SR*, 3: 174. Orders or warrants on the treasury were negotiable and circulated, though at greater discount than the state currency. They first became current in 1779 when demands on the treasury regularly began to exceed supplies; see Daniel Rodman and Samuel Woodbridge to Jon. Trumbull, Nov. 25, 1782, in *JT*, 17: 175. In January 1780 the legislature used the device of Pay-Table orders to settle with the Continental line, and a full description of them can be found in *SR*, 3: 21–23.

37. The report is appended to *ARC*, p. 46ff.; the schedule of taxes appears in table 1.

38. *SR*, 1: 471.

39. *ARC*, p. 48. Abatements for damage sustained during British raids did not become customary until taxation became oppressive in 1780; see *SR*, 3: 46–51, 187, 269–70, 321, 435–40, 524–25, 540–41.

40. *SR*, 3: 19, 321–22. The influx of refugees from Long Island did not at first affect abatements because they weren't considered inhabitants and did not have to hand in tax lists. As time went on and pressure on resources increased, listers began to require lists of them. At first the legislature answered their pleas for relief by granting abatements (2: 355); later they permitted them to return to the island (3: 64, 70, 75, 77–78).

41. *CR*, 13: 514; *ARC*, p. 48. Benjamin Gale, *Brief, decent, but free remarks* . . . (Hartford, 1782), pp. 17–21, drew attention to the power of the civil authority and selectmen to grant abatements.

42. See *JT*, 24: 105.

43. *SR*, 3: 45, 155; Selectmen and Authority of Newtown to Jon. Trumbull, Aug. 7, 1780, in *JT*, 12: 194; Oliver Wolcott to Trumbull, Aug. 17, in ibid., p. 231.

44. *ARC*, p. 48.

45. Before the tax reform of 1779, polls accounted on average for 34 percent of the list. The cohort between sixteen and twenty-one comprised about 16 percent of the polls; see *JT*, 24: 52–56, 99–104. In 1781 "E. W." (Erastus Wolcott) claimed the reform had reduced the proportion of the tax borne by polls only 1.7 percent, from 33.7 percent to 32 percent; see *CG*, Sept. 7, 1781.

46. *ARC*, table 1; Rog. Sherman to Jon. Trumbull, Dec. 30, 1779, in *7MHSC*, 2: 464.

47. *ARC*, tables 2 and 8.

48. *JT*, 24: 84*a–b*.

49. See, for instance, Guilford Town Records, Town Meetings, 2: 307; Saybrook Town Records, Town Meeting of Nov. 14, 1780; Killingworth Town Book, p. 52; Branford Town Records, 1691–1788, 341; Haddam Town Records, 2: 120; Middletown Votes and Proprietors' Records, 1735–98, 2: 391–92; Milford Town Records, 2: 96; New Haven Town Records, 1769–1807, p. 113; Hartford Town Votes, 2: 280; Lyme, Ex, Nov. 16, 1780; Francis O. Allen, *The History of Enfield* (Lancaster, Pa., 1900), 1: 458.

50. See Wm. Ledyard to Jon. Trumbull, Jan. 18, 1781, in *JT*, 14: 44; *SR*, 3: 292.

51. Washington to Jon. Trumbull, Apr. 10, 1781, in *5MHSC*, 10: 234–35; *SR*, 3: 361–62; Ralph Pomeroy Circular to the selectmen of various [Connecticut] towns, Apr. 13, 14, in WP; also, Pomeroy to Nathaniel Stevens, Apr. 16, and Timothy Pickering to Tench Tilghman, Apr. 29, in ibid.; Washington to Sam. H. Parsons, Apr. 30, in *WGW*, 20: 10.

52. Allen, *Enfield*, 1: 459; Ashford, Ex, Jan. 15, 1781; Bolton, Ex, Dec. 4, 1780.

53. See Canaan, Ex, Jan. 15, 1781. Towns such as Guilford authorized a special committee to pay whatever was necessary to collect the provisions; see Guilford Town Records, Town Meetings, 2: 308–14.

54. Hartford Town Votes, 2: 282; Middletown Votes 1735–98, 2: 400; Milford Town Records, 2: 97; New Haven Town Records, 1769–1807, p. 115; Guilford Town Records; Town Meetings, 2: 319; Woodbury, Ex, Nov. 20, 1780; Canterbury, Ex, Feb. 1, 1781; Canaan, Ex, Apr. 3; Fairfield, Ex, Mar. 27; Goshen, Ex, Mar. 22.

55. *SR*, 3: 312–13.

56. *JCC*, 11: 539; 18: 959–60, rank and file.

57. Washington's Circular to the States, Oct. 18, 1780, in *WGW*, 20: 204–10.

58. Guilford Town Records, Town Meetings, 2: 308, 315, 317; Branford Town Records, 1691–1788, p. 340; Middletown Votes, 2: 400; Milford Town Records, 2: 98–100.

59. See Danbury, Ex, Dec. 11, 1780.

60. See Bolton, Ex, Dec. 26, 1780; East Haddam Town Records, 1766–1822, p. 67ff.; Colchester, Ex, Dec. 18, 1780. Some came to the decision later than others; Woodbury, Ex, Sept. 6, 1781.

61. James A. Henretta, "Families and Farms: *Mentalité* in Pre-industrial America," *WMQ*, 3rd ser. 35 (1978): 6–9.

62. Haddam Town Records, 2: 120–21, 122, 124.

63. John Mead to Jon. Trumbull, Sept. 23, 1780, in *JT*, 13: 27; also Gold S. Silliman to Trumbull, Sept. 23 and Oct. 6, 13, 26, in ibid., pp. 28, 56, 69, 114.

64. SR, 3: 184, 248–49, 239.

65. Gold S. Silliman to Jon. Trumbull, Jan. 5, 1781, and Brigade Orders, Jan. 5, in JT, 14: 12–13.

66. *Articles of the Associated Loyalists . . .* (n.p., 1780), broadside in Evans 43764, 43933. For background, see *DAR*, 16: 127, 535, 1904, 1912, 2749, 19: 74, 106, 196.

67. *SHP*, pp. 327–28; also, Sam. H. Parsons to Wm. Heath, Jan. 25, 1781, in ibid., pp. 330–32.

68. Steph. St. John to Gold S. Silliman, Jan. 8, 1781, copy, in *JT*, 14: 20; also, Authority and Selectman of Norwalk to Jon. Trumbull, Jan. 19, in ibid., p. 48; David Austin and Tim. Jones to Trumbull, Feb. 4, and Edw. Russell to Trumbull, Feb. 7, in ibid., pp. 81, 109; also, Authority and Selectmen of Stratford to Trumbull, Mar. 31, in ibid., p. 167.

69. Gold S. Silliman to Jon. Trumbull, Jan. 20, 1781, in ibid., p. 53. Also Silliman to Ludlow, Sept. 23, 1780, in ibid., 13: 26; Silliman to Trumbull, Dec. 8 and Jan. 9, 1781, in ibid., p. 119, 14: 22; Silliman to Ludlow, Jan. 12, in ibid., p. 28; Ludlow to Silliman, Jan. 19, in ibid., p. 150.

70. *SR*, 3: 239, 317–19; also, 2: 456–59.

71. Ibid., 3: 235–36.

72. Ibid., pp. 307–8.

73. *CJ*, May 17, 1781; Steph. St. John to Jon. Trumbull, July 7, 1781, in JT, 14: 327. St. John was first paroled—see his letter to Trumbull, June 21, in ibid., pp. 305a–c—but the Board of Loyalists ordered him imprisoned

in June; St. John to the Board of Associated Loyalists, June 30, in ibid., p. 317. The board had larger objectives in mistreating him; see St. John to Trumbull, July 10, in ibid., p. 333. For the resolution of the controversy, see *SR*, 3: 475–76.

74. *CJ*, July 26, 1781; *SR*, 3: 377.

75. Washington to Jon. Trumbull, May 24 and June 15, 1781, in *5MHSC*, 10: 240, 242.

76. Thaddeus Betts, Eliph. Lockwood, Clapp Raymond, and Mejah Betts to Jon. Trumbull, Aug. 22, 1781, in JT, 15: 66*b*.

77. Extrapolated from Washington to Jon. Trumbull, June 25 and Aug. 2, 1781, in *5MHSC*, 10: 243, 250; *SOI*, pp. 194–205.

78. These inferences are drawn from *SOI*, pp. 206, 210; also JT, 24: 23*a*, 157, 166, 169.

79. Washington to Jon. Trumbull, May 24, 1781, in *5MHSC*, 10: 239.

80. See Jon. Trumbull to Thos. Chittenden, July 11, 1781, in JT, 20: 306; also, *SR*, 3; 475; Derby, Ex, Mar. 11, 1782; also, Fairfield, Ex, Mar. 27, 1781.

81. There were exceptions; see Ashford, Ex, Jan. 15, 1781; Colchester, Ex, May 4; Goshen, Ex, Feb. 15; Waterbury, Ex, Feb. 1, 15.

82. *SR*, 3: 390.

83. John Douglas to Jon. Trumbull, July 14, 1781, in JT, 15: 10; Selah Hart to Trumbull, n.d. (end of July?), ibid., p. 46.

84. See JT, 24: 135*a–g*; cf. ibid., pp. 127*a–u*, 140.

85. See *SR*, 3: 46–51, 187–88, 321, 323, 389, 4: 67, 178–82, for abatements granted on the various lists.

86. The censuses appear in *CR*, 14: 483–92; JT, 24: 178. A summary of the 1782 census was published under the title, *A return of the numbers of inhabitants in the State of Connecticut . . .* (n.p., 1782), in Evans 44184.

87. Edwin Hall, *The Ancient Historical Records of Norwalk, Conn. . . .* (New York, 1847), p. 140; Danbury, Ex, June 10, 1781, Mar. 6, 1782; Saybrook Town Records, July 17, 1781.

88. *SR*, 3: 462–63.

89. Return of Col. Samuel Canfield's regiment, Sept. 15, 1781, in JT; 24: 32*a*. For Norwalk, for instance, see Eli Lockwood and Uriah Raymond to Jon. Trumbull, Aug. 27, in ibid., 15: 77. The coastal towns were not heavily represented in the three-month detachment, and New Haven even succeeded in getting itself exempted; *SR*, 3: 465. Washington to Jon. Trumbull, Aug. 2, 1781, in *5MHSC*, 10: 250, Canfield to Trumbull, Aug. 2, in JT, 14: 328; Washington's Circular to the New England States, Aug. 2, in *WGW*, 22: 451–52.

90. *SR*, 2: 8.

91. Ibid., pp. 151, 240, 291, 385. See Memorial of the Officers of the Continental line to the Council of Safety, April 21, 1781, in JTP.

92. *SR*, 3: 384–86.

93. *ARC*, table 1.

94. See Returns in JT, 24: 183–84.

95. Washington to Jon. Trumbull, Apr. 12, 1777, in *5MHSC*, 10: 55.

96. The difficulties in procuring intelligence in this way were chronicled in Washington to Lord Stirling, Oct. 21 and Nov. 19, 1778, in *WGW*, 13: 120, 284; Washington to Wm. Livingston, Dec. 16, and to Lord Stirling, Jan.

8, 1779, in ibid., pp. 404, 496; Washington to Jos. Reed, Feb. 12, in ibid., 14: 101; Jon. Trumbull to Washington, Dec. 27, in 5*MHSC*, 10: 150–51; Sam. H. Parsons to Washington, Dec. 16, in *SHP*, p. 274. Nonetheless, Washington felt the benefits outweighed the disadvantages; see his letter to Trumbull, Jan. 14, 1780, in 5*MHSC*, 10: 154–55; also, his reply to Parsons, Dec. 18, 1779, in *SHP*, p. 275.

97. Jer. Wadsworth to Jon. Trumbull, Apr. 6, 1779, in 7*MHSC*, 2: 395; John Shipman to Trumbull, Jan. 13, 1778, in JT, 8: 43*a*. The depreciation of the new emission currency was also attributed to the illicit trade; Steph. St. John to Trumbull, July 3, 1781, in ibid., 12: 69.

98. Selectmen of Stratford to Jon. Trumbull and Thad. Betts to Trumbull, Jan. 21, 1778, in JT, 8: 51*a–b*, 51*c*; Thad. Burr to Trumbull, Jan. 22, in ibid., pp. 52*a–b*; Thos. Mansfield and Ephraim Humaston to Trumbull, Apr. 21, 1779, in ibid., 9: 180*a–b*; Samuel Lee, Jr. to Trumbull, June 13, 1781, in ibid., 14: 285.

99. *SR*, 1: 513, 517, 578, 2: 324, 440, 450–52, 502, 3: 13–14, 95, 172.

100. Gold S. Silliman to Jon. Trumbull, May 9, 1778, in JT, 8: 129; John Shipman to Trumbull, Mar. 2, 1779, and Wm. Worthington to Trumbull, June 29, in ibid., 10: 69, 256; Eli Lockwood to Silliman, June 13, 1780, in ibid., 12: 9; Saybrook Committee to Trumbull, Apr. 26, 1782, in ibid., 16: 103; Benjamin and Amos Mead to Trumbull, July 2, in ibid., 17: 6.

101. See Gold S. Silliman to Jos. Fish, Apr. 13, 1777, in SFC, box 2; also, Edw. Russell to Jon. Trumbull, Feb. 2, 1781, in JT, 14: 109; Silliman to Trumbull, June 20 and July 13, 1778, in ibid., 8: 145*a–c*, 159.

102. *SR*, 1: 514, 2: 163, 182, 213, 216, 230, 234, 341, 543.

103. Ibid., 2: 76–77, 113, 115, 150, 166.

104. Ibid., pp. 397–98.

105. Ibid., p. 504.

106. See Gold S. Silliman to Jon. Trumbull, Apr. 30, 1778, in JT, 8: 123; also petitions of Capt. Seth Holmes's company for his removal, Aug. 11, 1777, in ibid., 7: 16. Some disloyal elements had left in the early phase of the war, responding to British recruiting; see And. Adams to Trumbull, Dec. 6, 1776, in ibid., 5: 272; Autobiography of Stephen Jarvis in New York Historical Society.

107. The process was noticeable as early as 1777; see John Mead to Jon. Trumbull, Oct. 24, 1777, in JT, 7: 150*a–d*; Gold S. Silliman to Trumbull, June 20 and July 13, 1778, in ibid., 8: 145, 159; Mead to Trumbull, June 17, 1779, in ibid., 9:244, and Noadiah Hooker to Trumbull, June 29, in ibid., pp. 257*a–b*; Eli Mygatt to Trumbull, Apr. 19, 1780, in ibid., 11: 145; Mead to Trumbull, May 9, in ibid., p. 177; Gold S. Silliman to Trumbull, June 4, 26, in ibid., p. 239, 12: 50.

108. See "Report on the Past and Present Situation on the Western Frontier of the State," in ibid., 15: 304.

109. Gold S. Silliman to Jon. Trumbull, around June 6, 1780, in ibid., 11: 253; Levi Welles to Trumbull, Aug. 11, in ibid., 12: 202; John Mead to Silliman, Sept. 1, 8, in ibid., pp. 266, 280; Silliman to Trumbull, Oct. 26, in ibid., 13: 114.

110. "Report on the Past and Present Situation on the Western Frontier," in ibid., 15: 304.

111. ? to Jon. Trumbull, June 6, 1780, in ibid., 11: 253; John Mead to

Trumbull, Mar. 29, in ibid., p. 123; Gold S. Silliman to Trumbull, Nov. 4, in ibid., 13: 133.

112. This was suggested in "Report on the Past and Present Situation of the Western Frontier," in ibid., 15: 304. When Arnold tried using paroles in Virginia, Jefferson responded in such manner; see Jefferson to the County Lieutenants and Proclamation concerning Paroles, Jan. 19, 1781, in Julian P. Boyd, ed., *The Papers of Thomas Jefferson* (Princeton, N.J., 1950–), 4: 401–5.

113. See John Mead to Jon. Trumbull, Dec. 11, 1779, in JT, 10: 268, and nn. 107, 109, above.

114. Robt. Fairchild to Jon. Trumbull, Apr. 19, 1780, in JT, 11: 146; Thad. Burr to Trumbull, Aug. 16, and Oliver Smith to Trumbull, Sept. 8, in ibid., 10: 94, 145.

115. Thos. Young to Nath. Shaw, June 20, and Shaw to Jon. Trumbull, June 24, in ibid., 8: 146*a–b*, 148.

116. Benj. Henshaw to Jon. Trumbull, Apr. 13, 1779, in ibid., 9: 175; Wm. Ledyard to Trumbull, May 13, 1780, in ibid., 11: 218*c–d*.

117. Complaint of John Shipman, Samuel Field, William Hart, Levi Chapman, and Samuel Shipman, June 3, 1779, in CARW, 1st ser., 14: 171; Thad. Burr to Jon. Trumbull, Nov. 5, in 7*MHSC*, 2: 453–54; Wm. Worthington to Trumbull, June 29, in JT, 9: 256; And. Ward to Trumbull, July 12, 1780, in ibid., 12: 87; John Mead to Trumbull, Jan. 25, 1781, in ibid., 14: 37; Wm. Worthington to Trumbull, Jan. 30, in ibid., p. 69; Jab. Fitch to Trumbull, Oct. 13, in ibid., 15: 188.

118. Jon. Trumbull to Oliver Wolcott, Aug. 24, 1779, in JTP; *SR*, 2: 270.

119. *SR*, 3: 16–19, quote 17.

120. See Art. Lee to Jon. Trumbull, Apr. 6, 1779, in JT, 9: 166.

121. See Eli Lockwood to Gold S. Sulliman, June 13, 1780, in ibid., 12: 9; John Mead to Jon. Trumbull, Jan. 15, 1781, in ibid., 14: 37*a–b*. The British also succeeded in robbing the mail in areas under patriot control; see Wm. Heath to Trumbull, Nov. 15, 1780, in ibid., 13: 153; also, Sam. Huntington to Trumbull, Apr. 6, 1781, in ibid., 14: 176.

122. Washington to the President of Congress, Nov. 7, 1780, in WGW, 20: 314.

123. Civil Authority and Selectmen of Greenwich to Jon. Trumbull, Jan. 15, 1781, in JT, 14: 36*a–b*; R. Arthur Bowler, *Logistics and the Failure of the British Army in America* (Princeton, N.J., 1975), pp. 266–67.

124. Washington to Sam. H. Parsons, Feb. 22, 1781, in WGW, 21: 235–36.

125. *By Their Excellencies, Sir Henry Clinton . . . and Mariot Arbuthnot . . .* (New York, 1780), in Evans 43978; Roger P. Bristol misdated this because of a printing error in the proclamation. A version of the document also appears in *DAR*, 18: 261–63. For background, see ibid., pp. 155, 218–19.

126. For instance, the British squadron blockading the French in Newport was reported to be receiving supplies from Connecticut; Wm. Ledyard to Jon. Trumbull, Dec. 5, 1780, in JT, 13: 194; also, Thomas Niles and Amos Gore to Trumbull, Jan. 13, 1781, in ibid., 14: 32. British recruiters were also thought to be at work in Connecticut; Wm. Ledyard to Trumbull, Mar. 1, in ibid., p. 110. Reports of extensive networks of disloyal Americans within

Connecticut went back to 1779; see Jas. Prescott et al. to Trumbull, May 7, and Oliver Prescott to Trumbull, June 15, in ibid., 9: 202, 243. See also *CJ*, Apr. 20, 1780.

127. Sam. H. Parsons to Jon. Trumbull, Mar. 3, 1781, in *SHP*, pp. 341–43.

128. *SR*, 3: 307–8.

129. Ibid., pp. 308–9; Jon. Trumbull to Sam. H. Parsons, Mar. 16, 1781, in *SHP*, pp. 345–46.

130. Wm. Ledyard to Jon. Trumbull, Jan. 30, 1781, in JT, 14: 67; see also Richard Buel, Jr., "Time: Friend or Foe of the Revolution?" in Don C. Higginbotham, ed., *Reconsiderations on the Revolutionary War* (Westport, Conn., 1978), pp. 140–41. The patriots were guilty of overresponding to the suspension of the Prohibitory Act as it applied to New York; see Geo. Germain to Hen. Clinton, Feb. 15 and Aug. 3, 1780, in *DAR*, 18: 49–50, 131–32, 133.

131. Sam. H. Parsons to Thad. Burr, Mar. 16, 1781, in *SHP*, p. 346; Joseph Walker to Washington, Mar. 30, in ibid., p. 352; Parsons to Washington, Apr. 20, in ibid., pp. 354–55.

132. *SR*, 2: 292–93, 298, 366, 448, 483; also, Jon. Trumbull to Geo. Clinton, July 20, 1781, in *7MHSC*, 3: 250.

133. *CJ*, Apr. 5, 1781; Authority and Selectmen of Stratford to Jon. Trumbull, Mar. 31, 1781, in JT, 14: 167; Sam. Canfield and Thad. Burr in behalf of the Authority and Selectmen of Fairfield to Jon. Trumbull, Mar. 23, in JTP.

134. Geo. Clinton to Jon. Trumbull, Apr. 16, 1781, in *Public Papers of George Clinton . . .* (Albany, N.Y., 1904), 6: 758–59; also Caleb Brewster deposition, June 22; Selah Strong deposition, June 27; Resolves of the New York Senate, June 27; Clinton to Trumbull, June 30, in JT, 14: 303, 313, 316, 318.

135. *JCC*, 21: 836; New York's appeal to Congress is documented in Ezra L'Hommedieu to Geo. Clinton, July 31, 1781, and Thos. McKean to Clinton, Aug. 8, in *Papers of Clinton*, 7: 150, 176–77.

136. Jon. Trumbull to Geo. Clinton, July 20, 1781, in *7MHSC*, 3: 248–49, 250, also 251. This letter contrasts strongly with Trumbull's response to Clinton's initial protest; see Jon. Trumbull to Geo. Clinton, Apr. 27, 1781, in *Papers of Clinton*, 6: 803–4.

137. Jon. Trumbull to Geo. Clinton, July 20, 1780, in *7MHSC*, 3: 248, 250.

138. *NP*, Apr. 12, 1781.

139. Ibid., April 19 and May 4, 1781.

140. Eliph. Lockwood to Gold S. Silliman, June 13, 1780, in JT, 12: 9; *SHP*, p. 300.

141. Sam. H. Parsons to Eliph. Lockwood, Aug. 14, 1780, in *SHP*, pp. 300–301.

142. Wm. Williams to Jon. Trumbull, Mar. 29, 1780, in JT, 11: 122.

143. See chap. 5, n. 138, above.

144. *CC*, Apr. 2, 1782.

145. *SR*, 1: 212.

146. Ibid., pp. 378–79, 2: 98; Wm. Worthington to Jon. Trumbull, Apr. 1, 1779, in JT, 9: 147.

147. *SR,* 2: 283.
148. Ibid., p. 446, 468; also, CARW, 1st ser., 21: 213, 214.
149. See CARW, 1st ser., 21: 215–16.
150. Wm. Hart to Jer. Wadsworth, May 24, 1780, in JW, box 130.
151. Wm. Hart to Jer. Wadsworth, May 25, 1780, in ibid.
152. See *SR,* 3: 9.
153. CARW, 1st ser., 21: 221–22, 218*a–c.*
154. *SR,* 3: 405.
155. Ibid., 4: 113, 5: 203, 6: 10.
156. See the Memorial of sundry inhabitants of Saybrook, Jan. 26, 1781, in JTP, charging Shipman's company of guards with paying more attention to private than public business. Also Memorial of the Town of Branford, June 25, 1782, in 7*MHSC,* 3: 360. A similar fissure appeared between Fairfield and Green Farms in early 1783; *CJ,* Feb. 6, 1783. In a large town like New Haven the divisions may not have been geographic; see an account of the town meeting of July 24, 1780, that almost led to serious violence in *CJ,* Aug. 17.
157. Memorial of two justices and three selectmen of Killingworth, June 27, 1782, in JT, 16: 187.
158. See Jon. Trumbull to Sam. Whiting, Oct. 26, 1779, in ibid., 20: 217.
159. Sam. H. Parsons to the selectmen of Norwalk, Mar. 21, 1781, in *SHP,* pp. 349–50.
160. *AR,* pp. 330–31; Frances M. Caulkins, *History of New London . . .* (New London, 1895), pp. 545–46, 547–49.
161. Caulkins, *History,* pp. 558–59; "Stephen Hempstead's Narrative," in Charles Allyn, *The Battle of Groton Heights: A Collection of Narratives, Official Reports, Records, etc.* (New London, 1882), p. 49.
162. "Avery Downer's Narrative," in Allyn, *Battle,* p. 84.
163. Memorial of Gurd. Saltonstall et al. to Sam. McClellan, Apr. 22, 1782, in ibid., p. 125; Caulkins, *History,* p. 548.
164. See Allyn, *Battle,* p. 133. He may have been accompanied by another Stonington man; see ibid., p. 131.
165. New Haven Memorial, Sept. 1, 1781, in JT, 15: 87.
166. See Sam. H. Parsons to the Council of Safety, undated but before the end of August, 1781, in ibid., p. 325, also Jon. Trumbull to Wm. Greene, Sept. 5, in JTP.
167. *SR,* 3: 502.
168. Caulkins, *History,* p. 545.
169. Ibid., pp. 559–64.
170. See "Rufus Avery's Narrative," in Allyn, *Battle,* pp. 41–43, also 119–21.
171. Caulkins, *History,* p. 565.
172. "Experience of Jonathan Brooks," in Allyn, *Battle,* p. 78ff., also 114.
173. "Hempstead's Narrative," in ibid., pp. 49, 54; "Downer's Narrative," in ibid., p. 84, contests this point.
174. Caulkins, *History,* p. 559.
175. Gurd. Saltonstall et al. to Sam. McClellan, Apr. 27, 1782, in Allyn, *Battle,* p. 123.
176. Census of Feb. 1782, in JT, 24: 178.

177. Gurd. Saltonstall et al. to Sam. McClellan, Apr. 27, 1782, in Allyn, *Battle*, p. 123.

178. Washington to Jon. Trumbull, Jan. 31, 1782, in *WGW*, 23: 476; also, Trumbull to Jab. Bowen, Feb. 20, in *7MHSC*, 3: 316.

179. *SR*, 4: 5–8, 10–11.

180. Rog. Newberry to Jon. Trumbull, Oct. 16, 1781, and Feb. 24, 1782, in JT, 15: 196, 16: 47.

181. John Mead to Jon. Trumbull, Jan. 14, 1782, in ibid., 16: 15.

182. Jed. Huntington to Washington, June 10, 1782, in *WGW*, 24: 343 n.

183. *SR*, 4: 173.

184. Washington to Jon. Trumbull, May 4, 1782, in *5MHSC*, 10: 267; also, Jesse Root to Trumbull, May 11, in *7MHSC*, 3: 348; Jed. Huntington to Trumbull, Aug. 4, in ibid., p. 371.

185. *JCC*, 21: 1090; Jon. Trumbull to Jab. Bowen, Feb. 20, 1782, in *7MHSC*, 3: 316.

186. See Resolves of the Lower House, May 1782, in CARW, 1st ser., 22: 257*a–b*.

187. *SR*, 4: 8.

188. Ibid., pp. 105, 107–8.

189. In JT, 24: 183*a*.

190. *SR*, 4: 171; *ARC*, tables 1 and 8.

191. *CJ*, Aug. 8, 1782; Eliph. Dyer, Jesse Root, and Benj. Huntington to Jon. Trumbull, July 29, 1782, in *7MHSC*, 3: 368; Robt. Morris to Trumbull, Feb. ?, in ibid., pp. 325, 331; and Morris to Trumbull, Sept. 3, in JT, 17: 79.

192. *SR*, 4: 290.

193. Jab. Bowen to Jon. Trumbull, Jan 31, 1782, in JT, 18: 18.

194. *SR*, 5: 27.

195. *ARC*, table 8.

196. *SR*, 4: 17–18.

197. *JCC*, 2: 196. Oliver Wolcott and Richard Law to Jon. Trumbull, Apr. 29, 1782, in *7MHSC*, 3: 336–37.

198. Eliph. Dyer to Jon. Trumbull, Oct. 19, 1782, in *7MHSC*, 3: 393, also 391–92 n.

199. Jon. Trumbull, Jr., to Jon. Trumbull, Aug. 28, 1782, in ibid., p. 379.

200. *SCP*, 6: 92.

201. Pennsylvania had proposed putting the dispute to arbitration as early as 1779; see Resolution of the Pennsylvania General Assembly, Nov. 18, 20, 1779, and Jos. Reed to Jon. Trumbull, Dec. 8, in ibid., pp. 54–55. See also Eliph. Dyer and Benj. Huntington to Trumbull, July 1, 1782, in ibid., pp. 107–8.

202. Act of the Connecticut legislature in ibid., pp. 96–97; also, in *SR*, 4: 18–19.

203. *SCP*, 6: 120; also Eliph. Dyer to Jon. Trumbull, Sept. 25, 1782, in ibid., pp. 124–25.

204. Cf. Washington to the President of Congress, Feb. 18, 1782, in *WGW*, 24: 5.

205. *JCC*, 22: 76–77; Washington to the President of Congress, Feb. 20, 1782, in *WGW*, 24: 10–11.

206. Ebenezer Ledyard to Jon. Trumbull, Apr. 11, 1782, in JT, 16: 87; see also Washington to Adm. Digby and to the Secretary of War, June 5, in *WGW*, 24: 315–16, 317.

207. David Sproat to Nath. Shaw, Apr. 19, 1782, in JT, 16: 100*a–c*; Washington to Henry Knox and Gouverneur Morris, Mar. 11, in *WGW*, 24: 58.

208. Thos. Shaw to Jon. Trumbull, Apr. 30, 1782, in JT, 21: 100*a–c*; Wm. Pitkin to Trumbull, July 2, in ibid., 17: 5; *CG*, July 19, 1782.

209. See Thos. Shaw to Jon. Trumbull, May 23 and June 10, 1782, in JT, 16: 142, 165; *SR*, 4: 124, 126, 247–48.

210. *SR*, 4: 158–59; 251–52; Thos. Shaw to Jon. Trumbull, June 2, 1782, and Sam. McClellan to Trumbull, June 6, in JT, 16: 153, 162–63.

211. Washington to Hen. Knox and Gouv. Morris, Mar. 11, 1782, in *WGW*, 24: 57.

212. Washington to Abr. Skinner, June 12, 1782, in ibid., p. 336; Benjamin Lincoln to Washington, June 12, in ibid., p. 337 n.; Washington to Jon. Trumbull, July 3, in *5MHSC*, 10: 275.

213. See Thos. Shaw to Jon. Trumbull, July 1, 7, 1782, in JT, 17: 2, 11; Trumbull to Thos. Mumford, July 3, in JTP.

214. *CC*, Aug. 13, 1782.

215. See Washington to the President of Congress, July 9, 1782, in *WGW*, 24: 406.

CHAPTER SEVEN: PERILS OF PEACE

1. *CJ*, May 9, 1782; Jas. Madison to Art. Lee, May 7, 1782, in *LMCC*, 6: 345.

2. Guy Carleton and Robt. Digby to Washington, Aug. 2, 1782, in *CJ*, Aug. 15, 1782; John T. Gilman to Meschech Weare, Aug. 5; Jas. Madison to Edw. Randolph, Aug. 5; David Howell to Wm. Ellery, Aug. 10, in *LMCC*, 6: 413, 420, 440; also, Chas. Thomson's Notes, Aug. 12 and Sept. 16–17, in ibid., pp. 441, 473.

3. Jas. Madison to Edw. Randolph, Aug. 5, 1782; John T. Gilman to Mesch. Weare, Sept. 11, and to Josiah Barlett, Sept. 17; Virginia Delegates to Benj. Harrison, Sept. 17, in ibid., pp. 421, 471, 473–74, 478; *CC*, Oct. 29, 1782.

4. As reported in *CC*, July 23, 1782.

5. Ralph Izard to Mrs. Izard, Oct. 7, 1782; Izard to John Lowell, Oct. 23, in *LMCC*, 6: 497, 525; *CC*, Nov. 19, 1782. Carleton's proposal was made on Aug. 29; Washington's reply of Sept. 8 is printed in *CC*, Dec. 3; see also *CJ*, Dec. 12; *WGW*, 25: 137–38.

6. Elias Boudinot to Elias Dayton, Jan. 7, 1783, in *LMCC*, 7: 6; also *CC*, Jan. 7, 1783.

7. Jas. Madison to Edw. Randolph, Dec. 17, 1782, and Daniel Carroll to Wm. Paca, Dec. 21, in *LMCC*, 6: 564–65, 567.

8. Washington to John Sullivan, Feb. 4, 1781, in *WGW*, 21: 182–83;

also, Jon. Trumbull to Washington, Aug. 31, in *5MHSC*, 10: 203; "O.W.," in *CC*, Jan. 8, 1782.

9. Connecticut's growing difficulties in raising specie through taxation can be traced from data available in JT, 24: 156*a–b*. The departure of the French from Newport was probably as significant as the rise of the illicit trade in causing the difficulty.

10. Washington to the Secretary of War, Nov. 6, 1782, and to Jon. Trumbull, Nov. 13, in *WGW*, 25: 322, 325; Luzerne to Washington, Nov. 6, in WP; for Congress's response, see *JCC*, 22: 341.

11. See President of Congress (Sam. Huntington), Circular to the States, June 1, 1781, in JT, 14: 266.

12. Richard Buel, Jr., "Time: Friend or Foe of the Revolution?" in Don C. Higginbotham, ed., *Reconsiderations on the Revolutionary War* (Westport, Conn., 1978), p. 143.

13. Washington to the Secretary of War, Nov. 6, 1782, and to Jon. Trumbull, Nov. 13, in *WGW*, 25: 322, 335.

14. Washington had recommended such measures be taken in 1781; see his letter to John Sullivan, Feb. 4, in *WGW*, 21: 182–83; also, Washington to Wm. Livingston, Jan. 12–(13), 1782, in ibid., 23: 444–45. For the attitudes that prevented the states from acting on his advice, see Benj. Huntington to his wife, May 29, 1777, in Benjamin Huntington Papers, Connecticut Historical Society.

15. *SR*, 4: 161–62.

16. Ibid., pp. 9–12. Instead of allocating guards to the towns, the General Assembly gave them £9,190 to raise men.

17. See Washington to Thad. Burr, Dec. 26, 1782, in *WGW*, 25: 476; Benj. Talmadge to Jon. Trumbull, Jan. 4, 1783, in JT, 18: 2*a–c*, and to Washington, Jan. 4, in WP.

18. *SR*, 5: 22, 94.

19. Washington to Benj. Talmadge, Jan. 21, 1783, in *WGW*, 26: 55–56; also, Washington to the President of Congress, Feb. 26, in ibid., p. 166; Talmadge to Washington, Feb. 21, in WP; Talmadge to Jon. Trumbull, Feb. 8, in JT, 18: 22*a–c*.

20. *SR*, 4: 161.

21. See Benjamin Gale, *Brief, decent, but free remarks . . .* (Hartford, 1782), p. 37ff.

22. *CJ*, Dec. 19, 26, 1782. Dayton's two captures are reported in ibid., July 11 and Aug. 22, 1782; see also Louis F. Middlebrook, *Maritime Connecticut during the Revolutionary War* (Salem, Mass., 1925), 2: 223.

23. See *SR*, 4: 280, 5: 100. Dayton had never become a full member of the community; see *CJ*, Apr. 20, 1780.

24. Thos. Mumford to Jon. Trumbull, Jan. 18, 1783, in JT, 18: 7; *CG*, Apr. 4, 11, 1783; *SR*, 5: 64–65.

25. *CC*, June 25, 1782; also, Gale, *Brief remarks*, p. 51.

26. *CC*, Aug. 20, 1782. Some towns had acted before this; see Guilford Town Records, Town Meetings, 2: 330.

27. See *CC*, Aug. 27 and Sept. 10, 1782; *CJ*, July 25 and Aug. 22, 1782; *NP*, Aug. 15, 1782.

28. An obscure play, *The Double conspiracy; or, Treason discovered but not*

punished . . . (Hartford, 1783), depicts vigilante attitudes toward the illicit trade and the indignation which greeted resistance to such measures.

29. "The Watchman," in *NP*, Sept. 5, 19, 1782; Gale, *Brief remarks*, p. 38ff.; "Pacificus," in *CC*, July 30 and Sept. 3, 1782.

30. In JT, 20: 336*a*–*c*.

31. Gale, *Brief remarks*, pp. 4–8.

32. Ibid., pp. 8–9, 17–22, 24–27, 32–34. See also "Freeman," in *CJ*, Mar. 26 and Apr. 4, 1777, Sept. 9, 1779; Account of Norwich Town Meeting, Dec. 29, 1777, in *NP*, Jan. 5, 1778; Account of Branford Town Meeting, Mar. 9, 1780, in *CJ*, Mar. 15.

33. *CG*, Sept. 7–Oct. 5, 1781.

34. Ibid., Apr. 5–May 10, 1782, intermittently.

35. Ibid., Apr. 19, 1782.

36. *SR*, 3: 325. See also "A Constitutional Whig," in *CG*, Apr. 25, 1783.

37. *SR*, 4: 337, 338; Smith's story was restated in his memorial to the House of Representatives, Jan. 13, 1783, in CGAP, and CARW, 1st serv., 24: 101.

38. Increase Moseley's "Journal of the Proceedings of the House of Representatives," Jan. 1783, in CGAP.

39. This memorial can be found in CARW, 1st ser., 24: 102, and CGAP.

40. Jon. Trumbull to the Connecticut delegates in Congress, Feb. 24, 1783, in JT, 20: 343.

41. In CARW, 1st ser., 24: 103, and CGAP.

42. *SR*, 5: 37; Jon. Trumbull to the Connecticut delegates in Congress, Feb. 24, 1783, in JT, 20: 343.

43. *SR*, 5: 29; see also CARW, 1st ser., 24: 33, 34.

44. This memorial is in CGAP; see also Hartford Town Votes, 2: 299.

45. The countermemorial, without date, is in CGAP.

46. Moseley's "Journal of the Proceedings of the House of Representatives," in ibid.; also Oscar Zeichner, "The Rehabilitation of Loyalists in Connecticut," *NEQ* 11 (1938): 312.

47. Charles Allyn, *The Battle of Groton Heights* . . . (New London, 1882), pp. 28, 159.

48. CARW, 1st ser., 22: 284.

49. The intercepted letters appear in New York Historical Society, *Collections* 22 (1889) and are itemized on p. 501.

50. Thos. Mumford to Joshua Huntington, Feb. 1, 1783, in *CHSC*, 20: 167.

51. I rely here on McClellan's account in Sam. McClellan to Jon. Trumbull, Mar. 27, 1783, in JT, 18: 76*e*–*f*; see also the statement of Mumford et al., *CG*, Mar. 28.

52. *SR*, 5: 94–95.

53. Ibid., p. 95.

54. N. 40, above.

55. See John Chester to Josh. Huntington, Mar. 21, 1783, in *CHSC*, 20: 170–71. Chester seems to have exaggerated the response of the western towns; see Zeichner, "Rehabilitation," p. 312 n.

56. *CG*, Mar. 28, 1783.

57. See Jon. Trumbull's communication to the General Assembly, Jan. 24, 1783, in JT, 20: 342.

58. Moses Holmes to Wm. Williams, Mar. 20, 1783, and Jon. Trumbull to Williams, Mar. 20, in WW.

59. *CG*, Apr. 4, 1783.

60. John Chester to Josh. Huntington, Mar. 21, 1783, in *CHSC*, 20: 171. For Trumbull's role in Deane's disgrace, see Silas Deane to Jon. Trumbull, Oct. 21, 1781, and Trumbull's reply, May 15, 1782, in New York Historical Society, *Collections 22* (1889): 509–14, 23 (1890): 93–97.

61. *CG*, Apr. 4, 1783.

62. "Blunt," in ibid., Apr. 18, 1783.

63. Reported in *CC*, Mar. 25, 1783; quote from Samuel F. Bemis, *The Diplomacy of the American Revolution* (Bloomington, Ind., 1955), p. 261.

64. "Autobiography of Stephen Jarvis, 1775–1783," in the New York Historical Society.

65. Deposition of Sol. Ferris, Oct. 11, 1783, in CARW, 1st ser., 26: 110.

66. *CJ*, Apr. 17, 1783; memorial of the Town of Norwalk, Jan. 15, 1783, in CARW, 1st ser., 26: 247; Zeichner, "Rehabilitation," pp. 321–23.

67. Hartford Memorial of Jan. 29, 1783, in CGAP.

68. *SR*, 5: 109–10.

69. Journal of the House of Representatives, 1783–85, p. 31; "A Freeman of New Haven," in *CJ*, May 8, 1783.

70. *SR*, 5: 115; Zeichner, "Rehabilitation," p. 323.

71. *JCC*, 11: 502.

72. Washington to the President of Congress, Oct. 11, 1780, in WGW, 20: 158–59; also, *LOA*, pp. 17–20; *JCC*, 18: 958–59.

73. Sam. Huntington to Jon. Trumbull, Oct. 26, 1780, in *LMCC*, 5: 429.

74. Washington to Wm. Heath, Jan. 21, 1781, in WGW, 21: 124–25; Circular to the New England States, Jan. 5, in ibid., p. 62; Washington to Hen. Knox, Jan. 7, in ibid., p. 66.

75. See *SR*, 3: 290.

76. Ibid., p. 97.

77. Sam. H. Parsons to Jon. Trumbull, Feb. 5, 1781, in *SHP*, p. 325.

78. *SR*, 3: 320.

79. Ibid., p. 310; Committee of the Army to Jon. Trumbull, Feb. 3, 1781, in JT, 14: 73.

80. *SR*, 3: 382.

81. For details of the exchange see Sam. H. Parsons to Washington, June 26, 1781; Washington to Jon. Trumbull, June 28; Trumbull to Washington, July 9; Parsons to Trumbull, July 10; Trumbull to Parsons, July 16; Trumbull to Washington, July 17; Parsons to Trumbull, July 2; and the Committee of the Army to Trumbull, July 26, in *SHP*, pp. 370–71, 372, 372–73, 375–76, 377–78, 378–79, 380–84.

82. The quotations are from Jon. Trumbull to Washington, July 17, 1781, in ibid., p. 379.

83. Letter from sixty-seven Connecticut officers to Jon. Trumbull, July 26, 1781, in ibid., pp. 384–86.

84. *SR*, 3: 480–81, 487, 489, 493, 512; Hezekiah Wetmore to Jon. Trumbull, Sept. 2, 1781, in JT, 15: 88.

85. *SR*, 4: 12–14.

86. Ibid., pp. 211–13.

87. Ibid., p. 154.

88. Gale, *Brief remarks*, p. 8; *ARC*, table 8.

89. *LOA*, pp. 21–23.

90. Ibid., p. 24, 27–30, quotes 27, 29, 30.

91. In *JCC*, 25: 937.

92. Ibid., p. 938.

93. *LOA*, pp. 37–40, 40–42, quotes 38, 39, 41. See Richard H. Kuhn, "The History of the Newburgh Conspiracy: America and the Coup d'Etat," *WMQ*, 3rd ser. 17 (1970): 187–220, for the best general discussion of the incident.

94. *JCC*, 25: 938.

95. Ibid., 24: 207–8, quote 208.

96. Ibid., pp. 277–83, quote 282.

97. See Resolves of the Lebanon Town Meeting, Apr. 28, 1783, in *CG*, May 2; unsigned, in *CC*, May 13. Also Resolves of Farmington, Farmington Town Records, 2: 33–34. Farmington had appointed a committee to watch the army's activities on Feb. 6.

98. Memorial of the Massachusetts General Court, July 11, 1783, in PCC, item 65, 2: 185.

99. Journal of the House of Representatives, 1783–85, pp. 32–39.

100. Ibid., p. 38; the circular dated June 8, 1783, is in *WGW*, 26: 483–96.

101. *CC*, July 29, 1783.

102. Ibid., Aug. 12, 1783.

103. Hartford Town Votes, 2: 300.

104. *CC*, Aug. 26, 1783. "An Inhabitant of the Town of Hartford" subsequently protested that the committee had not been empowered to call a convention; ibid., Sept. 2.

105. Ibid., Sept. 9, 1783. In 1782 William Judd had petitioned Congress on behalf of the "deranged officers of the Connecticut Line" for half pay; see *JCC*, 22: 404 n., 418.

106. "An Inhabitant of the Town of Hartford," in *CC*, Sept. 2, 1783.

107. *CC*, Sept. 2, 1783.

108. See "An Inhabitant of the Town of Hartford," in *CC*, Sept. 2, 1783; "Amicus Patriae" and "A True Republican," in ibid., Sept. 9; "Decency," in ibid., Sept. 16; unsigned, in ibid., Sept. 30; "To the Printer," in ibid., Oct. 7; "Philo-Patriae," in ibid., Oct. 28. For a private response, see Heman Swift to Oliver Wolcott, Oct. 12, 1783, in OW, vol. 3.

109. "Honorius," in *CC*, Aug. 26, Sept. 2, 9, 16, 30, and Oct. 14, 21, 1783.

110. See Jab. Brown to Jon. Trumbull, Jan. 3, 1783, in JT, 18: 18.

111. See *CJ*, Sept. 17, 1783.

112. Ibid., June 19, 1783.

113. *SR*, 5: 15–19.

114. See *CJ*, July 9, 23, Aug. 6, and Sept. 13, 1783.

115. "Honorius," in *CC*, Sept. 2, 1783.

116. "Amicus Patriae," in *CC*, Sept. 9, 1783, and "Decency," in ibid., Sept. 16.

117. For Hugh Ledlie's early career, see Oscar Zeichner, *Connecticut's Years of Controversy, 1750–1776* (Chapel Hill, N.C., 1949), p. 52; Lawrence H. Gipson, *Jared Ingersoll* . . . (New Haven, 1920), pp. 183, 200. Ledlie was a member of the committee of correspondence established by the Sons of Liberty in 1766; Gipson, *Ingersoll*, p. 219. The only source on Street Hall's earlier career is the unreliable Samuel Peters in Kenneth W. Cameron, ed., *The Works of Samuel Peters of Hebron, Connecticut* (Hartford, 1967), p. 75. The report is so detailed as to suggest it is in some measure true, though, and Peters does give an account of why no other evidence survives.

118. Herbert Thomas, *Jared Eliot, Minister, Doctor, Scientist, and His Connecticut* (n.p., 1967), p. 117.

119. Thos. Seymour to Jon. Trumbull, July 10, 1779, in JT, 9: 281; Gentlemen of Wethersfield to Trumbull, July 10, 1779, in ibid., 10: 6*a*.

120. See *SR*, 4: 57–58; for Deane's apostasy, see Julian P. Boyd, "Silas Deane: Death of a Kindly Teacher of Treason?" *WMQ*, 3rd ser. 16 (1959): 518–50.

121. See CARW, 1st ser., 5: 64.

122. In JT, 8: 157*d*.

123. Woodward's authorship of the Torrington resolves is established by an undated verse reference to him in a composition by Mason Fitch Cogswell in Mason Fitch Cogswell Collection, Connecticut Historical Society. For a biography of Woodward, see Samuel Orcutt, *History of Torrington, Connecticut* . . . (Albany, N.Y., 1878), pp. 623–26. I am indebted to Peter D. Hall for drawing my attention to these materials. See also "A Freeman," in *CC*, Apr. 1, 1783, and *CJ*, Apr. 3; "Philanthropos," in *CG*, Apr. 4.

124. Jed. Huntington to And. Huntington, Sept. 19, 1783, in *CHSC*, 20: 446.

125. See "Philagathus," in *MG*, Mar. 13, 1786.

126. In his parting address to the legislature, Governor Trumbull inveighed against "the uncertain voice of popular clamour, which, most frequently, is excited and blown about by the artful and designing part of the community, to effect particular, and often times, sinister purposes"; *CC*, Nov. 25, 1783.

127. In *CJ*, Feb. 18, 1784.

128. *SR*, 5: 313.

129. *CC*, Nov. 4, 1783.

130. CARW, 1st ser., 26: 105*a*.

131. Journal of the House of Representatives, 1783–85, p. 64; a ms. copy of the remonstrance is in WW.

132. *JCC*, 25: 609–12.

133. *CJ*, Nov. 12, 1783.

134. *CC*, Dec. 22, 1783.

135. Ibid., Dec. 29, 1783.

136. See "A Political Creed," in ibid., Jan. 6, 1784; also, "A Connecticut Tory," in ibid., Jan. 20.

137. *SR*, 4: 154–55, 5: 25–26, 310–12.

138. See "Honorius," in *CC*, Sept. 2, 1783.

139. The series began in *CC*, Feb. 24, 1784, running intermittently through May 25; see also *CG*, Mar. 26–June 4. "Continentalist" argued the same position in *CJ*, Mar. 10–17; see also "To the Members of the Convention, Whether Good or Bad," *CC*, Apr. 6.

140. "C.H.," in *CC*, Jan. 6, 13, 20, 1784.

141. Quote from "Policy of Connecticut," pt. 2, in *CC*, Mar. 2, 1784, and *CG*, Apr. 9. See also Pelatiah Webster, *A Dissertation on the Political Union and Constitution of the Thirteen United States* (Hartford, 1783), p. 7; *Remarks on a Pamphlet, Entitled "A Dissertation . . ."* (New Haven, 1784), p. vi.

142. "Continentalist," in *CJ*, Mar. 10, 1784; "To the Public," in *CC*, Apr. 13.

143. See *SR*, 5: 277–79.

144. The disagreements that did arise when the state tried to settle its accounts with the continent are detailed in Oliver Wolcott, Jr.'s Report to the General Assembly, May 1786, in CARW, 1st ser., 32: 89*a–f*, 391, 392. "To the Public," in *CC*, Apr. 13, 1784; "Policy of Connecticut," pt. 4, in *CC*, Mar. 16, and *CG*, Apr. 20. The latter author played on the hope that Congress might compensate Connecticut for the difference between the value of the beef the state had supplied the army and the depreciated medium in which it had been paid.

145. Cf. *SR*, 5: 252–54, 315–17, and *CG*, Feb. 27 and May 28, 1784.

146. "A.D.," in *CG*, Apr. 9, 1784.

147. *SR*, 5: 313, 317.

148. *JCC*, 30: 48ff.

149. Ibid., 30: 95, 97. New Jersey rescinded her resolve; ibid., p. 222.

150. *SR*, 4: 171, ·101–2. See also "Political Paragraphs," in *MG*, June 19, 1786; "Public Creditor," in ibid., Nov. 20.

151. *SR*, 5: 122.

152. Ibid., p. 375.

153. "Honorius," in *CC*, Sept. 2, 1783.

154. *SR*, 5: 433–35.

155. Ibid., pp. 116, 256, 342, 438, 6: 160.

156. Ibid., pp. 257–77. Hartford, Middletown, and Norwich were also incorporated; ibid., pp. 343–73. For the advantages expected from incorporations, see "Policy of Connecticut," pt. 6, in *CG*, June 4, 1784.

157. *SR*, 5: 325–26; *CC*, June 1, 1784.

158. *SR*, 5: 150–51, 6: 63, 95, 121–22; *CC*, Oct. 19, 26, 1784, Oct. 3, 10, 1785.

159. *SR*, 5: 323–24. The reform proved to be controversial; see "An Aggrieved Freeman," in *CC*, Aug. 12 and Oct. 24, 1784; "A Contented Freeman," in ibid., Aug. 31, and "Publicola," in ibid., Sept. 7. The town of Waterbury even passed resolves on the subject (ibid., Apr. 19, 1785), which drew hostile comments in ibid., Apr. 26.

160. *SR*, 6: 11, 93.

161. Bruce C. Daniels, *The Connecticut Town . . .* (Middletown, Conn., 1979), 34–44, 185.

162. See "Senex," in *CC*, Aug. 21, 1786; ibid., Oct. 30 and Nov. 13; and "Political Paragraphs," in ibid., Nov. 20; unsigned, in ibid., Dec. 18; "A

Freeman," in *MG*, Sept. 4, 1786; "Political Paragraphs," in *MG*, June 19, also Oct. 30.

163. See *CC*, May 25, May 30, and Nov. 14, 1785; Oct. 23, 30 and Dec. 18, 1786; *MG*, Nov. 13, 1786ff.

164. "Yankee Doodle," in *CC*, Mar. 6, 1786.

165. Americans first learned of the restrictive British orders-in-council in Sept. 1783—see *CJ*, Sept. 17—but it was not clear how these would be enforced until reports arrived of seizures in the West Indies; see ibid., June 15, 1784; *MG*, Jan. 17, Feb. 20, 27, May 8, and June 12, 19, 1786; *CG*, June 3, 1785. See also *JCC*, 26: 270.

166. "A.B.," in *CC*, July 24, 1786; report in *MG*, Feb. 20; also, "Philagathus," in ibid., Mar. 13, and notices in ibid., July 17 and Nov. 6.

167. See *CC*, Sept. 28, 1784; Jan. 11 and Apr. 5, 1785; also *MG*, Jan. 24, Apr. 3, 10, 17, and Nov. 27, 1786; *CG*, Dec. 16, 1785.

168. *SR*, 6: 18–19; the selectmen could now grant abatements equal to one-eighth the taxes due.

169. Ibid., pp. 152–53, 155. James Wadsworth became the state's first comptroller.

170. See the advertisement of James Henshaw, *MG*, Jan. 31, 1786.

171. "A Farmer," in *CC*, Feb. 1, 1785, from *CG*, Jan. 7; unsigned, in *CG*, June 24, also Mar. 17 and June 9.

172. "Comparison," in *CG*, July 22, 1785; also, "A Citizen of Connecticut," in *CC*, Apr. 3, 1786.

173. *SR*, 5: 206, 376, 6: 101–2.

174. "State Creditors," in *MG*, Oct. 2, 1786.

175. "Modern Whig," in *CG*, Mar. 24, 1786. See also a letter from a New Haven merchant to Rev. Mr. ——— in London, in *CJ*, May 31.

CHAPTER EIGHT: EPILOGUE

1. See a letter from Virginia, in *CC*, Feb. 13, 1786.

2. Irwin H. Polishook, *Rhode Island and the Union* (Evanston, Ill., 1969), pp. 47–48; Albert E. Van Dusen, "The Trade of Revolutionary Connecticut" (Ph.D. thesis, University of Pennsylvania, 1948), p. 34.

3. Polishook, *Rhode Island*, pp. 60ff., 110.

4. Ibid., p. 124ff.

5. *Trevett* v. *Weeden* is discussed in ibid., pp. 132–34, and in Gordon S. Wood, *The Creation of the American Republic* (Chapel Hill, N.C., 1969), pp. 459–60.

6. Polishook, *Rhode Island*, pp. 141–42. For Connecticut's reaction to these developments, see *CC*, July 31, Aug. 14, and Sept. 25, 1786; *MG*, July 31.

7. Van Beck Hall, *Politics without Parties: Massachusetts, 1780–1791* (Pittsburgh, 1972), pp. 96, 107–9.

8. Ibid., p. 121.

9. Ibid., pp. 41, 121, 168, 204–12, 219–26, 234, 252.

10. See *CC*, Apr. 3, 1786; *CG*, Feb. 10 and Apr. 7.

11. "Justice," in *MG*, Mar. 6, 1786; "Public Faith," from the *Hampshire*

Herald, in ibid., Mar. 20; unsigned in ibid., Mar. 27. These notions were attacked by "Philagathus," in ibid., Mar. 13.

12. Ibid., Nov. 6, 1786; Dec. 25, 1786, and "Philagathus," in ibid., Mar. 26, 1787.

13. *SR*, 5: 277–78.

14. See "Agricola," in *CC*, Oct. 9, 1786. Because of their activities in Vermont and Pennsylvania, Connecticut's emigrants had acquired a reputation for being particularly aggressive in their quest for land.

15. *SR*, 6: 171–72 and n.

16. "Agricola," in *CC*, Oct. 9, 1786.

17. *SR*, 6: 237–38.

18. *JCC*, 31: 461–62; *SR*, 6: 232; *MG*, Aug. 14, 1786.

19. Neil A. McNall, *An Agricultural History of the Genesee Valley, 1790–1860* (Philadelphia, 1952), p. 12.

20. *CC*, Nov. 20, 1786; also in *MG*, Nov. 27.

21. *SR*, 6: 296.

22. *CC*, Nov. 20, 1786; also in *MG*, Nov. 27; "To the Public," from the *New Haven Gazette*, in *MG*, Dec. 11, 1786.

23. *CC*, Mar. 19, 1787. The meeting took place on Feb. 22.

24. "A Citizen of Connecticut," in *CC*, Mar. 26, 1787; "The Republican," in ibid., Mar. 5; "W," in ibid., Apr. 30; "Honestus," in ibid., May 14.

25. See ibid., May 28 and June 11, 1787.

26. *SR*, 6: 294–95 and n.; *CC*, May 28, 1787.

27. "The Republican," in *CC*, Mar. 19, 26, 1787; see also the debate in the General Assembly, in ibid., May 21.

28. In *MG*, Jan. 24–Feb. 26, 1787.

29. *SR*, 6: 292–93.

30. Christopher Collier, *Roger Sherman's Connecticut . . .* (Middletown, Conn., 1971), pp. 260–74; *SR*, 6: 355–56, 558–59, 569–71.

31. Ibid., p. 238 n.; *SHP*, pp. 549–52.

32. *SR*, 6: 238 n.; Helen M. Carpenter, *The Origin and Location of the Firelands of the Western Reserve* (Columbus, Ohio, 1935).

33. Harlan H. Hatcher, *The Western Reserve: The Story of New Connecticut in Ohio* (Cleveland, 1966), pp. 25–66. Uncertainty as to title continued to obstruct settlement, and the company sought a confirmatory act from Congress in 1800; see *SHP*, p. 553; *SR*, 6: 238 n.

34. Gaspare J. Saladino, "The Economic Revolution in Late Eighteenth Century Connecticut" (Ph.D. thesis, University of Wisconsin, 1964), p. 271ff.; Richard J. Purcell, *Connecticut in Transition, 1775–1818*, new ed. (Middletown, Conn., 1963), pp. 66–68.

35. Saladino, "Economic Revolution," chap. 11.

36. Ibid., pp. 81, 96, 247.

37. Ibid., p. 250.

38. Ibid., p. 256ff.

39. Ibid., p. 253.

40. Ibid., p. 340; Purcell, *Connecticut in Transition*, p. 108ff.

41. Saladino, "Economic Revolution," pp. 338–41; Purcell, *Connecticut in Transition*, pp. 78–84.

42. Saladino, "Economic Revolution," chap. 9 and p. 342; Purcell, *Connecticut in Transition*, p. 91ff.

43. See, for instance, "A Citizen of Connecticut," in *CC*, Mar. 26, 1787, who felt obliged to defend the state government against the charge that it was responsible for the emigration. The state's declining importance in the Union was not so traumatic for Connecticut as for Massachusetts, which had enjoyed clearer claims to preeminence. See James M. Banner, Jr., *To the Hartford Convention . . .* (New York, 1970), passim.

44. Saladino, "Economic Revolution," p. 243ff.

45. Richard Buel, Jr., *Securing the Revolution . . .* (Ithaca, 1972), p. 89; Purcell, *Connecticut in Transition*, chaps. 6–8.

Index

Albany, 53, 88, 120, 129
Allen, Ethan, 41
Amboy, N. J., 73
American Board of Customs Commissioners, 18, 19
Amherst, Sir Jeffery, 9
Angell, Captain James, 294, 295
Anglicans, 3, 16, 17, 27, 29, 312
Aquidneck Island, 49, 93, 153, 156, 204
Arbuthnot, Adm. Marriot, 229, 263
army, British, 29, 38; attacks from the north, 42, 67, 93, 120–23; attacks New Jersey, 82, 91, 101, 120, 125, 229; attacks New York, 46, 67, 72–73, 76–77, 81–82; attacks Philadelphia, 90, 120, 124, 129; attacks Rhode Island, 92–93; attacks Westchester, 88–90; conquest of the south, 235; Danbury raid, 111–14; deployment of, 41, 42, 53, 66, 72, 76, 86, 136–37, 152–53, 156–57, 159, 188, 204–5, 210, 226, 229, 233, 235, 282–83; detachments for the south, 60–61, 62, 72, 136, 152, 157, 164, 211, 263; devastates the Connecticut coast, 190–94; evacuates Boston, 46, 61–62; New London raid, 272–75; operations along the Hudson River, 107, 128–29, 186; recruiting in Connecticut, 70, 87, 88, 264; reinforcements from Europe, 42, 43, 44, 47, 53, 56, 67, 72, 73, 120, 124–25, 151, 154, 198; response to Bunker Hill, 48;

scales down operations in North America, 282; strength of, 38, 44, 47, 72–73; threatens Connecticut, 89–90, 177, 183, 193, 195
army, Continental: bounties offered recruits in, 53, 56, 68–70, 101–2, 106, 117–18, 173, 185–87, 216, 221, 223, 227, 232, 255; classing for, 110–11, 117–18, 172, 239, 249–50, 253, 275, 276; committee from requests compensation from Congress, 301–2; deployment of, 45, 63, 75, 87–88, 93, 101, 116, 120–24, 159, 186, 225; difficulties in recruiting for the long term, 100–102, 105–20, 215–16; formation of in 1776, 54–56, 58–59; growing unpopularity of in Connecticut, 177, 179–87, 209, 211, 212, 253; half pay for officers, 180–81, 297–98; hospital department, 101, 104; mutinies in, 130, 164, 181–82, 224, 237, 241, 263, 284, 298; new levies of 1776, 69–70, 71, 72, 73, 77, 91, 93, 99, 102; shortage of supplies for, 101, 143, 150, 206, 223–24, 233–34, 241–42, 248; strength of, 59, 71, 75, 77, 225
army, French: at Newport, 229, 233; at Yorktown, 238, 272; provisioning of, 159, 161, 163, 169, 224–26, 240–44; refusal of d'Estaing to commit in 1778, 156–57
army, standing, 81, 100, 105–18, 179, 182